Breaking Away from Broken Windows

Breaking Away from Broken Windows

Baltimore Neighborhoods and
the Nationwide Fight Against
Crime, Grime, Fear, and Decline

Ralph B. Taylor

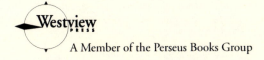
Westview
PRESS
A Member of the Perseus Books Group

Crime and Society

Copyright © 2001 by Westview Press, A Member of the Perseus Books Group

Published in 2001 in the United States of America by Westview Press, 5500 Central Avenue, Boulder, Colorado 80301–2877, and in the United Kingdom by Westview Press, 12 Hid's Copse Road, Cumnor Hill, Oxford OX2 9JJ

Find us on the World Wide Web at www.westviewpress.com

Library of Congress Cataloging-in-Publication Data to come
ISBN: 0-8133-9780-4

The paper used in this publication meets the requirements of the American National Standard for Permanence of Paper for Printed Library Materials Z39.48–1984.

10   9   8   7   6   5   4   3   2   1

In Memoriam

*As this volume was knitting itself together,
several people I knew passed on. Each is missed by many.*

*Warren Torgerson
Former professor at Johns Hopkins University
whose lucid writing still serves as a model for me*

*Francis L. Sutton
Favorite uncle, and trusted and practical adviser,
ever-ready to see the humorous*

*Clare Ryan
Good neighbor, good friend to Michele,
who redefined "World's Greatest Mom"*

*Primrose Gerrard
Artist, kind neighbor, and seer,
who loved beauty, and freely served for a time as
occasional, nearby, and valued grandmother to Mara*

*James ("Gerry") Gerrard
Good neighbor and friend, and a kind soul,
who gave me more than I can repay in my infrequent visits to
the hospital and nursing homes*

Contents

PART 3 QUALITATIVE EVIDENCE FROM COMMUNITY LEADERS

Tables and Figures

Acknowledgments

If people won't talk to social scientists, we're in trouble. Thankfully, people like to talk and researchers and interviewers like to listen. My greatest debt is surely to the Baltimore city residents and leaders who, over the years, have willingly answered questions and shared opinions.

In addition to talk, research requires funding. Federal tax dollars have generously underwritten my research over the years, in the form of research grants. The National Institute of Justice (NIJ) has funded much of this work. The latest grant underwrote the 1994–1995 round of data collection (93-IJ-CX-0022). A small grant funded the analysis of Minneapolis–St Paul data, discussed in a few places (94-IJ-CX-0018). I would not have been awarded that latter grant without Pam Lattimore's willingness to listen to my rebuttal of reviewer comments. Earlier NIJ grants included 80-IJ-CX-0077, 79-NI-AX-0063, and 80-IJ-CX-0104. Richard Titus of NIJ played a key role in supporting some of those earlier efforts. Steve Gottfredson, now dean at Virginia Commonwealth University, served as principal investigator on the latter two. Sally Shumaker, now at Wake Forest, served as project director on the first one and offered numerous insights, suggestions, and improvements on that project. I deeply appreciate the support and encouragement of my research provided by personnel currently or formerly at NIJ, including Jeremy Travis, Sally Hillsman, Christy Visher, Richard Titus, Fred Heinzelmann, and Pamela Lattimore, among others. The mid-1980s work was funded by the National Institute of Mental Health (NIMH) (Grants 1-RO1-MH40842-01A and 5-R01-MH40842-02). Tom Lalley played a key role in shepherding those grants through his agency. Doug Perkins, now at the University of Utah, was project director for the NIMH grants and spearheaded data collection for assessed incivilities on that project. Doris Hunt and John Meeks, along with Doug, braved bracing winter weather to collect the assessment information. Doug, in his various publications, has contributed significantly on his own to the area of incivilities as it links to key questions in community psychology, and I have benefited from his thinking in this and other areas.

A fellowship (96-IJ-CX-0067) from the National Institute of Justice during 1997 allowed me time to revise the first six chapters of this book, write the two more qualitative chapters, and explore data from four other cities to see how those results compared to what I was seeing in Baltimore (Chapter 3). That fellowship would not have happened were it not for the support of Jeremy Travis, Sally Hillsman, and Christy Visher at NIJ. With their comments, numerous personnel at NIJ helped enormously in my thinking about the issues discussed here: Steve Edwards, Bob Kaminski, Jeff Ross, Tom Feucht, Lois Mock, and Nancy LaVigne. Finally, the Office of the Provost at Temple University, under acting provost Corinne Caldwell, provided summer support in 1998 so that I could complete the analyses using 1987–1988 data on reactions to crime described in Chapter 6. Jennifer Robinson and Brian Lawton played key roles in bringing those analyses to completion. This generous support from the National Institute of Justice, the National Institute of Mental Health, and Temple University notwithstanding, the material here represents neither the opinions nor the official polices of the Department of Justice, the National Institute of Justice, or Temple University.

Over the years, the Baltimore Police Department has willingly provided requested data. I thank the late commissioner Frazier, and other past commissioners, who have permitted this access and still remember warmly my first meeting with the late Sgt. Emory Starry in the late 1970s.

The most recent 1994–1996 project depended on the skills and energy of several people and institutions. Sidney Brower at University of Maryland–College Park, coinvestigator on the project, provided insight and suggestions and helped tame the University of Maryland bureaucracy so that needed resources emerged. He sparked my interest in Baltimore neighborhoods over twenty years ago. His insights into residential life and the innovativeness with which he approaches these issues I find astonishing. The University of Baltimore graciously supplied our field office on North Calvert Street. Steve Pardue, now at the Federal Emergency Management Agency (FEMA), capably served as project manager, overseeing all phases of field data collection, supervising on-site assessors, contacting and interviewing local leaders, and photographing sites. The project would have gone seriously awry without his conscientious commitment. His dry, sardonic humor helped to break up our staff meetings. Mary Hyde, joining the project later, assisted ably in conducting leader interviews, as did several students from Sidney Brower's University of Maryland–College Park spring 1995 class. Pat Smith and Michael Clifton competently served as field assessors during the hot summer of 1994. Diane Burkom at Survey Research Associates (SRA) competently oversaw the telephone survey effort. Her professionalism and the skill of her colleagues at SRA were, as always, exemplary. At Temple, numerous graduate students assisted. Jianming Ding completed the census and crime data programming into neighborhoods accurately and speedily after a previous programmer disappeared without a trace, but with my CD-ROM of census data. Mary Blazofsky, Ruth Eichmiller, Dave Linne, and Mary Poulin competently performed a range of data processing, rating, and entry tasks. The untold contributions of this cadre spanned almost three years. Dave Linne also drafted the portion of Chapter 2 describing local events based on newspaper sources. Also at Temple, the Social Science Data Library and Scott Snyder, associate director, provided census data. Tracy Brown, director of the Mayor's Coordinating Council for Crime and Justice, provided key support for the project proposal.

Colleagues now or formerly in the Department of Criminal Justice at Temple University also contributed to the current effort in various ways. Alan Harland, Phil Harris, and Kay Harris were all understanding and supportive, helping facilitate needed project time over the years. Every academic should be so lucky. Jack Greene, now at Northeastern University, started me asking questions about community policing, and we published some of those questions in a book chapter many years—and even more policy changes—back. Conversations with George Rengert, John Goldkamp, and Wayne Welsh helped me sharpen my thoughts further on these topics here.

Various family members tolerated or encouraged the effort. Michele thought this project was interesting and somehow managed to complete her doctoral work amid all this. Thanks for tolerating my frequent absences as I commuted from Havertown to Baltimore and then later to D.C. To Nyssa and Mara: I apologize for the important events I missed. I owe you. Give me a ring when you want to go go-karting.

Lots of folks read over earlier drafts of various chapters. Several participants in a delightful session at the meetings of the Eastern Sociological Society in April 1997 provided thoughtful reactions to the material on city changes contained in Chapter 2. Chapter 3 never would have gotten started if Bob Langworthy had not encouraged me to undertake the theoretical critique contained in the first half of that chapter. Jeff Ross and Ron Davis provided insightful comments on Chapters 4 through 6. Ramiro Martinez spurred me to complete yet another revision and reanalysis for Chapter 5. Aaron Podolefsky, despite a broken leg and recently added administrative duties at the University of Northern Iowa, commented on Chapter 7. Steve Edwards, Mary Hyde, Ed Orser, and Steve Pardue read portions of Chapter 8, and their insightful remarks led to significant reworking of the material there. An anonymous reviewer of the entire volume for Westview provided further comments that helped better focus the effort.

A word is in order regarding local identities. Preapproach letters to local leaders soliciting their participation in interviews promised that no individuals would be identified using those data, nor would individual neighborhoods be identified using those data. To guard against potential loss of confidentiality, I: provide no maps showing locations of the sampled neighborhoods; provide place pseudonyms for all sampled neighborhoods, sometimes using more than one pseudonym; omit or alter minor details in the events recounted here; and change various attributes of the leaders interviewed, including gender. I recognize that the decision to maintain confidentiality has a high cost, especially when reading Chapters 7 and 8. It significantly reduces the interest Baltimore readers are likely to show in the volume. It probably reduces also the insight local leaders and policymakers might gain from the material. I regret these costs, and my colleagues, especially Sidney Brower, argued against incurring them. He may well be right, and I may be overcautious on this issue. Nonetheless, I felt bound by the promise extended to leaders to divulge neither their identities nor the neighborhoods they called home.

Of course, all remaining errors, inaccuracies, and sloppy thinking are, it goes almost without saying, mine alone.

Ralph B. Taylor
Havertown, PA
October, 2000

Acronyms

AHS	Annual/American Housing Survey
ANOVA	analysis of variance
B&O	Baltimore & Ohio Railroad
BID	business improvement district
CAPS	Chicago Alternative Policing Strategy
CATI	computer assisted telephone interviewing
CBD	central business district
CDC	community development corporation
C-H-M	Coldstream-Homestead-Montebello
COIL	Citizens Organized to Improve Life
COP	Citizens on Patrol
CPO	community police/policing officer
DEA	Drug Enforcement Administration
FEMA	Federal Emergency Management Agency
GSS	General Social Survey (GSS)
HGLM	hierarchical generalized linear models
HLM	hierarchical linear models
HUD	Department of Housing and Urban Development
ICPSR	Inter-University Consortium for Political and Social Research
IRS	Internal Revenue Service
MSA	metropolitan statistical area
NCS/NCVS	National Crime Survey/National Crime Victimization Survey
NFL	National Football League
NIJ	National Institute of Justice
NIMH	National Institute of Mental Health
NOI	Nation of Islam
OLS	ordinary least squares
P-P	percentile-percentile chart
SPR	social problem reduction
SRA	Survey Research Associates
USF&G	United States Fidelity and Guaranty Corporation
VP	victimization prevention

PART ONE

Background on the Place, the Theory, and Policies

1

Introduction

"From coast to coast, law enforcement officials are trying to combat so-called quality of life crimes that erode urban life." (2: B3)

Philadelphia, Pennsylvania

The Third and Fourth police districts in Philadelphia share a building, vintage 1960 urban school architecture with long horizontal windows and lots of brick, at Eleventh and Wharton Streets in southeast Philadelphia. I was headed there on a December afternoon in 1997 to talk to District Commander Captain John Fisher about quality of life initiatives in his district, the Fourth.

Visions of old and new Philadelphia slid past me as I drove north on Interstate 95 into South Philadelphia. The Philadelphia Naval Shipyard, opened in 1790 and closed in 1996, sprawled unused on the right, large gray ships bunched together in storage. It had employed tens of thousands at its peak. Exiting onto South Broad Street and driving north, I passed the new Corestates Spectrum basketball/hockey arena, now the First Union Center, on the right, gleaming far brighter in the December early afternoon sun than the mothballed fleet. Past the Corestates Spectrum is the old Spectrum arena, looking dated with its simple cylindrical shape; then Veterans Stadium, home of the Eagles and Phillies, ramps crisscrossing its sides. Revenue from taxes on blue-collar jobs like those at the old shipyard seem less important to cities these days than their take from the luxury skyboxes at the stadium and arena.

A block or so later, South Philly starts. Houses front Broad Street, then later you pass stores and businesses: nail care, delis, a post office, banks. Cars clog the center turn lane, a tradition in South Philly, and on every block there is at least one car double-parked. Stretching away on the narrow cross streets to the right and left are tightly packed row houses, mostly two stories high. Turning right on Wharton, after a block or so I spot an example of the topic of my upcoming conversation with Captain Fisher: about six male teens, white or Latino, slouching on cars or standing outside a corner store. The streets are narrow and the sun low, so even in early afternoon the entire street is in shadow.

Captain Fisher and I talk for about an hour in his office on quality of life initiatives, in particular, his "corner-clearing" operations in the Fourth District. He is tall and sizable, with short black hair going to gray and a direct manner. He wore black uniform pants, black polished shoes, white shirt, and uniform tie clipped with a department tie clip. We sat in two chairs in a corner of his office. To my left was a large desk; mounted on the paneled wall behind were plaques and a football team picture. To my right, a window looked out on a ramp for entering police vehicles, and occasionally Captain Fisher would wave to entering officers.

At the time of our conversation, a major corner-clearing initiative to improve residents' quality of life had been under way in the Fourth District for over a year. Residents' complaints about rowdy teens on the corners reached the office of a council member who lived nearby, and he started discussions with police on a solution. Police analyzed their radio calls and identified some forty "hot spots"—particular corners or a couple of nearby corners—generating many calls for service. Hot spots of crime have been examined for some time by criminal justice researchers, although questions about them persist (55). Adjusting policing practices in recognition of hot spots has become widespread in modern policing operations (e.g., 4).

District officers worked closely with a judge to be sure the initiative would be legally sound. In some cities, broad curfews targeted at teens had been challenged in court, and they wanted to be sure their initiative would stand up to such a challenge (11, 42). Being legal meant, according to the judge, only acting in specific locations where there was a documented problem, warning people before they were arrested, and treating similarly persons from different ethnic groups.

The district's analysis also showed that many calls coming in over the radio about corner complaints were not getting out over the airwaves to the officers. At that time, four different police districts were using the same radio frequency, and higher-priority calls about violent crimes, weapons, or drugs dominated airtime.

For the new initiative, a team of two volunteer officers is on shift from 6 P.M. to 2 A.M. five nights a week from about March to October. Their duties are mainly to respond to corner problems. Their car has a special call sign—"4-corner-1"—the dispatchers can use.

In the evening, the corner team will stop at problem locations and survey pedestrians to identify who is present. They will tell the people hanging out there that someone has complained; there has been a documented problem. If the officers return later in the evening, they can take to court those individuals still present. Adults will go to night court with Judge X, a motorcycle-riding, self-styled "Judge Dredd." He will give them a citation and make them pay a fine; juveniles will be held until their parents can come and get them out of jail.

For the residents, the activities of youth on the corners are *social incivilities:* street activity that is disorderly, troublesome, and threatening. Generally such social incivilities include things like rowdy teens; "hey honey" hassles; panhandlers; street "crazies"; public drunkenness; fights on the street; disorderly or sick drug users; and large numbers of persons hanging out, especially at odd hours.

Oakland, California

We can go to the other coast to illustrate a multiagency initiative focused on physical rather than social problems in neighborhoods. Lorraine Green Mazzerolle and her colleagues have documented an Oakland, California, multiagency "Beat Health" initiative. In contrast to the Philadelphia corner-clearing initiative addressing social conditions, the Oakland program targeted physical conditions (20, 33). The physical problems addressed by the Oakland program are *physical incivilities.* These include deteriorated housing; abandoned housing; poorly maintained properties, lots, sidewalks, and playgrounds; trash; graffiti; abandoned or burned-out cars; and vacant lots. They demonstrate that various land uses—residences, stores, lots, businesses—are not being kept up or used properly. Police researchers and practitioners have connected local physical conditions with other crime problems such as drug dealing, public drinking, and public drug use. I describe these connections in more detail in Chapter 3. In recognition of these connections, community policing efforts and community prosecution efforts have for the past decade or more considered fixing the physical problems as a way to fix the crime problem (3).

In Oakland, a large fraction of the sites visited by Beat Health officers had documented problems with drug dealing. The bulk of the physical problems addressed in these sites arose from housing conditions and rodent infestations linked to conditions in houses or yards (20: 41) If police received a complaint about a location, they visited the nuisance site, often accompanied by personnel from other city agencies; documented the problem; and, if possible, started establishing relationships with local owners and tenants. Police and the other agencies involved worked together to remedy the problems. For example, landlords might be encouraged to address code violations or evict troublesome tenants. The Oakland program is an example of using civil procedures to alleviate crime and crime-related problems (3). Evaluations of the Oakland program show that it did result in improved indoor and outdoor appearances at the sites and fewer visits from agency personnel afterward. Physical incivilities were successfully reduced in these locations.

These two programs—in Philadelphia and Oakland—both target community incivilities. Such targeting of incivilities, whether it be in the form of "grime fighting" or "zero tolerance policies," have become an axiomatic part of policing initiatives being adopted in numerous police departments across the United States (e.g., 4, 25). Sometimes disorder reduction efforts are folded into community policing innovations; at other times they appear antithetical to the spirit of community policing. Nonetheless, the presumption, as noted in the opening quotation, is that these disorders, or "quality of life crimes," "erode urban life."

Focus

The current volume focuses on the assumptions supporting initiatives like those described above. Such initiatives rest on a complex set of presumed connections between these incivilities and neighborhood fabric, neighborhood crime, and how residents feel about their own safety and their neighborhood's future. These presumed connections, particularly as they unfold over time, have rarely been investigated either by researchers or policymakers. This volume will focus on those connections.

The volume will *not* assess specific interventions implemented by police or other agencies to reduce incivilities. I will not evaluate programs like those described above to learn about their effectiveness or cost-effectiveness. Instead, my purpose is to examine, using empirical evidence, the linkages policymakers believe to exist. Such linkages provide an important part of the rationale for these interventions. The two central questions addressed are (1) What are the origins of incivilities? and (2) Do they erode urban life over time? These two general queries include the following concerns:

- Where do incivilities come from? What community conditions lead to more incivilities at a later point in time?
- What are the impacts of incivilities on later neighborhood decline? Do incivilities have *independent* impacts, separate from other community conditions that may be linked to disorder?
- Do incivilities have independent impacts on later changes in a neighborhood's crime rate?
- Do incivilities cause later increases in residents' safety concerns?
- Do incivilities reflect one, common, underlying feature of a neighborhood? Or are they a set of disparate issues, only loosely linked to one another?

Incivilities, Disorder, Social Disorganization, Collective Efficacy, and Social Capital

Amplifying for a moment on the last question in the list, we can adopt one of two views. We can consider the social and physical incivilities described above as the sole focus. Each physical or social incivility that concerns some number of residents is a separate problem to be solved. This is often the approach taken by community leaders and activists.

Alternatively, we can think of the incivilities as indicators pointing toward deeper, underlying problems, the causes of which may lie in the community or in events and actors beyond the community's boundary. In other words, we may think that the incivilities have one or more common but also less obvious causes. This approach is often adopted by the researchers studying the origins and impacts of incivilities. "What these conditions have in common is that they signal a breakdown of the local social order" (50: 2); "and residents react to them" (50: 4). In the first view, taken by local leaders, the incivilities are the disorder; in the second view, taken by researchers, the incivilities are signs of something deeper—a broader disorder.

A breakdown of the local social order, or community disorder, represents a far-reaching and at times slippery idea. Most would agree it refers to a set of social conditions and specific actions, separate and distinct from crime itself, reflecting an unpredictable, uncivil, and often threatening public street life; and a physical surround to that street life that is substandard, deteriorated, and unkempt.

Community disorder is related to, but distinct from, the venerable but still controversial sociological concept of social disorganization (39). This concept refers to a community's inability (1) to "govern" the behavior of its residents, including children and teens; or (2) to work toward common goals for the betterment of the neighborhood (6). Disorganized communities also lack sufficient ties to governing agencies and resources outside of the community itself (7). Social disorganization is distinct from juvenile delinquency, although socially disorganized communities can have high delinquency levels. Similarly, community disorder is distinct from high community crime rates, even though communities with high levels of disorder may have high crime rates now or in the future.

The reverse of social disorganization is collective efficacy, which has three components: shared and widespread participation in local social organizations; widespread and positive informal local ties among acquaintances, neighbors, and perhaps friends; and a willingness to intervene in troublesome situations (45). Another closely related term is social capital, the broader social networks among residents, both within and between households (8).

Delinquency and high community crime rates each may emerge from and amplify local social disorganization or weaken local collective efficacy or local social capital. Community disorder refers to a narrower set of conditions than social disorganization, collective efficacy, or social capital, even though community disorder may be evident in high-crime or high-delinquency neighborhoods.

Which perspective we adopt has implications for both how we think about incivilities and how we choose to fix them. From a research perspective, if there is a common, underlying cause in the broader disorder of the community, then different indicators of incivilities should closely match one another, and changes in one type of incivility should be reflected in changes in another type. From a policy perspective, a common cause suggests that a common solution or remedial program may be identified. On the other hand, if we do not presume incivilities are spawned by wider community disorder or social disorganization, researchers would not be surprised to find different types of incivilities changing in different directions, and policymakers would be content proposing various specific solutions for various specific incivilities.

The research and policy initiatives in this arena have reflected both perspectives. The corner-clearing initiative in the Fourth District in Philadelphia is one specific solution for a specific set of social incivilities. The Beat Health program in Oakland, by contrast, targets a range of physical incivilities, presuming that the problems and thus the solutions are inherently similar.

In short, there may be some underlying confusion here about how incivilities relate to the broader disorder or social disorganization in the community. This "fuzziness" appears when we look at the different theoretical models used in this area, as we will do in Chapter 3. It also surfaces in how we refer to the conditions themselves: signs of disorder, disorder, incivilities, signs of incivility, quality of life crimes, and soft crimes.

Broader Theoretical and Empirical Context of Current Approaches

The current volume examines three ways that "urban life" is eroded: through increasing neighborhood crime, through decreasing neighborhood quality, and by affecting residents' views about their neighborhood and their neighborhood safety. The statistical models examining these outcomes draw on three broad areas of empirical and theoretical work: new urban sociology, human ecology, and views about neighborhood quality and safety. Specific chapters describe the work and theorizing in each of these areas in more detail. Here I briefly review how each of these perspectives frames questions of neighborhood change, crime change, and reactions to crime.

New Urban Sociology

Within the past decade or so, a conflict-based perspective, called the new urban sociology, has gained popularity in the field of urban sociology. Similar shifts to a perspective focused on conflict also have occurred in other areas of sociology and in other social sciences. In general terms, a conflict perspective describes and understands interactions between groups, and societal changes, as resulting from fundamental conflicts between different segments of society for scarce "resources." "Resources" refer to any scarce commodity, such as land, good-quality housing, efficient government services, and perhaps even neighborhood safety. Urban scholars embracing this perspective, such as Molotch, Logan, Gottdiener, and Feagin, clarify how city changes emerge from these conflicts between institutional, corporate, citizen-based, and political entities.[1] According to this view, the conditions and changes we see in a locale represent the impacts of a political economy where a small number of powerful actors, such as large-scale businesses or development interests, perhaps in collaboration with public agencies, and larger numbers of less powerful actors, such as organizations, citizen groups, and small businesses, pursue their self-interests (31). Outsiders' pursuit of increased monetary value, called exchange value, is pitted against residents' efforts to maintain or increase neighborhood quality and functionality, called use value. The outsiders usually have an upper hand (18: 163).

Such a perspective points, in general terms, toward the importance of community socioeconomic status as a key influence on neighborhood futures. Socioeconomic status may be reflected in census variables such as house values, median household income, higher education levels among residents, or higher proportions of residents in managerial or professional occupations. Higher-status neighborhoods have a tax base that is more valued by local politicians and political clout exceeding that of poorer neighborhoods (21). The perspective suggests the best-off neighborhoods will get their way more often; they will garner more public services; and they can better resist changes threatening continued viability. Residents' enjoyment of their neighborhood quality—the use value they derive—may be more assured. Of course, differential access to power across urban neighborhoods based on current status or prestige is nothing new. The new urban sociology constantly reminds us that these dynamics are still with us.

The new urban sociology recognizes the political importance not only of status but also of neighborhood racial composition. A neighborhood's racial makeup, and changes in that makeup, powerfully influence the economic returns that strong political actors can reap from that locale, and thus the treatment of the locale by dominant local interests (46, 63). And of course, actions based on economic self-interest also may coincide with actions grounded in race-based biases (34).

For example, in one analysis that Jeannette Covington and I completed of Baltimore neighborhood deterioration in the early 1980s, we expected that rapid neighborhood racial change during the 1970s would "explain" why deterioration was so widespread in predominantly African-American neighborhoods in 1980 (57). But in replicated analyses, we found a different story. It was not the rapid racial change that was responsible for the deterioration. Rather, it was the resulting predominantly African-American neighborhood composition. The results suggested city service differentials, linked to neighborhood racial composition, in areas such as housing inspection or code enforcement, may have been partially responsible for the emergent deterioration.

Scholars of Baltimore neighborhoods readily admit the important roles that race has played in differential neighborhood development, change, and preservation (34, 36, 37). Unfortunately, although there are several predominantly African-American middle-class neighborhoods in the city of Baltimore, racial composition generally links strongly to socio-economic status. This makes it difficult in many instances to separate out impacts of racial composition per se. The conflict perspective suggests that race is important because it influences the economic interests of major local actors. Philadelphia in the late nineteenth century provided one stunning example: Local politicians there benefited by restricting the vice establishment to well-established African-American communities in central Philadelphia (29).

Human Ecology

University of Chicago researchers in the first half of the twentieth century, inspired by evolutionary theory, botany, and the dramatic changes taking place around them, connected community structure, location, and local social life with a human ecological framework. Wirth, Burgess, Park, McKenzie, Shaw, McKay, and others linked the features of a neighborhood, or the broader city, with social pathologies, as well as residents' "reactions" to the city and their immediate surrounds. The human ecological model, especially as it applies to social disorganization broadly, and outcomes such as delinquency, offender rates, and offense rates more specifically, has attracted renewed interest in the past dozen years or so and has had the benefit of two major updates (7, 44, 47).

Stated briefly, Shaw and McKay's model—in retrospect most applicable to large cities in the period prior to World War II—is as follows. City growth, as was witnessed in the first half of the twentieth century in the largest U.S. cities, causes expansion in the central business district (CBD) and construction of newer, higher-status residential areas on the outskirts of the city. The innermost zones, closest to the CBD, with their older, deteriorated housing, are the least desirable. Speculators, anticipating the area's demolition, buy properties but do not improve them, and the location becomes a "transition zone," with increasing deterioration and transient populations in low-rent accommodations.

Residents in the city sort themselves out, and get sorted, based on economics, which are linked to ethnicity and race, as well as immigration history. The newest in-migrating groups, and African Americans, are relegated to the poorest parts of the city with the least adequate housing and services. Delinquency is higher in poorer areas in part because of fewer economic opportunities, other social problems also evident in the locales, lack of agreement about appropriate public behavior, and a lack of commitment to neighborhood improvement. Unconcern about local conditions arises because most households focus on moving "up and out" to better locations. Families have little control over their children for several reasons. They are confronted with nontraditional or "deviant" subcultures, or both, but probably benefit from that subculture at the same time. "Thus, even if a family represents conventional values, some member, relative, or friend may be gaining a livelihood through illegal or quasi-legal institutions—a fact tending to neutralize the family's opposition to the criminal system" (47: 185). Thus, becoming delinquent or criminal may, Shaw and McKay admit, "make sense": "From the point of view of the delinquent's immediate social world, he is not necessarily disorganized, maladjusted, or antisocial. Within the limits of his social world and in terms of its norms and expectations, he may be a highly organized and well-adjusted person" (47: 316).

Shaw and McKay also recognized special difficulties faced by African-American households:

> The physical, economic, and social conditions associated with high rates of delinquents in local communities occupied by white population exist in exaggerated form in most of the Negro areas. Of all the population groups in the city, the Negro people occupy the most disadvantageous position in relation to the distribution of economic and social values. Their efforts to achieve a more satisfactory and advantageous position in the economic and social life of the city are seriously thwarted by many restrictions with respect to residence, employment, education, and social and cultural pursuits. These restrictions have contributed to the development of conditions within the local community conducive to an unusually large volume of delinquency (47: 187).

The above quotes may help rebut those marking the ecological model as "pro the status quo" (19). At least some ecological researchers, such as Shaw and McKay, have recognized status-based and race-based barriers to integration and achievement. They openly discuss the dynamics behind segregation and certainly do not downplay economic competition between different social groups. If key elements of the new urban sociology include viewing cultural and economic processes as primary, recognizing that social organization is dominated by class- and race-based interests, and acknowledging that real estate is a "second circuit of capital," then Shaw and McKay certainly represent this view.

Updates to the model support it in two ways. First, Sampson and Grove used data from a national British victimization survey to document empirical connections expected by the model. They found, as expected, ethnic heterogeneity and low neighborhood socioeconomic status led to both victimization and offending, because these features of the fabric weakened local social ties and local informal social control (44).

Bursik and Grasmick provided a conceptual extension of the model, moving it closer to the conflict perspective. They proposed that offending rates, offense rates, fear, and delinquency depend not only on control processes within the neighborhood but also on control processes linking the neighborhood with external coalitions and public agencies. They label these processes *public control* (7: 37–38). Political scientists, such as Crenson, call them neighborhood *foreign relations* (10). But the idea is the same. Some neighborhoods are "better connected" than others and more effective at funneling resources and services into their locale. Such connections dramatically influence not only neighborhood satisfaction and quality of life, but crime- and delinquency-related outcomes as well.

The ecological perspective perhaps makes its most important contribution by directing our attention simultaneously to the consequences of both community stability and informal social control in the neighborhood. Many households in the lowest-status locations may view their community as a temporary camp and thus be unwilling to work with others to maintain community standards.[2] And even if they exhibited such commitment, effective action may not result because their neighbors are recent, unfamiliar, and of a different cultural background (6, 15, 32). This is not to deny that numerous examples can be found of well-kept, cared-for, low-income communities where residents are strongly invested in their locale. But the factors working against collective involvement and improvement are stronger in these locations.

In short, the ecological perspective on disorder, at least as articulated by Shaw, McKay, Bursik, and Sampson, is complementary to the new urban sociology and fully recognizes the important impacts of class and race. It fills out our view on community by also pinpointing the roles of community stability and the processes associated with it, which can influence crime- and delinquency-related outcomes, as well as neighborhood viability.

Reactions to Crime

Fear of crime is people's emotional response to the possibility of victimization and is reflected, for example, in how safe people might feel in various locations. Fear is conceptually and empirically distinct both from people's concern about crime, or how serious they think the problem is, and from their perceptions of risk, or estimates of the likelihood of victimization (12). Detailed reviews of work on reactions to crime generally, and fear of crime more specifically, appear elsewhere (9, 14, 35, 58).

Of most concern to us is the specific question, do incivilities make people fearful? And if so, how and why? Despite considerable work on these questions (see Chapter 6), definitive answers have not yet emerged (35). The reason may lie in two different research traditions on fear of crime. Only when these two avenues of research are joined are we likely to gain complete answers.

One school of researchers treats fear as an ecological attribute, a reflection, in large measure, of how people gauge conditions in their immediate neighborhood. According to this line of argument, fear is driven by the actual, local conditions, and these are reflected in residents' perceptions of local disorders (e.g., 22, 49, 54, 57). This group has focused on neighborhood fear and links between neighborhood conditions and individual fear. These scholars, myself included, as I explain in Chapter 3, may have mistakenly put too much emphasis on fear of crime differences between neighborhoods and too little emphasis on fear of crime differences between neighbors; we may have lost sight of the fact that fear is largely a psychological issue and only secondarily an ecological issue.

A second group of scholars examines fear through a different lens. They argue that fear reflects an assessment of how much individuals are at risk of being victimized. These vulnerability assessments derive largely from characteristics of the perceiver (e.g., 26, 27, 30, 48, 60, 62). For example, women are much more fearful of crime for at least three reasons: Should they be attacked by a man, there is almost always the threat of rape. Ferraro calls this the "shadow of sexual assault" (14). And in an attack, it will be more difficult, on average, for them to fight off the attacker than it would be for a male. Third, women are more likely than men to be assaulted by those close to them—boyfriends, relatives, exspouses, and the like (51).

According to this second group, perceptions of disorder are relevant to fear, but these perceptions, and the resulting fear, do not really reflect neighborhood conditions. Instead they represent social constructions, residents' interpretations of how threatening conditions are for them, given their specific life circumstances. Answers to the question, "How much of a problem is there in the neighborhood with people fighting?"

reflect not just local conditions, but local conditions amplified or diminished based on each perceiver's personal context. Researchers such as Ferraro argue explicitly for such a symbolic interactionist framework (14). Stated differently, residents' perceptions of risk connect local conditions with resulting fear (27, 28, 61).

In short, one group of researchers has tried to more closely connect fear with neighborhood conditions. At the same time, another group has argued for disconnecting fear from neighborhood conditions, focusing instead on how those conditions are interpreted by various individuals. The first group sees the problem as ecological; the second, as psychological. Paralleling the conceptual differences in approach have been preferences for different data sets. The first group has opted for sets with extensive information about a relatively small number of neighborhood contexts, whereas the second has opted for representative surveys over a state or nationally. The latter surveys usually contain scant information from nonsurvey sources about specific neighborhood contexts.

More recently, researchers such as Rountree have attempted to bridge this gap between psychodynamically focused, individual-oriented studies and ecologically focused, neighborhood-oriented studies. She and her colleagues have linked fear to a range of neighborhood conditions and shown that some features of individuals have varying impacts on fear (40, 41; for other examples, see 9, 57).

The present effort, as it addresses fear of crime, extends the connections between the psychodynamic and ecological perspectives in two respects. It examines both the ecological impacts of neighborhood conditions, including incivilities, and the psychological impacts of perceived neighborhood conditions. Furthermore, it looks at the ecological relationships in a longitudinal framework, allowing us to more precisely gauge causal impacts of incivilities.

Evidence

The bulk of the evidence examined here comes from Baltimore, Maryland. I arrived there in the fall of 1973, having spent the previous fifteen months modifying the behaviors of "pre" delinquents in a residential treatment center in New Hampshire. Save for one year at Virginia Tech, I spent the next thirteen years going to graduate school, getting married, working in an urban research center at Johns Hopkins, raising two children, buying and selling my first house, and avidly following the Orioles to the 1979 and 1983 World Series. I moved out of the city in 1983 and out of the area in 1986.

While in Baltimore, I saw the fall City Fair mutate from a haphazard collection of tents, booths, and sometimes intriguing local bands to an annual mega-event drawing tens of thousands from the city and beyond. I witnessed the construction of Harbor Place and grudgingly admitted that I liked the aquarium I had thought was too expensive. I served on the Mayor's Vandalism Task Force and later on the Mayor's Coordinating Council for Crime and Justice.

I will never pretend to know the city of Baltimore the way that residents do who have lived there far longer than I, or the way that leaders do whose energy and commitment to the locale seems boundless, or the way that true local experts like Harold McDougall, Sherry Olson, Matt Crenson, Jacques Kelly, Ed Orser, David Harvey, Dick Cook, or Sidney Brower do, to mention just a few. I have assisted far fewer neighborhoods than I would have liked, have talked to far fewer residents and leaders than I would have liked, and have spent far less time in many neighborhoods than I would have liked. Those seeking a detailed history of the city or of certain sections of it can find those elsewhere (13, 36, 43).

A fuller description of the data collected and the methods used to gather them appears in an on-line appendix (http://www.rbtaylor.net/technical.htm). I offer a brief outline here. In 1978, in collaboration with city planners, Sidney Brower, Whit Drain, and I completed an ecological mapping of Baltimore's neighborhoods. The results of that mapping appeared sound in several respects, although it clearly reflected, in some locations, political dynamics limited to the period. The results of that mapping were published in 1979 (56). Later, following up on a project funded by the Mayor's Office, Allan Goodman and I recompiled 1970 and 1980 census information into those neighborhoods and did likewise for reported crime data (17).

Of course, as Suttles, Hunter, and others have argued, community is layered, and such a mapping artificially reifies neighborhoods, making them more static in time and place than they are. Layers of community, from the streetblock to the sector of the city, enfold the urban dweller and are sometimes manipulated or promulgated by outside actors (53). (The streetblock refers to both sides of the block face, between the two cross streets.)

But also think it can be a mistake to view neighborhood boundaries and names as completely fungible qualities. Baltimore boasts numerous neighborhoods the names or boundaries of which have persisted for decades and in some cases even match old parish or mill town boundaries (36). There is a texture and variation to Baltimore's settlement patterns, emerging from its history and topography, that is as much a part of its character as its downtown waterfront, its port, or its Mid-Atlantic location. Neighborhood character in other cities is similarly unique (e.g., 23).

In 1981, as part of another project, pairs of trained raters toured 20% of the streetblocks (n=848) in sixty-six randomly selected city neighborhoods. Using a closed-ended rating form, they assessed traffic, housing, land use, and deterioration (59).

In 1982, in each of those same sixty-six neighborhoods, interviewers at SRA interviewed about two dozen residents by phone or in person. The interview asked about perceptions of the neighborhood, local involvement, fear of crime, and related issues (54).

In 1987, in another fifty randomly sampled neighborhoods, SRA interviewed about eight residents on one streetblock in each neighborhood. This survey, conducted largely by phone, focused in particular on fear of crime and its mental health impacts (38). A year later, SRA successfully reinterviewed over three quarters of those original respondents. We also conducted open-ended interviews with leaders in about forty of the fifty neighborhoods. I will use the 1987–1988 data only in a portion of Chapter 6, looking at changes over one year's time in reactions to crime and neighborhood commitment.

The latest project, on which the current volume relies most heavily, began in 1994. Returning to thirty neighborhoods sampled from the originally sampled sixty-six neighborhoods, trained raters completed on-site assessments of block conditions in the summer of 1994. Sidney Brower, Steve Pardue, and I each selected three blocks in each of the thirty neighborhoods, choosing blocks where we had completed on-site assessments in 1981 and that had a substantial number of occupied households on them.[3] Where more than the required number of blocks were available, we sampled.[4] We included in our ratings some of the same items that had been used in the original assessments.

In the fall of 1994, SRA began telephone interviews with residents on those ninety blocks. The interviews included many items from the original 1982 survey, but added an additional battery of items concerned with neighborhood fabric (5). Interviewing began in September and ended in early November. A small number of additional blocks were added in a few neighborhoods.

Beginning in the late winter of 1994, Steve Pardue and Mary Hyde conducted semi–open-ended interviews with a range of local actors. We first interviewed district planners, asking about local conditions in different parts of the city and about special issues pertinent to our sampled neighborhoods. In each sampled neighborhood, we also attempted to interview a neighborhood leader who had been in the area for at least seven to ten years. We had a particular interest in how matters had changed in each neighborhood, and this restriction on length of residence made it difficult in some neighborhoods to find an eligible leader. Later, in 1995, we also sampled a number of additional neighborhoods (n=42) to better understand neighborhood redefinition between 1978 and 1990 and talked to leaders in as many of those neighborhoods as we could. Again, we concentrated on identifying leaders who had been in the area for at least seven to ten years, so that they could speak with some authority about the history of their neighborhood's boundaries.

In the spring of 1995, Steve Pardue and I revisited and photographed almost all of the blocks where interviews had taken place the fall before, going back to some blocks two or three times. We walked the blocks, talked to local residents, and chatted with shopkeepers. One of the latter wanted to know who he had to pay off to get his liquor license. On several blocks, even very early in the morning, it did not feel safe to conduct these walking tours, and we did not.

For the period around the survey, we scanned the *Baltimore Sun*, cutting out articles that related to project themes or neighborhoods. David Linne and I used these items to describe how the media portrayed events during the project period. Of course, the media's selection of stories serves its own purposes and may not accurately depict what is "really happening" in these communities. Nevertheless, it provides us with one way to describe high-profile events during the time of the survey.

We obtained 1990 census data and programmed that into our original 1979 neighborhoods. We also obtained reported crime for the period 1980 through 1992 and programmed that similarly. To recompile this updated information into the neighborhoods, it was necessary to reconstruct our mapping of all census blocks in the city to specific neighborhoods. The next section describes how we organized our examination of this evidence to address specific questions surrounding the incivilities thesis.

The Argument and the Chapters Ahead

Data are limited largely to one city, although I do in places draw on studies completed in other cities across the country (Chicago, Atlanta, Seattle, Spokane, Minneapolis–St. Paul). Consequently, some time is spent in the following chapter considering whether the changes seen in Baltimore over the past quarter century—the population shifts, the economic transformations, and the changes in reported crime—are typical of what took place in comparably sized cities during the period.

Academics and policymakers are often adept at dismissing results not to their liking. Those who find themselves displeased with the results to follow can most easily discount them by arguing that the findings are limited only to Baltimore. But the typicality of Baltimore's situation, combined with the similarity between findings here and those seen in several other cities, suggest otherwise.

Furthermore, it is not possible to provide the different kinds of detailed data used here, of several different varieties, and simultaneously collect that information from a nationally representative sample of cities. Simultaneous depth and breadth are not feasible.

Finally, for those concerned about generality, it is worth remembering that some of our most powerful insights about urban neighborhoods come from observations collected in just one city, often just one or two neighborhoods, whether it be interviews in a renovating Boston neighborhood in the 1950s (16), reflections on Greenwich Village's Hudson Street at the end of the 1950s (24), observations on neighborhood social life in the Adams area of 1960s Chicago (52), or insights into street life in two racially and economically mixed neighborhoods in West Philadelphia at the close of the 1980s (1).

Turning from the data background to the theoretical background, the arguments advanced about incivilities—the incivilities thesis—receive close scrutiny in Chapter 3. About twenty-five years ago, the incivilities thesis started out connecting fearful urban residents with socially chaotic and physically deteriorated neighborhood conditions. Since that time, the thesis evolved in three important ways. Researchers shifted their focus from differences between neighbors to differences between neighborhoods. For example, the question shifted from why is Ms. Able so much more fearful than Ms. Baker to why are residents of West Hills so much more fearful than residents of East Hills? In addition, researchers suggested that incivilities affected additional outcomes beyond just fear itself: neighborhood crime rates and the fundamental quality and stability of the neighborhood itself. Finally, attention shifted from a cross-sectional view to a longitudinal one. In short, the argument became progressively ecologized and longitudinal and moved beyond the initial focus on fear. Yet the data to support the argument in its newer form have not yet appeared, and fundamental questions persist about the independent contribution of incivilities to changes in neighborhood fear, crime, and fabric.

Although the conceptual ground has shifted under the incivilities thesis, work has continued to rely heavily on one type of incivilities indicator: problems perceived by residents and reported through surveys. Alternate data sources from newspapers or on-site assessments of conditions appear far less often. Turning back to the question addressed earlier, if incivilities have a common underlying cause, such as disorder or lack of collective efficacy or lack of social capital, we might expect that different indicators of incivilities would shift in the same way over time. Chapter 4 considers changes over time in incivilities perceived by residents and as reflected in on-site conditions. Several features of the results suggest incivilities may not share strong connections to a common, underlying cause. Further, different types of incivility indicators change in different ways over time. A neighborhood where residents see problems as more serious than previously may be a neighborhood where vacant housing has decreased. In addition, the causes of changing incivilities are somewhat different depending on the type of indicator. It appears that the indicators used may reflect a variety of only loosely related conditions rather than a single, broader underlying disorder.

Turning next to the impacts of incivilities on changes in crime, Chapter 5 considers whether incivilities, assessed or perceived, contributed to decade-long relative changes in crime rates or changes in fundamental neighborhood fabric. For violent crime changes, independent impacts of incivilities emerge, after controlling for contemporaneous structure, on homicide, rape, and assault. Different types of indicators, however, prove relevant to each crime. Looking at structural decline, results show independent impacts of incivilities on increasing disadvantage, but not on shifts in stability or status.

Thus, Chapter 5 shows independent, lagged, ecological impacts of incivilities on three out of four subsequent violent crime changes, and one out of three pathways of structural decline. These results provide empirical support for the longitudinal, ecological version of the incivilities thesis. The longitudinal results provided here partially support the cross-sectional ecological findings of other authors.

That pattern of partial support continues in Chapter 6, which examines lagged impacts of incivilities on fear of crime and local commitment. Lagged, ecological impacts of incivilities appear for two out of the six outcomes examined. More striking, however, are the extremely consistent and strong connections between perceived incivilities and reactions to crime at the *neighbor* rather than the *neighborhood* level.

The support for the longitudinal, ecological version of the incivilities thesis is described as only partial, however, for three reasons. First, the ecological, longitudinal version of the incivilities thesis may have overreached when specifying its ecological outcomes. Initial incivilities linked to only one of the three pathways of later decline. Second, the empirical support seen in Chapter 5 is not only inconsistent across outcomes, it also is inconsistent across indicators. For no single crime or structural outcome was a significant impact of incivilities observed that persisted across two different indicators for incivilities. The lack of consistent impacts observed across various indicators, coupled with a failure (Chapter 3) of the different indicators to correlate closely with one another leaves open important questions about convergent validity of the indicators used, as well as more fundamental questions about the disorder construct. Third, the pattern of lagged incivility impacts deserves consideration in the context of the performance of other predictors, especially initial status and initial racial composition. Initial status influenced two later crime changes; it also influenced later changes in psychological outcomes. The far-reaching impacts of relative neighborhood standing speak to the power of neighborhood exchange value. Once a relatively privileged position has been obtained in the urban community status hierarchy, a range of social and political processes are set into motion (see Chapters 7 and 8) that help protect those advantages. The result is that crime and fear both grow less in these locales than elsewhere.

Race also matters; it consistently influenced changing homicide rates, in all the equations examined. Increasing violence in predominantly African-American neighborhoods corresponds closely to a volume of cross-sectional work on communities and crime. But race also provided several unexpected results. To take just one example, for four outcomes of the six considered in Chapter 6, neighborhoods that were more predominantly African-American at the beginning of the decade were *less* likely to show increasing concern or decreasing commitment over time. Race also linked in unexpected ways to changing deterioration. The connections between neighborhood racial composition and the outcomes considered here need a lot more examination.

The message to take home from the central chapters testing hypotheses generated by the longitudinal, ecological version of the incivilities is that incivilities *do* matter for crime changes, for structural changes, and for fear changes. But—and this is an important "but," as they say—incivilities do not matter for as many outcomes as proponents of this thesis have suggested; nor do they matter as consistently as other features of neighborhood fabric, especially status; nor do they matter consistently, regardless of the indicator used. Further, in the case of reactions to crime, the individual-level impacts of incivilities are more strongly confirmed. For this set of outcomes, the individual-level thesis appears far stronger than the ecological version.

The perhaps even more important message to take home is the need for broader theoretical integration. Theorizing on incivilities needs to reconnect more firmly with works in the areas of urban sociology, urban political economy, collective community crime prevention and organizational participation. Changes in neighborhood fabric, neighborhood crime rates, and residents' safety concerns are each tangled topics with a range of causes. To gain a clearer picture of these processes, it is necessary to break away from broken windows per se, and broaden the lines of inquiry. In Chapters 7 and 8, the author attempts to take his own advice.

To incorporate neighborhood leaders' perspective on incivilities and reconnect with the field of community crime prevention, Chapter 7 examines what leaders are doing to address these and other crime-related concerns. In other words, what is the broader array of collective crime prevention initiatives undertaken by local leaders and how does incivilities reduction fit into that? A conceptual framework developed by Aaron

Podolefsky about two decades ago, prior to the "crack invasion" of the mid to late 1980s, suggests residents can pursue activities designed either to prevent the specific crimes of concern or to address deeper social problems. We find leaders still engaged in both types of initiatives; which type they favor depends heavily on the economic and racial makeup of the neighborhood, as Podolefsky previously predicted. The reduction of incivilities represents an important strategy adopted by local leaders for enhancing neighborhood safety, but for the most part, such initiatives do not overshadow other approaches to reducing crime and related problems. In other words, despite the considerable attention lavished on reducing incivilities, we ought not lose sight of the broad range of prevention strategies pursued by leaders.

Chapter 8 widens the view even further, looking at political-organizational changes over time in neighborhoods. Such shifts appear as changes in neighborhood names or boundaries, or both. If police are to cooperate with citizen groups in coproducing public safety, they need to identify the locale and the groups who are their partners. Potential impediments to the formation of such partnerships are shifts in neighborhood names and boundaries. Chapter 8 considers such changes: How frequent are they? Are they patterned, more likely to occur in some types of neighborhoods than others? And what types of changes do we see? The purpose here is to describe the types of shifts witnessed and to consider how police departments seeking to stabilize community policing partnerships might address such shifts. These descriptive materials testify to the local political clout of better-off neighborhoods, the names, boundaries, and organizations of which appear more salient and more stable over time. Ironically, the neighborhoods with the highest relative status have given up on coproduction, opting instead to finance private policing. The locales where the political leadership is most stable and neighborhood contours most clearly defined—the higher-income, predominantly white neighborhoods—and thus the locations where coproduction would present the fewest interorganizational impediments, have turned their back on coproduction.

The "Bottom Line"

For the time-pressed reader who would rather grade exams, go to the beach, write a memo, bake bread, make a new policy, talk to family members, or write another article rather than read the rest of this volume, what is the "bottom line?" Enter the dreaded two-handed social scientist who makes people wish desperately for the one-handed version.

On the one hand, the longitudinal, ecological version of the incivilities thesis receives support in each of the three outcome areas examined.

How much deterioration or disorderly social behavior was noted initially in a neighborhood either by its residents or by outside raters did have an independent impact on later, relative violent crime changes (three out of four), later unexpected structural decline (one out of three pathways), and changing reactions to crime, including local commitment (two out of six). The longitudinal work does support results seen previously with only cross-sectional analyses. Further, it does underscore for reactions to crime and local commitment the independent importance of physical problems in a locale. The incivilities thesis is not just a repackaged social disorganization theory.

But, on the other hand, the support for the ecological, longitudinal version of the thesis is only partial. It is partial for the following reasons. First, initial incivilities did not affect as many outcomes as the theory has suggested. Second, which indicator was used for incivilities mattered a lot. For both decline and crime changes, no impact was observed across two different incivilities indicators. The inconsistency across indicators, when coupled with loose connections among the indicators themselves, suggests that incivilities may not reflect an underlying disorder, but rather a constellation of only loosely connected, somewhat separate problems that may each require somewhat unique policy responses. Third, incivilities do not show overwhelming impacts when contrasted with either initial structure or with initial crime rates. Generally, initial status, racial composition, and crime rates are as important as initial incivilities in shaping later changes. Given this broader array of ecological causes, broader theoretical integration is needed. Researchers and policymakers alike need to break away from broken windows per se and widen the models upon which they rely, both to predict and to preserve safe and stable neighborhoods with assured and committed residents.

Do the present results mean that police administrators ought to abandon grime-fighting initiatives like the Oakland Beat Health initiative or zero tolerance policies like the Fourth District's corner-clearing initiative? No. The present results do not provide evaluations of specific programs. Such initiatives may be able to achieve noticeable improvements. At the same time, the current results caution against hoping that a cumulation of such initiatives will "turn around" a neighborhood. It is one thing to show short-term improvements in local calls for service or feelings of personal safety. It is another to achieve improvements that will last over a decade or more. In addition, the current results might encourage police administrators to reevaluate the *relative* value of grime-fighting initiatives, compared to other traditional or community policing initiatives. Such administrators should not a priori decide that grime fighting is the best approach. Other strategies may deserve equal consideration.

Similarly, officials responsible for urban redevelopment ought not hope that grime-fighting initiatives by themselves will restore the fundamental fabric of neighborhoods which has been damaged by decades of inadequate city services, declining employment opportunities for its adults, and declining educational quality for its youth. That fundamental fabric continues to cause shifts, unfolding over time, in how residents view their locale and in what it is like to live there.

Perhaps the most important policy direction suggested by the current results is that officials—and researchers as well—should develop a more integrated perspective. The central dynamics described by the incivilities thesis need to be folded into the broader work in human ecology, urban sociology, and reactions to crime. We know a fair amount about the multiplicity of factors affecting urban neighborhoods over time and how residents view those neighborhoods. Work on the incivilities thesis has been pursued too often apart from this other work. A more complete picture will better guide program initiatives and theoretical development.

Notes

1. There are, of course, important differences between some of these authors in their views (18).

2. Of course, there are numerous important exceptions, such as the households living for thirty years in a public housing community.

3. In the sampling of streetblocks in 1981, we assessed locations regardless of whether there were occupied houses on them.

4. In 1994, since we also wished to complete residential interviews on the same blocks where we had assessed conditions, we limited ourselves to blocks with at least twelve residential addresses.

References

(1) Anderson, E. (1991) *Streetwise: Race, class and change in an urban community*, University of Chicago Press, Chicago.
(2) Boccella, K. (1996) Police cracking down on street-corner gatherings. *Philadelphia Inquirer* May 5, B1, B3.
(3) Boland, B. (1998) The Manhattan experiment: Community prosecution. In *Crime and place: Plenary papers of the 1997 Conference on Criminal Justice Research and Evaluation*, pp. 51–68. Washington, DC: National Institute of Justice.
(4) Bratton, W. (1998) *The Turnaround*, Random House, New York.
(5) Brower, S., and Taylor, R. B. (1997) Qualities of ideal and real-world neighborhoods. In *Evolving environmental ideals: Changing ways of life, values, and design practices* (Gray, M., ed), pp. 99–106. Kungliga Tekniska Hogskolan, Stockholm.

(6) Bursik, R. J. (1988) Social disorganization and theories of crime and delinquency. *Criminology* 26, 519–551.

(7) Bursik, R. J., and Grasmick, H. G. (1993) *Neighborhoods and crime: The dimensions of effective social control*, Lexington Books, New York.

(8) Coleman, J. S. (1988) Social capital and the creation of human capital. *American Journal of Sociology* 94, Supplement S95–S120.

(9) Covington, J., and Taylor, R. B. (1991) Fear of crime in urban residential neighborhoods: Implications of between and within-neighborhood sources for current models. *Sociological Quarterly* 32, 231–249.

(10) Crenson, M. (1983) *Neighborhood politics*, Harvard University Press, Cambridge, MA.

(11) Crowell, A. (1996) Minor restrictions: The challenge of juvenile curfews. *Public Management* August, 4–9.

(12) Dubow, F., McCabe, F., and Kaplan, G. (1979) *Reactions to crime: A critical review of the literature*, Government Printing Office, Washington, DC.

(13) Fee, E., Shopes, L., and Zeidman, L. (1991) *The Baltimore book: New views of local history*, Temple University Press, Philadelphia.

(14) Ferraro, K. F. (1994) *Fear of crime: Interpreting victimization risk*, State University of New York Press, Albany.

(15) Fisher, J. D., Bell, P. A., and Baum, A. (1984) *Environmental psychology*, Holt, Rinehart and Winston, New York.

(16) Gans, H. J. (1962) *The urban villagers*, Free Press, New York.

(17) Goodman, A. C., and Taylor, R. B., eds. (1983) *The Baltimore neighborhood fact book*, Center for Metropolitan Planning and Research, Johns Hopkins University, Baltimore.

(18) Gottdiener, M. (1994) *The social production of urban space* 2nd ed., University of Texas Press, Austin.

(19) Gottdiener, M., and Feagin, J. R. (1988) The Paradigm shift in urban sociology. *Urban Affairs Quarterly* 24, 163–187.

(20) Green, L. (1996) *Policing places with drug problems*, Sage, Thousand Oaks, CA.

(21) Henig, J. R. (1982) Neighborhood response to gentrification: Conditions of mobilization. *Urban Affairs Quarterly* 17, 343–358.

(22) Hilson, R., Jr. (1995) Neighbors vow to fight juvenile jail plan. *Baltimore Sun* February 26, B1, B4.

(23) Jablonsky, T. J. (1993) *Pride in the jungle: Community and everyday life in Back of the Yards Chicago*, Johns Hopkins University Press, Baltimore.

(24) Jacobs, J. (1968) Community on the city streets. In *The search for community in modern America* (Baltzell, E. D., ed), pp. 74–93. New York: Harper and Row.

(25) Kelling, G., and Bratton, W. (1993) *Implementing community policing: The administrative problem*, July 1993, National Institute of Justice, Washington, DC.

(26) Kennedy, L. W., and Silverman, R. A. (1985) Significant others and fear of crime among the elderly. *International Journal of Aging and Development* 20, 241–256.

(27) LaGrange, R. L., and Ferraro, K. F. (1989) Assessing age and gender differences in perceived risk and fear of crime. *Criminology* 27, 697–719.

(28) LaGrange, R. L., and Ferraro, K. F. (1992) Perceived risk and fear of crime: Role of social and physical incivilities. *Journal of Research in Crime and Delinquency* 29, 311–334.

(29) Lane, R. (1986) *Roots of violence in black Philadelphia 1860–1900*, Harvard University Press, Cambridge, MA.

(30) Liska, A. E., Sanchirico, A., and Reed, M. D. (1988) Fear of crime and constrained behavior: Specifying and estimating a reciprocal effects model. *Social Forces* 66, 827–837.

(31) Logan, J. R., and Molotch, H. (1987) *Urban fortunes*, University of California Press, Berkeley.

(32) Maccoby, E. E., Johnson, J. P., and Church, R. M. (1958) Community integration and the social control of juvenile delinquency. *Journal of Social Issues* 14, 38–51.

(33) Mazzerolle, L. G., Kadleck, C., and Roehl, J. (1998) Controlling drug and disorder problems: The role of place managers. *Criminology* 36, 371–404.

(34) McDougall, H. A. (1993) *Black Baltimore: A new theory of community*, Temple University Press, Philadelphia.

(35) Miethe, T. (1995) Fear and withdrawal from urban life. *Annals of the American Academy of Political and Social Science* 539, 14–27.

(36) Olson, S. H. (1997) *Baltimore: The building of an American city*, revised and expanded bicentennial ed., Johns Hopkins University Press, Baltimore.

(37) Orser, E. (1997) *Blockbusting in Baltimore: The Edmondson Village story*, University of Kentucky Press, Lexington.

(38) Perkins, D. D., Meeks, J. W., and Taylor, R. B. (1992) The physical environment of streetblocks and resident perceptions of crime and disorder: Implications for theory and measurement. *Journal of Environmental Psychology* 12, 21–34.

(39) Rosenfeld, R. (1994) Review of *Neighborhoods and crime*. *American Journal of Sociology* 99, 1387–1389.

(40) Rountree, P. W., and Land, K. C. (1996) Burglary victimization, perceptions of crime risk, and routine activities: A multilevel analysis across Seattle neighborhoods and census tracts. *Journal of Research in Crime and Delinquency* 33, 147–180.

(41) Rountree, P. W., and Land, K. C. (1996) Perceived risk versus fear of crime: Empirical evidence of conceptually distinct reactions in survey data. *Social Forces* 74, 1353–1376.

(42) Ruefle, W., and Reynolds, K. M. (1995) Curfews and delinquency in major American cities. *Crime & Delinquency* 41, 347–363.

(43) Ryon, R. N. (1993) *West Baltimore neighborhoods: Sketches of their history: 1840–1900*, University of Baltimore, Institute for Publications Design, Baltimore.

(44) Sampson, R. J., and Grove, W. B. (1989) Community structure and crime: Testing social disorganization theory. *American Journal of Sociology* 94, 774–802.

(45) Sampson, R. J., Raudenbush, S. W., and Earls, F. (1997) Neighborhoods and violent crime: A multi-level study of collective efficacy. *Science* 277, 918–924.

(46) Sampson, R., and Wilson, W. (1995) Toward a theory of race, crime, and urban inequality. In *Crime and inequality* (Hagan, J., and Peterson, R., eds), pp. 37–54. Stanford University Press, Stanford.

(47) Shaw, C. R., and McKay, H. D. (1969 [1942]) *Juvenile delinquency and urban areas* 2nd ed., University of Chicago Press, Chicago.

(48) Silverman, R. A., and Kennedy, L. W. (1985) Age, perception of social diversity and fear of crime. *Environment and Behavior* 17, 235–251.

(49) Skogan, W. (1986) Fear of crime and neighborhood change. In *Crime and justice: A review of research,* Vol. 8: *Communities and crime* (Reiss, A. J., Jr., and Tonry, M., eds), pp. 203–230. University of Chicago Press, Chicago.

(50) Skogan, W. (1990) *Disorder and decline: Crime and the spiral of decay in American cities,* Free Press, New York.

(51) Stanko, E. A. (1995) Women, crime, and fear. *Annals of the American Academy of Political and Social Science* 539, 46–58.

(52) Suttles, G. D. (1968) *The social order of the slum,* University of Chicago Press, Chicago.

(53) Suttles, G. D. (1972) *The social construction of communities,* University of Chicago Press, Chicago.

(54) Taylor, R. B. (1996) Neighborhood responses to disorder and local attachments: The systemic model of attachment, and neighborhood use value. *Sociological Forum* 11, 41–74.

(55) Taylor, R. B. (1998) Crime in small scale places: What we know, what we can do about it. In *Research and Evaluation Conference 1997,* pp. 1–20. Washington, DC: National Institute of Justice.

(56) Taylor, R. B., Brower, S., and Drain, W. (1979) *A map of Baltimore neighborhoods,* Center for Metropolitan Planning and Research, Johns Hopkins University, Baltimore.

(57) Taylor, R. B., and Covington, J. (1993) Community structural change and fear of crime. *Social Problems* 40, 374–397.

(58) Taylor, R. B., and Hale, M. (1986) Testing alternative models of fear of crime. *Journal of Criminal Law and Criminology* 77, 151–189.

(59) Taylor, R. B., Shumaker, S. A., and Gottfredson, S. D. (1985) Neighborhood-level links between physical features and local sentiments: Deterioration, fear of crime, and confidence. *Journal of Architectural Planning and Research* 2, 261–275.

(60) Warr, M. (1984) Fear of victimization: Why are women and the elderly more afraid? *Social Science Quarterly* 65, 681–702.

(61) Warr, M. (1985) Fear of rape among urban women. *Social Problems* 32, 238–250.

(62) Warr, M. (1990) Dangerous situations: Social context and fear of victimization. *Social Forces* 68, 891–907.

(63) Wilson, W. J. (1996) *When work disappears: The world of the new urban poor,* Knopf, New York.

2

The Baltimore Context, and Its Context

WITH CHARLES DAVID LINNE

The War Has Been Won?

In February 1995, the mayor of Baltimore, Kurt L. Schmoke, in the midst of his primary campaign for a second term (33), announced that the battle had been won. He declared success in his campaigns against crime, racial and ethnic discrimination, physical decay, and governmental rule restrictions (136).

Schmoke's announcement came at a curious time. His administration was embattled on several fronts: there was unflattering, extensive, in-depth newspaper coverage of at least two city departments (police and housing) had recently appeared; and violent crime rates remained stubbornly high despite dropping rates in some other nearby cities. Later in this chapter, we review some of the coverage on crime and disorder at the time Schmoke was seeking reelection, and we were interviewing residents and leaders. But before doing that, we review structural and crime changes in Baltimore and in nearby and comparable cities. What were the *structural* challenges facing Schmoke during his first and second terms, and how long had these problems been brewing?

Baltimore, founded in 1797 on a branch of the Patapsco River, off the upper Chesapeake Bay, had thrived during and immediately after World War II, population and manufacturing jobs growing to meet the needs of the wartime and later the postwar economies, the population cresting at just over a million in 1950. During the 1960s, growing suburban locations proved more attractive, and the city experienced its first decade of sizable postwar population losses, as well as riots in the spring of 1968. Under

Mayor William Donald Schaefer (1971–1986), Baltimore drew nationwide attention as a city roaring back. "*Esquire* called Schaefer the country's best mayor, and *Time* nicknamed Baltimore the 'Renaissance City'" (110: 389). During Schaefer's reign, new shops, an aquarium, and entertainment venues emerged in the Inner Harbor, a revitalized former dock area of the downtown; and city sales of "dollar houses" to renovators helped gentrify decaying neighborhoods, resulting in seemingly wholesale makeovers of several communities near the downtown. These and other developments drew the public's attention. At the same time, overall city spending was cut, and school budgets were trimmed about a quarter (110: 398; 98). Detractors talked about the decay beneath the glitter.

Whether Schaefer's strategy was successful or sorely misdirected is an argument that is likely to continue for some time. Nonetheless, the popular impression held by many was that the city did well under Schaefer (20: 680–690). Schmoke, born in the city, with degrees from Yale University and Harvard Law School, after serving as Assistant U.S. Attorney (1978–1981) and in elected office as State's Attorney (1981–1987), took over the mayoralty in 1988 from "Du" Burns, former chair of the city council, who briefly held the position following Schaefer's "retirement." (Schaefer went on to serve as governor.) Schmoke was the first African American elected to the office of mayor in Baltimore (6). Hopes were high.

But criticism proved unending. Even though Schmoke's administration touted achievements in literacy, housing, economic redevelopment, and safety, his announced victory noted above coincided with unflattering newspaper analyses of the police department and his housing commissioner, Donald Henson. A pilot privatization program in city schools, important to Schmoke, given his strong interest in literacy, touted higher test scores, but it later turned out additional resources had quietly been targeted to these schools. Leaders in African-American neighborhoods criticized his administration as distant and uncaring about their concerns (102). Maybe it was inevitable that so many would be disappointed, since expectations had been so high. In 1999, Schmoke announced that he would not seek a third term as mayor.

Unfortunately for Mayor Schmoke, not only were hopes for his success perhaps unrealistically high before he took office, and not only was he following one of the city's reputedly most successful and certainly most colorful mayors in several decades, he took office just as the "crack invasion" was appearing on Baltimore's streets and violent crime rates nationwide were starting to run up. We will turn to crime and census data to see how Baltimore changed in the 1970s and 1980s. We suggest that the structural challenges confronting Schmoke as he took office—what had been happening in the 1970s and 1980s in Baltimore and in other large, older cities—were far more formidable than those facing Schaefer when he took office. Comparing Baltimore's changes in structure and crime indicate that the city was suffering under numerous burdens at the end of the 1980s, and these were typical of what had happened elsewhere. The examination also suggests that under Schaefer matters may not have improved as much as many thought. The purpose in this section is not to evaluate either Schaefer's or Schmoke's administrations. Rather, we want to describe the changes taking place during their watches. They had scant control over many of them.

Describing the Baltimore context hints at some conclusions that may be unexpected. Both structural and crime shifts suggest that Baltimore suffered far worse in the 1970s—when it was viewed as prospering—than it did in the 1980s—when it was viewed as struggling. Job losses were more sizable, and crime increases were more marked in the earlier decade. Distributions of neighborhood crime rates suggest that low-crime, relatively safe neighborhoods disappeared largely in the 1970s, not the 1980s. In line with this pattern, we also see that despite worsening citywide physical deterioration in the 1980s, the typical Baltimore resident was *not* more fearful, generally, in 1994 than in 1982; nor did this typical resident see his or her neighborhood as more problem-plagued.

Purpose

This chapter describes the context in which our research took place. Its purposes are to describe events related to the incivilities thesis and crime taking place at the time of our 1994–1995 data collection, as reported by the local paper; to describe just a few of the structural changes taking place in Baltimore in the 1970s and 1980s; to see how Baltimore compares to a few other cities around the country on these changes; to describe changes in Baltimore crime rates in the 1970s and 1980s and to see how these changes compare to those taking place in the nearby cities of Philadelphia and Washington, D.C.; and to examine citywide changes in fear and incivilities using our 1982 and 1994 surveys as well as physical changes on the 1994 study blocks between 1981 and 1994. The purpose here is largely descriptive, to fill in the context surrounding our research. We want to provide the reader with a better sense of concerns about crime and incivilities at the time of the study and a view of recent structural and crime changes.

At the same time, when we look at the context of the context—what was happening in other cities at the time—we think a case can be made that Baltimore's changes are relatively typical of shifts seen in other cities of about the same size.[1] Certainly, every city has its unique history. But major changes in city fabric, population, and crime seen in Baltimore appear far from atypical when examined in the context of changes in other cities.

Changes in People, Housing, and Jobs

Most scholars accept that many big cities in the United States have changed considerably in the past quarter century. Those changes, particularly as they affect the lives of workers, have been documented elsewhere (12, 95, 114).

> Since the 1970s urban areas in the United States and in other industrialized nations have been subjected to a series of unprecedented changes. Two of the most fundamental involve, on the one hand, the restructuring of the economic base and the shift from mass industrial production to high technology manufacturing and information processing, and, on the other, the demographic diffusion of population on a massive scale across metropolitan regions. (53: 1)

Both these shifts are evident in Baltimore. Between 1970 and 1995, the region lost 90,000 factory jobs (110: 392); firms such as Bethlehem Steel, General Motors, and W. R. Grace reduced workforces in the 1980s, often dramatically. Although the losses reflected ongoing deindustrialization nationwide and echo the closing of the Philadelphia shipyard noted in Chapter 1, the changes may have been worse in Baltimore, given its curse: It has always been a "branch" town. "Branch plants don't make decisions" (110: 392). Growth in the region boomed, adding 454,000 persons from 1970 to 1990, even as the city population dropped by about a fifth, slipping below 700,000 in 1995 (110: 455; 16).

To contrast changes happening in Baltimore during the 1970s and 1980s with other cities of about the same size or smaller, we selected a sample of moderately large cities, spread geographically around the county, with populations between 300,000 (El Paso) and 800,000 (Washington, D.C.) in 1970.[2] Baltimore's 1970 population was over 905,000. We also included Philadelphia, even though its 1970 population, just a shade under 2 million, was much greater. Including both Philadelphia and Washington, D.C., we compared Baltimore to its two closest large neighboring cities. We chose a small number of population and economic factors on which to compare the various cities. The purpose was simply to see if the types of changes occurring in the different locations are similar. Did the changes between 1970 and 1990 in Baltimore appear also in other locations? If the changes and trends observed were comparable, they would suggest that what Baltimore may have experienced in the period is comparable to what other cities experienced. Granted, every city is different and has a unique character and history. Nonetheless, the different locations may be confronted by similar challenges.

If we find, in terms of both structural change and crime change, that Baltimore is comparable to some other cities, it also shapes how we think about the generalizability of the results discussed in the later chapters. It would suggest that the dynamics observed and conclusions reached may apply elsewhere. Of course, the question of whether findings from one location do actually apply to another location can only be answered with data from that other location. External validity is always an empirical question. But points of similarity between Baltimore and other cities would suggest, at the least, that there is nothing atypical about the study location.

On a final orientation note, the results we examine here refer to changes within the city of Baltimore. From an ecological perspective, that city's role in the larger urban-suburban region has changed over the period, and some of the data we see here reflect that shifting role. As the region has grown and the city has lost population, it also has lost political power (110: 397). The city and surround are more split racially and economically (110: 396) than formerly. These differences result in a closer mapping of racial and class divisions onto political divisions than was previously the case. Since we are not looking at the surround, save in one series examining crime changes in the 1980s, we "overlook" this repositioning of the city in the broader metropolitan fabric. We focus on a location that plays a different "role" in the region than it did a quarter century ago.

"Losing" People

Baltimore, like many other eastern, or "rustbelt," cities, lost population from 1970 to 1990, going from around 900,000 to just over 700,000 people. The same percentage drop, around 20%, also afflicted Philadelphia and Washington, D.C., the two closest large cities. Cleveland experienced a slightly bigger drop, around 30%. Milwaukee and Boston also lost residents, but only about one tenth of their 1970 numbers. Of course, southern and western cities like El Paso, San Jose, and Phoenix, by contrast, all witnessed substantial growth with the move of population to the Sunbelt and annexation by some cities of outlying areas.

When the losses happened for the older, eastern cities proves surprising. For Baltimore; Philadelphia; Washington, D.C.; Cleveland; Milwaukee; and Boston, most of the drop took place in the 1970s, not the 1980s. In other words, the population losses occurred largely in the 1970s, and for these cities, at least, slowed considerably by the 1980s.[3] For Milwaukee and Boston, the figures for 1980 and 1990 are almost equivalent.

The Elderly and African Americans

Not only are there fewer people in these cities than a quarter century ago, the composition of the remaining city dwellers has changed as well. They are older and more likely to be African-American. In Baltimore, those sixty-five and up grew as a percentage of the population, up to almost 14% from around 11%. Philadelphia and Washington, D.C., showed roughly comparable percentage increases, as did the farther-away cities of Cleveland, Milwaukee, Indianapolis, and Memphis. Boston bucked the trend and "got younger," the proportion age sixty-five and up dropping from 13% to 11%.

Those remaining behind in these cities are not only more likely to be elderly; they also are more likely to be African-American. This racial shift nationwide, to the increasing location of poor, African-American households in segregated neighborhoods in central cities, has been documented elsewhere (51, 100) and is discussed at more length in Chapter 4. Baltimore followed this national shift, going from about 45% to almost 60% African-American during the period. Milwaukee and Memphis demonstrate comparably sized increases of 15% to 20% in the relative predominance of African Americans. The percentage shift (7% increase) appears much smaller in Philadelphia, but that is also a much larger city. Washington, D.C., goes against the trend here, becoming slightly less predominantly African-American during the period 1970–1990 (72% to 65%), but it had started out as the most African-American of the cities in the group of cities we examined.

Jobs, Unemployment, and Income

In Baltimore, manufacturing jobs as a percentage of all employment dropped precipitously, from about 26% in 1970, to about 18% in 1980, to about 12% in 1990. Philadelphia, Cleveland, Columbus, Indianapolis, and Milwaukee all saw comparably large percentage dips over the two decades. The drops in manufacturing in the 1970s and 1980s seem about comparable in these cities. Washington, D.C., being a government town, boasts little manufacturing, and the proportion in that sector remained steady over the period at about 5%. The manufacturing drop helps lay the groundwork for increasing incivilities in several ways; Chapter 4 will discuss those dynamics.

The loss of manufacturing jobs, however, is not mirrored clearly in increasing unemployment or increasing poverty. Both of these indicators show markedly worsening conditions in the 1970s, with modest improvements in the 1980s for Baltimore and its larger neighbor. In Baltimore, unemployment spurted from about 4% to 11% from 1970 to 1980, dropping back slightly to around 9% by 1990. Philadelphia showed a comparable pattern. Changes in the same direction, albeit not as large, also appeared in Indianapolis and Columbus (OH).

For Baltimore and Philadelphia, the changes in poverty mirror the changes in unemployment. Matters got a lot worse in the 1970s and improved slightly in the 1980s. In Baltimore, poverty went from 4% to 11% to 9%; in Philadelphia the percentage changes were about the same. Washington, D.C., and Boston show the same pattern. Again, by contrast, some cities, such as Cleveland, experienced increasing poverty over both decades. On this indicator of changing economic conditions, the 1970s appears to be the more important decade of the two for Charm City and its two neighboring cities. The 1970s were a period of loss, the 1980s a period of improvement.

Given markedly increasing poverty and unemployment in the 1970s and slightly improving conditions in the 1980s in Baltimore, it is no surprise to see changes in family income follow a similar pattern. In Baltimore, median family income, in constant 1983 dollars, dropped from around $23,000 to around $18,000 in the 1970s, gaining to around $22,000 by 1990. Roughly comparable patterns appear in Philadelphia, Indianapolis, and Memphis. Milwaukee and Cleveland appear to present worst case scenarios for this group of cities, with constant income dropping steadily over the two decades.

Housing

Median house prices in 1983 dollars increased steadily in Baltimore ($25,000 to $35,000 to $41,000) and in several other cities, such as Philadelphia, Indianapolis, San Antonio, and Memphis. Some cities, such as Boston; Washington, D.C.; Seattle; and San Francisco, experienced extremely dramatic increases during the period. Among the cities examined, Cleveland presents the worst case scenario, with prices dropping steadily through the period.

On vacant housing, including both for sale and for rent, as well as vacant and boarded up, Baltimore presents a slightly different picture than do its neighboring cities. In Baltimore, the vacancy rate stayed steady at about 7% through the 1970s, increasing markedly in the 1980s to around 9%. By contrast, vacancies increased somewhat in Washington, D.C. (6% to 8% to 10%) and Philadelphia (6% to 9% to 10%) during both decades. Cleveland's changes, however, look comparable to Baltimore's (8% to 8% to 11%).

The lag in the increased vacancies shown by Baltimore may be related to the numerous and widely publicized housing initiatives undertaken by Mayor Schaefer during the 1970s (20: 662–664). In addition to developing Harbor Place, he used low-interest, subsidized loans to lure home rehabbers into downtown neighborhoods such as Gay Street, Barre Circle, Ridgely's Delight, and others. And of course, gentrification without public assistance was ongoing elsewhere in the city (23).

These housing initiatives in the 1970s concentrated on some of the highest-vacancy neighborhoods in the city, but these were also a small

TABLE 2.1   Baltimore Community Changes in Vacancies and Homeownership,
1970–1990

Year	1970	1980	1990
Vacancy rate (average/median)	5.6% / 4%	7.4% / 5.1%	8.3% / 5.9%
Homeownership rate (average/median)	42.2% /44.4%	46.7% / 48.9%	50.8% / 53.1%

number of neighborhoods, probably less than two dozen, out of the city's 200+ neighborhoods. Consequently, if we examine changes in the community vacancy rates, rather than the citywide rate, we might see a different picture for the 1970s.

We do. The community rates suggest steady increases in both decades. Unweighted average and median vacancy and ownership rates, across communities, appear in Table 2.1.[4] The median rate, probably a more appropriate indicator given the highly skewed distribution of the rates, suggests roughly comparable increases in the vacancy rate during both decades or perhaps a slightly weaker increase in the 1980s. We also see homeownership has increased in both decades as more marginal rental housing has become unoccupied or destroyed during the period. Issues of vacant housing are covered in more detail later in the chapter, where we review initiatives undertaken by Schmoke's administration.

Summary

The changes affecting Baltimore look a lot like the changes affecting other, comparably sized cities in the east or the "rustbelt." Baltimore, like these other cities, has gotten smaller, with higher proportions of elderly and African Americans. Manufacturing jobs have dwindled markedly in the job mix. Unemployment and poverty have increased, but for Baltimore, and some other cities, the more sizable shifts on these issues occurred in the 1970s. Housing, in constant dollars, is more expensive, at the same time that vacancies are more widespread.

Changes in Crime: The City as a Whole

This section examines crime changes in Baltimore in relationship to crime changes in the comparison cities mentioned above and in relation to the surrounding area. For each Part I crime, save arson, we contrasted how the crime rate changed in Baltimore relative to all the comparison cities; in comparison to the two closest large cities of Philadelphia and Washington, D.C.; and, for the 1980s only, in comparison to the surrounding metropolitan statistical area (MSA). The MSA is a census-defined region, comprising a major city, sometimes two, and the surrounding suburbanized counties that depend on, or are linked to, the central city or cities. In comparing Baltimore with all the comparison cities, we look both at the raw data and at the percentage changes from the 1970 crime rate. The eight most serious, Part I, crimes, as defined by the FBI, are murder, rape, robbery, aggravated assault, burglary, larceny, motor vehicle theft, and arson. Since Baltimore is larger than most of the comparison cities, we would expect its crime rates to be higher. But our interest here also focuses on how crime changes in Baltimore either track or fail to track the changes occurring over time in the other cities. Although we looked at all Part I crimes, we report in detail here just the results for robbery. They were fairly typical of the patterns seen for the other violent crimes.[5] The years covered, except for the MSA comparison, are 1970 to 1992. These years correspond to the three decades of crime data used in the later analyses: 1970–1972 average; 1980–1982 average, and 1990–1992 average. Our purpose is to describe the crime context leading up to the 1994 study, not to provide an up-to-the-minute review of Baltimore's neighborhood crime rates.

Examining robbery rates, and changes in those rates, shows that Baltimore is less safe than many of the cities in the comparison group and that year-to-year changes in Baltimore roughly tracked changes seen in the comparison group. Furthermore, Baltimore's rate matched that of Washington, D.C., for much of the period, diverging only in the late 1980s.

Baltimore's robbery rate in 1970 (1200/100,000 population) started at about three times the rate seen in the comparison cities[6] (see Figure 2.1). But Baltimore's rate dropped through the early and mid-1970s, reaching around 950/100,000 by 1977, whereas the average rate for the other cities slowly climbed to about 500/100,000. From 1978 until about 1988, Baltimore's shifts shadowed shifts in the group average, except that the average fluctuated in a narrower range. For Baltimore and the cross-city average, rates climbed in the late 1970s, peaking in 1981 (almost 1,400/100,000 in Baltimore), then dropping through the mid-1980s. By 1988, Baltimore's rate was still below 1,000/100,000, whereas the group's average was around 500/100,000. Thereafter, Baltimore's robbery rate started to climb dramatically, moving steadily upward to about 1,700/100,000 by 1992. The average rate climbed more modestly for a couple of years, leveling out at about 650/100,000 in 1991 and 1992. The marked rise in all Baltimore crime rates from the late 1980s through the early 1990s has been widely attributed to the arrival of crack cocaine; emergency room data for Baltimore (see Chapter 7) appears to confirm this reading. Despite this marked divergence for the last four years of

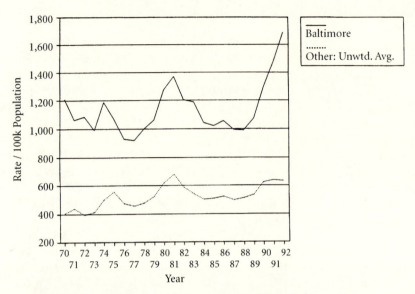

FIGURE 2.1   Baltimore and Comparison Cities: Robbery Rates,
1970–1992

the series, the growth in rates for 1970–1992 are not that different. Baltimore ended up with a rate about 55% higher than the one with which it started, whereas the comparison group's 1992 average rate was about 40% higher than where it started.

Looking at Baltimore's robbery rates relative to those of Washington, D.C., suggests relatively similar rates and shifts from about 1972 to 1990, although there was more volatility in Washington, D.C. The rate spiked higher in 1982 and dropped lower in the mid-1980s. The last two years (1991 and 1992) of the series show another discrepancy, with the rate in Washington, D.C., holding steady at about 1,200/100,000 and Baltimore's rate running up to about 1,700/100,000. Philadelphia's rate was much lower than the rates in the other two cities and did not fluctuate nearly as much. The Philadelphia police department has been suspected for some time of unfounding crimes at a high rate; in the spring of 1999 Commissioner John Timoney announced he was officially looking into the issue and taking steps to correct the situation (7).

Unfounding is a routine feature of police work. When a crime is reported, police will determine, typically based on subsequent investigative work, that a crime did or did not occur. If they conclude it did not, the crime is "unfounded." A wife comes home, finds the front door open and a broken pane in the door. She calls the police to report a burglary. The inves-

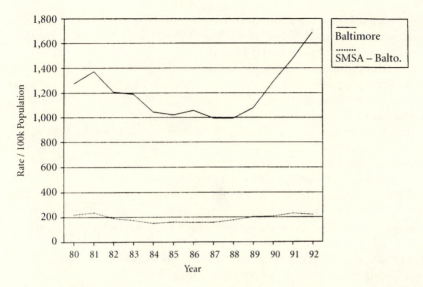

FIGURE 2.2   Baltimore and Surrounding Metropolitan Area: Robbery
Rates 1980–1992

tigating officer shows up and learns that the husband came home, broke in
because he lost his house key, then ran out for an Elks Club meeting and
left the door open. The officer would unfound the reported burglary. The
rate at which police unfound reported crimes is the unfounding rate.

If we look at Baltimore's robbery rates in the 1980s and contrast them
with the rates for the surrounding MSA, we see a disturbing pattern that
also appears for all other violent crimes (Figure 2.2). For most of the
1980s, Baltimore's robbery rate was a declining multiple of the rate in the
surrounding MSA, going from about seven times the MSA rate in 1981 to
about five times the MSA rate in 1988. But then the city rate takes off,
ending the period at over eight times the rate in the surrounding MSA.
The safety differential between the city and the surrounding counties
narrowed, then later widened noticeably. I will return to the widening
safety differential between Baltimore and the surrounding MSA when I
take up the question of changes in fear of crime.

To sum up on crime, Baltimore's rates, and the way those rates have
changed over time, do not appear unique. On many crimes, either the
rate change or the percentage change, or sometimes both, closely shadow
the multicity comparison group. Changes in rape and larceny and percentage changes in murder, for example, show relatively close parallels
between Baltimore changes and the comparison group. There is some

suggestion on a few crimes that Baltimore's pattern begins to diverge for the last two to four years of the series. But in the main, for several crimes, we see close parallels over much of the period

When we compare Baltimore to its large, neighboring sister cities, we also see some parallels. Baltimore's levels and changes in robbery, burglary, and larceny match those of Washington, D.C., except for the last couple of years in the series. It appears that for most of the period, we have roughly the same forces driving the changes in the two locations, at least for these crimes.

The above points are not to deny the third point: Each city is unique, as is each reported crime rate. With each city, there are differences in local history, we also have differences in citizen reporting practices, police recording practices, and police unfounding rates. We see some evidence of this specificity. Why does the murder rate in Washington, D.C., after having roughly paralleled Baltimore's rate from 1970 until about 1987, suddenly skyrocket? What was taking place in Washington, D.C., that was not taking place forty miles up Interstate 95?

Pulling apart these differences goes beyond the scope of the current effort. But the more important point is that the pattern of similarities and differences reviewed here suggest that Baltimore's reported crime rates from 1970 on, and the changes in those rates, were in no way unique or "peculiar." They look fairly comparable, on many crimes, to what was happening elsewhere. There is no suggestion that the crime context in Baltimore was unique.

Furthermore, for several crimes, the dramatically increasing crime rates of the late 1980s were not unprecedented. Rates almost as high, and in some cases higher, had been seen before, either at the beginning of the 1970s or the beginning of the 1980s. This appears to be the case with robbery; burglary; motor vehicle theft; and, to a lesser extent, murder.

Take the case of robbery in Baltimore. By the mid-1980s, the citywide rate was about 1,000/100,000 population/year. This rate was about 20% lower than the rate in 1970 and about 33% lower than the rate in 1981. The rate also stayed steady in the 1,000 range for several years, before beginning its dramatic increase in about 1989.

Motor vehicle theft presents an even clearer example. Rates in Baltimore dropped steadily from 1970 until about 1982. In the comparison cities, the rate dropped more gradually. But in Baltimore, the 1982 rate was about *half* the 1970 rate.

If the rates and the increases seen in the mid to late 1980s were not unprecedented, how are we to explain the dramatic increases in concern about crime and especially violent crime? The typical answers are that there had been a shift in the nature of the violence; it became more lethal or it involved youth more often than previously (48).

But the explanation may be simpler and rooted in the recent trends we have reviewed. What may have made the crime increase seen for several of these crimes from the mid-1980s on so troubling for residents is that the increase followed several years of decreasing, or at least steady, crime rates. For several of these crimes, we have seen the storm following the calm, and that contrast itself has served to deepen residents' and policy-makers' concerns.

Another contrast—at least in Baltimore—may have contributed to the public's anxiety attack over increasing urban crime rates from the late 1980s on: the increased rate differential between the city and the surrounding areas. The differential between the central city crime rate and the crime rate in the remainder of the MSA for the period 1980–1992 increased sharply for *all* crimes in the latter half of the period. For most crimes, the differential in the early 1980s was a ratio of city to surround of about 2:1. By the early 1990s, for most crimes, the differential was close to 3:1. In Baltimore during the last four to six years of the series, the relative dangerousness of the city, as compared to the surrounding area, increased markedly.

But we want to move beyond describing the city as a whole. Next we examine more specifically the crime changes taking place within Baltimore in the 1970s and 1980s and how neighborhood crime rates changed during the period.

Baltimore Neighborhood Crime Rates

In 1942, Clifford Shaw and Henry McKay in *Juvenile Delinquency in Urban Areas* documented the dramatic shrinkage of low-delinquency communities in Chicago during the first thirty years of the twentieth century. For example, using the delinquency commitment series, between the beginning of the century and 1930 the portion of the city with the lowest delinquency rate areas—that is, the bottom quarter, or quartile—shrank from 52% of the city to less than 30% (121: 70, Table 8). In this section, looking at changes in Baltimore crime rates for the period 1970 to 1992, we find an even more dramatic shrinkage in low-crime neighborhoods taking place within just one decade.

We examined the neighborhood crime rates in four different ways: (1) We looked at the average population-weighted neighborhood reported crime rate over time. Each neighborhood's 1990 population was used as the weight. We included both the downtown and the public housing neighborhoods in the city. (2) We also reexamined the weighted average rate after removing the downtown and the public housing communities. Our intention was to get an idea of how crime rates were shifting over time for "typical" neighborhoods. (3) Next, we examined crime rate changes in the thirty 1994 survey neighborhoods, considering both rates weighted by neighborhood population and unweighted rates, and compared those to rates in nonstudy neighborhoods. (4) Finally, we looked at the distribution of neighborhood crime rates in Baltimore at the beginning of the 1970s, the beginning of the 1980s, and the beginning of the 1990s to see how these distributions had shifted.

In brief, we found the following. For violent crimes, the thirty sampled neighborhoods had crime rates slightly lower than the citywide average community crime rates. Nevertheless, the sample demonstrated roughly comparable trends over time. For property crime, the sample rates more closely matched the average overall community rates, sometimes slightly exceeding them. As with violent crime trends, property crime trends in the sample matched the overall trends. Consequently, at least in terms of crime rates, from a purely descriptive perspective, the sample looked comparable to the city overall.

To more closely compare sample versus nonsample neighborhood crime rates, we tested the null hypothesis that at the beginning of each decade the sample average did not differ from the nonsample average.[7] We carried out a multivariate analysis of variance for each crime; the three dependent variables were the percentile scores based on 1970–1972, 1980–1982, and 1990–1992 rates. Since we have seven different crimes, and the different crimes are themselves related to one another, we carry out a Bonferroni adjustment of our alpha level, and use .05/7 or .007. The predictor was whether the community was in the 1994 sample or not. The downtown and public housing communities were excluded. For five of the seven crimes, the multivariate F was < 1, for robbery it was 1.9, and for motor vehicle theft it was 1.21. All these multivariate Fs are highly nonsignificant. In sum, the percentile crime rates for our thirty sampled neighborhoods are, on average, not markedly different from the average percentile crime rates in nonsampled neighborhoods. Results showed that they did *not* differ.

Changing Distributions of Neighborhood Crime Rates

So far we have been concentrating on average reported crime rates, or average crime percentiles. These averages, of course, do not capture all of the features of the crime rate distributions. To look more closely at the distributions and how they may have shifted over time, we computed measures of central tendency, dispersion, and quartiles for each of the crime distributions for each of the three periods: 1970–1972, 1980–1982, and 1990–1992. The comparisons across the decades showed the most sizable shifts in the distribution of neighborhood crime rates took place in the 1970s. For all of the crimes save motor vehicle theft, the most dra-

matic changes in means, medians, and twenty-fifth and seventy-fifth percentiles took place between 1970–1972 and 1980–1982. In the case of several crimes, the 1990–1992 figures were *lower* than the 1980–1982 figures.
From the figures reviewed earlier, we know that during the early 1980s
there was a peak or a bump in the crime rates. On several crimes, a
decade later, city neighborhoods look safer. But the peak or bump witnessed in the early 1980s is of interest because it coincided with our first
survey.

Another way to examine how the shape of the neighborhood crime
rate distributions have changed over the period is to see how different
points on the percentile distribution relate to specific crime rates and
how these correspondences have shifted over time. To get at this, we
plotted the weighted neighborhood crime percentile scores against the
logged neighborhood crime rates. Each figure displays the weighted percentile on the Y axis, and the logged crime rate on the X axis. The chart,
in essence a variation on a P-P (percentile-percentile) chart, shows how
the distribution of each crime shifts from decade to decade. These figures
told a simple story: Except for motor vehicle theft, the most noticeable
shifts in Baltimore's community crime rates took place in the 1970s. It
was during that period that large numbers of relatively safe, low-crime
neighborhoods disappeared.

Graphically, the change appears in two ways. See, for example, robbery, shown in Figure 2.3. The line shifts further to the right as the rate
increases from one decade to the next. In addition, as the large number
of safe neighborhoods disappear, the curve changes its shape. The steep
increase in the lower percentile ranges seen in 1970 is replaced by a
much flatter, stretched-out curve for the lower percentile neighborhoods.

In the early 1970s, a weighted robbery percentile crime score of 50 corresponded to a robbery rate of about 20/100,000 population. In other
words, if you lived in a neighborhood with this robbery rate, about 50%
of the residents in the city lived in neighborhoods with rates this low or
lower. Look also at the twentieth percentile for robbery in the early 1970s.
About 20% of the city's population lived in neighborhoods with robbery
rates of about 8 or lower.

By the early 1980s, both of these percentiles had shifted up noticeably.
Only about 5% of residents (down from 20%) lived in neighborhoods
with a robbery rate of 8 or lower. Only about 10% (down from 50%) of
residents lived in neighborhoods with robbery rates of 20/100,000 or
lower. The large number of relatively safe neighborhoods evident in
1970–1972 largely disappeared by 1980–1982. Changes in the distribution, of course, continued to take place between 1980–1982 and
1990–1992. But they were nowhere near as striking.

42

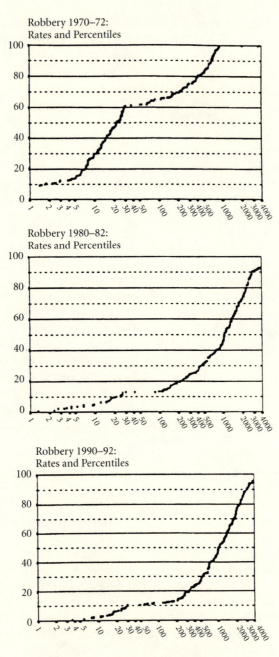

Robbery 1970–72:
Rates and Percentiles

Robbery 1980–82:
Rates and Percentiles

Robbery 1990–92:
Rates and Percentiles

FIGURE 2.3   Changing Distributions of
Baltimore Neighborhood Robbery Rates,
per 100,000 population, on log scale:
1970–1972, 1980–1982, 1990–1992

Assault looks similar. In the early 1970s, about one fifth of the neighborhoods, the safest 20%, had assault rates of 5/100,000 or lower. By the early 1980s, only about 3% to 4% of the neighborhoods had rates this low or lower.

Not only did the low-crime neighborhoods disappear in the 1970s, the number of extremely high crime neighborhoods increased. For robbery, in the early 1970s no neighborhoods had rates above 100/100,000 population. But by the early 1980s, about *half* of the city population lived with a neighborhood crime rate this high or higher.

Summary on Crime Changes

The thirty neighborhoods where we surveyed residents in 1994 have neighborhood crime rates typical of average neighborhood crime rates in the city on property crime, but perhaps slightly lower than average on violent crime. The weighted crime percentiles of the sampled neighborhoods, however, were no different from the weighted crime percentiles of the nonsampled neighborhoods. Furthermore, the trends over time seen in the study neighborhoods matched fairly closely the changes seen in most city neighborhoods for both property and violent crime.

Perhaps the most striking finding is the disappearance of large numbers of relatively safe neighborhoods during the 1970s and the appearance of large numbers of high-crime neighborhoods during that same time. For most crimes, matters continued to deteriorate during the 1980s. But the major shifts occurred during the 1970s. Motor vehicle theft appears to be the only marked exception to this pattern.[8]

These shifts do not accord well with public perceptions of Baltimore's renaissance and the subsequent stalling of that renaissance. Many view the 1970s as a period of significant achievement for the city, with the rise of the Inner Harbor and other downtown projects. Many also view the late 1980s and 1990s, the Schmoke years, as far less successful. But what we see here is that the safe neighborhoods virtually disappeared off the map during the 1970s, at the same time that gentrification and the renaissance were in full swing. These more extreme crime changes in the 1970s fit with the more extreme structural changes witnessed during that decade.

We are not suggesting that Mayor Schaefer deserves less kudos than he has received or that Mayor Schmoke deserves more. Evaluating the achievements of and challenges confronting each administration is a task far beyond the scope of this volume and our expertise. Others have begun those discussions (e.g., 98, 102, 110). The only point being made here

TABLE 2.2   Descriptive Information on Observed Streetblock Characteristics, 1981 and 1994

Characteristic	1981			1994		
	Mean	SD	% scoring	Mean	SD	% scoring
N Total occupied units	28.34	15.2	–	29.35	14.7	–
N Boarded-up houses per block	.31	.81	83% score 0	.51	1.48	79% score 0
% Boarded-up houses	01.0	.03	83% score 0	02.1	.05	79% score 0
% Houses boarded up or for sale or rent	01.8	.03	68% score 0	04.0	.08	50% score 0
% Residential frontage	90.84	14.21	53% completely residential	88.5	18.8	52% completely residential
Graffiti-free (1=no, 2=yes)	1.82	.36	79.5% graffiti-free	1.67	.45	63% graffiti-free
Maintenance[a]	–	–	–	3.55	.95	–
Structural condition[b]	–	–	–	3.55	1.05	–
Extent outdoor plantings[c]	–	–	–	2.49	.88	–
Total people	3.96	7.75	–	5.05	5.14	–
Traffic volume[d]	2.19	.94	–	1.78	.89	–

NOTE: n=88 for 1981 assessments; n=91 for 1994 assessments.
a. proportion of houses and buildings well maintained: 1=none; 2=small number; 3=about half; 4=well more than half; 5=all.
b. proportion of houses and buildings in good structural condition: same rating format as above.
c. extent of flowers, shrubs, flower boxes and/or plantings in good condition: same format as above.
d. volume of vehicular traffic:1=very light; 2=light; 3=moderate; 4=heavy; 5=very heavy.

TABLE 2.3   Statistical Tests for Changes on Study Blocks, 1981 versus 1994

Characteristic (n=87 pairs)	Rank Change			
	1994 < 1981	1994 > 1981	Z	p < (2-tailed)
N vacant, boarded-up houses	9	14	−1.33	.20
% residential units are vacant, boarded-up houses	7	19	−2.76	.01
% residential units are for sale or rent	14	26	−2.09	.05
% empty (units boarded up or vacant for sale or rent)	17	35	−3.19	.01
Graffiti-free	21	4	3.11	.01
Total people	24	54	−3.34	.001

NOTE: Results from nonparametric Wilcoxon matched-pairs, signed-ranks tests.

is that the citywide structural changes seen over the two decades and the shifts in neighborhood crime rates present a picture of these two decades markedly discrepant from the one commonly held.

The next section drills down deeper for a more detailed look at changes taking place, focusing specifically on the period 1981–1982 to 1994. We examine changing deterioration on approximately ninety blocks assessed by raters in both 1981 and 1994. Following, we look at shifts in residents' perceptions of neighborhood incivilities and in their concerns about safety. Using these sites and residents as windows onto citywide conditions and sentiments, do we find increasing citywide deterioration and fear?

Shifting Incivilities: 1981–1994

Did incivilities increase on streetblocks assessed by on-site teams of raters in both 1981 and 1994? If they did, was the rise significant? This section looks into these questions.[9] Table 2.2 describes the changes seen on this sample of streetblocks between 1981 and 1994, using averages across the two raters on each block at each point in time. Table 2.3 reports the results of nonparametric Wilcoxon tests of the significance of the change for the eighty-seven pairs of streetblocks including measures at both points in time.[10] The streetblocks have not been weighted, at either point in time, to reflect the relative population size of the respective neighborhood.

Boarded-Up Units

If we focus just on boarded-up vacant houses, the total number on the assessed streetblocks increased about 71%, from twenty-seven to forty-six.

The number changed from one boarded-up house every third streetblock to one boarded up-house every other streetblock. The prevalence rate, however, increased only slightly. Whereas 17% of the streetblocks had one or more boarded-up units in 1981, about 21% had one or more boarded-up units in 1994. If we take into account the number of units on each streetblock and develop an incidence rate, we see that it basically doubled during the period, from .01 boarded-up addresses per total streetblock addresses, to .02 boarded-up addresses per total addresses. This is a significant increase. Whereas seven streetblocks ranked lower on this rate in 1994 than in 1981, nineteen ranked higher. The different patterns for incidence and prevalence rates suggest the shifts are due somewhat to expansion of vacant housing to new neighborhoods, but are in the main driven by intensification of the problem in neighborhoods where it was already in evidence in 1981.

We looked at the locations where the number of vacant, boarded-up houses on streetblocks changed the most. Two streetblocks in a predominantly African-American, near-westside neighborhood showed increases (3.5→10; 2→3.5), and one streetblock there showed a decrease (4.5 →3). A streetblock in another, partially gentrifying near-westside neighborhood showed the largest increase, from none to seven. Two streetblocks in a near-southwest neighborhood also increased (2.5→3.5; 0→1). One streetblock in a near-eastside neighborhood also experienced an increase (0→2).[11]

Changes from 1981 to 1994 on these sample streetblocks extend a trend noted between 1970 and 1980 (148). In that earlier analysis, looking at census tract vacancy rates, Tom Webb and I learned that the vacancy rates were higher *and increasing faster* in the near-eastside and near-westside sections of town, as compared to other portions, and that the within-city regional disparities were increasing over time. This trend has continued through the 1980s and into the 1990s, particularly in the near westside. Although most blocks in the northern, northeastern, or far eastern sections of the city remained without vacancies, vacancies increased on a few near-eastside and several near-westside streetblocks.

Equally troubling was the expansion of vacant housing—albeit at a low rate—to the city's fringes, locations where it was previously largely unknown. One block in each of two southern-tier neighborhoods, adjoining either Baltimore or Anne Arundel County, had boarded-up units in 1994. None had been seen by raters in 1981 on those streetblocks.

There were spots where boarded-up units had decreased. On one streetblock in each of six neighborhoods, raters had both observed a boarded-up unit in 1981 and failed to observe one in 1994. One of these improving streetblocks was located in the same neighborhood where we also had witnessed the largest increase in the number of boarded-up units on a streetblock. There were also other blocks where the number of vacant units had decreased, albeit not to zero.

Empty Units

If we include both vacant units that are boarded up and vacant units for sale or rent, we can gauge the amount of empty housing units on streetblocks. Whereas 32% of the streetblocks had one or more empty residential units in 1981, by 1994 the prevalence rate had increased to 50%, a 56% increase. If we take into account not just the presence versus absence of empty units, but the numbers occurring, we can construct an incidence rate of empty residential structures as a percentage of total residential structures. The incidence rate of empty units more than doubled from 1.8% in 1981 to 4.4% in 1994, suggesting a significant shift citywide. Whereas seventeen of eighty-seven streetblocks ranked lower on this vacancy rate in 1994 than in 1981, thirty-five streetblocks ranked higher on the rate in 1994.

Graffiti

At both points in time, raters gauged the presence versus absence of graffiti. In 1981, about 80% of the streetblocks were graffiti-free; in 1994 that portion had declined to 63%. Or if we focus on the presence of graffiti, in 1981 both raters agreed that 20% of the blocks had them, and in 1994 both raters agreed that 37% of the blocks had them, an increase of over 89%. The increase in the prevalence rate of graffiti is significant.[12]

People

The presence of people on the street during weekday afternoons certainly should not be considered a sign of disorder. Nevertheless, we wished to explore how this presence might have changed. The presence of people did increase significantly, from four per streetblock in 1981 to five per streetblock in 1994. Although this increase is significant, it should be interpreted cautiously. The number of people on the street is highly sensitive to both time of day and temperature. Differences in the proportions of observations made in mornings versus afternoons in 1981 versus 1994 may partially account for the difference. In addition, the volume of people on the street is highly responsive to local economic conditions, variations in household composition, and availability of alternate gathering places.

Correlates of Empty Houses

Vacant or empty (for sale or rent, plus abandoned or boarded-up) houses, whether abandoned and open, abandoned and boarded up, or vacant and for sale or rent, create "holes" in the fabric of informal, resident-based territorial control over streetblock activities (96, 146). If this is the case, then we might expect more people to gather on streets where the proportion of empty housing, vacant for any reason, is higher. Also we might expect more litter and graffiti from the increased volume of people on the street.

Regression analyses allowing for curvilinear relationships suggest that the volume of empty housing is indeed linked to the presence of people, whether we use all empty units, residential and nonresidential ($R^2 = .16$); empty residential units only ($R^2 = .19$); or the rate of empty units ($R^2 = .14$). The presence of empty units helps us predict not only the volume of people, but the volume of graffiti ($R^2 = .16$) as well. These analyses, which should be interpreted merely as descriptive, suggest that the incidence of unoccupied housing, large numbers of people on the street, and the lack of street and structural maintenance tend to co-occur. Of course, this may be a spurious correlation driven in part by social class. But the point is that on the specific streetblocks, these conditions coexist.

Summary Comments on Changes

Significant changes in city fabric took place in Baltimore and in other cities during both the 1970s and 1980s; the changes taking place in Baltimore appear typical of what took place in several other cities during the period. To move to a more specific focus on crime, the crime rate trends in Baltimore as a whole look similar in many ways to the changes taking place in other cities, including the two largest neighboring cities. To some extent, depending on the crime, Baltimore's pattern diverges from that of Washington, D.C. or Philadelphia, especially during the late 1980s and early 1990s. But the overall picture does not suggest that Baltimore's crime changes are markedly atypical of what took place in other cities.

Examining changes in neighborhood crime rates in Baltimore showed that crime worsened most significantly during the 1970s, not during the 1980s. It was during the earlier decade that large numbers of relatively safe neighborhoods disappeared and large numbers of high-crime neighborhoods appeared. For several crimes, matters continued to worsen during the 1980s, but the fundamental shift was earlier. The only crime representing a clear exception was motor vehicle theft.

Given such crime patterns, why did the *perceptions* of city danger suddenly increase in the late 1980s? Part of the answer may lie in the changing gaps between crime rates in the city versus the rest of the MSA. In

Baltimore's case, the discrepancy between city: surround crime rates stayed relatively constant during the early 1980s. But in the late 1980s and the early 1990s, the differential increased noticeably for several crimes. Consequently, a lot more people may have started thinking the city was extremely dangerous because its dangerousness relative to immediately surrounding locales was increasing.

Turning to incivilities, we only have detailed information for the 1980s. In the eighty-seven streetblocks where assessments were completed in both 1981 and 1994, dramatic increases in both vacancies and graffiti appeared; these two incivilities were assessed at both points in time.

A pattern appears for the increasing incivilities, particularly vacancies. They intensified most in inner-city locations, near-eastside and near-westside neighborhoods where they were already relatively frequent by 1980. Conditions were most likely to deteriorate in areas already afflicted by blight. In the case of vacancies, the shifts from 1981 to 1994 appear to continue a trend, first noted in the 1970s, of increasing spatial differentiation of the problem. Some areas, usually outer-city locations, were not experiencing increases, and areas with preexisting problems were worsening. This differentiation, continuing across decades, may represent a dynamic pattern of urban change that has been at work for several decades.

But a second, less dominant pattern was that in some neighborhoods incivility-free in 1981, incivilities were occurring at a low rate in 1994. Two neighborhoods on the southern edge of the city represent cases in point. The problems were cropping up in locations previously thought to be stable, middle class, and not needing attention from policymakers. This shift, not seen in the prior decade of the 1970s, may represent a dynamic process of urban change originating in the 1980s in Baltimore and not seen in previous decades.

The trends reported here raise interesting questions about people's perceptions of incivilities and their safety concerns. One commonly held view is that crime got markedly and unprecedentedly worse in the late 1980s with crack cocaine's arrival in Baltimore and other big East Coast and rustbelt cities. But violence rates were high earlier, in the early 1980s. What made the increasing crime so noticeable in the late 1980s may have been that it followed several years of low or declining rates. Given this perspective—quite different from the general view—we might *not* find Baltimore residents interviewed in late 1994 markedly more fearful than those residents interviewed in mid-1982.

Likewise, an argument can be made either way for expecting or not expecting a shift in perceived incivilities. Deterioration worsened, as shown by the physical changes seen on some ninety-odd blocks. Taking those as a sample of city streetblocks suggests an overall increase. But at the same time, the most sizable increases surface in just a couple of sectors of the city, so we might not see perceived incivilities worsening citywide. The next section takes up these shifts.

The Questions of Fear and Neighborhood Problems

Nathaniel Hurt is a retired steelworker and neighborhood stalwart who shot a teen vandal and later stood trial for it; more details on his case appear below. His defense attorney, Stephen Miles, perhaps better known for his ads on late night local television touting his skills with accident and workers' comp cases, attempted to introduce evidence about the "urban fear syndrome" in Hurt's defense. Although this initiative was turned aside by the judge for technical reasons, many would probably agree that city residents are much more concerned about their personal safety than in the past.

But is the urban fear syndrome "legit"? Granted, urbanites' safety concerns have routinely outstripped those of suburban and rural residents. For example, the General Social Survey (GSS), which conducts nationwide, representative surveys yearly, asks respondents if there is anywhere nearby—within a mile—where they would be afraid to walk alone at night. Looking at all the data from 1973 through 1996, about 44% of urban residents, about 41% of suburban respondents, and about 28% of rural respondents respond positively to this item. But have fear levels reached unprecedentedly high levels? Have they gone up over time, as Hurt's defense attorney would have us believe?

The data from national polls do not find Americans are more afraid now than they were ten or fifteen years ago. The Harris Poll, a national survey of households, has asked people since the mid-1960s, "Compared to a year ago, do you personally feel more uneasy on the streets, less uneasy, or not much different?" If we looking at the period from 1980 on, the proportion reporting "more uneasy" has ranged from 48% to 24%, with the percentage dipping in the mid-1980s. The 1981 portion feeling more uneasy was 48%; the corresponding 1993 figure was 42%.[13] The Gallup Poll, another national public opinion survey, asks respondents, "Is there any area near where you live—that is, within a mile—where you would be afraid to walk alone at night?" This is apparently the same item as the GSS item. Since 1972, the portion saying yes has bounced around between 40% and 45%. The 1981 and 1983 figures were 45%; the 1993 figure was 43%.[14]

Focusing more closely on just urban residents and using the GSS fear item similarly confirms *no trend upward* in fear in urban locations. Analyses of these data show the proportion of fearful urban respondents has ranged between 42% and 50% from 1973 to 1996. Only the year 1982 stands out, when about 56% of urban residents reported being afraid. No long-term, upward trend is visible. Fear increased modestly in the mid-1970s, dropped in the early to mid-1980s, and remained steady around 45% for most of the late 1980s and early 1990s, the only exception being 1994, when it went up to 50%. But when we take sampling error into account, all of the numbers for the entire twenty-three-year series overlap. *Nationwide, urban fear levels have not increased.*

Certainly, these figures have limitations. And the questions used may not be the best items for gauging fear of crime (45: chap. 3).[15] Nevertheless, however limited the specific items might be, the results fail to support the idea that fear of crime has increased nationally or among urban residents in the past ten to fifteen years.

In short, given the fear figures, those for the population as a whole and for just urban residents, and given the information reviewed earlier on neighborhood crime rate shifts in the 1970s versus the 1980s, perhaps we should *not* expect Baltimore residents' personal safety concerns to be stronger in 1994 as compared to 1982.

Standing opposite the "no change" expectation is a "change" expectation grounded in the incivilities thesis. As further explained in Chapter 3, the longitudinal, ecological version of the incivilities thesis expects that as neighborhoodwide physical deterioration increases, so too should residents' fear. Treating our random sample of streetblocks as representative citywide of occupied residential neighborhood streetblocks, statistical tests (Table 2.3) showed significant increases in both graffiti and vacant housing from 1981 to 1994. Therefore, the incivilities thesis argues, citywide fear should climb as well.

The same line of argument applies to perceived incivilities. The longitudinal, ecological version of the incivilities thesis anticipates not only that residents' concerns about physical neighborhood problems should deepen as deterioration advances, but so too should worries about unseemly or threatening behaviors on the street. Chapter 3 describes more fully the reasoning and processes behind these anticipated connections. The only point we want to establish here is that we need not rely only on popular—and, as just shown, incorrect—notions of the urban fear syndrome to ground an expectation of increasing fear and increasing perceived social and physical incivilities between the 1982 and 1994 surveys. The conceptual framework provided by the incivilities thesis provides a sound foundation for the same expectation, given the increased deterioration documented.

Simply put, on the one hand, national data at variance with the popular image suggest we should *not* expect increased fear in Baltimore from 1982 to 1994. Across the nation, or across the nation's cities, we do not see increasing fear in the 1970s or the 1980s through to the mid-1990s. On the other hand, documented increases in Baltimore's physical deterioration, coupled with the incivilities thesis, anticipate a citywide increase in fear, perceived physical incivilities, and perceived social incivilities. But before turning to the results, two additional complications—one psychological, one behavioral—deserve attention.

Even if assessed physical deterioration was significantly higher in 1994 as compared to 1992, perceived incivilities might not be correspondingly elevated due to psychological adaptation. In earlier work, Sally Shumaker and I have suggested that residents in high-problem neighborhoods may "tune out" some of the surrounding disorder (147). That work showed the impact of neighborhood physical deterioration on fear of crime weakened at higher levels of deterioration. If significant cognitive adaptation is taking place, residents may not be more fearful than they were twelve years ago despite a more deteriorated context.

The behavioral reason to not see increased perceived problems or fear despite more widespread deterioration arises from the differential exodus thesis. This thesis will emerge repeatedly throughout the volume as a way of "explaining away" various findings. The argument is simply this: Those who, at Time 1, saw more neighborhood problems or were more concerned for their personal safety were more likely, by Time 2, to have moved out of the neighborhood and perhaps out of the city altogether. Consequently, if perceived incivilities or fear are *not* higher at Time 2, it is because those most afraid, or the most problem-concerned, have vacated the premises. So, in effect, we are looking at the wrong outcome (fear rather than mobility) and misleading ourselves because we have failed to interview the same people at both times. The differential exodus thesis can be applied to findings at the individual, block, or neighborhood levels.

Several points, however, argue against the differential exodus thesis. First is its ahistorical character: It assumes that something different started happening right at Time 1, rather than admitting that the changes from Time 0 to Time 1, or from Time –1 to Time 0, are the same as the changes taking place from Time 1 to Time 2. Baltimore's population losses in the post–World War II era have never been egalitarian. For example, following school desegregation, "from 1954 to 1970, white children withdrew from the city schools at the rate of ten thousand a year to enter schools in the suburban counties" (110: 370). In short, for the differential exodus thesis to apply to the analyses shown here, it would have to demonstrate that exit dynamics from 1982 to 1994 were markedly different from those between, say, 1970 and 1982. Second, the mobility literature does not strongly confirm that people move because of bad neighborhood conditions (52, 142). Particularly tough to demonstrate have been impacts of crime on actual mobility. The influence of "pull" factors, such as the attractiveness of the destination, may be more important than

conditions left behind. The most important influence on mobility of all
appear to be issues such as stage of life cycle and employment changes.
Third, differential exodus ignores constrained mobility. Many who might
like to leave find it difficult because of limited economic means; inability
to sell their house; or, in the case of African Americans, few destinations
to move to where they would feel accepted (46).

Finally, three findings specific to Baltimore suggest the differential exodus thesis ought not be applied to the outcomes of interest. This thesis,
applied ahistorically, expects moving intentions to be stronger in 1982
than in 1994, because by 1994 all those intolerant of the high fear and
problem levels would have left. But moving intentions were about the
same at both points in time. In 1982 about 59%, ± 4%, reported ever seriously considering moving out of their neighborhood. This is slightly
higher, but not significantly so, than the 1994 percentage of 54% ± 4%.[16]
Furthermore, a 1978–1979 survey of Baltimore residents in twenty-one
neighborhoods found that those who perceived more serious local problems and who were more concerned about crime were the residents most
attached to the neighborhood, as shown by their ability to furnish the
neighborhood name (24: 120, 124). (For an explanation of the use of
neighborhood name as an index of attachment, see 145.) And a 1978–1979
study in another twelve Baltimore neighborhoods showed that local perceived incivilities failed to interfere with attachment to place (145). Given
these empirical findings, almost as strong an argument can be made that
perceived incivilities enhance attachment, or certainly do not interfere
with it, as can be made that incivilities drive people out of their neighborhood.

So to go back to the question at hand: Taking sampling error into account, do we see more fear and perceived problems, citywide, in 1994 as
compared to 1982?[17] We take sampling error into account by focusing on
the confidence intervals around the "best" estimate of each population
mean, at each point in time, on each outcome. Throughout, we use the
99% confidence interval, in an effort to partially counterbalance the large
number of outcomes examined here.[18] Although we only report here the
results using our thirty neighborhoods where residents were interviewed
both in 1994 and in 1982, we also looked at the results using all sixty-six
neighborhoods where residents were interviewed in 1982, both before
and after weighting. Use of the sixty-six neighborhoods, as compared to
the thirty, resulted in noticeably smaller confidence intervals, given the
larger sample size. But the specific conclusions discussed here are identical, whether we focus on the 1982 results with sixty-six neighborhoods,
weighted or unweighted, or the 1982 results with thirty neighborhoods,
weighted or unweighted. To simplify presentation, we show only the results based on the thirty neighborhoods. If the confidence intervals at the

two times *fail* to overlap, a significant shift has probably taken place in the broader population of Baltimore neighborhood residents.

Four different indicators, asked about fear during the day and at night, on the streetblock and elsewhere in the neighborhood. Would we expect to see fear increasing for all four indicators? Nighttime situations can be especially fear-inspiring for some (151). So nighttime fear levels may be the most likely to elevate over time. Furthermore, fear may be less likely to increase on the streetblock compared to elsewhere in the neighborhood. The streetblock provides a regular pattern to locals' activities, and these rhythms provide a consistency and predictability to the activities there (143). Thus streetblock dynamics may help to "buffer" residents from ongoing neighborhood changes. Consequently, fear on the streetblock may be less likely to increase as compared to fear elsewhere in the neighborhood.

Fear

We examined responses to four fear items. They were

How safe would you feel being out alone in your neighborhood during the day? (Q29)
How safe would you feel if you were out alone at night in your neighborhood? (Q30)
How safe would you feel if you were out alone on your block during the day? (Q49)[19]
How safe would you feel if you were out alone on your block at night? (Q50)

Total variance for questions on daytime items increased 24% for neighborhood fear and 28% for streetblock fear from the 1982 to 1994 surveys. By contrast, fear differences at night decreased in total size: 7% for neighborhood fear and 6% for streetblock fear. In short, considering everyone in the thirty neighborhoods: People disagreed with one another somewhat more in 1994 as compared to 1982 on how afraid they felt during the day; how much they disagreed with one another about nighttime safety remained relatively unchanged. The latter result has implications for the differential exodus thesis. Following that thesis, and assuming the level of fear among low-fear residents remained relatively unchanged, total fear variation should have decreased from the first to second interviews. Instead, the shift in total variation depends on the fear item in question. The pattern observed casts some doubt on the idea of highly fearful residents fleeing the city in the 1980s; such a pattern should have resulted in compressing fear variation more in the 1994 interviews.

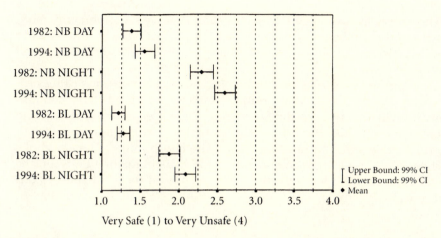

FIGURE 2.4   Empirical Bayes Estimates of Population Means, 1982 and 1994, for Four Fear of Crime Items with 99% Confidence Intervals, Based on Thirty Neighborhood Results for Each Time Period. Results are unweighted. Results with weighted samples virtually identical. Results using all 66 neighborhoods for the 1982 sample are also virtually identical. NB = neighborhood; BL = block.

Figure 2.4 displays the sample means by item and the 99% confidence "band" within which the citywide mean for each item probably lies. Going down the vertical axis we display results for neighborhood-day, neighborhood-night, block-day, and block-night. For each fear question, going down, we display the 1982 thirty-neighborhood sample mean and the 1994 thirty-neighborhood sample mean. Both samples are not weighted. The horizontal axis, from left to right, displays scores ranging from very safe (1) to very unsafe (4).

Confidence intervals for 1982 and 1994 overlap in three of the four items. Only in the case of neighborhood fear at night is there *no* overlap. Citywide, people appear significantly more fearful when abroad in their neighborhood at night in 1994, compared to twelve years earlier. Whereas the estimated population mean used to lie closer to "somewhat safe" than "somewhat unsafe," now the reverse is true. In the three other cases, the means have shifted up, but the confidence intervals continue to overlap noticeably. The "average" Baltimore resident, in 1994, felt as safe on his or her streetblock and as safe when out in the broader neighborhood during the day as he or she did in 1982.

A second finding revealed by the figure relates to the differentiation by time and location of residents' fear. In 1982, we saw no citywide difference between how safe people felt in their neighborhood during the day and how safe they felt on their streetblock during the day. The mean differences were, as we would expect, that people felt safer on their streetblock. But the daytime-neighborhood and daytime-streetblock confi-

dence intervals overlapped. By contrast, in 1994 we see a more differenti-
ated pattern. Now, citywide, residents report feeling significantly safer
on their streetblock during the day than elsewhere in their neighborhood
during the day.

The streetblock serves as a relatively safe arena, both connecting residents to and buffering them from the broader, less predictable community. Moving away from the home, the resident experiences decreasing
control over events and who occupies which spaces (144). This lack of
control is reflected in residents' fear. The city population as a whole,
when thinking of nighttime scenes, clearly distinguished between the
two levels on both surveys. But only recently in the 1994 surveys did
people make a similar distinction when thinking about the daytime.

Perceived Incivilities

In the survey, respondents were asked if various problems were "not a
problem (0), somewhat of a problem (1), or a big problem (2) in your
neighborhood?" The issues addressed were

A. Vandalism, like people breaking windows or spray painting
   buildings?
B. B. Vacant housing?
C. C. People who don't keep up their property or yards?
D. D. People who say insulting things or bother other people when
   they walk down the street?
E. E. Litter and trash in the streets?
F. F. Vacant lots with trash or junk?
G. G. Groups of teenagers hanging out?
H. H. The amount of noise in the area?
I. I. Bad elements moving in?
J. J. People fighting and arguing?
K. K. Crime?

How had the relative salience of different perceived neighborhood
problems changed for residents between the two surveys? Figure 2.5
shows the ordering of the citywide averages and the associated 99% confidence interval, based on the 1982 surveys in thirty neighborhoods
(panel A) and the 1994 surveys (panel B).[20] For both periods, crime heads
the list, getting the highest overall rating as a serious neighborhood problem. For 1982, the citywide average was about halfway between "not a
problem" and "somewhat of a problem." The city average for 1994 lies
somewhere around a score of 1.0, corresponding to "somewhat of a problem." Citywide, residents perceive the severity of the crime problem in

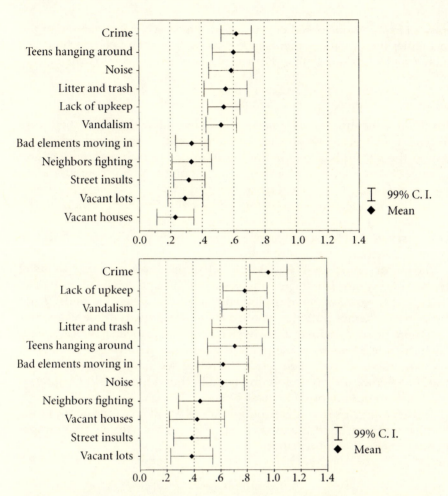

FIGURE 2.5   Relative Severity of Different Perceived Incivilities, 1982 and 1994
NOTE: Results based on 30 neighborhoods sampled in both 1982 and 1994. Empirical Bayes estimates of unweighted population means shown.

their neighborhood as significantly higher in 1994. The 1994 and 1982 confidence intervals fail to overlap. *Concern about neighborhood crime, citywide, appears higher than a dozen years earlier.*

Somewhat more surprising is the corresponding failure of perceived incivilities to also increase. *Citywide, we do not see unequivocal increases in any of the other perceived incivilities.* The sample means, of course, have shifted up, as can be seen. Some of these shifts are barely noticeable, others are more obvious. But the increases are not so marked that sampling error can be ruled out as the cause. The confidence intervals overlap. This is contrary to expectations based on the longitudinal, ecological version of the incivilities thesis. City residents in 1994 do not see their neighborhoods as more problem-ridden than did the residents of twelve years earlier.

Summary on Shifting Fear and Perceived Incivilities

Baltimore residents are *not generally* more fearful in 1994 than they were in 1982. They feel as safe on their streetblock and while abroad during the day in their neighborhood as they did a dozen years before; they are, however, more concerned for their safety at night in their neighborhood. We see bounded rather than broad-gauged increases in feelings of vulnerability. In addition, except for the perceived crime problem in the neighborhood, respondents in 1994, as compared to those from a dozen years earlier, did not see their neighborhoods as more problem-ridden; perceived incivilities have not intensified.

The rhetoric often used to describe urban residents, such as Nathaniel Hurt, who *in general* are increasingly terrified and perceive themselves as living in increasingly deteriorating and disorderly neighborhoods, is not supported. Neither national data from the past twenty-three years, nor Baltimore data on changes over twelve years confirm such an argument. Such rhetoric blinds us to the perhaps more important question: In what communities and for which residents do we see significant increases in fear and significantly deteriorating neighborhood quality? In Chapters 4 to 6, we turn our attention to those issues.

This chapter closes by describing in more detail concerns about crime and incivilities around the time of our 1994 survey. We rely on newspaper reports for that information.

In the News

This section provides details about stories related to crime, incivilities, and neighborhood quality that received media attention in Baltimore around the time of our 1994–1995 resident and leader interviews. In a few cases, we supplement newspaper coverage with information provided by interviewed leaders. Our purposes here are descriptive only. We provide the most detail on the police department, its responses to crime, other major crime stories, housing issues, and neighborhood development.

Police

Leadership, Morale, and a Tale of Two Commissioners.   In February 1994, the *Baltimore Sun* reporter David Simon, author of *Homicide: A Year on the Killing Streets*, wrote a series of investigative articles on the Baltimore City Police Department (132, 133, 134, 135). Drawing on interviews with more than 100 officers, supervisors, former police officials, law enforcement experts, and other police representatives (133), he detailed several serious problems in the department. The series found Mayor Schmoke's crime-fighting reputation wanting.

> While rising violence is a constant preoccupation among city residents, from housing projects in the poorest neighborhoods to the well-tended enclaves of Roland Park and Guilford, the mayor's most visible priorities seem to be Baltimore's schools, or neighborhood revitalization, or better housing. . . . But Mr. Schmoke has been far more reticent in setting goals about dealing with crime. (133: A1)

Much of the controversy centered on the leadership provided the department by Commissioner Ed Woods, originally appointed in 1990 and reappointed by Schmoke in 1994 amid rising homicide counts and deteriorating police performance. Many considered him lackluster and little more than a caretaker, content to let the department be largely reactive and to overlook strategic planning (133).

Woods's initiatives included a community-oriented policing pilot project in the Eastern District and a violent crimes task force, focusing on homicide, started in late 1992. In the eyes of some, these projects proved ineffective, in part because of internal problems facing the department at the time. Personnel losses were high and morale was low. In 1991, city agencies faced a hiring freeze. The department also placed more officers in command positions. As a result of these departmental policies, many investigative units lost officers; this, in turn, increased an already heavy workload for remaining officers. Not surprisingly, arrest and clearance rates dropped (133, 134).

In short, in the minds of some, Woods failed to deal with attrition, did not address officer morale, and was too politically attached to city hall but at the same time unable to use those connections to benefit the department. After a four-year tenure, Woods was forced out by Schmoke (134). Seeking to mend his reputation and his policies toward crime reduction, Schmoke recruited Thomas Frazier, a San Jose, California, deputy chief (133). "Mr. Frazier was the first commissioner to come from outside the Baltimore agency in more than a dozen years. This was seen as suggesting a mandate for change and reform" (133: A12). On appointment in 1994, Frazier identified the following top priorities:

> Creating a major intelligence unit to gather information on gangs, drug organizations and intrastate criminal groups, and to target them for undercover operations . . . Revamping the department's 911 system to speed up service . . . Shifting the Baltimore department's drug enforcement efforts to-

ward investigating large-scale and violence-prone organizations and away
from the current practice of arresting street-level dealers and drug users . . .
Moving the department's internal investigations unit into his office to speed
up the disciplining of wayward officers and to increase accountability to the
public and to district commanders . . . Instituting a department wide rotation policy that will force officers to change jobs every three to six years. (59)

Frazier followed through on many of these priorities. Reviewing his
work after about a year, reporter Peter Hermann noted,

Soon after becoming commissioner, Mr. Frazier launched a series of major
drug raids, a tactic differing from previous police sweeps, which had targeted low-level dealers and users. . . . The raids—and a harsh winter—
helped reduce crime during his first year in the job. . . . Mr. Frazier draws
high marks for filling depleted investigation units including the rape squad,
which at one time in 1993 had only one detective; for securing more equipment; and for fighting for raises. He also decentralized the department, giving district commanders much more power to run their dominions (70:
A27).

Frazier continued as commissioner until December 1999, being succeeded by Ronald Daniel following Martin O'Malley's win in the November 1999 mayoral election. In the late 1990s, Frazier had resisted efforts, pushed by O'Malley and others, to clone New York City's "zero
tolerance policies" (see Chapter 3), focusing instead on getting guns off
the street and busting high-level drug dealers. At the end of July 1999, he
began a replication of Boston's Operation Cease Fire, highlighting severe
penalties for major gang leaders involved in violence, together with multiagency coordination. Twenty-two arrests in two drug organizations in
East Baltimore were made on July 29, 1999. But a high-level news conference planned for earlier in the month announcing the multiagency approach was canceled because it was not clear all agencies were "on
board" (42).

Community-Oriented Policing.

Lauded by national experts, community-oriented law enforcement attempts
to reduce reliance on the 911 system by dedicating specially trained officers
to neighborhood intervention and problem solving, ranging from crime-
fighting to truancy to trash removal. (131: A12)

Commissioner Frazier proposed to revive community policing in Baltimore, implemented in some Baltimore locations in the late 1980s (112). A

lack of available personnel, however, created operational challenges. The department had had trouble staffing units, let alone undertaking a city-wide plan of community policing. With such critical personnel shortages, what could community policing accomplish in Baltimore? Did this style of policing reduce crime or merely the fear of crime? Soon after Frazier's limited revival of community policing, some neighborhoods, such as Berea and Orangeville, reported good results, in part because homeowners were invested in the locale and worked closely with the police (131).

The results from our leader interviews provided an intriguingly different perspective on this issue. In the past, the city had targeted certain key areas for community policing efforts, sometimes, as in Reservoir Hill, in response to serious drug problems (112). And there were other parts of town, such as Charles Village, where a community policing officer (CPO) on foot or cruising down the alleys in a Cushman cart was a familiar sight even in the 1970s. But from the viewpoint of leaders with whom we spoke, CPOs were not a major or steady presence.

A couple of leaders reported that there had been a CPO assigned to their locale for a time, they had gotten on well with the officer and viewed his or her presence as a contribution, but then the officer "disappeared." Some suggested these officers had been near retirement and had not been replaced after leaving the force. In a couple of incidents described to us where leaders identified a particular problem related to drug selling, they were able to eventually enlist police cooperation in documenting the problem, but the support came from regular patrol officers, not a CPO. In short, Frazier supported the goals of community policing, which, at least from some neighborhood leaders' perspective, had not been a major presence. He also recognized the enormous implementation problems confronting such a goal. (And later, circa 1997, when city council leaders wanted community policing to become zero tolerance policing, he resisted those pressures [101].)

Personnel shortages may have been partially corrected by a shake-up plan in late April 1995. It called for the reassignment of 300 officers from desk jobs to street patrols, with desk positions to be filled with civilian employees. The reassignments were prompted by a consultant's study showing that 42% of officers were not patrolling local streets (68).

Drug Raids. Commissioner Frazier followed through on his promise to carry out large-scale drug raids, believing that only large-scale raids would have a lasting impact on a community (63). Questions arose, however, about the effectiveness of these high-profile raids: Were drug dealers being removed or were they merely moving to different neighborhoods? In addition, concerns arose about the lasting impact of raids as well as the inherent risks. Residents of the neighborhoods expressed some optimism, and the officers gained satisfaction from making dents in drug networks (63). The drug raid initiative started with Operation Midway in March 1994; fourteen houses were raided in the vicinity of Greenmount Avenue. Four months later, twenty houses were raided in the Middle East community, near Johns Hopkins Hospital. These raids were followed by raids in Perkins Homes public housing (August) and Druid Heights (September) (63).

Again, neighborhood leaders' comments on the drug raids provide a different slant on the issue. In an East Baltimore neighborhood, part of which was included in the Operation Midway sweep, the neighborhood leader commented on the lack of communication about such initiatives. For obvious intelligence reasons, the police department cannot alert local leaders to upcoming raids. But nevertheless, when a raid does occur, some leaders may view it, as this one did, as another example of "the City coming in here, and doing whatever they want, without telling anybody anything."

Local drug sellers in some locations appear eager to find out what they can from local leaders about upcoming initiatives. A leader in a neighborhood along the York Road corridor in north Baltimore admitted that she knew who the big drug dealers were: they were always trying to find out what the police were up to. She invited them to community meetings, and they sometimes came. She felt it was better that you knew who they were, and for the dealers to know what her organization was about.

In the Greenmount Avenue area where our leader interview came about two weeks after a large-scale raid, a longtime local leader admitted that the raid had reduced drug activity on the street "for a while"; she expected it would be back to preraid levels before long. A citizen leader in Walbrook expressed a similar view.

> Walbrook residents were hopeful yesterday that the arrests of 50 people in weekend raids aimed largely at drug hot spots in their high-crime community will not be the last. "It gets better, but then it gets bad again. We have to keep working on it. It's a constant battle," said the elderly chairwoman of Citizens for Community Improvement, a group of community activists who challenged Police Commissioner Thomas C. Frazier to clean up their neighborhood last summer. "Now my concern is will we have to go back and do more," she said. The neighborhood leader—like many others who have lived in the area for decades—did not want to be named publicly. (19: B2)

Back in the Greenmount area, the elderly leader we interviewed viewed the drug issue not in law enforcement terms, but in personal terms. (Chapter 7 discusses different approaches taken by leaders to local drug problems.) For her, the way to end the problem was to take care of people that you knew, friends, friends of friends, and relatives. She recounted a story of a relative of a friend who had finally gotten off drugs after a rehab program and with substantial support from friends and relatives. For her, the drug problem was personal, involving people she knew. The way to solve it was to get the people that you knew about and cared for off of drugs (141).

In late October 1994, Frazier and the State's Attorney Stuart O. Simms were preparing to publicize the use of civil law (Maryland's 1991 nuisance abatement law) that allowed for action against homeowners who constantly rent to drug dealers. This initiative echoes the first chapter's description of Oakland's Beat Health initiative. In Baltimore, it was discovered that at the first house targeted for this action, 1812 East Pratt Street, the neighboring house was also involved in drug dealing. Officers made four arrests. Both houses were owned by the same person (61). The nuisance abatement law "provides for expedited proceedings in District Court and gives judges broad power to issue orders to property owners. Under the law, the judges can order yards to be cleaned, determine who can and can't live at troublesome properties and even order the demolition of houses" (61: B3).

And in late 1994, large drug raids continued. Thirteen houses were raided in East Baltimore's Oliver community and twenty people were arrested (3). Later that month Operation Southside targeted Walbrook on the westside and fifty arrests were made there (19). Operation O'Donnell Heights focused on a predominantly white community in southeast Baltimore and took place in mid-February 1995; twenty-one houses were raided and twenty-one persons were arrested (79). Later in February, Operation Hatchet targeted homes in the Winchester neighborhood, a near-westside African-American community. Twenty homes were raided and twenty-seven persons were arrested (93). In April 1995, police stumbled on a suspected heroin operation in the two southwest Baltimore communities of Shipley Hill and Pratt-Monroe (69).

But gaining quick intelligence about dealers or targeting nuisance sites is effective only if residents are willing to supply information. Unfortunately, in many of the most drug-plagued communities, many residents are reluctant to do this (for details on the processes involved, see Chapter 7). In one near-eastside neighborhood, the leader we interviewed admitted that almost all residents were afraid to provide any information for fear of retaliation. Of course, those residents also might be benefiting monetarily from the munificence of local drug dealers, but that topic did not surface. According to her, residents' concerns about retaliation were so strong that not only were they unwilling to supply information, they were reluctant to serve on local community organization boards. They feared that after a location had been targeted, those cited or arrested would come looking for them, figuring organization members were the logical information source.

Apparently residents' concerns are well founded. Around the time of the Pratt-Monroe raid (April 1995), a neighborhood leader we interviewed in a community close by reported that organization members had been threatened face to face by local dealers. As a result, the organization was moving to a "secret surveillance" effort, one the leader was unwilling to discuss. Again, Chapter 7 provides more details. These sentiments and incidents underscore the difficulties police face in gaining good drug intelligence from local leaders and residents.

The drug raids not only put dents in drug networks; they spawned delays in the courts and overcrowding in the detention center. The backlog caused several problems, most notably cases lost due to speedy trial rules and resources diverted from other cases. In early 1995, those awaiting trial averaged a seven-month wait, and, of course, if they could not post bail, that time was spent in the detention center (120).

Changes in Crime.   In 1994, for the first time in a decade, gun-related violence dropped in the city; homicides dropped as well. In 1993, there were 353 homicides, compared to 321 homicides in 1994. There was also a 3.7% drop in overall violent crimes during the first ten months of 1994 (66). Of course, at the same time violent crime was dropping in other big cities as well, including New York (14, 18, 41). Frazier, nonetheless, was quick to pin credit for Baltimore's homicide drop on the drug raids in the city's most violent neighborhoods, as well as routine targeting of open-air drug markets (66). To put matters in context, however, murders in 1988, 1989, and 1990 totaled 234, 262, and 305 (130: 626).

Crime in the Neighborhoods.   In this section, we provide a brief sample of the more newsworthy crimes afflicting Baltimore citizens during the period. Crime even hit close to home for the mayor.

Golfing on city golf courses got riskier, as golfers were asked to turn over their wallets to fairway robbers. In August 1994, the Baltimore Municipal Golf Corporation beefed up its security after a second armed robbery in less than a week. Robbers had been reported on previous occasions in several of the five public golf courses, including one in the northwest section of the city (99).

In February 1995, the mayor reported that his father and stepmother were robbed at gunpoint outside their West Baltimore home. This was the second time a member of his family had been victimized while he was in office. In 1989, the mayor's son was robbed of a leather jacket and twelve dollars in cash while walking to Reistertown Road Plaza (127).

In March 1995, eleven-year-old Natishia Moore was found dead, having been raped, strangled, and set on fire in the 2800 block of Rayner Avenue in West Baltimore. (The case bore troubling similarities to the never-solved murder of eleven-year-old Latonya Kim Wallace in Reservoir Hill in 1988 [130: 59].) The police arrested a seventeen-year-old (81, 118).

Later in March 1995, police feared a possible serial killer, after four women were slain in close proximity to each other in the vicinity of Perkins Homes public housing project and the southern edge of Washington Hill. All had been strangled, and all had similar drug use patterns. Homicide detectives came to believe, however, that the killings were unrelated, and later located multiple suspects (73).

Also in March, Charlie Christensen, a man who could not speak, was killed. It happened while he was waiting for a bus at Park Circle in the lower northwest part of town. A witness reported seeing two teen-aged boys hollering at Christensen before he was shot. As Christensen lay bleeding to death, cars kept driving by, and a few people even walked by. A man named Johnny Dow tried to help, but could not communicate with Christensen. He died approximately an hour after he was shot (106).

Perhaps the highest-profile crime case during the period centered around the killing of a thirteen-year-old boy by a retired steelworker, Nathaniel Hurt. The incident place on the 800 block of East North Avenue. In October 1994, after a group of kids had thrown rocks shattering Hurt's car windshield, the sixty-one-year-old man shot thirteen-year-old Vernon Holmes (62). The incident drew wide attention, and strong support for Hurt from many nearby residents. Neighbors collected donations to raise money for Hurt's bail of $200,000. Many saw Hurt as a community stalwart; he had even worked as a block captain. This collection of money and support was troubling for police and the mayor. Residents and parents were cautioned against vigilantism and to keep an eye on their children (64).

> The community raised money to gain Mr. Hurt's release, and in a radio interview, Mr. Hurt said that he felt sorry that the boy died, but did not regret what happened. There was no intent, according to Mr. Hurt, to hurt anybody, he just wanted to scare the 20–30 youths who threw the rocks at his car. Mr. Hurt justified his actions on the belief of protecting his property and life. (154: B2)
>
> At trial, Mr. Hurt was charged with murder and a weapons charges, the latter carrying a mandatory sentence requirement. At the beginning of the trial, witnesses for the prosecution painted Mr. Hurt as a neighborhood bully. Prosecution argued that Mr. Hurt was in no immediate harm and could have

relied on 911. (According to one report, the boy had been shot while running away.) Defense attorney Stephen Miles, not well known in Baltimore for his criminal practice, painted Mr. Hurt as a law abiding citizen, who experienced "urban fear syndrome" after months of threats and harassment. One of the prosecution witnesses allegedly received a beating from Mr. Hurt after he had admitted vandalizing Hurt's property. (10: B1, B5)

The fear issue was brought up at trial. Miles stated that the urban fear syndrome especially afflicted older African Americans.[21] Syndrome defenses have been on the rise. Although this one is not medically recognized, the apparent hope was to gain sympathy votes (113). On a technicality, relevant material was ruled out, the judge deciding that defense lawyers had not shared appropriate documents with the prosecution (9).

Hurt rejected the offer of a last-minute plea bargain. When the jury returned, he was convicted of manslaughter and a weapons charge. He reported that he had felt confident of an acquittal because jury deliberations took only twelve hours (11). Many lawyers criticized Miles for not prompting Hurt to take the plea offer. The police complained that Miles had unjustifiably cast aspersions on their professionalism (8, 11).

In June 1995, Judge Ellen Heller sentenced Hurt to a five-year prison sentence, emphasizing that Hurt had no right to take the law into his own hands. Hurt was released while his prison sentence was being appealed (119).

The Hurt incident was not without precedent. In 1979, a man was charged with killing a young man who pelted his home with snowballs in the Dundalk area. In 1991, a thirteen-year-old boy was shot by a forty-nine-year-old man reportedly because the youth and others continuously rang the door bell and ran. In May 1994, a seventeen-year-old was shot after bumping a truck and setting off the alarm (62).

Even if we leave aside the urban fear syndrome, Hurt's case raises a number of interesting questions. He came from the same general area where the leader had told us residents were extremely reluctant to do anything about crime because of fear of retaliation. Hurt himself had apparently played a high-profile role in neighborhood maintenance in the past, as a block captain, and was known to not tolerate attacks on his property. It seems that in a neighborhood where many keep their heads down, one who does not is perhaps bound to draw attention.

Youth and Crime.   Hurt's case also raises questions about youth involvement in vandalism and more serious crime. Youth violence was visible on school grounds during this period. In November 1994, it was reported that violence was becoming a routine feature in Baltimore's public school system. Incidents involving guns were on the rise. These incidents in-

FIGURE 2.6   Baltimore Police Department Patrol Officers on Bicycles, Waiting for "Rush Hour" Outside Northern High School. Photo by author.

cluded assaults and robberies, as well as firearms possession. The number of incidents rose from 47 in 1992–1993 to 67 in 1993–1994. Weapons assaults increased from 56 to 104, and armed and unarmed assaults jumped 14.7%. Arrests also rose from 2,609 to 2,790. The school system attributed much of this increase to more efficient detection and reporting. Nonetheless, many critics leveled complaints against ineffective school security. Many agreed the schools were becoming increasingly dangerous (50).

The city council, in response to this information, initiated a probe into violence in schools. Many urban schools across the United States use metal detectors, surveillance cameras, and randomized searching. Baltimore's school superintendent emphasized conflict resolution classes in place of other methods for dealing with the violence problem (50).

Despite measures taken to increase school safety on the inside for students, teachers, and other staff, people are not necessarily safer on the school grounds outside. For example, in January 1995, a shootout in front of Northern High School resulted in one person dead and another critically wounded. The dispute reportedly involved two neighborhood gangs and may have stemmed from an earlier basketball game. The victims were not students at the high school (75). In the spring of 1995, we talked with some police officers on bicycles on post outside Northern High School. These officers reported that they were on site at the school every day around the time school let out. We did not ask when their assignment there had begun.

Prevention/Programs.   Crime was reported to have dropped in the downtown area between 1993 and 1994. This drop was in part attributed to the Clean and Safe Program, part of the business improvement district (BID) activities in the downtown. A business surcharge pays for forty-four public safety guides who patrol the downtown streets. These safety guides give directions, assist motorists in distress, and help police catch criminals (74).

Baltimore started a program called Project Disarm. This program was an effort to get guns off the streets by targeting repeat offenders accused of misdemeanor handgun crimes. These offenders appear before a federal court, which delivers longer sentences and no parole. The program was reportedly meeting with some success (67).

In November 1994, Baltimore was slated to receive $2 million from the federal Bureau of Justice Assistance. This money was to be spent on programs such as community policing (mentioned earlier), drug courts, and midnight basketball, according to federal and city officials (4).

Youth Crime Prevention/Programs.   Several churches in East Baltimore joined together to form "safe haven networks" to provide a refuge for children who were frightened by the crime-ridden neighborhoods surrounding the schools (49, 152). Student leaders came together to tackle the violence problem in schools. Approximately 125 junior and senior high school student council members pledged to report weapons in the school and to support legislation to aid in decreasing the amount of weapons in the schools (17). The school district used "breakthrough teams" to decrease the violence in the schools. The teams generally consist of two to five adults from the community who have a rapport with the students. It was hoped that these teams could go in and discuss behavior problems with troublesome students (84).

The city also enacted curfew laws to help reduce youth crime. The laws include penalties for parents (13, 150). Around the same time other cities, such as Chester, Pennsylvania, and Camden, New Jersey, publicized existing curfew laws or enacted new ones. Curfews continue to be a problem-ridden approach for addressing youth crime and delinquency, given constitutional challenges and implementation difficulties (25, 115).

Issues of Color

Baltimore has always been a city where issues of color played major roles in settlement patterns; business; politics; and, more recently, crime. Olson in her comprehensive history of the city, and McDougall, in his more recent discussion of Park Heights, Harlem Park, and Upton, address these broader forces (102, 110). Here are some race-related issues linked to crime, communities, and disorder that drew media attention around the time of the 1994 survey.

History of Edmondson Village Appears. An American Studies scholar at the University of Maryland–Baltimore County drew attention with the release of his book chronicling the rapid racial turnover in Edmondson Village in the 1950s and 1960s (111). According to Orser, real estate block-busting, racism, realtors' unwillingness to deal with African-American clients, and panic peddling all contributed to the rapid shift (15). Several neighborhoods in the area continue to have high crime rates in the 1980s and 1990s. The area also has witnessed significant reconfiguring of neighborhood boundaries in the past twenty years (Chapter 8). Both of these phenomena may be partially attributable to the rapidity of the racial turnover taking place there in the 1950s and 1960s.

The Citizen's Patrol in the Northwest and the Commander. In the Upper Park Heights section of Baltimore, citizen anticrime activities staffed largely by Orthodox Jewish participants drew fire. The Northwest Citizens Patrol volunteer organization, a "citizens on patrol" operation, drove the streets of the area to prevent crimes. Auto theft had been a particular problem in this location. The patrol even received national media exposure.

But members were exclusively male Orthodox Jews. They explained that the exclusivity created a strong religious bond among members and ensured survival of the patrols. African Americans had been excluded, but not because of their race (97).

African-American citizens of the Upper Park Heights neighborhoods expressed concern about the arrangement. This rift between African-American citizens and Jewish citizens came to a climax in September 1994 over a "misunderstanding." At the center of the controversy was the transfer order for Major Barry Powell, the African American commander of the Northwest District. African-American leaders believed his ousting to have been instigated by local Jewish leaders. Police Commissioner Frazier urged African-American and Jewish leaders to talk with each other.

In the truce agreement between these two groups, Frazier said that Powell would remain on the job indefinitely; African-American leaders agreed that the Jewish community did not instigate the transfer; and the Northwest Citizen Patrol agreed to open up its membership to all residents (65, 116). The plan to keep Powell in place lasted until April 1995, when he was reassigned as part of a broader departmental shake-up (72).

Daniel Henson and Michael Olesker. In June 1995, racial remarks allegedly made by Daniel P. Henson, commissioner of Housing, further underscored racial tension in the city. Henson, who faced several controversies at the time (see below), was accused by Michael Olesker of blaming the Jews for the decline of neighborhoods in the northwest section of the city (39, 109). Olesker, an author and longtime columnist for the *Baltimore Sun*, also appears regularly on a local news show.

> Mr. Henson was quoted in Michael Olesker's column as saying the administration had not abandoned Park Heights, a Northwest Baltimore neighborhood scarred by large numbers of boarded up properties. "The abandonment didn't just start," he was quoted as telling Mr. Olesker. "It was you." Mr. Olesker asked, "What do you mean me? You mean white people? You mean Jews?" To which Mr. Henson reportedly replied "Yes." (39: B1)

Henson stated that he was misquoted and offered a different version of the story (39, 109).

Housing

Vacant Houses.   Henson, as commissioner of Housing, was responsible for spearheading efforts to reduce vacant housing. Henson and Schmoke had both received criticism for their lack of progress on this front. In the early years of Schmoke's administration, they had tried to sell city-owned vacant houses at auction. They also had tried renovating city-owned abandoned properties and then selling them. In a second phase of the attack on vacant housing, in the fall of 1994, Schmoke threatened to flatten landlords' abandoned properties that were not improved. Then, in the spring of 1995, he turned his attention to private vacant units, hoping to assist in the sales of those unoccupied homes in six targeted "teetering" neighborhoods.

Before we describe Schmoke's strategies circa 1994–1995, some historical background on housing is warranted. During the 1970s, with a rapidly appreciating national housing market, Mayor Schaefer had successfully targeted for revitalization several inner-city neighborhoods with extensive vacant housing. He sold the houses for a dollar and provided low-interest loans to renovate the housing; the buyers in turn promised that the units would be habitable within a specific period of time. Neighborhoods such as Barre's Circle, Ridgely's Delight, Gay Street, and others were substantially redone. These and other neighborhoods showed significant signs of gentrification in the 1970s (23).

But by the early 1980s, volumes of vacant housing were still a problem in the city, numbering about 4,300 in 1983 (2). A study at that time by the Citizens Planning and Housing Association focused on a sample of 132 vacant and abandoned units located in five neighborhoods: Sandtown-Winchester, Harlem Park, Pratt-Monroe, Coldstream-Homestead-Montebello (C-H-M), and East Baltimore Midway. They found that the owners were likely not to be big-time slumlords, but, in 90% of the cases, "inexperienced property owners with fewer than 10 holdings" (2: B8). Seventy-five percent of the units were owned by individuals rather than corporations. Inexperienced owners would buy property, planning to rehabilitate it, then realize how expensive and extensive the renovation would be, leading them to abandon the property before they could "recycle" it. In addition to the owners' problems, the report suggested, neighborhood arson and vandalism also contributed to abandonment, but strong, active neighborhood organizations, such as could be found in C-H-M, could help prevent abandonment.

Ten years later, the volume of vacant, abandoned units had roughly doubled. Schmoke had tried auctioning off city properties and helping to rehabilitate the sites. Auctioned properties moved into new owners' hands at a glacial pace, and investigations showed rehabilitation costs often far outstripped house values. In short, nothing seemed to be working, and the volume mounted steadily.

Now we are back where we started, in October 1994. Mayor Schmoke touted a plan for vacant and dilapidated properties: Landlords would be told to fix them up or the city would flatten them. Housing Commissioner Henson also wanted to raise fines and prosecution rates of absentee landlords. The number of vacant houses was expected to reach 8,000 in 1995. Henson perspicaciously attributed the problem of deteriorating homes to population losses in the city. Schmoke sought to place the burden on property owners, but only wanted to deliver the "fix it or we raze it" ultimatum if owners failed to respond or pay fines (28). Schmoke and Henson asked community leaders for lists of properties for razing. Community leaders and activists welcomed the plan; they thought it made sense to demolish unsalvageable properties. Henson stated that the first demolitions would likely involve entire blocks of dilapidated row houses. The mayor stressed that he wanted to work with community leaders on this project (40).

The campaign started in December 1994, when three dilapidated houses, two privately owned, were destroyed in the Walbrook neighborhood. The properties in question were known drug hangouts. The residents applauded the demolition and planned to put gardens on the site (26).

Initially, the campaign appeared aggressive. But in June 1995, it was reported that only fourteen homes had been knocked down. The number of vacant houses had increased to 8,500 from 7,500 in the fall of 1994. Henson blamed the slow start on lengthy legal notifications required for private property owners, as well as problems hiring wrecking crews. According to the mayor, the slow pace could also be attributed to the need for redevelopment plans for the newly vacant lots. Henson promised that things would speed up, forecasting 400 vacant houses torn down by the end of 1995. To help speed up the process, the city trained its own demolition crew and bought a fifty-ton crane (34).

Hoping to restore some of the vacant units to occupation, the city developed a plan to attract people into vacant homes. As part of the plan, the city agreed to pay for renovations with block grants if the owner would pledge to live in the property for ten years. The plan appeared to run into problems early on. Repairs were done by city contractors shoddily or not at all, according to some reports. The volume of units acted on was smaller than anticipated. Henson stated that the problems with the program were due to credit and renovation program limitations (32, 37).

As mentioned above, in the spring of 1995 Henson also targeted private properties that had been for sale for an extremely long period of time. Focusing on six "teetering" neighborhoods, he sought to make these units more attractive to buyers. We quote extensively from an article by JoAnna Daemmrich from that period, because it provides an overview of the programs attempted:

> For the third year in a row, Baltimore is trying a different gambit to attract homeowners to older neighborhoods where once well-kept streets have begun to slip into disrepair. . . . The latest strategy to restore luster to fading neighborhoods has the city offering incentives to help owners sell houses that have been on the market for some time. . . . Housing officials are teaming up with real estate agents to auction off about 50 privately owned houses in six middle class neighborhoods. . . . This year's sale is a marked departure from the past two vaunted auctions designed to get boarded-up city-owned properties renovated and back on the tax rolls. Both of the city's earlier ambitious efforts to attract new owners for its growing inventory of vacant houses have faltered. . . . Housing Commissioner Daniel P. Henson III said the previous auctions were hindered by complications involving property appraisals, income verifications and extensive renovations required for houses that were little more than vacant shells. . . . "Last time we went to the hard core vacant properties . . . this year we're trying to market specific neighborhoods. . . . The Greater Baltimore Board of Realtors is going through its lists of houses that have been on the market for 90 days or longer to find at least 50 suitable properties." . . . Traditional brick rowhouses and eclectic freestanding houses line many of the streets in Baltimore-Linwood, Callaway-Garrison, Edgewood, Waverly, Better Waverly, and Mid-Govans. But all six neighborhoods have begun to show signs of decay, from the first boarded-up houses to overgrown lots and a growing number of rental prop-

erties. . . . As a result the city has designated these mid- to outer-city neighborhoods "conservation areas" and is attempting to stabilize them by offer-
ing extra public improvements, loans and grants to boost homeownership,
school repairs, business services, and the like. . . . "We're concentrating on
these areas because they are not teetering yet, but without some special assistance they could," Mr. Henson said.

Houses in the six neighborhood generally sell for $40,000 to $50,000. . . .
The city will chip in $5,000 to $7,500 towards the closing and settlement
costs for each house, depending on the buyer's income. The program could
cost the city roughly $300,000 in community block grants. . . .

Last April's auction of vacant houses owned by the city and state . . . resulted in only 52 of 152 houses being sold.

Thirteen of the successful bidders failed to qualify for mortgages or gave
up on the program, while another 13 still are waiting for renovations
promised by the city.

In the end, the city spent nearly $4,000,000 renovating 42 of the houses,
which were sold for $1,800,000. The average renovation bill, paid by the city
mostly with block grants, was $94,000, and several houses had to be rebuilt
for more than $100,000. . . .

Mayor Kurt L. Schmoke and Mr. Henson have acknowledged that the last
two auctions ultimately failed to live up to expectations. Last year's effort
was dogged by renovation problems and red tape; and a complex foreclo-
sure process resulted in only 350 of the 1500 vacant houses being sold in a
highly touted tax sale in the spring of 1993.

. . . [Mayoral candidate Mary Pat] Clarke . . . has continued to criticize his
administration for failing to develop a comprehensive strategy for the growing inventory of boarded up houses. The city, she said, has been forced into
"demolition by neglect." . . .

As many as 1,041 blocks now have at least one vacant property, most privately owned. (29: B4)

Controversies Around Public Housing.   Two controversies related to
public housing surfaced during this time. One concerned irregularities in
contracts to renovate public housing, the other the hiring of the Nation of
Islam to provide public housing security.

"No bid" contracts were given to contractors for renovating public
housing units. (With a "no bid" contract, a competitive bidding process is
not followed for contracting out the work.) In a series of articles in the
Baltimore Sun, fraud and shoddy workmanship were alleged. The federal
Department of Housing and Urban Development (HUD), in response,
demanded the city of Baltimore pay $725,759 for costs inflated by the
Housing Authority and contractors. HUD warned that contracts without

bids could not be awarded without the department's approval. But Henson maintained that he did not need this type of permission to award no-bid contracts (78). The scandal spurred anger from some in Congress, who charged that Mayor Schmoke misused federal government money (76). Members of the Baltimore city council also criticized Schmoke and Henson and, in a divided vote, decided that the Housing Commission should hold a hearing instead of an investigation by the full council (31, 35, 104).

The accusations leveled against the mayor and Henson involved $25.6 million of no-bid contracts for work at the sites. Friends of both men received many of the contracts, the costs were inflated, jobs were not done or were done very poorly, work was not monitored, and work was handed down to inexperienced African-American firms even as qualified African-American firms were not given contracts (107). Henson defended the no-bid program, stressing that if mistakes were made, it was due to the urgent need for housing (104).

Baltimore's Housing Authority was also involved in another scandal involving federal regulations. The Nation of Islam (NOI) security agency received a $4.6 million contract to provide public housing security. The NOI group, however, was the highest bidder. HUD investigated the NOI contract after the Wells Fargo security agency sued the Housing Authority. The Wells Fargo bid was the lowest at $3.5 million. Baltimore was faced with possibly paying $1 million to the federal government (77). Henson supported the NOI contract, stating that the company with the lowest bid does not always do the best job. The Nation of Islam security agency was found to have less experience than the Wells Fargo company (36). This issue, the subject of an episode on the TV series *Homicide*, evoked strong feelings among the citizenry. Many claimed that the NOI guards, in addition to providing security, played active roles in rehabilitating African-Americans with drug problems. As one person who spoke to us on the issue put it, the regular guards would just step over a crackhead found in the stairwell. But the NOI guards would take in, feed, and try to rehabilitate the addict. On the other hand, some criticized the "strong arm" tactics allegedly used by NOI. Four NOI guards were charged in a beating incident. The investigation uncovered that some of the guards had no experience, and one of them was a former police officer who had been removed for use of excessive force (44, 71).

The Nation of Islam security agency had its own problems with the federal government. It was suspected of racial and religious discrimination by the federal government (82). In addition, the Internal Revenue Service (IRS) stated that NOI owed $58,846 in income taxes withheld from employees (155).

The Mayor and the Report.   One last housing-related issue surfaced during this period. In 1993, the mayor commissioned a $47,909 study of the Baltimore Housing Authority, which was facing problems placing 33,000 poor families in vacant apartments. The author of the study, a close legal friend of Schmoke, briefed the mayor on his findings, but at the request of the mayor no written report was prepared. At the heart of the controversy was whether the report should be made public because the bill was paid with city funds. The mayor did not think so and claimed the results could be kept undisclosed by invoking the lawyer-client privilege. The mayor did provide an eleven-page outline after being challenged by the city council. The outline contained information on management restructuring, new buildings, and strengthening security (38).

Neighborhood Maintenance and Redevelopment

During the 1994–1995 period, numerous redevelopment and revitalization efforts were under way throughout the city. Here we mention just a few to provide a flavor for the initiatives being pursued at the time. We outline in more detail a few of these that directly affected some of our study neighborhoods.

In Brief.

Near the Pimlico racetrack, a community development corporation (CDC) continued buying and rehabilitating a number of homes located between Park Heights Avenue and Reistertown Road. Begun in 1989, and still going strong in 1995, the CDC hoped to turn over at least eighty units (103).

• In the same section of town, in October 1994, a $5.3 million, eighty-four–unit apartment complex was planned for the 5400 block of Park Heights Avenue, replacing a center that had been vacant for years and finally demolished in October 1993 (153).

• In November 1994, the Enterprise Foundation launched a campaign to raise funds to be used in West Baltimore to replicate the Sandtown-Winchester revitalization project. The latter project had placed several blocks of new housing in the area and received national media coverage, although it does have its critics (102). The new campaign was titled "Communities for Change: New Home, New Hope." The goals include rebuilding depressed neighborhoods and providing affordable housing, employment opportunities, and other services for low-income residents (117).

• In February 1995, a redevelopment plan for the Rosemont section surfaced. The Lutheran Hospital, closed for several years, was targeted for conversion. The plan was to provide shops and apartments for the elderly. It was hoped the project would help ease "urban blight" in the adjoining communities (85). In our district planner interview for this area, the planner did highlight resident concerns about the hospital. The site had been of concern even before it closed, with some residents alleging medical waste had washed up in their toilets.

• Schmoke announced plans in November 1994 to turn Baltimore's Howard Street corridor, the heart of Baltimore's downtown before the Inner Harbor era, into an "Avenue of the Arts." Vacant buildings in the area were to be converted to galleries and artist housing. Other plans for the corridor included a performing arts center and the reopening of the Mayfair theater (54).

• In February 1995, Baltimore agreed to buy the Fishmarket for $2.4 million. The large property, which lies two blocks from the eastern part of the Inner Harbor, was to be converted to a children's museum (122).

• Henson announced plans in May 1995 to demolish the first of the decaying high-rise towers at the Lafayette Courts public housing community. The plans were to replace "the buildings with townhouses, a daycare center and a health clinic" (30: B1). The demolition and reconstruction plans of Lafayette Courts were the beginning of a seven-year, $293 million plan to overhaul four public high-rise campuses and to provide new neighborhoods for the poor (30). The demolition, when it did happen, was woven into another *Homicide* television episode.

• The government made a $10 million investment in midtown Baltimore for a parking garage at Pennsylvania Station, its AMTRAK passenger station. Many hoped the move would help draw people and investors into the Penn North community and adjoining locations and perhaps even halt the spread of drugs and crime. (94)

Some development proposals drew fire rather than accolades.

• Residents of several East Baltimore communities sought to block the building of a juvenile justice facility to be located at Hillen Street and Fallsway. Within walking distance of the proposed facility was the state penitentiary, the city detention center, and the supermax facility for extremely violent offenders. Residents claimed that property values would go down (80).

• In Little Italy, residents opposed apartment plans, charging that a developer misled them about plans to include low-income units. The neighborhood is surrounded by subsidized housing areas such as Flag House Court, Douglass Homes, and Perkins Homes. Residents opposed further subsidized or low-income housing in and around their neighborhood. As a result, the city delayed funding (83).

Eastern High School.   On Thirty-Third Street, sitting just across from Memorial Stadium, home to the Baltimore Orioles from the 1950s through 1991, as well as the Baltimore Colts for a somewhat shorter span, sits shuttered Eastern High School. The site is south of the Ednor Gardens Lakeside neighborhood and is catercorner from the southern boundary of the Waverly neighborhood. About six to seven blocks due east, the Johns Hopkins Homewood campus begins, the entrance stairway topped by a mossy bust of the founder.

Eastern was built in 1939 and closed in 1986. Residents in adjoining neighborhoods have expressed strong concern about the site, given its visible location and the much reduced use of Memorial Stadium across the street after the Orioles moved to their new stadium, Oriole Park at Camden Yards, beginning with the 1992 season. High school and college football games have continued at the stadium. It became the home to a Canadian Football League team in the early 1990s, and for the 1996 and 1997 season the newly relocated National Football League (NFL) Baltimore Ravens, formerly the Cleveland Browns, used it for home games. But the long-term future of Memorial Stadium remained unclear at the time of the study. Thus residents express especially strong interest in recycling the Eastern High site.

In January 1995, a proposal was submitted to convert the site to a commercial center. Some believed, however, the proposal would detract from other commercial interests in the area (56). In March 1995, Johns Hopkins made a bid for the property to be used as a satellite campus. In the 1980s, Hopkins Hospital had successfully converted the old City Hospital site on Eastern Boulevard in southeast Baltimore into a research/medical site. On the Homewood campus, building projects through the 1980s have used up almost all of the remaining open space. By the mid-1990s, some Hopkins offices were housed in high-rise towers off campus, on the northern side of University Parkway. Homewood needed additional space if it was to add activities.

Community members strongly supported the proposal, many believing it would bring additional employment opportunities into the area. They also felt it would help "shore up" the surrounding neighborhoods, such as Waverly, Better Waverly, Ednor Gardens–Lakeside, and Coldstream-Homestead-Montebello (5, 47, 57, 86).

Fells Point, Development, and Mega-Bars. The Fells Point section of the city, emotionally if not geographically centered at the base of Broadway in East Baltimore, and the adjoining neighborhoods with harbor frontage such as West Canton and Canton, experienced considerable development during the 1980s. Along Boston Street, at least one high-rise went in, and condominiums were constructed on the vacant land along the water. Some sites look not unlike the vacant lot just south of the abandoned Continental Can factory where Barry Levinson placed the diner for his mid-1980s movie *Diner*.

Fells Point has had for a number of years, and continues to have, an active night life, built in part on excellent seafood like Bertha's Mussels and large numbers of small bars. In February 1995, some developers decided it was time to try and do things big time.

Developers asked the city to consider adding 1,200 restaurant and bar seats along the harbor from Fells Point to Canton. The proposal called for open-air bars and restaurants carrying exotic names and props such as tiki huts and palm trees (92).

The proposal immediately drew fire. Opponents argued the exotic decor would clash with neighborhood architecture and that more rowdy young drinkers would be drawn to the waterfront (92). As one local politician put it, residents did not want to make money by having people come into the neighborhood and get falling-down drunk.[22]

The city's zoning board rejected one proposal for the first open-air bar and restaurant along the Fells Point waterfront (90). In March, plans to build the restaurant and bar in Canton were killed when the city liquor board denied the project a license (89).

In April 1995, the General Assembly of Maryland passed a bill banning large waterfront bars—large meaning over 150 seats—from Little Italy, located west of Fells Point, to Canton, located east of Fells Point. The bill prohibited the transfer of liquor licenses to such businesses in these locations. Licenses would only be granted if these places took in 80% of profits on food (88).

But then the newly elected governor Parris Glendening stepped in. He vetoed the bill that would have banned the waterfront bars. An aide explained: The governor vetoed the bill because there was no public hearing and new restaurants could be prevented from obtaining liquor licenses (87). John Pica, a state senator from Baltimore, also pushed for the veto of the bill, stating that the requirement for a restaurant to take in 80% in food profits was too restrictive. This decision sparked anger from neighborhood residents who are still trying to find a way to ban the mega-bars (91).

Special Tax Districts.   In December 1994, residents of Charles Village approved a plan to increase their property taxes. Underlying this seemingly irrational behavior was their desire for more city services.

The special tax district they proposed and approved was loosely modeled on downtown BIDs (business improvement districts), where storeowners pay an extra assessment for extra services like street cleaning or foot patrol officers. The downtown BID in Baltimore sponsored, among other activities, "crime and grime patrols," started in March 1995 with a staff of twelve to fourteen public safety officers and a two- to four-member clean team. Teams in distinctive uniforms could be seen trimming grass around trees and cleaning sidewalks.

Charles Villagers hoped they could get safer and cleaner streets with their extra funds. The taxation plan was expected to provide $400,000 for the district and to be supplemented by $100,000 from Johns Hopkins University, the Homewood campus of which is directly east of Charles Village (105, 137). Two years later, as Charles Village celebrated its 100th anniversary in 1997, the benefits district leader credited the initiative with helping to reduce crime markedly in the locale (139).

In March 1995, another special tax district was proposed for the residential neighborhoods just north of the downtown, from Centre Street north to Twentieth Street, and from the Jones Falls Expressway on the east to Howard Street on the west (126). The special taxing districts appear to have growing appeal. Some hope it might help keep the middle class in the city (123).

Talking Trash and Graffiti.   Baltimore, like every other major city, has trash problems. In September 1994, Mayor Schmoke reorganized the Bureau of Solid Waste and mounted nightly patrols. The latter were intended to deter illegal dumping in alleys and vacant lots (27). In January 1995, a new battle plan was developed to make the city cleaner. It called for dividing the city into twenty sections. Monthly, each section would be invaded on designated days by groups of collectors and trucks. The city also planned to target alleys, streets, and vacant lots, as well as removing bulk trash and graffiti (124). Schmoke hoped that the city's cleanup efforts would help city residents to feel better about themselves and their community (128).

Schmoke's graffiti prevention initiative echoed Mayor Schaefer's wide-ranging antivandalism initiatives of the early 1980s, when he had formed a mayor's task force on the issue. At that time, city hall had a mayor's antivandalism coordinator for the city, Dan Lipstein, and had vigorously prosecuted several graffiti writers. One of those caught turned out to be an art student at the Maryland Institute of Art (149).

Population and Job Shifts.   The somber-hued backdrop for these efforts was continued population losses. These losses had afflicted the city of Baltimore and Washington, D.C., since 1950 (20: 773). They continued apace in the early 1990s. According to the U.S. Census Bureau, the number of Baltimoreans dropped from approximately 736,000 in 1990 to an estimate of 703,000 in 1994, as many city residents moved to the suburbs (16). It has been reported that those leaving the city were middle-class families who had struggled with high property taxes, a fear of drugs and crime, a failing public education system, and the belief that nothing would get better in the city (108).

Accompanying the city population losses was the increasingly African-American population in the inner suburban ring, first noted at the end of the 1970s (51). A June 1995 report predicted that Baltimore County was changing so quickly it could be 30% African-American by the year 2005. The report showed that many African Americans were making the exodus from the city of Baltimore, a trend noted nationwide since 1970 by William Julius Wilson (156). But whereas middle-class African-American households had moved out in earlier decades, the influx into surrounding Baltimore County in the 1990s contained more working-class and poor households. Their migration into the county was beginning to burden infrastructure in the inner-ring suburbs (21).

Families were not the only ones making an exit from the city. The historic Har Sinai congregation voted to sell its property on the 6300 block of Park Heights Avenue and move to the suburbs following the departing members of the congregation (1, 55). Even major African-American churches have considered an exodus from the city (138).

Along with families and churches, numerous businesses, some quite large, have left the city. United States Fidelity and Guaranty Corporation (USF&G), the tawny tower of which symbolized the Inner Harbor revitalization and the Baltimore renaissance of the 1970s, and the upper stories of which had been home to eagles, announced plans to vacate (22). Given such losses, Schmoke proclaimed as a major victory Alex Brown and Sons' decision to keep its headquarters downtown. Schmoke's office had apparently lobbied hard to keep the firm (129). Brown's financial activities in Baltimore dated back to the War of 1812 (20: 199). In June 1995, it was reported that Baltimore was able to hold city job losses to their lowest level in five years. Meanwhile, the metro area continued to grow. "Taken as a whole, metropolitan Baltimore added 14,600 jobs last year, growing by 1.3 percent, to a total of 1.11 million, the Labor Department said. Many of the jobs were in the commercial construction, service industries and health care" (58: A9).

Will the Empowerment Zones Empower?

As our field effort was winding down in Baltimore in the spring of 1995, the city was selected as an empowerment zone site (125). These zones represented one of the major initiatives of President Clinton's first term. The goal was to use federal funds to help create economic development in disadvantaged cities. Specific sites in each location were specified as the empowerment zone. Cities and sometimes regions competed to be chosen. Six were finally selected. Baltimore was one. Improvement efforts were to be targeted at some of the worst-off sections of the city.

Figure 2.7 displays a billboard thanking President Clinton for the empowerment zone funds. The sign is next to a recently reopened and

FIGURE 2.7   Just East of Midtown Belvedere, Looking Toward Downtown. Residents Thank President Clinton "for Our Empowerment Zone." Photo by author.

promptly graffiti-covered bridge, just east of Midtown, the neighborhood where we had our field office during the course of the study. On this clear, spring morning in April 1995, the view looks toward the downtown. Although the geographer David Harvey has detailed the job losses and internationalization of commerce reflected in the downtown landmarks, it is almost easy to be hopeful (60).

But when the view shifts closer, it is a little harder. Just next to the sign are abandoned houses. On the street around the corner, Steve Pardue and I walked on broken glass and saw more vacant houses with no windows, as well as kids playing in the street, watched over by a few older women. As we traveled east from this site, further from the downtown, moving through neighborhoods like Middle East, the volume of vacant, boarded-up housing and unemployed men sitting about grew substantially. We do not yet know how many of those houses will still be windowless and abandoned and how many of those men will still be sitting out on sunny, spring weekday mornings when the empowerment zone funds are spent and gone.

Notes

David Linne generated the first draft of the material reporting on newspaper accounts, which originally appeared as a separate chapter. He also assisted in preparing the data for the multicity crime and structural comparisons.

1. Those seeking more comprehensive reviews of significant events in Baltimore taking place before 1970 would do well to consult 110. For Maryland history, see 20.

2. Those other cities, and their 1970 populations were:

EL PASO	322,261
SAN JOSE	446,504
JACKSONVILLE	528,865
SEATTLE	530,890
COLUMBUS	539,377
PHOENIX	581,600
MEMPHIS	623,755
BOSTON	641,053
SAN ANTONIO	654,289
SAN FRANCISCO	715,674
MILWAUKEE	717,124
INDIANAPOLIS	744,570
CLEVELAND	751,046
WASHINGTON, D.C.	756,510
PHILADELPHIA	1,948,609

3. Of course, some of these cities began losing population before 1970, but those broader trends go beyond the scope of the current project.

4. 1970 and 1980 figures are rates per census tract (148).

5. Readers seeking detailed information on changes for other Part I crimes will find them in the final report for Grant 93-IJ-CX–0022, available from the National Criminal Justice Reference Service (on-line at http://www.ncjrs.org).

6. For the comparison cities, we report unweighted average rates across cities, ignoring city size. To have weighted by size would have given too much weight to Philadelphia.

7. In carrying out this test, and in describing crime changes, we made use of a standardized, weighted crime percentile measure. We first averaged the crime rate for the three years at the beginning of each decade: 1970–1972, 1980–1982, and 1990–1992. Then, for each average, we found its population-weighted percentile score. For more details, see Chapter 4. Each population-weighted percentile score looks at the proportion of the city population with a score at or below *that* community's score. So if a neighborhood has a percentile score of 75 for robbery, it means that its robbery rate is higher than is found in neighborhoods containing 75% of the city's population.

Choice of 1990 versus 1980 versus 1970 population seems somewhat arbitrary. We examined the figures using different weighting schemes and found no marked differences.

It is possible for several neighborhoods to have a percentile score of zero, if they all have a crime rate of zero. They are all "tied" for the safest position. Only one neighborhood, however, can have a percentile crime score of 100.

The percentile crime distributions are not normal; rather they are uniform, or flat, in appearance. They are too platykurtic. But this deviation from normality is a lot less serious than problems with skewness and extreme outliers that crop up when using crime rates or logged crime rates.

Some percentile crime distributions are slightly positively skewed if a large proportion of neighborhoods score zero on the crime in question. Murder is the only crime where this results in noticeable skewness. But the skewness statistic is still well within the acceptable range.

8. Are there changes in crime reporting practices rather than changes in crime per se in the 1970s that might explain these shifts? By the early 1980s, we did see the implementation of 911 technology. But the police commissioner through the 1970s was Donald Pomerlau, so there were none of the high-level political shifts that can so often drive shifts in crime levels. And the changes we see appear across a number of crimes, including homicide, the crime least likely to be influenced by technological or political crosscurrents.

9. Interrater reliability for all the items of interest here, with the exception of litter, were about .70 or higher (see Chapter 3). Given litter's unacceptably low reliability, it was not analyzed.

10. We go from ninety streetblocks to eighty-seven streetblocks because one streetblock assessed in 1981 was dropped since it was not residential, even though we surveyed residents at an adjoining apartment complex in 1994; one streetblock assessed in 1981 (unit block East Biddle St.) was confused with an adjoining streetblock (unit block West Biddle St.) and no 1981 assessments were available for the streetblock where residents were interviewed in 1994; and a streetblock added in 1994 to the survey did not have 1981 assessment information.

11. The "half a house" in these figures is due to the averaging across two raters.

12. In 1994, raters also counted graffiti, but they did not do so in 1981.

13. K. Maguire and A. L. Pastore, eds. (1996), *Sourcebook of Criminal Justice Statistics 1995* (Washington, D.C.: USGPO), page 152, Table 2.31.

14. *Sourcebook of Criminal Justice Statistics 1995*, page 151, Table 2.32. Baltimore, of course, is predominantly African-American and has been so since the 1980s. If we look at the portion of African Americans saying yes to this question, there is still no discernible trend (Table 2.33, pp. 152–153). The 1982 figure for African Americans and others is 61%; the 1994 figure is 56%.

15. Ferraro and LaGrange, among others, have criticized many fear indicators. In Ferraro's view many of the items are "less than stellar" (1995: p. 32). Chapter 6 considers this debate in more detail.

16. A 95% confidence interval is used here.

17. Since the results exclude the downtown, public housing locations, and a small number of unorganized areas, the results, strictly speaking, do not apply to all types of residential locations in the city. But they still apply to the wide range of other residential settings.

18. Stated more technically, we are attempting to manage the inflation of Type I error levels by using this more restricted error level. We opted for the 99% intervals levels because for each topic under discussion, fear and perceived problems, we had multiple, related outcomes. Therefore, to have used a conventional alpha of .05 and the associated 95% confidence intervals would have resulted in an inflated alpha level.

Strictly speaking, it would have been most appropriate to use a Bonferroni-adjusted alpha level. This would have been .0125 for the fear items and .0045 for the perceived problems. Communicating these specific alpha levels is somewhat technical for the general reader, so we compromised by setting alpha at .01 and the confidence intervals at 99%.

The results reported here were generated using hierarchical linear models. More specifically, we carried out one-way analysis of variance (ANOVAs), with no Level I predictors and no Level II predictors, to estimate grand means on each outcome and the confidence interval around each grand mean. These means and the confidence intervals are based on Empirical Bayes estimates of "true" scores, taking into account variations in data quality in each neighborhood and variations in sample size in each neighborhood.

For the 1982 results based on thirty neighborhoods and the 1994 results based on those same neighborhoods, we show unweighted results. We also examined the results if we weighted respondents to take into account relative neighborhood size and our slight underrepresentations of renters, African Americans, and men. Those weighted results, for 1994 and 1982, were virtually identical to those reported here and resulted in conclusions no different from those described here.

19. Block had been defined earlier in the interview as the streetblock—the two sides of the block face between the two cross streets.

20. Again, as with the fear items, the means shown are empirical Bayes population estimates.

21. Earlier evidence showed that urban fear has not been increasing nationwide since the 1970s. The General Social Survey data provided information on fear in urban African Americans, and urban, elderly African Americans. Again, fear was not demonstrably increasing through the 1980s for either of these groups.

22. As a Philadelphia aside, along the Delaware waterfront, mega-bars such as Hooters and Dave and Buster's abound. But these sites are not contiguous to a viable residential neighborhood.

References

(1) Alvarez, R. (1995) Har Sinai congregation may move to Owings Mills. *Baltimore Sun* January 12, A1, A16.

(2) Anonymous. (1983) Vacant housing found to be mostly problem of small owner. *Baltimore Sun* July 31, B1, B8.

(3) Anonymous. (1994) Baltimore raids net 20 suspects. *Baltimore Sun* November 2, B3.

(4) Anonymous. (1994) City receives $2 million as anti-crime grant. *Baltimore Sun* November 21, B3.

(5) Anonymous. (1995) Hopkins plan backed for former school site. *Baltimore Sun* April 11, 1995, B3.

(6) Anonymous. (1999) *Kurt L. Schmoke, mayor: Official biography* [on-line: http://cw.bi.baltimore.md.us/mayor/bio.html; retrieved August 2, 1999].

(7) Anonymous. (1999) Major crimes climb in Philadelphia. *Philadelphia Inquirer* January 17 [on-line: Article ID 9901190077, http://www.philly.com/newslibrary; retrieved August 2, 1999].

(8) Apperson, J. (1995) Lawyer takes blame for Hurt doing time. *Baltimore Sun* April 13, 1B, 11B.

(9) Apperson, J. (1995) Officer contradicts Hurt's defense. *Baltimore Sun* April 8, B1, B3.

(10) Apperson, J. (1995) Trial under way for man charged in teen's death. *Baltimore Sun* March 31, B1, B5.

(11) Apperson, J., and Shatzkin, K. (1995) Hurt convicted, faces imprisonment. *Baltimore Sun* April 12, A1, A20.

(12) Barlett, D. L., and Steele, J. B. (1996) *America: Who Stole the Dream?* Andrews and McNeel, Kansas City.

(13) Blum, J. (1994) In Baltimore, both sides shrug off new youth curfew. *Washington Post* August 1, B1, B2.

(14) Blumstein, A., and Rosenfeld, R. (1988) Explaining trends in U.S. homicide rates. *Journal of Criminal Law and Criminology* 88, 1175–1216.

(15) Bock, J. (1994) A history lesson in black and white. *Baltimore Sun* November 5, B1, B3.

(16) Bock, J. (1995) City population likely to dip below 700,000 this year. *Baltimore Sun* February 9, A1, A16.

(17) Bowler, M. (1994) Student leaders pledge to fight school violence. *Baltimore Sun* November 17, B1, B2.

(18) Bratton, W. (1998) *Turnaround*, Random House, New York.

(19) Brill, P. (1994) After raids, Walbrook hopes for more. *Baltimore Sun* November 21, B1, B2.

(20) Brugger, R. J. (1988) *Maryland: A middle temperament*, Johns Hopkins University Press, Baltimore.

(21) Carson, L. (1995) Balto. Co. minorities increase. *Baltimore Sun* June 6, B1, B2.

(22) Conn, D. (1995) USF&G to leave its tower. *Baltimore Sun* January 20, A1, A11.

(23) Covington, J. C., and Taylor, R. B. (1989) Gentrification and crime: Robbery and larceny changes in appreciating Baltimore neighborhoods in the 1970's. *Urban Affairs Quarterly* 25, 142–172.

(24) Crenson, M. (1983) *Neighborhood politics*, Harvard University Press, Cambridge, MA.

(25) Crowell, A. (1996) Minor restrictions: The challenge of juvenile curfews. *Public Management* August, 4–9.

(26) Daemmrich, J. (1994) 3 sites of drug use demolished by city. *Baltimore Sun* December 1, B4.

(27) Daemmrich, J. (1994) Night patrol told to curb illegal trash. *Baltimore Sun* September 16, B1, B2.

(28) Daemmrich, J. (1994) Schmoke warns landlords: Fix it, or city will raze it. *Baltimore Sun* October 7, A1, A15.

(29) Daemmrich, J. (1995) Baltimore again backs house sales: In third auction try, city will help buyers in six neighborhoods. *Baltimore Sun* April 15, 1A, 8A.

(30) Daemmrich, J. (1995) City high rises will be demolished. *Baltimore Sun* May 24, B1, B4.

(31) Daemmrich, J. (1995) City housing woes debate stirs rivalries on council. *Baltimore Sun* February 28, A1, A12.

(32) Daemmrich, J. (1995) City sale of vacant homes ends "beautifully" for pair. *Baltimore Sun* March 12, B1, B2.

(33) Daemmrich, J. (1995) Clarke dives into campaign. *Baltimore Sun* February 12, C1, C4.

(34) Daemmrich, J. (1995) Demolition of derelict buildings gets slow start. *Baltimore Sun* June 21, A1, A10.

(35) Daemmrich, J. (1995) Hearing set on home repair effort. *Baltimore Sun* March 2, B1, B4.

(36) Daemmrich, J. (1995) Henson insists NOI contract proper. *Baltimore Sun* March 11, B1, B4.

(37) Daemmrich, J. (1995) Housing program stumbles. *Baltimore Sun* March 5, A1, A21.

(38) Daemmrich, J. (1995) Housing study outlined. *Baltimore Sun* May 6, B1, B4.

(39) Daemmrich, J., and Siegel, E. (1995) Henson's resignation demanded. *Baltimore Sun* June 31, B1, B4.

(40) Daemmrich, J., and West, N. (1994) Neighbors welcome city plan to demolish abandoned, tumbledown houses. *Baltimore Sun* October 9, B2.

(41) Donohue, J. J. (1998) Understanding the time path of crime. *Journal of Criminal Law and Criminology* 88, 1423–1451.

(42) Dorsey, G. (1999) 22 Charged as police begin new anti-violence plan. *Baltimore Sun* July 30 [on-line: http://www.sunspot.net; retrieved July 30, 1999].

(43) Elliott, D. S., Wilson, W., Huizinga, D., Sampson, R., Elliott, A., and Rankin, B. (1996) The effects of neighborhood disadvantages on adolescent development. *Journal of Research in Crime and Delinquency* 33, 389–426.

(44) Farabaugh, M. (1995) Four NOI guards charged in beating. *Baltimore Sun* March 27, B1, B10.

(45) Ferraro, K. F. (1994) *Fear of crime: Interpreting victimization risk,* State University of New York Press, Albany.

(46) Fischer, C. S., et al., eds. (1977) *Networks and places,* Free Press, New York.

(47) Folkenflik, D., and Gunts, E. (1995) Hopkins makes bid for Eastern High site. *Baltimore Sun* March 1, A1, A6.

(48) Fox, J. A. (1996) *Trends in juvenile violence: A report to the United States Attorney General on current and future rates of juvenile offending. Executive Summary.* [on-line: http://www.ojp.usdoj.gov/bjs/abstract/tjvfox.html; retrieved October 14, 1999].

(49) Gately, G. (1994) Churches offer havens for students. *Baltimore Sun* October 4, B4.

(50) Gately, G. (1994) Growing violence troubles schools. *Baltimore Sun* November 14, A1, A7.

(51) Goodman, A., and Talalay, R. (1981) *Racial changes in Baltimore region in the 1970's.* Census Note 1, Center for Metropolitan Planning and Research, Johns Hopkins University, Baltimore.

(52) Gottdiener, M. (1994) *The new urban sociology,* McGraw Hill, New York.

(53) Gottdiener, M., and Pickvance, C. (1991) Introduction. In *Urban life in transition* (Gottdiener, M., and Pickvance, C., eds), pp. 1–11. Newbury Park, CA: Sage.

(54) Gunts, E. (1994) City sees Howard St. as Baltimore's SoHo. *Baltimore Sun* November 8, A1, A9.

(55) Gunts, E. (1995) Historic Har Sinai votes to sell property, leave city. *Baltimore Sun* January 23, B1, B3.

(56) Gunts, E., and Hancock, J. (1995) Developers look at Eastern High site. *Baltimore Sun* January 16, B1, B2.

(57) Gunts, E., and Sugg, D. (1995) Hopkins plan seen creating jobs. *Baltimore Sun* March 3, B1, B3.

(58) Hancock, J. (1995) City's job drain slows; area hiring up. *Baltimore Sun* June 1, A1, A9.

(59) Haner, J. (1994) Police chief vows reforms focusing on street patrols. *Baltimore Sun* February 9, A1, A13.

(60) Harvey, D. (1991) A view from Federal Hill. In *The Baltimore book: New views of local history* (Fee, E., Shopes, L., and Zeidman, L., eds), pp. 227–252. Temple University Press, Philadelphia.

(61) Hermann, P. (1994) Cocaine rains from window next door. *Baltimore Sun* October 28, B1, B3.

(62) Hermann, P. (1994) Fatal shots were fired in frustration. *Baltimore Sun* October 12, A1, A12.

(63) Hermann, P. (1994) High-profile raids show force, carry risks. *Baltimore Sun* October 3, A1, A5.

(64) Hermann, P. (1994) Neighbors try to collect bail in fatal shooting. *Baltimore Sun* October 14, B1, B4.

(65) Hermann, P. (1994) A truce in furor over police. *Baltimore Sun* September 20, A1, A12.

(66) Hermann, P. (1995) After rising for years, Baltimore slayings, shootings fall. *Baltimore Sun* January 8, A1, A21.

(67) Hermann, P. (1995) Armed thugs feeling the crackdown. *Baltimore Sun* April 6, B1, B2.

(68) Hermann, P. (1995) Baltimore to put 300 more police on street patrol. *Baltimore Sun* April 26, A1, A15.

(69) Hermann, P. (1995) City police stumble on suspected heroin operation. *Baltimore Sun* April 9, B3.

(70) Hermann, P. (1995) Morale issues shadow city police chief's successes. *Baltimore Sun* February 12, A1, A27.

(71) Hermann, P. (1995) New questions arise about NOI. *Baltimore Sun* March 28, B1, B2.

(72) Hermann, P. (1995) Police commander moved out of Northwest District. *Baltimore Sun* April 28, B1, B4.

(73) Hermann, P. (1995) Slayings of four women linked to different killers. *Baltimore Sun* March 19, C1, C2.

(74) Hermann, P., and Matthew, T. (1995) Drop in downtown crime praised. *Baltimore Sun* March 24.

(75) Hermann, P., and Thompson, J. (1995) Shootout outside school leaves 1 dead, 1 injured. *Baltimore Sun* January 24, B1, B4.

(76) Higham, S., and Myers, M. (1995) Congressmen irate over Baltimore's housing woes. *Baltimore Sun* February 23, A1, A16.

(77) Higham, S., and Myers, M. (1995) HUD finds city in violation on NOI contract. *Baltimore Sun* March 10, A1, A11.

(78) Higham, S., and Simmons, M. (1995) HUD demands $725,759 from city. *Baltimore Sun* February 22, A1, A10.

(79) Hilson, R., Jr. (1995) 21 arrested in raids in O'Donnell Heights. *Baltimore Sun* February 18, B3.

(80) Hilson, R., Jr. (1995) Neighbors vow to fight juvenile jail plan. *Baltimore Sun* February 26, B1, B4.

(81) Hilson, R., Jr. (1995) Teen charged with murder in death of girl, 12, who was strangled, set afire. *Baltimore Sun* March 15, B4.

(82) Hilson, R., Jr., and Matthews, T. (1995) Muslim guards are praised by tenants who see no evidence of discrimination. *Baltimore Sun* January 20, B14.

(83) Jackson, H. (1994) City delays funding decision after Little Italy residents oppose apartment plans. *Baltimore Sun* November 10, B3.

(84) Jackson, H. (1995) Amprey vows to restore "breakthrough teams" to reduce violence. *Baltimore Sun* January 28, B3.

(85) Jackson, H. (1995) Old hospital may become apartments for elderly. *Baltimore Sun* February 14, B1, B5.

(86) Jacobson, J. (1995) Community elated by Hopkins bid. *Baltimore Sun* March 2, B1, B4.

(87) Jacobson, J. (1995) Glendening veto revives mega-bar. *Baltimore Sun* May 24, A1, A12.

(88) Jacobson, J. (1995) Last-minute bill bans "mega-bars" for waterfront. *Baltimore Sun* April 12, B1, B2.

(89) Jacobson, J. (1995) Liquor board denies pier project a license. *Baltimore Sun* March 24, B2.

(90) Jacobson, J. (1995) Proposal for open-air bar in Fells Point rejected. *Baltimore Sun* February 8, B1, B2.

(91) Jacobson, J. (1995) Residents meet on waterfront mega-bars; governor to visit area. *Baltimore Sun* May 31, B4.

(92) Jacobson, J. (1995) Waterfront bars could multiply. *Baltimore Sun* February 7, A1, A12.

(93) James, M. (1995) Police raid 20 homes, arrest 27, seize drugs in 2-day "Operation Hatchet." *Baltimore Sun* February 26, C2.

(94) Jensen, P. (1995) Garage may put Penn Station on track. *Baltimore Sun* May 26, A1, A16.

(95) Kasarda, J. D. (1992) The severely distressed in economically transforming cities. In *Drugs, crime and social isolation: Barriers to urban opportunity* (Harrell, A. V., and Peterson, G. E., eds), pp. 45–98. Urban Institute Press, Washington, DC.

(96) Kurtz, E., Koons, B., and Taylor, R. B. (1998) Land use, physical deterioration, resident-based control and calls for service on urban streetblocks. *Justice Quarterly* 15, 121–149.

(97) Larson, E. (1994) Neighborhood patrol carries out its duty, hopes to be bored. *Wall Street Journal* May 23, A1, A4.

(98) Levine, M. L. (1987) Downtown redevelopment as an urban growth strategy: A critical appraisal of the Baltimore renaissance. *Journal of Urban Affairs* 9, 103–123.

(99) Libit, H., and Hermann, P. (1994) Golf courses tighten security after holdup. *Baltimore Sun* August 31, B1, B4.

(100) Massey, D., and Denton, S. (1993) *American apartheid: Segregation and the making of the underclass*, Harvard University Press, Cambridge, MA.

(101) Matthews, R. G. (1997) Criminal justice leaders criticized. *Baltimore Sun* September 23, 3B.

(102) McDougall, H. A. (1993) *Black Baltimore: A new theory of community*, Temple University Press, Philadelphia.

(103) Mirabella, L. (1995) Face lift for Pimlico. *Baltimore Sun* February 26, L1, L10.

(104) Myers, M., and Daemmrich, J. (1995) Few questions, fewer answers at hearing on housing repairs. *Baltimore Sun* March 8, A1, A10.

(105) Obermayer, J. (1994) Neighbors split over tax boost. *Baltimore Sun* October 1, B1, B2.

(106) Olesker, M. (1995) As Charlie bleeds to death, so does a neighborhood. *Baltimore Sun* March 14, B1, B3.

(107) Olesker, M. (1995) City housing troubles take on a political hue. *Baltimore Sun* February 23, B1, B3.

(108) Olesker, M. (1995) Middle-class flight shrinks hope for Baltimore's future. *Baltimore Sun* February 12, C1, C8.

(109) Olesker, M. (1995) Racial remark nothing to be proud of either. *Baltimore Sun* June 4, C1, C6.

(110) Olson, S. H. (1997) *Baltimore: The building of an American city*, revised and expanded bicentennial ed., Johns Hopkins University Press, Baltimore.

(111) Orser, W. E. (1991) Flight to the suburbs: Suburbanization and racial change on Baltimore's west side. In *The Baltimore book: New views of local history* (Fee, E., Shopes, L., and Zeidman, L., eds), pp. 203–226. Temple University Press, Philadelphia.

(112) Pate, A. M. (1989) Community oriented policing in Baltimore. In *Police and policing: Contemporary issues* (Kenney, D. J., ed), pp. 112–135. Praeger, New York.

(113) Pemberton, M. (1995) "Urban fear" led man to kill boy, defense argues. *Washington Post* March 3, B3.

(114) Peterson, G. E., and Harrell, A., eds. (1992) *Drugs, crime and social isolation*, Urban Institute Press, Washington, DC.

(115) Ruefle, W., and Reynolds, K. M. (1995) Curfews and delinquency in major American cities. *Crime & Delinquency* 41, 347–363.

(116) Ruhl, S. (1994) Jewish residents give haven vibrant identity. *Baltimore Sun* September 25, K1, K14.

(117) Sachs, A. (1994) $78 million housing campaign launched by Rouse foundation. *Baltimore Sun* November 17, B4.

(118) Shane, S. (1995) Girl, 11, found dead in rowhouse. *Baltimore Sun* March 6, B1, B2.

(119) Shatzkin, K. (1995) Hurt sentenced to 5 years in fatal shooting of teen. *Baltimore Sun* June 13, A1, A7.

(120) Shatzkin, K. (1995) Mass drug sweeps causing a backlog. *Baltimore Sun* June 22, A1, A10.

(121) Shaw, C. R., and McKay, H. D. (1969 [1942]) *Juvenile delinquency and urban areas*, 2nd ed., University of Chicago Press, Chicago.

(122) Siegel, E. (1995) Baltimore to buy Fishmarket. *Baltimore Sun* February 9, B1, B2.

(123) Siegel, E. (1995) Citizens willing to pay for a say in services. *Baltimore Sun* March 29, A1, A16.

(124) Siegel, E. (1995) "Complete cleanup" of Baltimore will follow 20-section battle plan. *Baltimore Sun* January 19, B1, B12.

(125) Siegel, E. (1995) Empowerment zone planning begins. *Baltimore Sun* February 6, B1, B3.

(126) Siegel, E. (1995) "Grime and crime" district is proposed for midtown. *Baltimore Sun* March 25, B1, B2.

(127) Siegel, E. (1995) Mayor says his parents robbed, he sees merit in canning proposal. *Baltimore Sun* February 17, B2.

(128) Siegel, E. (1995) Mayor touts plan to cleanup city. *Baltimore Sun* March 24, B2.

(129) Siegel, E., and Daemmrich, J. (1995) Deal helps Schmoke quiet critics. *Baltimore Sun* June 1, B1, B2.

(130) Simon, D. (1991) *Homicide: A year on the killing streets,* Ballantine, New York.

(131) Simon, D. (1994) Hot trend in Baltimore cools elsewhere. *Baltimore Sun* February 9, A12.

(132) Simon, D. (1994) In police front lines, sense of duty falters. *Baltimore Sun* February 8, A1, A10.

(133) Simon, D. (1994) Lackluster policing starts at the top. *Baltimore Sun* February 9, A1, A12.

(134) Simon, D. (1994) A police department in decline. *Baltimore Sun* February 6, A1, A20, A21.

(135) Simon, D. (1994) Police policy of street arrests proves ineffective. *Baltimore Sun* February 7, A1, A6.

(136) Smith, C. (1995) Schmoke declares victory, but image is bruised. *Baltimore Sun* February 26, F1, F6.

(137) Snyder, B. (1995) Crime and grime patrols may not start until March. *Baltimore Sun* January 6, B2.

(138) Somerville, F. (1995) Black churches may join exodus from Baltimore. *Baltimore Sun* January 29, A1, A23.

(139) Stiehm, J. (1997) Charles Village celebrates 100th. *Baltimore Sun* February 24, 3B.

(140) Taylor, R. B. (1988) *Human territorial functioning,* Cambridge University Press, Cambridge, UK.

(141) Taylor, R. B. (1995) Community crime prevention, Podolefsky's model, and responses to drugs. Paper presented at the annual meetings of the American Society of Criminology, Chicago, November.

(142) Taylor, R. B. (1995) Impact of crime on communities. *Annals of the American Academy of Political and Social Science* 539, 28–45.

(143) Taylor, R. B. (1997) Social order and disorder of streetblocks and neighborhoods: Ecology, microecology and the systemic model of social disorganization. *Journal of Research in Crime and Delinquency* 33, 113–155.

(144) Taylor, R. B., and Brower, S. (1985) Home and near-home territories. In *Human behavior and environment: Current theory and research,* Vol. 8: *Home environments* (Altman, I., and Werner, C., eds). New York: Plenum.

(145) Taylor, R. B., Gottfredson, S. D., and Brower, S. (1984) Neighborhood naming as an index of attachment to place. *Population and Environment* 7,
101–111.

(146) Taylor, R. B., Koons, B., Kurtz, E., Greene, J., and Perkins, D. (1995) Street-
blocks with more nonresidential landuse have more physical deterioration:
Evidence from Baltimore and Philadelphia. *Urban Affairs Review* (formerly
Urban Affairs Quarterly) 30, 120–136.

(147) Taylor, R. B., and Shumaker, S. A. (1990) Local crime as a natural hazard:
Implications for understanding the relationship between disorder and fear
of crime. *American Journal of Community Psychology* 18, 619–642.

(148) Taylor, R. B., and Webb, T. (1982) *Changes in owner occupancy and vacancy levels in Baltimore census tracts*. Census Note 4, Center for Metropolitan Planning and Research, Johns Hopkins University, Baltimore.

(149) Twigg, R. (1983) City's "not a graffiti town," and aides like it that way. *Baltimore Sun* July 31, B8.

(150) Valentine, P. W. (1994) New curfew in Baltimore: Parents of violators face
tougher penalties. *Washington Post* July 29, A1.

(151) Warr, M. (1984) Fear of victimization: Why are women and the elderly more
afraid? *Social Science Quarterly* 65, 681–702.

(152) West, N. (1994) After school, the wary walk home. *Baltimore Sun* October
14, B1, B4.

(153) West, N. (1994) Apartment complex for elderly welcomed in Park Heights.
Baltimore Sun October 31, B3.

(154) West, N. (1994) Man charged in shooting of boy, 13, has no regrets. *Baltimore
Sun* October 10, B1, B2.

(155) West, N. (1995) NOI firm is hit by tax lien. *Baltimore Sun* March 18, B1.

(156) Wilson, W. J. (1987) *The truly disadvantaged*, University of Chicago Press,
Chicago.

3

The Incivilities Thesis: Theory, Measurement, and Policy

The incivilities thesis, outlined briefly in the first chapter, deserves close reexamination. It has received a lot of attention from policymakers and the press. Coverage in the popular media has included such outlets as the *New York Times*, the *Christian Science Monitor*, and *U.S. News and World Report* (37: 292), to name just a few. If we look just at the first two months of 1997, for example, Jerry Skolnick was arguing in *Newsday* that policing strategies based on the incivilities thesis helped bring crime down (88); and in the *Washington Post*, George Kelling, one of the "founding fathers" of the incivilities thesis, squared off against Richard Moran, a frequent contributor to National Public Radio on social science topics. Kelling said the new policing strategies deserved credit for the crime drop, whereas Moran said we just could not be sure (45, 62). At about the same time, just up the road from Washington, D.C., in Baltimore, city council leaders harshly criticized Police Commissioner Frazier and Mayor Schmoke for *failing* to mount policies similar to New York's "zero tolerance" for disorder (57, 58). Zero tolerance policies include aggressive police arrest policies targeted at those committing misdemeanor crimes on the street such as public urination, public drinking, disturbing the peace, vagrancy, and so on. New York Police Commissioner William Bratton, who had been inspired by the incivilities thesis to mount disorder-reduction initiatives in the subways, was applying it to the streets of the city (7: 152) amid a rising volume of complaints about police brutality (37: 299). Policing strategies grounded in the incivilities thesis received credit for much of the crime decline witnessed in large cities beginning in the early 1990s (37: fn7, fn11).

The incivilities thesis has drawn so much controversy because it forms part of the conceptual core of several new policing approaches, including problem-oriented policing (28), where officers work with other agencies and local citizen leaders to identify community problems and bring the needed resources to bear on those; community policing, involving, among other elements, "a re-orientation of patrol in order to facilitate two-way communication between police and the public" while assuming "a commitment to broadly-focused, problem oriented policing" (86: 5); third-party policing (9), where police work alongside other regulatory agencies; and zero tolerance policies or order maintenance policing for low-level misdemeanor crimes (7, 46, 106).

Of course, community policing, third-party policing, and problem-oriented policing are strategies and orientations to policing in which concern goes far beyond issues of social and physical incivilities (15). These initiatives address police-community interaction and consultation (2, 3, 8, 10, 34), together with departmental attitudinal and organizational shifts (32, 33, 48a, 56, 63), and raise new questions of process and outcome evaluation (19, 85, 86, 104). The range of available strategies in the realm of community or problem-oriented policing go far beyond reducing social and physical incivilities. The purpose here is not to evaluate all aspects of community or problem-oriented policing, even though the present discussion has implications for that broader policy context; nor is it to examine the meta-philosophical underpinnings of these strategies, as Harcourt (37) has done.

Rather, the current chapter pursues two more modest goals. First, it examines the evolution of the incivilities thesis over the past twenty-five years. The thesis has emerged in five relatively distinct versions over that period. In addition, in the course of that evolution, focus has shifted in three important ways: from differences at one point in time to differences over time, from differences between neighbors to differences between neighborhoods, and from a focus on fear of crime to a focus on increasing crime and neighborhood decline. In short, due to conceptual drift there are several different versions of the incivilities thesis currently being floated; we want to be clear how each may be relevant, in different ways, to policy proposals and evidence reviewed.

The second goal pursued is the clarification of two distinct but related measurement questions raised by the incivilities thesis and its evolution. As mentioned in Chapter 1, some presume that incivilities result from broader neighborhood conditions of disorder or social disorganization; if this is so, different indicators of incivilities should tie strongly together. The close connection should show at one point in time and in shifts over time. It also should appear even if different data sources are used for the indicators. A high degree of interrelatedness among the indicators would reflect their convergent validity, a desirable quality from a measurement perspective (91: 133). Also of interest, theoretically and for measurement purposes, is whether the incivilities indicators demonstrate discriminant validity (12). Again, this is a desirable property, one we hope the indicators share. If the incivilities indicators have it, they will link more strongly to one another than to indicators for different but related constructs.

Data from several Baltimore studies are used, as well as information from several other cities around the United States, to address these measurement questions. The evidence reviewed, I suggest, fails to adequately and consistently demonstrate the desired properties of convergent and discriminant validity across different approaches to data collection and different levels of aggregation.

Organization

Five distinct variants of the incivilities thesis have been proposed by Wilson-Garofalo-Laub, Hunter, Wilson and Kelling, Lewis and Salem, and Skogan. I describe the central processes highlighted by each theory. Placing these versions of the incivilities thesis in a temporal ordering reveals several clear shifts in emphasis and scope over the period, which are described. The following section briefly summarizes empirical support to date for some of the key hypotheses in each version of the theory. Following that, the measurement questions raised above receive detailed consideration, using data from five different cities. The chapter closes with a discussion of the policy, practice, and theory implications of these measurement results.

Variations on a Theme

This section summarizes five different versions of the incivilities thesis. After reviewing the processes of central interest to each, shifts in thinking on this topic are described.

Wilson 1975/Garofalo and Laub 1978

In *Thinking about Crime*, Wilson asks why are urban residents so fearful for their safety when personal victimization is still a relatively rare event? He suggests it is not just crimes that they find troubling. The daily hassles they are confronted with on the street—street crazies, panhandlers, rowdy youth, and "hey honey" hassles—and the deteriorated conditions that surround them—trash-strewn alleys and vacant lots, graffiti, deteriorated and abandoned housing—inspire concern (105).

In a closely related vein, Garofalo and Laub suggest that fear of crime reflects a more general "urban unease" rather than a specific concern just

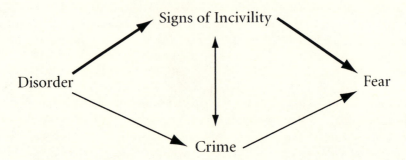

FIGURE 3.1   Hunter's Incivilities Thesis (From 43; reprinted by
permission)

about crimes that have occurred or may occur (25). This led to their dic-
tum that "fear of crime" was more than "fear" of "crime." Again, the key
idea is that urban conditions, not just crime, are troublesome, inspiring
residents' concern for safety.

These theories emerged in the wake of the first analyses of the National
Crime Survey showing residents' fear was far more widespread than
their victimization (14, 20). They attempted to explain this slippage. For
all three theorists, the outcome of interest was fear of crime, an affective
state reflecting safety-related concerns about possible street victimization
(23). Fear is distinct from perceptions of risk, a more cognitive assessment of the likelihood of victimization (51). It is also separate from worry
about property crimes while away or worry about the potential victimization of family members (20, 100).

In both theories, the authors provide no explicit specification of the relationship between these concern-inspiring conditions and actual crime
or victimization, except to note that the conditions are far more prevalent
than crime or victimization. In short, they do not try to either connect the
causes of incivilities to or disconnect them from the causes of crime.

One further similarity: Both statements focus on *individuals,* on psychological rather than community dynamics. Although community differences are implicitly acknowledged, the key focus is why are so many
more *people* afraid than would be expected given the prevalence of victimization.[1] High fear levels and neighbor-to-neighbor fear differences
are of central interest.

Hunter 1978

Hunter presented a paper titled "Symbols of Incivility" at the 1978 meetings of the American Society of Criminology (43).[2] As in the Wilson-
Garofalo-Laub version of the incivilities thesis, the outcome in question

was still fear of crime, and it was assumed that incivilities were far more prevalent than crime or victimization.[3] Figure 3.1 depicts Hunter's causal model.

Hunter's framework elaborates on the earlier statements of the thesis in four major ways. Perhaps most important, he describes in some detail how residents may interpret signs of incivility; he considers what residents "read into" these conditions. He proposes that local residents attribute disorderly actions and deteriorating physical conditions to two sets of factors. On the one hand, residents may think local deterioration and problems indicate neighbors and local, citizen-based organizations are unable to manage or preserve the neighborhood. On the other hand, observers also may conclude that public agencies outside the neighborhood, such as various city services, are either incapable of preserving order as they are chartered to do or unwilling to do so. Seeing that matters are out of hand in the neighborhood and that local actors or external agencies, or both, cannot or will not intercede, residents feel vulnerable and at risk of victimization.

Hunter's description of these processes is important because it suggests how the causal attributions residents make—their conclusions as to why incivilities occur and persist—shape their fear. It is not just the presence of the signs of incivilities that is threatening, it is the meaning attached to them. Ferraro has continued this symbolic interactionist interpretation of incivilities and fear (23). Hunter suspects residents blame actors both within and outside the community for these conditions.

Hunter's second contribution is to nonrecursively link crime with incivilities. Each causes the other; one does not precede the other. This view suggests that extensive incivilities will be found in high-crime neighborhoods, and high crime will be found in neighborhoods with extensive deterioration and disorderly street behavior.

Third, Hunter's model connects incivilities and crime in a second way, through a common underlying exogenous cause: neighborhood disorder. It is not clear, however, if by disorder he means specifically social disorganization, the inability of a community to regulate itself and work toward common goals (11, 49), or the community characteristics more generally associated with high offense or high offender rates (1, 39).

Finally, Hunter's model moves us from the individual-level processes described by Wilson and Garofalo and Laub to a contextual model (6). The focus earlier was on psychological processes. Here these processes are elaborated, but within the context of neighborhood crime rates and mutual impacts of crime and incivilities. In short, these psychological processes are linked to varying community contexts.

Hunter's elaboration of the thesis leads to specific empirical predictions. (1) Communities with higher crime rates should have more exten-

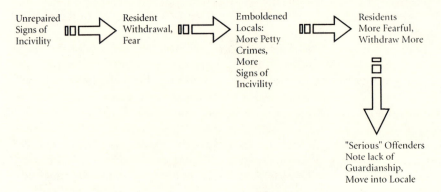

FIGURE 3.2   Wilson and Kelling's Incivilities Thesis

sive incivilities. (2) High community crime rates and extensive incivilities should share common structural origins, such as instability, low status, and more extensive minority populations. But even after putting these common origins aside, (3) crime and incivilities should still "feed" one another. Controlling for the structural origins, crime should have an independent impact on incivilities and vice versa.

Wilson and Kelling 1982

In their first of two *Atlantic Monthly* pieces on the topic, Wilson and Kelling elaborate the thesis in three important ways (106). This article has proved enormously influential on researchers examining fear of crime (23) and on policy analysts in community policing (35).

First, Wilson and Kelling inject a temporal perspective, describing a specific, multistep process whereby persistent physical or social incivilities lead to higher neighborhood crime rates; see Figure 3.2. The proposed sequence is as follows. A sign of incivility such as a broken window is not important per se. Some windows are always getting broken, some homes are always deteriorating, and some homes are always being abandoned. More important is how long the broken window remains unrepaired, the house remains dilapidated, or the building stays abandoned. If the condition is not repaired in a relatively short time, *then* residents will infer that resident-based informal control on the streetblock is weak and that residents do not care about what is happening in the neighborhood. They will infer the neighborhood is socially disorganized.[4]

Making such a judgment, residents become increasingly reluctant to use public spaces or to intervene in disorderly situations. As the withdrawal becomes more general and residents' informal control weakens, their concerns about safety rise. In the language of routine activity theory, natural guardians and place managers grow more reluctant to act (21). In Jane Jacobs's terms, there are fewer eyes on the street (44).

At the same time, local "lightweight" offenders—spray-painting teens or heckling corner groups—become emboldened, causing further resident apprehension and withdrawal. For local delinquents and predelinquents, the persistent physical incivilities symbolize opportunities for delinquency (13, 99).

After the above conditions have been in place for a time and local, resident-based control has weakened markedly, motivated, "heavy duty" potential offenders from outside the neighborhood become aware of altered conditions, and the lower risks of detection or apprehension associated with offending in that locale. If offender motivation is high enough and if enough targets are available, such persons move into the locale to commit street crimes.

In short, the authors temporally sequence the connections between physical deterioration, increasing local delinquency, decreasing resident-based control, and increasing serious street crime.[5] Time not only shapes the sequence, it also influences the interpretation attached to incivilities by residents and other users of the local spaces.

Kelling and Coles recently updated the thesis and placed it in a broader legal context (46). They further developed the rationale for order maintenance policing around social incivilities, but also pointed up the challenges in police and community working closely on reducing disorder (46: 168). In addition, they clarified why disorderly conduct and physical deterioration have increased so dramatically in cities. They argue police have retreated—unwisely—from order maintenance, instead concentrating on serious crime. This shift has been partially encouraged by modifications in civil law, placing overly stringent limits on police and other agents of public control. These shifts have facilitated increasing incivilities, especially social ones.

As is apparent from the above-suggested dynamics, a second major difference in Wilson and Kelling's thesis, compared to prior incarnations, is the expanded range of outcomes. Individual and group behaviors as well as physical neighborhood quality are added outcomes of interest. The authors move beyond fear per se to encompass resident-based informal social controls over street life; the vitality of street life itself; and, perhaps most important, increasing neighborhood crime rates. Their inclusion of neighborhood crime rates as the ultimate outcome of interest justifies policing initiatives to reduce social incivilities or to mobilize other public agencies and work with them, reducing physical incivilities.

Given their concern for community policing, Wilson and Kelling also address the geography of deployment, a third difference from prior treatments.[6] They roughly separate communities into three groups: those with assured stability, those deteriorated beyond hope, and those previously stable but currently threatened with an uncertain future, not unlike the "teetering" neighborhoods that were the focus of one of Housing Commissioner Henson's initiatives described in the previous chapter. They suggest that incivilities and reduction of incivilities will have the strongest impacts on behavioral, crime, and emotional outcomes for this last set of neighborhoods. Therefore these places merit remediation efforts, including community policing.

The above focus brings us to the final contribution of the model. Wilson and Kelling state specific roles police officers can play in helping communities fight incivilities. In essence, the job of community or problem-oriented police is to learn what conditions are troubling residents and merchants in these teetering neighborhoods and help them address these concerns.[7] The officers might move rowdy groups out of an area, notify agencies so that landlords are cited for needed repairs, or arrange to get junked cars towed or trash-filled lots cleaned. These problem-solving roles for community police officers have received some attention in different demonstrations and evaluations (36, 89).

Lewis and Salem 1986

Returning to a sole focus on fear of crime, and a cross-sectional as opposed to longitudinal perspective, in their 1986 volume Dan Lewis and Greta Salem argue that both the extent of signs of incivility and crime levels contribute synergistically to fear (53a). They suggest that if crime and signs of incivility are *both* at high levels, residents will exhibit the highest fear levels. If crime is high but signs of incivility are not, or vice versa, residents will be less fearful. In analysis of variance terminology, it is the two-way interaction effect that most strongly influences fear, not the main effects of each. Lewis and Salem support their argument using data from a three-city, multineighborhood survey conducted as part of the 1975–1980 Northwestern "Reactions to Crime" project.

Lewis and Salem's model continues the trend of separating the causes of crime and incivility. By implication, if one can be high and the other low, each has some unique causes. If the origins of each are distinct, we have a stronger rationale for addressing each with separate initiatives.

Skogan 1990

The last version considered here extends the theoretical and empirical investigation to the neighborhood level (83, 84). Skogan's variant of the incivilities thesis focuses on neighborhood change as the ultimate outcome of interest. Labeling signs of incivility as disorder (84: 2), he "argues that disorder plays an important role in sparking urban decline." His definition of disorder is "[it] reflects the inability of communities to mobilize resources to deal with urban woes. The distribution of disorder thus mirrors the larger pattern of structured inequality that makes inner city neighborhoods vulnerable to all manner of threats to the health and safety of their residents" (84: 173). In short, as with Hunter's model, there are two causes of disorder: social disorganization within the community itself and inequality resulting from broader urban dynamics operating outside the neighborhood. This interpretation of incivilities ties us again to the social disorganization literature and, simultaneously, to the work on urban inequality (107).

Incivilities lead to a range of psychological, social-psychological, behavioral, and ultimately ecological outcomes, such as neighborhood decline. First, echoing Wilson and Kelling, Skogan suggests incivilities undermine informal social control (84: 65). Second, as did prior theorists, he proposes disorder "sparks concern about neighborhood safety, and perhaps even causes crime itself. This further undermines community morale" (84: 65). Third, incivilities "undermine the stability of the housing market" (84: 65). Impacts of neighborhood crime on house values have been well established in the literature (54, 92); separate impacts of incivilities, net of other factors, have not.

In short, Skogan argues, "Disorder can play an important, *independent* role in stimulating this kind of urban decline" (84: 12, emphasis added). Current theorists, given Skogan's arguments and evidence, accept as proven that "disorder, both directly and as a precursor to crime, played an important role in neighborhood crime" (46: 25). Skogan's work has proved enormously influential. Harcourt, however, after reanalyzing Skogan's data, has questioned the conclusions drawn (37).

Skogan's version takes us beyond Wilson and Kelling's model in three ways. He focuses explicitly on neighborhood change, in the form of decline, as the ultimate outcome of interest. It was included but not emphasized in Wilson and Kelling's treatment. Skogan promotes it as the outcome of most interest to residents and policymakers alike. High fear and weak informal local social control may be important in their own right, but gain added significance because they contribute to later decline. The evolution in this series of models—from a focus solely on psychological outcomes in Garofalo and Laub's version to one solely on ecological outcomes—is now complete.

Second, Skogan expands the scope of mediating dynamics given his interest in neighborhood change. The first versions of the thesis focused on fear; subsequent versions expanded to include weak informal social control and withdrawal from street life. Skogan augments the relevant proces-

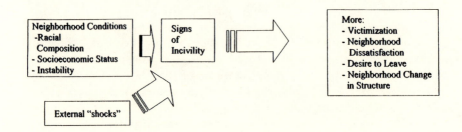

FIGURE 3.3   Skogan's Longitudinal Ecological Incivilities Thesis

sual dynamics further, drawing in intent to move, neighborhood satisfaction (84: 88 ff.), community solidarity (84: 70 ff.), and involvement in privatistic crime prevention. Other authors before Skogan (e.g., 47) argued that perceptions of neighborhood deterioration act "as a major catalyst in provoking a move" (47: 183), or contribute independently to neighborhood decline (24). The literature, however, has failed to consistently link crime or crime-related neighborhood conditions with actual mobility (92).

Third, in several analyses Skogan explicitly acknowledges that structural conditions give rise to signs of incivility. He reports that poverty, instability, and racial composition all contributed equally to signs of incivility and crime in the form of robbery victimization rates (84: 75). In his analyses, signs of incivility almost totally mediate the impacts of neighborhood structure on victimization. Furthermore, in an earlier statement of the thesis, he suggests "random shocks" arising from developments outside the neighborhood itself also can influence the expansion of incivilities (83). In short, his is the first model to start systematically examining links between incivilities and community structure (see Figure 3.3). Nonetheless, his modeling of incivilities as mediating variables seems counter to his statement (84: 12) that incivilities make independent contributions to outcomes such as neighborhood decline (37). Further, it leaves open the question of the appropriate policy focus. The question of the causal position of incivilities—vis-à-vis fundamental neighborhood features such as status, stability, and racial composition—is important practically as well as theoretically. Skogan concludes that since disorder mediates impacts of structure on robbery victimization, "direct action against disorder could have substantial payoffs" (84: 75). But at the same time, his data show that structural factors explain 65% of disorder itself (84: 75, Figure 4-3). If disorder is so heavily determined by basic neighborhood fabric, does it make sense to try and take direct action against disorder, or instead to focus on neighborhood fundamentals?

Evolution of the Perspective.

The main variants of the incivilities thesis reveal numerous differences. In four areas, these differences reflect a clear evolution in the perspective applied.

Expansion of Outcomes. The models progress from concerns about fear of crime (Wilson-Garofalo-Laub, Hunter, Lewis and Salem) to neighborhood street life and crime (Wilson and Kelling) to neighborhood structural decline (Skogan). The enlargement of outcomes increases the importance of the thesis; it becomes relevant not only to reactions to crime but also to the stability and viability of the larger urban community fabric. The broadening scope also provides additional rationales for neighborhood stability or order maintenance policing initiatives.

Shifting Levels of Analysis. As the theorists have augmented outcomes, they also have shifted levels of analysis upward. Garofalo and Laub adopted a psychological perspective. Hunter and Lewis and Salem provided contextual models, pointing up impacts of community as well as psychological factors. Wilson and Kelling's discussion includes both streetblock and neighborhood outcomes, but the most central dynamics appear to be at the streetblock level (97). Skogan moves us explicitly to the neighborhood level, using both neighborhood predictors and neighborhood outcomes. Reactions to crime, such as fear, and other person-environment transactions, such as neighborhood satisfaction or intention to move, are modeled at the neighborhood level because they may link to long-term neighborhood stability. Ecological dynamics occupy center stage.

   In an examination of measurement issues, two concerns surface related to this shift in interest. The migration of interest across levels of analysis presumes that the reactions to crime and person-environment transactions seen as part of the neighborhood-level dynamics have substantial ecological components, that is, that sizable between-neighborhood variance exists in these variables, relative to the pooled within-neighborhood variance. In addition, the migration suggests researchers might want to use ecologically based rather than psychologically based incivilities indicators. These measurement issues receive consideration below.

Shifting Temporal Perspective. The models evolve in their temporal perspective. The theorists start out discussing why some people are more afraid than others at one point in time (Wilson-Garofalo-Laub, Hunter) and end up focusing on changes over time in fear, informal social control, street life, neighborhood crime rates, and neighborhood structure (Wilson and Kelling, Skogan). Wilson and Kelling provide the most detailed

temporal sequencing. Despite their sequencing, however, they do not describe how long it will take for the entire process to complete a cycle.

Again, as with the change in levels of concern, there are measurement
implications. One would expect, given the shift from cross-sectional to
longitudinal processes, that indicators would change correspondingly,
and researchers would start to look at changes in fear, neighborhood
structure, and incivilities, for example.

Progressive Unlinking of Crime and Incivilities.   The early models (Wilson-Garofalo-Laub, Hunter) suggested a common origin for both crime
and incivilities. Incivilities were presumed to vary from neighborhood
to neighborhood, roughly paralleling crime differences from neighborhood to neighborhood, but appearing at higher rates and thus influencing more residents. Hunter's model provides incivilities and crime with
a common cause. Skogan, by contrast, explicitly anticipates that incivilities will make independent contributions to neighborhood change, net
of neighborhood structure and, presumably, neighborhood crime, although indicators for the latter were not available in his data set.[8] And
Lewis and Salem anticipate that crime and incivilities can vary independently, leading to situations where one is high and the other not.
The modeling implication is that neighborhood crime rates and neighborhood incivilities can be separated from one another in a cross-sectional model and that changes in each can be separated in a longitudinal model.

Empirical Support for Hypotheses

Before turning to a detailed discussion of measurement issues, I provide
a brief summary of what we know about some of the key hypotheses
generated by each version of the incivilities thesis. I organize the evidence by theory version. I do not consider the extensive evaluation research on community policing programs based on some version of this
thesis; for recent reviews of this work see 22: 8–27; 46; 81: 3–7. That evaluation work often fails to provide sufficient detail about timing of measurement and scope of indicators, making it difficult to address specific
hypotheses mounted in these models.

Wilson-Garofalo-Laub

Multiple studies support the key idea that those perceiving more neighborhood problems are more concerned for their safety. Initial analyses of
individual-level outcomes confounding differences between neighbors
and neighborhoods (e.g., 53) have been confirmed by later studies parti-

tioning predictor variance (16), correctly modeling within-neighborhood correlated errors, and controlling for direct and indirect victimization experiences (96). In short, we have strong evidence that those who are more afraid than their neighbors see more local problems than do their neighbors. It is not clear at this time, however, whether social or physical disorders are more troubling to residents. Nor is it certain whether the perceived problems cause the fear, or vice versa, or both, or if some as-yet-unspecified psychological factor, such as anxiety, causes both fear and the perception of problems.

Hunter

Hunter's key idea is that both incivilities and local crime rates may contribute independently to outcomes such as fear. One study using assessed incivility indicators could not test this thesis because incivilities and crime were so closely linked (95). It is the case that, controlling for neighborhood crime rates, individuals who perceive more local problems than their neighbors are more fearful than their neighbors (96). Data from Seattle neighborhoods suggest that average perceived incivilities in a neighborhood and the neighborhood burglary rate both contributed independently to burglary-specific fear of crime (74) and to perceived crime risk (73).[9]

The work so far suggests that, net of local crime rates, both individual and community differences in perceived incivilities contribute cross-sectionally to reactions to crime such as fear and perceived risk. We do not yet have studies *simultaneously* examining impacts of individual and community perceived incivilities while controlling for local crime or victimization rates.

Wilson and Kelling

Numerous studies claim to find support for portions of the Wilson and Kelling thesis. These studies vary in the degree to which they apply needed statistical controls. The suggestion that streetblocks with more incivilities have more crime problems gains support from a Baltimore study using perceived indicators of each incivility, after controlling for streetblock composition and layout (65).[10] This streetblock analysis, however, does not confirm that tenet in the longitudinal manner in which it was framed. A further limitation of the study is that land use mix on the block, which may be more important than incivilities as an influence on block crime (50), was not taken into account.

Another analysis attempting to link incivilities and drug crime problems at different times fails to focus clearly on changes. Returning to neighborhood leaders in the 1990s—neighborhoods where residents had been interviewed in the late 1970s and early 1980s—Chicago researchers (87) find that perceived social and physical disorder reported seven to twelve years previously strongly predicted severity of current drug problems in the neighborhood. The authors concluded these results "point strongly in the direction of the 'broken windows' hypothesis: that levels of noncriminal decay and social disruption can spawn more serious problems in the future by undermining the capacity of communities to respond to crime" (87: 525).

The conclusion, however, may be premature. The authors did not control for the earlier level of perceived drug problems in the communities, thus their outcome did not reflect community change. In addition, their data source, with just a small number of communities, did not easily permit removing the influence of community structure from the relationship. So the researchers could not gauge the independent impact of incivilities.

Another longitudinal hypothesis receiving some cross-sectional support is Wilson and Kelling's suggestion that incivilities have the strongest impacts in teetering neighborhoods. In sixty-six Baltimore neighborhoods in the early 1980s, the impacts of assessed social and physical incivilities on fear of crime were most evident in neighborhoods of moderate stability (103). Separate analyses on the same data showed extremely weak impacts of incivilities on fear in the most deteriorated neighborhoods (102). Both analyses, however, failed to simultaneously control for all relevant features of community fabric.

Empirical research on interactions between incivilities and other predictors as they influence reactions to crime appears to have moved beyond the theoretical groundwork already laid out. For example, how incivilities-infested residents see their locale may alter the connections between race and risk perception (73). The relevant conceptual underpinnings for such a moderating effect are not clear.[11]

Far better developed is the theoretical basis for interactions between perceived disorder, at the individual level, and social support on fear of crime. Weaker impacts of perceived disorder on fear appear among those with more local ties (72). This represents an example of the buffering hypothesis developed in the social support literature (41). According to the buffering hypothesis, the deleterious effects associated with confronting significant stressors are weaker among those with more available coping resources. Social support represents one such resource. In this study mentioned, however, the moderating effect was extremely small in size compared to the main effect. In short, at least for outcomes such as reactions to crime, it appears that individual-level impacts of incivilities are conditioned by other factors or that incivilities themselves alter the connections between personal characteristics and these outcomes. So far, the size of both these types of moderating effects is modest.

A third feature receiving empirical support is Wilson and Kelling's suggestion that increasing incivilities may signal delinquent opportunities to local teens and other "lightweight" offenders. Replicated contextual models in one Baltimore study linked neighborhood assessed deterioration with residents' agreeing that unsupervised teen groups are a problem in their neighborhoods (99). Again, regrettably, this confirmation was cross-sectional rather than longitudinal, as the hypothesis has been stated. Nonetheless, this finding begins to document links between incivilities and social disorganization processes. (Such connections have been anticipated by social disorganization theorists (11a). Reports of unsupervised peer teen groups have been used as a key indicator of weak local informal social control (77).

Skogan

Skogan joined data from forty neighborhoods in six cities, originally collected in different studies completed between 1977 and 1983. Eighteen of the neighborhoods were natural areas of Chicago, some of which were surveyed three times (84: 188). The studies operationalized incivilities using subjective, survey-based responses where respondents indicated how serious they perceived different incivilities to be in their own neighborhoods. He analyzed neighborhood-level outcomes using simple and multiple regressions and path analyses. Treating the time of the surveys as roughly comparable, he analyzed all the data in a cross-sectional design.

Skogan examined the causes of incivilities (84: 60, his Fig. 3-3). He found that nonwhite neighborhood racial composition, poverty, and instability were all linked to higher incivility levels. He also examined a range of consequences of incivilities. He found that in neighborhoods where incivilities were perceived to be more intense, neighbors were less willing to help one another (84: 71), robbery victimization was more extensive (84: 75), residential satisfaction was lower, and more people intended to move (84: 82). He also found some extremely strong correlations (> .80) between signs of incivility and indicators of neighborhood structure, such as unemployment (84: 173).

Harcourt's recent, detailed critique points to several shortcomings of Skogan's analyses and data treatment, including the treatment of missing data in the incivilities indices, inattention to a small number of neighborhoods with undue influence on the outcomes for some analyses, and the choice of robbery victimization as an outcome (37). One conclusion Harcourt reaches after this careful reexamination is the same point being raised here: The independent contribution of incivilities is still an open question.

Using census and crime data for Cleveland and Washington, D.C., Harrell and Gouvis proposed to test Skogan's thesis using census tracts as the unit of analysis (38). They wanted to learn if leading indicators of decay helped predict later crime changes. Unfortunately, questions arise about the decay indicators. The ones they chose did not focus on incivilities per se, but instead were rates for crimes such as arson (see also 71). Their study showed that some crime rates helped predict later shifts in other crime rates.

Summing Up on Empirical Support

To date, we have the strongest confirmation for the Wilson-Garofalo-Laub psychological model. Studies routinely find extremely strong connections between individual differences in perceived incivilities and individual differences in fear of crime; these remain after controlling for neighborhood crime rates and neighborhood structure. Studies also find contextual impacts of neighborhood-level perceived or assessed incivilities on individual-level outcomes such as fear, suggesting multilevel impacts may be operating. We do not yet have studies using the same indicator and comparing individual and contextual incivility impacts.

The effects of incivilities observed at the individual level and at the community level sometimes appear contingent on other factors. At the community level, Wilson and Kelling's thesis predicts disorder impacts contingent on community stability; Lewis and Salem's model predicts impacts contingent on local crime rates. Some empirical support has been obtained for the first, although further testing is needed with more adequate statistical controls. Testing of Lewis and Salem's hypothesized interaction effect—incivilities prove especially problematic in high-crime locales—has not yet been carried out. Part of the problem with doing so is that, especially with assessed indicators, disorder usually correlates very strongly with local crime rates. Researchers have begun suggesting that individual-level impacts of perceived incivility may be conditioned by other personal attributes, and work looking at these contingent impacts is beginning.

Also receiving substantial support is Hunter's version of the thesis. It suggests *both* crime and incivilities contribute to fear. This idea receives support using perceived disorder indicators at the individual level controlling for other personal or neighborhood features. Assessed disorder at the community level correlates too strongly with crime to test for independent contributions without committing the partialling fallacy (26, 95).[12]

But in contrast, support is essentially nonexistent when we turn to explicitly longitudinal versions of the incivilities thesis. Even though researchers interpret results from several cross-sectional studies as lending support to the thesis, these are still just cross-sectional data. To test Wilson and Kelling's version of the thesis, we need longitudinal studies of streetblocks—in communities, using a large number of communities and the ability to partial out the independent contributions of incivilities to *changes*, over time, in fear of crime, resident-based informal controls, perception of risk, and offender movement patterns. To test Skogan's version of the thesis, we need comparable community-level data sources so we can gauge impacts of incivilities, net of community structure and crime rates, on neighborhood structural changes and changes in crime. These studies have not yet been completed.

A Theoretical Aside on Demographic and Structural Issues

The incivilities thesis and its variations, despite a widening scope of outcomes over time, has maintained a narrow focus on the input side. Versions of the theory have largely failed to incorporate other community and individual factors linked to outcomes such as fear, changes in neighborhood crime, and neighborhood decline. We know a fair amount about the latter connections (e.g., 60, 78, 80; more generally, see 30, 55). To prove practically and theoretically useful, work on the longitudinal, ecological version of the incivilities thesis will need to be integrated with this established body of work. This integration is beginning to occur (79).

The only pattern of findings that would justify continued separate development of this version of the thesis would be one showing independent impacts of incivilities regardless of community composition. Cross-sectional results so far already point away from such a picture of only free-standing impacts, suggesting instead some contingent impacts. Those contingent impacts depend on features of community, such as stability, that also influence the outcomes of interest here (103). Some work, such as Skogan's neighborhood-level analyses, suggests a different type of connection, whereby neighborhood features that we know influence crime also shape incivilities, and the latter affect the outcomes of interest. So here the connection between structure and incivilities is not contingent, but rather a mediating one; incivilities "carry" the impact of prior structure. In short, the work to date already points toward the need for a fuller integration between current understandings of communities and crime with longitudinal, ecological impacts of incivilities. Similarly, along the lines of Garofalo and Laub's version, we have begun to see impacts on outcomes such as fear that may depend on community factors. So for this version as well, broader integration seems warranted.

The purpose of the current volume is not to complete that integration, but rather to lay the groundwork for it. That more modest purpose is accomplished by (1) clarifying the causes of incivilities, (2) examining the relationships among incivilities indicators, and (3) looking at the impacts of incivilities in that broader context. We turn now to the second of these questions.

From Theory to Research: Incivilities Indicators

Three important measurement questions arise from the incivilities thesis. First, all variants presume incivilities refer to a construct independent of related ones. At the individual level, this means incivilities indicators would be separate from indicators for perceived risk, anxiety, fear of crime, territorial cognitions, sense of community, attachment to place, or neighborhood confidence and satisfaction. At the neighborhood level, this means incivilities indicators would be separate from indicators for neighborhood structure (status, stability, racial composition, and ethnic heterogeneity) and crime. In short, discriminant validity (12) has been presumed for incivilities indicators. In this section, a small number of data sets are examined to see whether the evidence supports such a presumption.

A second important measurement question is multimethod convergent validity. As noted above, incivilities theorizing began with a focus on psychological dynamics (Wilson-Garofalo and Laub), moved to an interest in social-psychological processes (Wilson and Kelling), and evolved finally into a focus on community dynamics and outcomes (Skogan). Paralleling this drift across levels of analysis have been shifts in the incivilities indicators used. For psychological processes, researchers used survey-based perceptions of incivilities. To capture social-psychological and ecological variation in incivilities, most researchers have averaged survey-based perceptions across residents in a streetblock or in a neighborhood. A smaller number of researchers have responded to the shift toward ecological processes by gathering on-site assessment data, including site and streetblock features, and aggregating those items to the streetblock level for social-psychological investigations or to the neighborhood level for ecological investigations.[13]

Our confidence in the construct validity of incivilities will be boosted if both convergent and discriminant validity appear: incivilities indicators from different methods converging with one another and simultaneously separating from indicators of related constructs. Ideally, at each level of aggregation, different indicators of incivilities, based on different data collection procedures, would correlate closely with one another and would correlate little with related constructs (12). Researchers have not yet investigated this question.

Finally, the latest variant of the incivilities thesis focuses on changes over time. But as yet, researchers have not extensively examined the relationships among changing incivilities. When we examine changes, as required by the ecological, longitudinal version of the thesis, we will be most confident that different indicators tap into one broad incivilities construct if the various changes correlate strongly with one another and, simultaneously, prove relatively independent of other aspects of community change.

Such measurement questions go to the heart of what incivilities are. As mentioned in Chapter 1, many presume incivilities reflect a broader problem, variously called disorder, social disorganization, lack of social efficacy, or some other attribute. Although theorists may attach these meanings to the indicators, the connections they draw may presume too much. These connections need to be empirically established, not just stated. The process of verifying these connections is a process of establishing construct validity and deciding what meaning to attach to the indicators (17, 91). Such decisions about meaning depend crucially on examinations of convergent and discriminant validity.

Discriminant Validity

Does evidence suggest that incivilities indicators are distinct from other features of community, such as its structure, its crime rates, and its land use patterns?

Structural Dimensions of Community.   Researchers utilizing census data to describe community structure generally refer to three independent dimensions: socioeconomic status, stability, and racial and youth composition (4, 42, 42a, 43).[14] These dimensions appear when researchers analyze census data from U.S. and foreign cities. These three dimensions also can be used to describe the structural pathways along which neighborhoods may change over time (43, 98).

Status is captured by variables reflecting income levels, house values, occupational and educational levels, and the extent of poverty and unemployment. *Stability* is best captured by variables reflecting the extent of homeownership and the proportion of households at the same address five years prior to the census. Housing type, such as the percentage of one-unit structures, is also relevant. *Race and youth composition* is reflected in percentages Hispanic and African-American and the proportions of the population between zero and five years or between six and thirteen years of age.

Assessed incivilities indicators link strongly to neighborhood structure. Using 1981 data from on-site assessments of 800+ streetblocks in Baltimore, aggregated to the neighborhood level (n=66), Sally Shumaker, Steve Gottfredson, and I completed an exploratory principal components analysis of assessment-based incivilities and land use indicators (103). We defined a general incivilities index based primarily on physical items, such as graffiti and abandoned buildings.[15]

We found moderate-to-strong links between this index and both total reported crime and community structure. The simple correlations were crime (.64), instability (.59), income (−.53), and proportion African–American (.40). Neighborhood structure explained 63% of the variation in assessed signs of incivility and 55.8% of the variation in residents' perceived signs of incivility.

To better understand the connections among the different indicators, I carried out several exploratory principal components analyses. In such an analysis, underlying linear composites "explaining" the connections among the variables are recovered (48). (This analysis is closely related to factor analysis, a procedure that recovers underlying factors, or dimensions, from a matrix of correlations or covariances.) Each recovered component can be forced to be orthogonal to each other recovered component; thus each component can be independent. Furthermore, the analysis reports how much each observed variable "loads" on each recovered component. This is analogous to saying how much each variable correlates with each recovered component. Confirmatory factor analyses represent more advanced structural equation modeling techniques wherein the researcher specifies beforehand how many dimensions to recover and which observed variables link to which dimensions (5). In these exploratory principal components, if different incivilities indicators load on the same component, even when the indicators are based on different data collection procedures, this would suggest convergent validity; if incivilities indicators load on components that are separate from the components where indicators of different constructs load, this would suggest discriminant validity.

Exploratory principal components analyses of the 1981 incivilities data and 1980 census data from sixty-six Baltimore neighborhoods closely connect this same incivilities index with a structural component capturing poverty, low education, and neighborhood instability. Even if we rotate four components (of community structure plus incivilities), incivilities continue to load highly on a poverty component.

Minneapolis–St. Paul data for twenty-four small commercial centers and their residential surround (for information on the data, see 59) showed that neighborhood instability correlated .62 with assessed vacancies in small commercial centers, and assessed graffiti correlated .87 with percentage of the neighborhood that was African-American (93, 96). Exploratory principal components analyses of these Twin Cities data linked graffiti with the racial dimension of neighborhood structure, and vacancies with instability in the surrounding neighborhood.[16]

These two analyses using assessed disorder indicators for two study sites suggest disorder is not readily separable from neighborhood structure. What do perceived disorder indicators show?

As mentioned earlier, Skogan reported strong correlations, up to .8, between neighborhood structure and *perceived incivilities*. Comparably strong links emerge from the British Crime Survey (40).

To obtain a more detailed picture of these connections with perceived indicators, Ellen Kurtz and I completed a secondary analysis using data sets spanning 216 communities in five cities: Atlanta (6 neighborhoods) (31), Baltimore (30 neighborhoods) (94), Chicago (56 neighborhoods) (52), Minneapolis–St. Paul (24 neighborhoods) (59), and Seattle (100 neighborhoods) (61). Only the six Atlanta neighborhoods were used by Skogan in his community-level analyses, so these data sets provide us with a fresh view on these questions.

All five data sets shared three perceived incivilities—vandalism, troublesome teens, vacant buildings. Aggregating perceived incivilities to the community level, an exploratory principal components analysis included those items along with neighborhood structure and one crime indicator: neighborhood assault or robbery rates. Five components were retained and rotated: three for community structure and one each for incivilities and crime.

The three incivilities separated out from the other community features, emerging on their own component (I). Each incivilities variable had a loading above .60 on the component; this would be considered a fairly strong "correlation" between the component and each indicator. Component II captured instability with both relevant variables—proportion living there for five years and proportion homeowners—showing strong negative loadings. Component III captured crime and had only one high loading—assault rate (.94). Component IV reflected both status and racial composition, the loadings suggesting that higher-status neighborhoods were less likely to have a high proportion of African-American residents. Component V had only one high loading, the robbery rate (.79).

In short, in this set of cities, except for a moderate connection between incivilities and low status, perceived incivilities appear to be relatively independent of crime and structure at the neighborhood level. This analysis is limited, of course.[17] Reanalysis with more indicators or a confirmatory rather than exploratory approach would be desirable.

The relative independence of perceived incivilities from both neighborhood structure and crime using these five cities' data contrasts with the stronger connections seen both in Baltimore and in Minneapolis—St. Paul between assessed incivilities and neighborhood structure. How people think about the problems they see in their neighborhoods appears less closely connected to fundamental neighborhood fabric than are the conditions on which they are reporting.

What are the connections at the individual level? Using these same variables from the same five cities, less the crime rate variable, a series of exploratory *individual-level* principal components analyses, should produce four components: status, stability, race, and incivilities (n=8,195). Again, as with the ecological-level principal components analyses, the incivilities indicators formed their own separate component. No other variables loaded above .40 on the incivilities component.[18] At the individual level, perceived incivilities separate clearly from other sociodemographics. When two indicators for person-environment bonds were added (neighborhood satisfaction, attachment to place) and five components were requested, perceived incivilities and person-environment bonds each associated with different components.

Such results suggest that at the individual level, perceived incivilities are readily separable both from characteristics of the perceiver and from person-place bonds such as attachment to place (82). Although these analyses use only data from one method source—surveys—they suggest that perceived incivilities at the individual level do have discriminant validity.

Crime.   Using the same five-city data set described above, neighborhood-level connections between neighborhood perceived incivilities and neighborhood crime rates, before and after controlling for neighborhood structure, were explored. The number of neighborhoods ranges from 6 in Atlanta to over 100 in Seattle.

Hunter's model in particular suggests that crime and incivilities are linked in two ways: because of their common structural origins and because each "feeds" the other. If he is correct, we should see strong connections between crime and incivilities; we also should see connections that are noticeably weaker but still of moderate strength after removing the effects of neighborhood structure.

The results appear in Table 3.1. The first column shows the city-by-city correlations of community-level perceived problems with vandalism, teens, and abandoned buildings and the community reported robbery rate. The second column repeats these correlations after partialling for (removing the influence of) percentage African-American, percentage homeowners, and average education. The third and fourth columns repeat the same information for the reported assault rate. Correlations are averaged across the five cities at the bottom of the table. I also show the median (middlemost) correlation from each column. Given the small

TABLE 3.1   Neighborhood-Level Correlations: Crime Rates and Perceived Incivilities

		Crime			
		Robbery Rate		Assault Rate	
City	Incivility		Partialled		Partialled
Atlanta	Vandalism	.53	.69	−.13	.99
	Rowdy Teens	.32	.81	.52	.06
	Abandoned Buildings	.76	.88	.94	.92
Baltimore	Vandalism	.10	.14	.10	.03
	Rowdy Teens	.09	.18	.32	.05
	Abandoned Buildings	.34	.33	.54	.26
Chicago	Vandalism	.22	.45	.23	.38
	Rowdy Teens	.30	.25	.38	.34
	Abandoned Buildings	.56	.30	.67	.50
Minn.–St. Paul	Vandalism	.72	.40	.73	.45
	Rowdy Teens	.32	.22	.46	.46
	Abandoned Buildings	.68	.38	.73	.63
Seattle	Vandalism	.71	.49	.72	.51
	Rowdy Teens	.51	.15	.62	.15
	Abandoned Buildings	.54	.18	.65	.31
Average	Vandalism	.46	.43	.33	.47
	Rowdy Teens	.31	.32	.46	.21
	Abandoned Buildings	.58	.41	.71	.52
4-City Average	Vandalism	.44	.37	.45	.34
	Rowdy Teens	.31	.20	.45	.25
	Abandoned Buildings	.53	.30	.65	.43
	Median	0.51	0.33	0.54	0.38
	Median (4 city)	0.425	0.275	0.58	0.36

NOTE: Four-city average ignores Atlanta data, with only six neighborhoods.

number of neighborhoods (n=6) in Atlanta, the numbers are reaveraged after dropping data from that city.

The correlations in Table 3.1 suggest several points. Perceived incivilities link both to local crime rates and to community structure. Before removing the influence of community structure and after averaging across different types of perceived incivilities, community crime rates explain about one quarter of the community variation in perceived incivilities (median r = .51 and .54 for robbery and assault, respectively; .42 and .58 if we ignore Atlanta). But crime's connection to community-level perceived problems is noticeably lower after we remove the connections due to structural origins; thereafter the overlap is only about 10% to 15% (median r = .33 and .38; .28 and .36 if we ignore Atlanta).[19] See Figure 3.4.

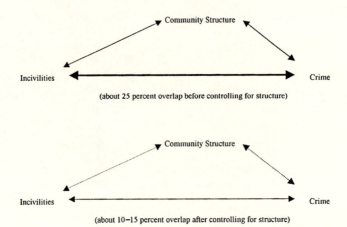

FIGURE 3.4   Community-Level Correlations Between Incivilities
and Crime Before and After Controlling for Neighborhood Structure

Land Use Features.   Using the 1981 general index of assessed incivilities
based on information from sixty-six Baltimore neighborhoods (103), we
were able to separate signs of social and physical incivility from indicators of residential versus nonresidential land use mix. The resulting component loadings appear in Note 15. In short, these results suggested signs
of incivility could be discriminated from land use and block layout patterns and that indicators of signs of incivility converged as expected.

We were similarly successful in Baltimore and in Philadelphia, using
two additional streetblock data sets, and more rigorous analytic techniques. In the early 1990s, Barb Koons, Ellen Kurtz, and Jack Greene collected on-site information from a large number of blocks in one north
Philadelphia neighborhood, Logan. Using this information, along with
the on-site assessments from fifty Baltimore blocks collected in the late
1980s, we successfully separated land use mix from signs of incivility using confirmatory factor analyses (101). I am not aware of any other available data sources available that would permit examining connections between land use and assessed incivilities.[20] The current Chicago
Neighborhoods Human Development Project is gathering and analyzing
extensive assessed and perceived incivility data, as well as land use information, but these data are not yet publicly available (79).

If we turn to other micro-level features in the urban residential environment, such as *defensible space features* and *territorial signage* (90), we do not
yet know if they can be separated from signs of incivility. Multimethod-
multitrait investigations at the block and neighborhood level are needed.
Block-level investigations conducted in New York City by Perkins, Wan-

dersman, Rich and Florin, and in Baltimore by Perkins and me, contain both incivilities and territorial variables, but the requisite analyses have not yet been completed (see especially 68; see also 64, 65, 66, 67).

Summing Up on Discriminant Validity. Are incivilities at the community level separable from community structure and crime? Yes, if we use indicators based on aggregated, resident perceptions. Incivilities are not as clearly separable from structure if we rely on on-site assessments. Analyses at the streetblock level in two different cities and at the neighborhood level in one city clearly separate assessed incivilities from land use features. In short, at the community level, discriminant validity depends in part on the type of indicator used.

At the individual level, incivilities appear easily separable from other constructs, such as person-environment bonds, when both constructs rely on the same data collection instrument. Researchers have not yet investigated connections between incivilities and related constructs, such as territorial signage, where the two constructs rely on different data collection methods.

Convergent Validity and Multiple Assessment Modes

A key idea behind the multitrait-multimethod approach to validity is that expected convergences and divergences within and between constructs, respectively, should appear even when multiple methods provide indicators of the same construct (12). When we turn to multiple methods, focusing on cross-sectional or longitudinal perspectives, incivilities indicators from different data sources fail to converge as expected.

Using cross-sectional data from fifty Baltimore streetblocks collected in 1987, I carried out an exploratory principal components analysis of incivilities and crime. (For details on data collection, see 66.) These data came from three different sources: resident surveys (perceived social incivilities, perceived physical incivilities), on-site assessments (residential deterioration, nonresidential deterioration, males on the street), and counts of crime and disorder events in the neighborhood from local newspapers (serious crime news, quality of life crime news, and disorder news). The analysis suggested two independent dimensions.[21]

Unfortunately, the multitrait-multimethod matrix did not generate strong evidence of convergent and discriminant validity independent of assessment method. Results for the first component look promising initially.

Three variables from two different data sources had high loadings on the first component and refer to incivilities: perceived social incivilities

TABLE 3.2   Correlations Between Four Indicators of Unexpected Changes in Incivilities

	Assessed		Perceived	
	Vacant	*Graffiti*	*Physical*	*Social*
Graffiti	0.364			
	0.473			
Physical	0.138	0.286		
	0.140	*0.362*		
Social	0.078	0.097	0.274	
	0.104	*0.107*	*0.378*	

NOTE: Number of observations: 30 neighborhoods. Gamma coefficients; Spearman rank order correlations in italics. Vacant = average counts of vacant housing across blocks in the neighborhood; Graffiti = probability both raters agree graffiti present on average block; Physical = perceived physical incivilities; Social = perceived social incivilities. All indicators are measures of unexpected change (observed - expected) calculated using multilevel models. The predictor was the corresponding indicator from 1981 or 1982; the outcome was from 1994.

(.85), perceived physical incivilities (.94), and assessed incivilities of on-block households (.85). The first component clearly refers to incivilities. Serious crime news, measured from newspaper stories, however, also loads substantially on the component (.639), suggesting more than incivilities may be represented here.

On the second component, the item with the highest loading is disorder news from the newspaper stories. Nonresidential assessed incivilities, males hanging out, and other crime news also load highly on the component, as does serious crime news. In short, the second component contains indicators of both signs of incivility and crime from two different methods. The second component appears to favor items based on the newspaper sources.

The results from these fifty blocks are somewhat encouraging, in that two survey-based incivility items and one assessment-based incivility item appeared together. But they are discouraging because one component seems to favor the survey items, whereas the second component favors newspaper- or assessment-based items. Such results need to be considered with great caution given our small number of cases here.

The incivilities thesis, especially as stated by Wilson and Kelling and Skogan, emphasizes the importance of *changes* in incivilities. The streetblock data described in Chapter 2, when aggregated to the neighborhood level and combined with the survey data available, permit learning how unexpected changes in perceived incivilities and unexpected changes in assessed incivilities relate to one another. Each variable in the analysis here reflects unexpected change at the neighborhood level—1994 scores after partialling for respective 1981–1982 scores—in perceived physical incivilities; perceived social incivilities; changes in vacant, boarded-up houses; and changes in graffiti.

The relationships among the four changing incivilities indicators appear in Table 3.2.[22] It shows both gamma and rank-order coefficients, in consideration of some outliers in the data. These figures show moderately strong correlations within change indicators of the same type (assessed or survey-based) and generally weaker connections across different types of indicators. The exploratory principal components analyses appear to confirm the separation by data collection mode. After rotating to a varimax solution (see 29 for rationale), perceived social (.91) and perceived physical (.84) incivilities changes load strongly on the first component whereas vacant housing changes (.83) and graffiti changes (.82) have strong loadings on the second component.[23]

Some researchers might argue that we should have tried a solution rotating to correlated components rather than orthogonal components and simple structure. Oblique rotations, however, raise extremely serious concerns about construct clarity (29). Furthermore, looking at the factor loadings suggested clear orthogonality between the two components.

These analyses using different data sources raise questions. Changes in incivilities may be far less unitary than previously thought. Neighborhoods where perceptions of disorder were increasing unexpectedly were not necessarily the same neighborhoods where on-street conditions were worsening dramatically, nor were they the same neighborhoods where relative crime rates were unexpectedly rising. More details on some of these discrepancies are discussed in Chapter 4.

The divergent patterns apparent in the latter analysis suggest two possible interpretations. One is that changes in different incivilities indicators may be driven by different processes. Factors changing residents' perceptions, for example, may be heavily influenced by media reports and certain high-profile events in the neighborhood, whereas changes in vacancies may be driven by longer-term trends in local housing markets and job markets. Another possible interpretation is that perceptions are not responsive immediately to ongoing changes in the locale. The perceptions may be "sticky" and slow to incorporate more recent events.[24]

Conclusions on Measurement Questions

This portion of the chapter addressed three measurement questions raised by the incivilities thesis.

The first question is, can we separate incivilities indicators from related constructs? Are incivilities at the neighborhood level distinct from community structure and community crime rates? The answer is yes, if we use aggregated indicators based on residents' perceptions. If we use assessed indicators, it is harder to separate them from community structure and crime, but they are distinct from land use features. At the individual level, perceived incivilities appear easily separable from related constructs such as attachment to place. In short, discriminant validity for survey-based items appears acceptable, but not so for assessment-based items.

The second and third questions asked about cross-sectional and longitudinal convergent validity: Do incivilities indicators based on different data collection methods converge as expected? The data examined suggest they do not. Cross-sectionally, at the streetblock and neighborhood levels, indicators tend to converge as much by method as by construct. When examining longitudinal data, focusing on unexpected changes in neighborhoods over an extended period, such as a decade, indicators also cluster by method.

Other researchers using shorter time frames have observed comparable patterns. In an analysis around a Spokane housing community for the elderly, for example, researchers noted that different assessed incivilities indicators changed in divergent ways, and residents' changes in perceptions did not neatly reflect those changing conditions (27). Analyses of assessed and perceived incivilities in low-income public housing communities in Chicago revealed similarly divergent patterns (69). Residents' patterns of perceived problems shifted more in response to episodes of gang war versus gang peace than they did in response to actual cleanups. These parallel findings from the Midwest and Northwest show that the longitudinal divergences across indicators observed here are not limited just to the study site and the change period.

Implications for Policy, Practice, and Theory

There are four approaches to gauging the amount of disorder in a locale: surveys, on-site assessments of conditions by trained raters, census data, and archival data. Most of the work on the incivilities thesis has used indicators based on the first two methods. Census data provide only one indicator, vacant housing. Archival data usually can only supply indirect data, such as property tax delinquencies (70) or newspaper reports (66). Practitioners or policymakers evaluating initiatives geared to reducing incivilities need to choose the type of data on which they will rely for evaluating program impact. The foregoing analyses suggest which type they choose will have important implications for their evaluations.

Should practitioners or policymakers choose survey-based assessment, they are focusing on an outcome more readily separable from fundamental community fabric. Therefore, it should be "easier" to generate changes on survey-based outcomes compared to assessment-based outcomes, because the former are less structurally dependent. In short, if analysts choose survey-based measures they can more easily argue that incivilities are a problem separate from neighborhood fabric and neighborhood crime, and they can more easily get results. This is a practice often followed (for example, 86).

But the analyses presented, in particular the investigation into changes in incivilities, warn against assuming conditions have improved just because residents think they have. Over a long period, such as a decade, it appears that different incivility indicators tap into different pathways of neighborhood change. Residents' perceptions might worsen while neighborhood conditions improve—or the reverse. Other researchers, using much shorter time frames of one to two years, also find divergence between perceived incivility changes and assessed incivility changes (27, 69). In short, if evaluators rely on survey-based incivility indicators, they may more readily find resident views improved, but will not necessarily know how conditions have actually changed.

In sum, what we know about incivilities and how to fix them depends on the theory we are using to frame the issue and the type of indicators used. The version of the theory receiving strongest empirical support to date is the Wilson-Garofalo-Laub individual-level one. In addition, the incivilities indicators it views as appropriate, survey-based reports of neighborhood problems, have demonstrated the expected convergent and discriminant validity patterns. These indicators point most clearly to a separate problem deserving a separate policy focus.

By contrast, for the later versions of the incivilities thesis, shifting from an individual focus to a community one and from a cross-sectional perspective to a longitudinal one, empirical support is lacking, and measurement questions persist. To date, we have no longitudinal tests of the independent contributions of incivilities to neighborhood changes in fear, crime, or structure. Chapters 4 to 6 examine new data relevant to these issues. In addition, it is not clear if we should rely on on-site assessments or aggregated resident perceptions to gauge incivilities. The two types of indicators appear to reflect different, relatively independent dynamics, failing to demonstrate convergent validity when indicators from more than one method are used.

Researchers and practitioners may want to widen the scope of inquiry into incivilities to consider two additional issues: a group that has been left out and a concept that has been left out. Researchers have overlooked the many others who use neighborhoods besides the residents: business personnel working at local establishments, service providers such as UPS drivers passing through, cable technicians, or phone repair personnel. Researchers have not considered their perspectives. What types of local conditions draw their attention? Do they make inferences comparable to those made by residents or are their conclusions markedly different? In short, are the attributions made dependent on the type of interpreter? We have one study from Minneapolis–St. Paul where the impacts of assessed incivilities on business personnel were opposite from what was expected based on research with residents (96).

Turning back to theory, researchers have not explored the connection between incivilities and social disorganization. An extraordinarily rich conceptual and empirical literature exists on the latter topic (49, 75, 76, 77). One of the premier items used to gauge the presence of social disorganization is the presence of unsupervised teen groups. Such groups also have been labeled as a key social incivility. Are social incivilities little more than indicators of social disorganization? Or do they refer to a related but distinct set of local processes? If we want to make such a differentiation, how should we go about it? If we are concerned that social incivilities and social disorganization have common origins or similar geographic patterns, how do we lay those concerns to rest? Is the Wilson-Garofalo-Laub incivilities thesis no more than the psychological counterpart of community social disorganization dynamics? By considering the relationship between incivilities and social disorganization, research in this area will at least become less theoretically insular.

Notes

Portions of earlier versions of this paper were presented at the annual meetings of the American Psychological Association, New York City, August 1995, and at the first National Institute of Justice–sponsored conference, "Measuring What Matters," Washington, D.C., November 1995. A somewhat different version appears in R. Langworthy, ed. (1999) *Measuring what matters*. Washington, D.C.: National Institute of Justice/Office of Community Oriented Policing Services.

1. Skogan and Maxfield's (87a) indirect victimization model also attempts to address this same question. But instead of moving beyond crime per se to consider other conditions, the authors discuss how crime impacts can be amplified through local social networks.

2. This presentation significantly influenced workers in the field at that time and merits attention here. Hunter's influence can be seen in publications such as 53 and Skogan and Maxfield (87a).

3. Hunter appears to be the first to coin the term "symbols (or signs) of incivility."

4. Whereas Hunter allowed that residents would make inferences either about residents and organizations in the neighborhood or about public agencies outside the neighborhood, or both, Wilson and Kelling suggest the inference made refers to internal actors, i.e., other residents.

5. Unrepaired signs of incivility inspire nonserious crime initially, but contribute to later increases in serious crime, the latter arising from offender in-migration. Unfortunately, Wilson and Kelling fail to explain how prior crime levels might contribute to unrepaired signs of incivility in the first place. Their view appears to be different from that of Hunter, who suggests that crime and incivilities have the same structural origin and are nonrecursively locked in an escalating loop.

6. This "triage" feature of their model has drawn enormous criticism, especially from critical criminologists. Those debates are not directly relevant to the features of the model being examined here.

7. Kelling and Coles develop in detail what actions are relevant and some of the issues surrounding officer-community cooperation.

8. Skogan uses robbery victimization as an outcome variable, but does not carry out analyses using victimization as a predictor so that its impacts can be separated from the impacts of perceived incivilities.

9. Researchers did not test contributions of perceived incivilities at the individual level to fear of crime or to perceived risk, after controlling for the local victimization rate.

10. The partial impact, however, exceeded the coefficient linking perceived vandalism with assessed vandalism on the block, suggesting that on-site incivilities may influence local crime in ways that do not involve residents' perceptions.

11. With a moderating effect, a third variable influences or conditions the strength of the relationship between two other variables.

12. A researcher commits the "partialling fallacy" when he or she tries to separate out the independent influence of several predictors on an outcome when the predictors correlate too strongly with one another. After partialling—removing the influence of a particular predictor—very little of the other predictor(s) remains.

13. The only previously archived data set containing *extensive* assessed as well as perceived incivilities at the Inter-University Consortium for Political and Social Research (ICPSR) is from Minneapolis–St. Paul (59). The Skogan and Annan (85a) data set contains only a limited number of assessed incivilities indicators and no land use data.

14. Prior to 1970, variables describing youth population related to the stability dimension, also called, before 1970, a familism dimension. For 1970 and thereafter, however, youth population relates more closely to the race dimension in urban communities. Thus we refer to the latter as a race and youth dimension.

15. The individual items and the principal component loadings are shown in the following table:

	I Incivilities	II Commercial/ residential
Small groups	.86	.06
Graffiti	.78	.33
Volume of males on street	.72	-.04
Vacant houses	.71	.23
Housing density/block size	.69	.32
Litter	.69	.46
Commercial/industrial/ inst. land use	.13	.86
Percent residential frontage	-.35	-.84
Parking lots	.04	.77
Amenities drawing foot traffic	.31	.64
High traffic/high volume streets	.08	.52
Vacant lots	.14	.50
Lambda	5.25	1.79

16. The exploratory principal components analyses reported here for Baltimore and Minneapolis–St. Paul need to be interpreted with extreme caution, given the extremely low ratios of cases to variables.

17. Although this exploratory principal components analysis has an acceptable ratio of cases to variables (216:9), it is problematic in that for status and racial composition we have only one indicator variable each. Thus these components cannot be clearly defined. Nonetheless, we have three perceived incivilities indicators, permitting relatively clear definition of this component.

18. Removing Seattle from the analysis, since its over 5,000 cases "drove" the analysis, and reanalyzing the remaining 2,893 cases, produced slightly different results. Most notably, education almost reached a sizable negative loading (–.39) on the incivilities component, suggesting that low status and perceived neighborhood problems related. But the incivilities indicators continued to load tightly together.

19. The table hints at a couple of additional points qualifying the main pattern. First, the incivilities-crime connection may depend to some extent on the specific incivilities in question and on the city. In Baltimore, perceived problems with abandoned buildings connect more strongly to crime than the other two incivilities. In Seattle, all three connect to crime with about equal strength. Second, the removal of neighborhood structure may have varying influences on the incivilities-crime relationship, depending on the incivility and the city.

20. The Greenberg and Rohe (31) data set from Atlanta contains *perceived* incivilities along with land use information. It does not contain information on assessed incivilities.

21. These results should be viewed cautiously since the ratio of variables to cases exceeds the recommended ratio of 1:10.

22. All indicators are neighborhood-level indicators. Unexpected change = (1994 actual score – 1994 predicted score), where the actual score is an Empirical Bayes estimate of true neighborhood score derived from hierarchical linear models (HLM), or hierarchical generalized linear models (HGLM), and the predicted score is likewise derived from HLM or HGLM. n = 30 neighborhoods.

For the on-site assessment items, the period of change is 1981 to 1994 and the same blocks were assessed in 1981 and 1994. For the survey items, the period of change is 1982 to 1994. Excellent interrater reliability was obtained for both assessment items at both time points. For vacant houses, the reliability coefficients were .78 (1981) and .93 (1994) using Cronbach's alpha. For graffiti present/absent on each block the reliability coefficients were .78 (1981) and .83 (1994) using Kappa as the reliability coefficient.

The perceived problems were obtained by the standard format survey item where respondents were asked if the issue was not a problem (0), somewhat of a problem (1), or a big problem (2) (see Chapter 2). We carried out a principal components analysis of the perceived problems, extracting two eigenvalues explaining 60% of the total variance. Rotating the two components to a varimax solution, one component picks up just physical problems: vacant houses, vacant lots, people who do not keep property up, and litter. A second component focuses on social problems: insults, teens, noise, bad elements moving in, and people fighting. Vandalism had moderate loadings on both components. Putting vandalism together with the other physical problems, we created an index with a reliability (Cronbach's alpha) of .80. The reliability of the social problems was .86.

23. I repeated the analysis adding reactions to crime, such as changes in avoidance. Again, the survey items related closely to one another, loading better than .80 on their dimension. And the two assessment items loaded better than .80 on a separate dimension. Repeating the analysis again adding unexpected changes in three crimes—robbery, assault, and larceny—provided a diffuse pattern as well. The crime variables went together on one dimension, the survey items went together on a different dimension, and the assessment variables clustered by themselves. A two- rather than three-component solution, resulted in a slightly less clean pattern of loadings, but the assessment-based variables were still separated from the survey-based variables.

24. I am indebted to Pam Lattimore and Jack Riley for this suggestion.

References

(1) Baldwin, J., and Bottoms, A. E. (1976) *The urban criminal*, Tavistock, London.
(2) Bayley, D. H. (1994) International differences in community policing. In *The challenge of community policing* (Rosenbaum, D., ed), pp. 278–281. Sage, Thousand Oaks, CA.
(3) Bennett, S. F. (1995) Community organizations and crime. *American Journal of Policing* 539, 72–84.
(4) Berry, B. J. L., and Kasarda, J. D. (1977) *Contemporary urban ecology*, Macmillan, New York.

(5) Bollen, K. (1989) *Structural equations with latent variables,* Wiley Interscience, New York.

(6) Boyd, L. H., and Iversen, G. R. (1979) *Contextual analysis: Concepts and statistical techniques,* Wadsworth, Belmont, CA.

(7) Bratton, W. (1998) *Turnaround,* Random House, New York.

(8) Buerger, M. E. (1994) The limits of community. In *The challenge of community policing* (Rosenbaum, D., ed), pp. 270–274. Sage, Thousand Oaks, CA.

(9) Buerger, M., and Mazerolle, L. G. (1998) Third-party policing: A theoretical analysis of an emerging trend. *Justice Quarterly* 15, 301–328.

(10) Buerger, M. L. (1994) A tale of two targets: Limitations of community anti-crime actions. *Crime & Delinquency* 40, 384–410.

(11) Bursik, R. J. (1988) Social disorganization and theories of crime and delinquency. *Criminology* 26, 519–551.

(11a) Bursik, R. J., and Grasmick, H. (1993) *Neighborhoods and crime,* Lexington Books, Lexington, MA.

(12) Campbell, D., and Fiske, D. (1959) Convergent and discriminant validation by the multitrait-multimethod matrix. *Psychological Bulletin* 56, 81–105.

(13) Cloward, R. A., and Ohlin, L. E. (1960) *Delinquency and opportunity,* Free Press, New York.

(14) Cook, F. L., and Skogan, W. G. (1984) Evaluating the changing definition of a policy issue in congress: Crime against the elderly. In *Public policy and social institutions* (Rodgers, H. R., Jr., ed), pp. 287–332. JAI, Greenwich, CT.

(15) Cordner, G. (1997) Community policing. In *Critical issues in policing: Contemporary readings,* 3rd ed. (Dunham, R. G., and Alpert, G. P., eds). Waveland, Prospect Heights, IL.

(16) Covington, J., and Taylor, R. B. (1991) Fear of crime in urban residential neighborhoods: Implications of between and within-neighborhood sources for current models. *Sociological Quarterly* 32, 231–249.

(17) Cronbach, L. J., and Meehl, P. E. (1955) Construct validity in personality tests. *Psychological Bulletin* 52, 281–302.

(18) de Leeuw, J., Kreft, I. G. G., and Aiken, L. (1995) The effects of different forms of centering in hierarchical linear models. *Multivariate Behavioral Research* 30, 1–22.

(19) Dietz, A. S. (1997) Evaluating community policing: Quality police service and fear of crime. *Policing* 20, 83–100.

(20) Dubow, F., McCabe, F., and Kaplan, G. (1979) *Reactions to crime: A critical review of the literature,* Government Printing Office, Washington, DC.

(21) Eck, J. (1995) Review Essay: Examining routine activity theory. *Justice Quarterly* 12, 783–797.

(22) Eck, J. (1997) Preventing crime at places. In *Preventing crime: What works, what doesn't, what's promising* (Sherman, L. W., Gottfredson, D., MacKenzie, D., Reuter, P., and Bushway, S., eds). Office of Justice Programs, U.S. Department of Justice, Washington, DC.

(23) Ferraro, K. F. (1994) *Fear of crime: Interpreting victimization risk,* State University of New York Press, Albany.

(24) Fisher, B. (1991) A neighborhood business area is hurting: Crime, fear and disorders take their toll. *Crime & Delinquency* 37, 363–373.

(25) Garofalo, J., and Laub, J. (1978) The fear of crime: Broadening our perspective. *Victimology* 3, 242–253.

(26) Gordon, R. A. (1968) Issues in multiple regression. *American Journal of Sociology* 73, 592–616.

(27) Giacomazzi, A. L., McGarrell, E. F., and Thurman, Q. C. (1997) *Reducing disorder, fear and crime in public housing: An evaluation of a drug crime elimination program in Spokane, Washington.* Draft Final Report.

(28) Goldstein, H. (1990) *Problem-oriented policing,* Temple University Press, Philadelphia.

(29) Gordon, R. A. (1968) On the interpretation of oblique factors. *American Sociological Review* 33, 601–620.

(30) Gottdiener, M. (1994) *The new urban sociology,* McGraw Hill, New York.

(31) Greenberg, S., and Rohe, W. (1986) Informal social control. In *Urban neighborhoods: Research and policy* (Taylor, R. B., ed), 79–118, Praeger, New York.

(32) Greene, J. R. (1989) Police officer job satisfaction and community perceptions: Implications for community-oriented policing. *Journal of Research in Crime and Delinquency* 26, 168–183.

(33) Greene, J. R., and Decker, S. H. (1989) Police and community perceptions of the community role in policing: The Philadelphia experience. *Howard Journal of Criminal Justice* 28, 105–124.

(34) Greene, J. R., and Pelfrey, W. V. (1997) Shifting the balance of power between police and community. In *Critical issues in policing: Contemporary readings,* 3rd ed. (Dunham, R. G., and Alpert, G. P., eds), 37–51, Waveland, Prospect Heights, IL.

(35) Greene, J. R., and Taylor, R. B. (1988) Community-based policing and foot patrol: Issues of theory and evaluation. In *Community policing: Rhetoric or reality?* (Greene, J. R., and Mastrofski, S. D., eds), pp. 195–224. Praeger, New York.

(36) Greene, R., and McLaughlin, E. (1993) Facilitating communities through police work: Drug problem solving and neighborhood involvement in Philadelphia. In *Drugs and the community* (Davis, R. C., Lurigio, A., and Rosenbaum, D. P., eds), pp. 141–161. Charles C. Thomas, Springfield, IL.

(37) Harcourt, B. E. (1998) Reflecting on the subject: A critique of the social influence conception of deterrence, the broken windows theory, and order-maintenance policing New York style. *Michigan Law Review* 97, 291–372.

(38) Harrell, A., and Gouvis, C. *Community decay and crime.* Final report, Grant NIJ-IJ-CX-K016, The Urban Institute, Washington, DC.

(39) Harries, K. D. (1980) *Crime and the environment,* Charles C. Thomas, Springfield, IL.

(40) Hope, T., and Hough, M. (1988) Area, crime and incivility: A profile from the British Crime Survey. In *Communities and crime reduction* (Hope, T., and Shaw, M., eds), pp. 30–47. Her Majesty's Stationary Office, London.

(41) House, J. S., Umberson, D., and Landis, K. R. (1988) Structure and processes of social support. *Annual Review of Sociology* 14, 293–318.

(42) Hunter, A. (1974) *Symbolic communities,* University of Chicago Press, Chicago.

(42a) Hunter, A. (1974) Community change: A stochastic analysis of Chicago's communities 1930–1960, *American Journal of Sociology* 19, 923–947.

(43) Hunter, A. (1978) Symbols of incivility. Paper presented at the Annual Meeting of the American Society of Criminology. Dallas, Texas, November.

(44) Jacobs, J. (1961) *The death and life of great American cities,* Vintage, New York.

(45) Kelling, G. (1997) Restore order and you reduce crime. *Washington Post* February 9, C3.

(46) Kelling, G. L., and Coles, C. M. (1996) *Fixing broken windows: Restoring order and reducing crime in our communities*, Free Press, New York.

(47) Kirschenbaum, A. (1983) Sources of neighborhood residential change: A micro-level analysis. *Social Indicators Research* 12, 183–198.

(48) Kline, P. (1994) *An easy guide to factor analysis*, Routledge, London.

(48a) Klinger, D. A. (1997) Negotiating order in police work. *Criminology* 35, 277–306.

(49) Kornhauser, R. R. (1978) *Social sources of delinquency*, University of Chicago Press, Chicago.

(50) Kurtz, E., Koons, B., and Taylor, R. B. (1998) Land use, physical deterioration, resident-based control and calls for service on urban streetblocks. *Justice Quarterly* 15, 121–149.

(51) LaGrange, R. L., and Ferraro, K. F. (1989) Assessing age and gender differences in perceived risk and fear of crime. *Criminology* 27, 697–719.

(52) Lavrakas, P. J. (1982) Fear of crime and behavioral restrictions in urban and suburban neighborhoods. *Population and Environment* 5, 242–264.

(53) Lewis, D. A., and Maxfield, M. G. (1980) Fear in the neighborhoods: An investigation of the impact of crime. *Journal of Research in Crime and Delinquency* 17, 160–189.

(53a) Lewis, D. A., and Salem, G. (1986) *Fear of crime*, Transaction Publishers, New Brunswick, NJ.

(54) Little, J. T. (1976) Residential preferences, neighborhood filtering and neighborhood change. *Journal of Urban Economics* 3, 68–81.

(55) Logan, J. R., and Molotch, H. (1987) *Urban fortunes*, University of California Press, Berkeley.

(56) Mastrofski, S. D., Worden, R. E., and Snipes, J. B. (1995) Law enforcement in a time of community policing. *Criminology* 33, 539–563.

(57) Matthews, R. G. (1997) Criminal justice leaders criticized. *Baltimore Sun* September 23, 3B.

(58) Matthews, R. G. (1997) Schmoke talking high-tech on crime. *Baltimore Sun* January 24, 1A, 13A.

(59) McPherson, M., and Silloway, G. (1986) The role of the small commercial center in the urban neighborhood. In *Urban neighborhoods: Research and policy* (Taylor, R. B., ed), pp. 144–180. Praeger, New York.

(60) Miethe, T. (1995) Fear and withdrawal from urban life. *Annals of the American Academy of Political and Social Science* 539, 14–27.

(61) Miethe, T. D., and Meier, R. F. (1994) *Crime and its social context*, State University of New York Press, Albany.

(62) Moran, R. (1997) New York story: More luck than policing. *Washington Post* February 9, C3.

(63) Pate, A., and Shtull, P. (1994) Community policing grows in Brooklyn: An inside view of the New York City Police Department's model precinct. *Crime & Delinquency* 40, 384–410.

(64) Perkins, D. D., Florin, P., Rich, R. C., Wandersman, A., and Chavis, D. M. (1990) Participation and the social and physical environment of residential

blocks: Crime and community context. *American Journal of Community Psychology* 18, 83–115.

(65) Perkins, D. D., Meeks, J. W., and Taylor, R. B. (1992) The physical environment of street blocks and resident perceptions of crime and disorder: Implications for theory and measurement. *Journal of Environmental Psychology* 12, 21–34.

(66) Perkins, D., and Taylor, R. B. (1996) Ecological assessments of disorder: Their relationship to fear of crime and theoretical implications. *American Journal of Community Psychology* 24, 63–107.

(67) Perkins, D. D., and Taylor, R. B. (1996) Ecological assessments of community disorder: Their relationship to fear of crime and theoretical implications. *American Journal of Community Psychology* 24, 63–107.

(68) Perkins, D. D., Wandersman, A., Rich, R., and Taylor, R. B. (1993) Physical environment of street crime: Defensible space, territoriality and incivilities. *Journal of Environmental Psychology* 13, 29–49.

(69) Popkin, S., Gwiasda, V. E., Amendiola, J. M., Anderson, A. A., Hanson, G., Johnson, W. A., Martel, E., Olson, L. M., and Rosenbaum, D. P. (1997) *The hidden war: The battle to control crime in Chicago's public housing.* Draft Final Report, 93-IJ-CX–0037; 95-IJ-CX–0011, Abt Associates, Chicago.

(70) Rengert, G. (1996) *The geography of illegal drugs,* Westview, Boulder.

(71) Rosenfeld, R. (1994) Review of: Neighborhoods and crime. *American Journal of Sociology* 99, 1387–1389.

(72) Ross, C. E., and Jang, S. J. (1997) Community disorder, fear and distrust: The buffering role of incivilities. Paper presented at the annual meetings of the American Society of Criminology, Chicago, November.

(73) Rountree, P. W., and Land, K. C. (1996) Burglary victimization, perceptions of crime risk, and routine activities: A multilevel analysis across Seattle neighborhoods and census tracts. *Journal of Research in Crime and Delinquency* 33, 147–180.

(74) Rountree, P. W., and Land, K. C. (1996) Perceived risk versus fear of crime: Empirical evidence of conceptually distinct reactions in survey data. *Social Forces* 74, 1353–1376.

(75) Sampson, R. J. (1988) Local friendship ties and community attachment in mass society: A multilevel systemic model. *American Sociological Review* 53, 766–779.

(76) Sampson, R. J. (1991) Linking the micro- and macro-level dimensions of community social organization. *Social Forces* 70, 43–64.

(77) Sampson, R. J., and Grove, W. B. (1989) Community structure and crime: Testing social disorganization theory. *American Journal of Sociology* 94, 774–802.

(78) Sampson, R. J., and Lauritsen, J. L. (1994) Violent victimization and offending: Individual, situational- and community-level risk factors. In *Understanding and preventing violence,* Vol. 3: *Social influences* (Reiss, A. J. J., and Roth, J. A., eds), pp. 1–114. National Academy Press, Washington, DC.

(79) Sampson, R., and Raudenbush, S. (1999) Systematic social observations of public spaces: A new look at disorder in urban neighborhoods. *American Journal of Sociology* 5, 603–651.

(80) Schwirian, K. P. (1983) Models of neighborhood change: A review. *Annual Review of Sociology* 9, 83–102.

(81) Sherman, L. W. (1997) Communities and crime prevention. In *Preventing crime: What works, what doesn't, what's promising* (Sherman, L. W., Gottfredson, D., MacKenzie, D., Reuter, P., and Bushway, S., eds), chapter 3. Office of Justice Programs, U.S. Department of Justice, Washington, DC.

(82) Shumaker, S. A., and Taylor, R. B. (1983) Toward a clarification of people-place relationships: A model of attachment to place. In *Environmental psychology: Directions and perspectives* (Feimer, N. R., and Geller, E. S., eds), pp. 219–256. Praeger, New York.

(83) Skogan, W. (1986) Fear of crime and neighborhood change. In *Crime and justice: A review of research,* Vol. 8: *Communities and crime* (Reiss, A. J., Jr., and Tonry, M., eds), pp. 203–230. Chicago: University of Chicago Press.

(84) Skogan, W. (1990) *Disorder and decline: Crime and the spiral of decay in American cities,* Free Press, New York.

(85) Skogan, W. (1994) The impact of community policing on neighborhood residents. In *The challenge of community policing: Testing the promises* (Rosenbaum, D., ed), pp. 167–181. Sage, Thousand Oaks, CA.

(85a) Skogan, W., and Annan, S. (1993) Drug enforcement in public housing. In *Drugs and the community* (R. C. Davis, A. Lurigio, D. Rosenbaum, eds.), pp. 162–174, Charles Thomas, Springfield, IL.

(86) Skogan, W., and Hartnett, S. (1997) *Community policing, Chicago style,* Oxford University Press, New York.

(87) Skogan, W., and Lurigio, A. J. (1992) The correlates of community anti-drug activism. *Crime & Delinquency* 38, 510–521.

(87a) Skogan, W., and Maxfield, M. (1981) *Coping with crime,* Sage, Beverly Hills, CA.

(88) Skolnick, J. H. (1997) Making sense of the crime decline. *Newsday* February 2, G6, G15.

(89) Spelman, W., and Eck, J. E. (1987) *Problem-oriented policing,* National Institute of Justice, Washington, DC.

(90) Taylor, R. B. (1988) *Human territorial functioning,* Cambridge University Press, Cambridge, UK.

(91) Taylor, R. B. (1994) *Research methods in criminal justice,* McGraw Hill, New York.

(92) Taylor, R. B. (1995) Impact of crime on communities. *Annals of the American Academy of Political and Social Science* 539, 28–45.

(93) Taylor, R. B. (1996) *Responses to disorder in Minneapolis–St. Paul: Relative impacts of neighborhood structure, crime, and physical deterioration.* Unpublished Final Report 94-IJ-CX-0018 to the National Institute of Justice, Department of Criminal Justice, Temple University, July.

(94) Taylor, R. B. *Impacts of crime and grime on reactions to crime, neighborhood crime changes, and changes in neighborhood structure.* Draft Final Report 93-IJ-CX-0022, National Institute of Justice, Department of Criminal Justice, Temple University.

(95) Taylor, R. B. (1996) Neighborhood responses to disorder and local attachments: The systemic model of attachment, and neighborhood use value. *Sociological Forum* 11, 41–74.

(96) Taylor, R. B. (1997) Relative impacts of disorder, structural change, and crime on residents and business personnel in Minneapolis–St. Paul. In *Community crime prevention at the crossroads* (Lab, S., ed), pp. 63–75. Anderson, Cincinnati, OH.

(97) Taylor, R. B. (1997) Social order and disorder of streetblocks and neighborhoods: Ecology, microecology and the systemic model of social disorganization. *Journal of Research in Crime and Delinquency* 33, 113–155.

(98) Taylor, R. B., and Covington, J. (1988) Neighborhood changes in ecology and violence. *Criminology* 26, 553–589.

(99) Taylor, R. B., and Covington, J. (1993) Community structural change and fear of crime. *Social Problems* 40, 374–397.

(100) Taylor, R. B., and Hale, M. (1986) Testing alternative models of fear of crime. *Journal of Criminal Law and Criminology* 77, 151–189.

(101) Taylor, R. B., Koons, B., Kurtz, E., Greene, J., and Perkins, D. (1995) Streetblocks with more nonresidential landuse have more physical deterioration: Evidence from Baltimore and Philadelphia. *Urban Affairs Review* (formerly *Urban Affairs Quarterly*) 30, 120–136.

(102) Taylor, R. B., and Shumaker, S. A. (1990) Local crime as a natural hazard: Implications for understanding the relationship between disorder and fear of crime. *American Journal of Community Psychology* 18, 619–642.

(103) Taylor, R. B., Shumaker, S. A., and Gottfredson, S. D. (1985) Neighborhood-level links between physical features and local sentiments: Deterioration, fear of crime, and confidence. *Journal of Architectural Planning and Research* 2, 261–275.

(104) Thurman, Q., Bogen, P., and Giacomazzi, A. (1993) Program monitoring and community policing: A process evaluation of community policing in Spokane, Washington. *American Journal of Police* 7, 89–114.

(105) Wilson, J. Q. (1975) *Thinking about crime,* Basic Books, New York.

(106) Wilson, J. Q., and Kelling, G. (1982) Broken windows. *Atlantic Monthly* 211, 29–38.

(107) Wilson, W. J. (1996) *When work disappears: The world of the new urban poor,* Knopf, New York.

PART TWO

Quantitative Evidence on Origins and Impacts

4

Origins of Incivilities

A Story About One Broken Window

The April morning sun shone, but failed to dispel the mid-morning chill on the corner where Steve Pardue and I stood in Midtown, a neighborhood not too far north of downtown Baltimore. The earlier steel crush of downtown-bound commuters had drained away, and it was almost quiet on the block. Stretching north from the corner, the block seemed almost stately: well-kept, dignified stone or brick four-story row houses dating from the beginning of the twentieth century lined the street. The houses have been converted to apartments and, on the east side, occasional law offices. It was one of the better-kept blocks in Midtown. The sober brick and stone facades notwithstanding, the neighborhood is diverse. We were a few blocks from a well-known gay nightclub. The neighborhood is home to numerous students. Small and medium-sized businesses or offices can be found on many of the blocks. Since this particular block was well maintained, we were surprised to see across from us a broken, boarded-up fourth-story window.

As we twirled the lenses on our cameras, preparing to take shots, a middle-aged African American crossed the street to us. He had a mustache and glasses and wore a leather Chicago Bulls cap and a blue windbreaker. He was carrying a broom and had on rubber gloves. Naturally, he wanted to know what we were doing. We explained, and he told us about the building, where he was the caretaker, and its tenants.

He stressed to us that all types of folks live in the building. "You want blue hair, I got it. You want green hair, I got it. You want purple hair, I got it." But, he emphasized, those looking nattiest on the outside may have the worst-kept apartments. "We got folks dressed nice with apartments you cannot believe the mess." We asked for the story behind the window.

The fourth-floor tenant, a woman, was a long-term renter. A few years ago, she suddenly changed all her locks, got a large dog, and started refusing to let anyone into the apartment. Then, a couple of years ago, the window got broken. She boarded it up herself and told the maintenance man it was not a problem. In explaining his "live and let live" attitude, the Bulls fan stressed that the neighborhood has lots of different kinds of folks, and some tolerance is required for getting along. Permitting her to keep her broken window appeared to be part of that requirement.

Focus and Organization

That morning we heard a story about one out-of-place broken window. In this chapter, assessment, census, and survey data ground a broader story: Where do neighborhood deterioration and residents' perceptions of neighborhood problems come from? The incivilities, or broken windows thesis, as explained in Chapter 3, suggests a range of consequences for individuals and neighborhoods. But far less attention has been given to the *causes* of social and physical incivilities, especially as they shift over time.

Understanding the causes of these fluctuations may prove important. On a practical level, it may help us predict areas where deterioration will emerge in future. In a theoretical vein, clarifying the sources of shifting incivilities may help us explain how they intertwine with other neighborhood qualities and processes.

The next section recounts different perspectives on the origins of incivilities. The analyses following use assessment-based indicators. Finally, controlling for the views of residents in 1982, I look at how residents' perceptions of local problems in those same neighborhoods had shifted by 1994.

Perspectives on the Origins of Incivilities

In general, four different perspectives on the origins of incivilities appear in the literature: historical focusing on legal shifts, structural, racial, and random urban dynamics.

The Historical-Legal Perspective

The courts are largely to blame, according to Kelling and Coles's presentation of the historical legal perspective on increasing incivilities (22). They argue (22: Chapter 2) that long-term shifts in legal views over the past three decades have facilitated the emergence of widespread incivilities in urban communities. Courts have backed away from the rights of communities to maintain orderly street life in favor of the individual rights of the homeless, panhandlers, and others. Coupled with this legal shift have been modifications in policing, with increasing attention devoted to serious index crimes and less effort expended on order maintenance. This has led to "bad public policy" (22: 5).

Such a perspective provides a broad historical framework for understanding how variations in criminal justice processing may have contributed to increasingly disorderly street conditions and the lack of countermeasures. Of course, numerous other factors outside of the criminal justice system may have contributed to increasingly uncivil street behavior, including cultural and institutional shifts (e.g., 24). But Kelling and Coles's argument may help us understand how such shifts went unchallenged. Their views would appear to be most useful when considering disorderly street behaviors such as harassment, public urination, public drunkenness, and dealing, for example.

But at the same time, the perspective also seems limited. The argument sheds less light on increasing physical deterioration in urban communities than on increasing disorderly behavior. In addition, the perspective's macro-level focus, although relevant to multidecade trends, does not help us understand differences between neighborhoods in one city and how those differences might widen or narrow over time. The framework seems to imply that between-neighborhood differences arise solely from differences in enforcement patterns. Although such differentials undoubtedly contribute to spatial variations in incivilities (23), they may not be the most powerful contributor.

The Structural Perspective

By contrast, an expanded human ecology model, one more in keeping with the new urban sociology, would expect the increases in incivilities to be spatially patterned (11, 18). It would expect dramatic increases to occur in locations where there has been a failure of public control.

Public control is strong when the neighborhood, through its connection with local political powers, is able to ensure that outside resources flow into and help maintain the neighborhood (11, 20). In neighborhoods where local organizations have failed to maintain successful working relationships with city hall and public control is weaker, decreases in service result. Street cleaning occurs less often; it takes the city longer to board up abandoned houses or to tear down unsalvageable structures. Residents are less likely to receive assistance from local authorities in carting away junk from abandoned lots. Police make fewer efforts to clear the streets of disorderly youth, should they gather there, and are less likely to respond to other minor disturbances (23).

Such differentials in service delivery or enforcement emerge from the relative location of the community in the broader political economy (19,

29). As the location's economic value to outside interests—its exchange
value—declines, so too does its power and the services it receives. Where
Kelling and Coles's perspective focuses on broad shifts over time, this
structural framework concentrates instead on differences between communities, seeking the origins of witnessed differences in incivilities in
community fabric differentials linked to socioeconomics.

The structural framework also has implications for changes over time.
It would expect that increasing incivilities will occur in politically weaker
locations. In Baltimore, this means neighborhoods that are of lower status, and/or less stable, and/or, according to some analysts, more predominantly African-American. As status and stability decline, residents
contribute less to local income and property tax revenues. Furthermore,
in unstable or increasingly unstable locations, it becomes more difficult
to mobilize the widespread resident support needed for initiatives that
could increase public control.

The systemic, ecological perspective also anticipates that crime itself
may spur increased incivilities. The mediating processes might be several. For example, we know that crime influences house prices (34, 47).
Crime may lead investors to reconsider maintaining owned properties
they live in or rent out. Alternatively, turning to social incivilities, the relevant dynamics may center around street activity and crime's ability to
erode orderly street life while impairing residents' willingness to try and
regulate that street life (48).

Those supporting the neighborhood from outside, as well as the residents themselves, might be affected by a neighborhood's increasing
crime rates. Rates ratcheting up might signal to those outsiders on whose
service and intervention the neighborhood depends, such as, for example, realtors, that the future of the neighborhood is in jeopardy (34).

Outside agents such as police may play key roles in the crime-to-de-
cline sequence as well. The crime level in a community influences patrolling officers' attitudes toward and responses to minor crimes and incivilities (23). Officers may respond more leniently and display less
vigor—less willingness to initiate official processing of an event—in
higher-crime locales. But regardless of the responsible dynamic and
whether those processes involve residents or outsiders, or both, the systemic model anticipates crime may lead to increased deterioration and
perception of neighborhood problems.

The Racial Perspective

Racial composition represents a key element in community structure.
Whereas ecologists such as those described above include racial composition as a feature of neighborhood fabric equivalent in importance to
other features of structure, another group of scholars accord race a pre-

eminent position, arguing that racial composition is more influential than status or stability. The theories they develop provide a different perspective on the origins of social and physical incivilities.

Historical connections between social incivilities and urban neighborhood racial composition can be traced at least to the late nineteenth century. In Philadelphia, Lane argues that discrimination at that time against the largest African-American community, located near the city center, served not only to keep violence and vice levels high in the locale but disorderly behavior and drunkenness as well (26: 159). Despite the complaints of African-American middle-class and professional leaders and strong political support at the polls for the dominant Republican politicians and their machine, it was more expedient for local political leaders to zone the community for vice. Lane further makes the case that members of the African-American community were systematically excluded from emerging employment opportunities in "good" industrial jobs (26: 134) and from comparable educational opportunities (26: 27), thereby limiting legitimate earning opportunities. It seems plausible, then, that in such a context residents would have less resources to maintain housing, landlords would experience less pressure to maintain properties, or both. Lane's thesis suggests an important historical perspective for the link between community racial composition and incivilities.

Moving us forward about seventy years, for several predominantly African-American West Baltimore neighborhoods, McDougall argues for a connection between racial composition and incivilities driven most recently by demolition and subsequent public housing construction in the 1950s (32: 54). Discussing Upton, at the base of Pennsylvania Avenue, he suggests the demolition shredded neighborhood fabric, and the influx of households from all over the city to the new public housing further eroded community ties. To meet this new demand, "Dives and prostitution infested lower Pennsylvania Avenue" (32: 54). Empirical work in Chicago has established that the siting of public housing communities does destabilize the surrounding neighborhoods (10). McDougall argues that in the Baltimore case, historical patterns of mayoral neglect of predominantly African-American communities have continued into the present, even under Mayor Schmoke, an African American.

Consequently, given the more distant and more recent political histories described here, we would expect both social and physical incivilities to be high and to increase more markedly in predominantly African-American communities, controlling for other factors, as well-established patterns of neglect or weaker service delivery and code enforcement persist.

Turning from a political to an economic perspective on race, William Julius Wilson highlights the increasing concentration of urban African Americans in extremely poor neighborhoods, with poverty rates over 40%. He links racial composition with social and physical disorder in urban communities, but for economic reasons rather than service delivery reasons (54). Manufacturing has declined, as shown in Chapter 2, and many jobs have moved out of the city (22); lacking a work routine people are more likely to stay out late and be rowdy. In addition, an economy based on drug dealing has replaced the legitimate economy in many poor, urban, African-American communities. This economy spawns settings that breed social disorder: open-air and in-house drug markets.

Although Wilson does not directly address physical deterioration, his argument can be easily extended to this concern. In a poor neighborhood, those who own their homes are unlikely to be able to afford upkeep. Their means are too limited. Those who rent are likely to be renting from landlords spending minimal funds on upkeep. In the case of dilapidated rental units, Wilson's argument would probably be close to Logan and Molotch's discussion of minimizing investments in low return—that is, low exchange value—locations.

Wilson's argument focuses on severely distressed communities where unemployment is extremely high. But even in locations where economic disadvantage is less extreme, racial composition may link to higher incivilities due to changes in the nature of available jobs. Crutchfield and Pitchford argue that labor stratification mediates or connects community economic structure and violent crime (15). They distinguish the primary labor market—employees are valued and trained, receive decent wages, and expect job security—from the secondary labor market—employees are treated as temporary help, receive little training and low wages, and can expect little stability or advancement. As one African-American, inner-city, Washington, D.C., informant put it over thirty years ago, a hard-working dishwasher just becomes a hard-working dishwasher (28).

When secondary employment dominates in a locale as the primary labor market shrinks, as has happened with manufacturing jobs moving out of central cities, individual residents and those around them have fewer connections to their employment. The discipline and rationality demanded for holding down a manufacturing job—showing up for work, every day, at 7:30 A.M., sober—no longer applies. If a resident loses his or her "McJob," he or she figures it is no great loss. Thus chances of involvement in drug use, drinking, or rowdy behavior all may increase. Not only may social incivilities increase, but so too may physical incivilities, as working residents' relatively poor long-term employment prospects make it more difficult for them to secure mortgages and those who already are owners have fewer funds to maintain housing.

What Crutchfield and Pitchford describe, as industrialism gives way to postindustrialism, is the historical reversal of the salutary effects experienced by Irish immigrants in big cities in the latter half of nineteenth century and by urban African Americans in the middle third of the twentieth century as industrial jobs opened up (26). These shifts have clear implications for levels of social incivilities. The implications for changes in physical incivilities are present as well, but more indirect.

The focus on labor stratification illuminates what may be happening in predominantly African-American communities before unemployment gets to the extremely high levels described by Wilson. It suggests that prior to reaching this stage, shifts in the labor market, with secondary employment opportunities dominating, also may encourage more widespread social and physical incivilities.

One additional perspective on race, linked to Wilson's discussion, may help us understand the spatial patterning of incivilities. Although Wilson folds in the impacts of segregation combined with economic disadvantage, Massey concentrates more exclusively on the spatial pattern. He has documented increasing patterns of urban racial segregation over the past few decades (30, 31). He points out that despite fair housing laws, African Americans remain systematically segregated in specific urban locations. He uses the term hypersegregation to describe current conditions in extremely disadvantaged African-American communities where residents are segregated on several dimensions and may not see any whites for days on end (30). The extreme isolation emerges because African-American urban communities are sizable; since these communities have high scores on several different dimensions of segregation, their residents were more residentially segregated and spatially isolated than other minority populations, such as Hispanics and Asians, in both 1980 and 1990. Given such extreme isolation and the "compact spatial configuration" in these locations, and given the older housing there, we would expect physical incivilities to increase faster in African-American communities than in Hispanic, Asian, or low-income white locations. The more compact spatial configuration leads to a given prevalence rate[1] of physical incivilities having a stronger visual impact. If the incivilities, such as, for example, vacant houses, are packed into a smaller area, neighborhood conditions would look worse than if the same rate of vacant housing were spread over a wider area. The stronger visual impact is likely to lead to faster withdrawal of lending capital, more rapid abandonment of marginal properties by landlords, and the like. In other words, Massey's argument implies some physical incivilities, such as abandoned housing and abandoned stores, will increase faster in African-American communities because of their more spatially compact and isolated form.

Random Urban Dynamics

Some incivilities theorists assume that incivilities can increase in any place, at any time. Such upswings, according to this view, are part of dynamic urban living. Increases in incivilities, when they do occur, probably arise from external causes; they are part of the "random shocks" that go with modern urban life and can befall any community (43). Or the shocks may be less random, a part of broader trends, such as a downturn in house prices in a certain part of the city. This view sees shifts in incivilities operating more independently of the structural features of the community and more independently of community-city relationships. What is important is not where and why the incivilities show up, but rather how speedily they are addressed and remediated by local actors. If such random shocks are important and the predominant feature shifting incivilities in a locale, efforts to predict such shifts, using earlier structural attributes of neighborhoods, should prove fruitless.

An Unexciting, but Necessary, Methodological Aside on Change

In the work presented in this and the following two chapters, we will be looking at different temporal relationships between our predictors and outcomes. Which approach we take depends in part on the available data and in part on our theoretical aim. It is necessary here to briefly explain the approach taken to operationalizing change. Unfortunately, this is an area where experts have disagreed for some time and continue to do so (1, 2, 5, 25, 37, 38, 39). I will illustrate our approach to operationalizing change by considering the relationship between crime and house prices.

In examining how crime might have changed house prices, the first question is how will we get each variable into the most usable form? House prices have several undesirable properties. Across a range of neighborhoods, there are likely to be a large number of lower-priced locations and a much smaller number of higher-priced locations, with some of the higher-priced locations having extremely high scores. Such a distribution is "skewed," because there are more lower than higher cases and the higher-scoring cases are more spread out than the lower-scoring cases. For a number of reasons, these are undesirable features of the variable. Of course, we also have the problem of inflation across a decade, driving house prices up generally and making it difficult to directly compare 1970 with 1980 house prices, for example.

One transformation making house prices more manageable is to use a population-weighted percentile at each decade (12). Each neighborhood is placed on a scale, from 0 to 100, its score reflecting its house price and the percentage of the total city population where the average neighborhood house price is lower than that neighborhood's price. A house with a neighborhood house value percentile of 25 is a neighborhood compared to which 25% of the city's population lives in neighborhoods with less expensive housing and 75% of the city's population lives in neighborhoods with more expensive housing. If a neighborhood's house value percentile score is 90%, then the corresponding figures are 90% of the city's population lives in neighborhoods with cheaper average housing and 10% live in neighborhoods where average prices are more expensive. For each decade—1970, 1980, and 1990—we can standardize house prices at that time, so the figures reflect how the neighborhood stacked up against other neighborhoods in the same city in terms of house prices at that time. The higher-priced neighborhoods will have higher house value percentile scores.

Similarly, we can construct, for the beginning of each decade, weighted percentile crime rate scores for each crime. For the beginning of each decade, three years of crime data were averaged (1970–1972, 1980–1982, 1990–1992) before calculating percentiles weighted by neighborhood population. Again, as with the house price figures, the weighted crime percentiles indicate how the neighborhood stacked up against other neighborhoods in the city, at that time, on that crime rate. If you live in a neighborhood with a weighted robbery percentile score of 10, 10% of the city's population live in neighborhoods with lower robbery rates, and 90% of the city's population live in neighborhoods with higher robbery rates. The *higher*-crime neighborhoods will have *higher* percentile scores.

The logic of these percentile scores is inherently comparative. The focus is on how each neighborhood compares to other neighborhoods in the city. This comparative logic is inherent in a broader ecological perspective examining the roles played by different communities in the broader urban fabric (8).

Capturing Unexpected Change

Change across a decade has two portions: first, that amount predictable from the neighborhood's position at the beginning of the decade and affecting all neighborhoods during the period; and, second, that piece *not* predictable from the foregoing. I label the latter *unexpected change*.

Imagine, for example, that the average neighborhood racial composition increased from 45% African-American to 55% over the course of a decade. Imagine further—and this is an unrealistic assumption, necessary just to simplify this theoretical example—that the amount of the increase was the same in almost all neighborhoods, regardless of initial racial composition. Consequently, we would expect each neighborhood's racial composition to increase by about 10% African-American. This would reflect an expected change, given the overall city changes taking place during the period. Thus, if a neighborhood decreased its percentage African-American population by 20% or increased its percentage African-American population by 30%, these are changes that deviate

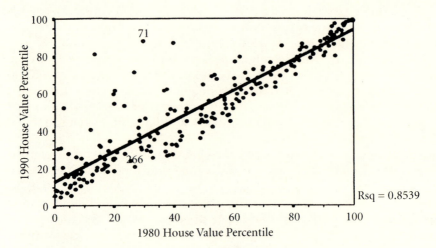

FIGURE 4.1   Predicting 1990 House Value Percentile Scores with 1980
Scores

from the expected. As a result of an unexpected change taking place in a
particular neighborhood, its relative position on the variable might
change. This shift in the neighborhood's relative position in the ordering
on this variable would represent unexpected change.

We can separate expected and unexpected portions of change using regression techniques. Returning to the question of house values, if we predict 1990 house price percentile scores with 1980 house price percentile
scores, using all neighborhoods in the city, we see the results shown in
Figure 4.1[2]

Two neighborhoods are identified on the chart: number 71 corresponds
to an East Baltimore neighborhood between the downtown and Patterson
Park that hosts a lively night scene and number 266 corresponds to a small,
predominantly African-American neighborhood close to the Edmondson
Village area. Each started with a 1980 house value percentile score of about
30. By the end of the decade, number 71's score was much higher than expected, as shown by its location high above the regression line. The vertical
distance between the observed 1990 score (about 90 on the Y axis) and the
corresponding expected score shown by the corresponding value on the
regression line (about 35 on the Y axis) is a residual. Its size and direction
captures the type and amount of unexpected change experienced by that
community in that time period on this variable.

By contrast, number 266's relative house value had slipped somewhat
more than expected, as shown by its position below the regression line.
The amount of unexpected change is much less for the westside neigh-

borhood than it is for the eastside neighborhood. Number 266 ended the 1980s having moved lower on house value, relative to the other neighborhoods, during the period.

Comparable unexpected change scores for other features of neighborhood change, such as homeownership, racial composition, and crime were constructed; for some indicators unexpected changes for a different decade, from 1970 to 1980, were viewed as well.

In examining neighborhood structural and crime changes, information from all of Baltimore's neighborhoods, excluding the downtown and public housing, is used. It is all the neighborhoods in the city that "set the stage" for the unexpected changes.[3] When considering assessed incivilities, most analyses using these unexpected change scores concentrate on sixty-six or thirty neighborhoods, for the most part widely separated from another throughout the city. But when looking at survey *and* physical assessment data with information from two points in time, unexpected change measures can be construed only for the blocks or neighborhoods supplying both types of data. Regardless of the data source, when referring to unexpected change, it is these residual scores that are referenced.

Since the 1920s, ecologists such as McKenzie have recognized the adverse impacts that unexpectedly rapid change may have on how a community functions (33). More recently, Bob Bursik has documented longitudinal links between unexpected community changes and shifting delinquency rates (8, 9). The focus on unexpected change via the residuals described above is grounded in this perspective.

Varying Temporal Perspectives

One temporal perspective looks at changes occurring simultaneously. For example, we might ask how did unexpected robbery changes from 1980–1982 to 1990–1992 link to unexpected changes in house values from 1980 to 1990? Such an approach does not allow one to clearly state that one change is causing the other, because both changes are taking place in the same time frame. But one can see if one change accompanies the other. I label this a *dynamic* perspective.

Potentially providing more causal insight is a perspective linking beginning-of-the-decade scores with unexpected changes taking place as the decade later unfolds. One might ask how the robbery percentile score for 1980–1982 linked with unexpected house value changes from 1980 to 1990. The assumption here is that conditions at the beginning of the period set the stage for and shaped what followed over the next ten years. I call this a *partially longitudinal perspective* because the predictor, although its measurement precedes the changes captured in the outcome, is static, looking at conditions at one point in time.

Finally, and also providing causal insight, one can link unexpected changes in one decade with unexpected changes in the following decade. For example, how did unexpected increases or decreases in robbery in neighborhoods between 1970 and 1980 influence unexpected changes in house prices in those neighborhoods in the following decade, between 1980 and 1990? Such a cross-decade framework assumes that unexpected changes have a reverberating importance, setting in motion processes that echo forward into the next decade. I label this a *fully longitudinal perspective* because it captures dynamics over a two-decade cycle.

Each of these perspectives conceptualizes linkages between predictors and outcomes in different ways and uses different indicators. The different perspectives may provide different answers.

Another Necessary, but Unexciting, Aside on Multilevel Models

In some of the analyses to follow, I have carried out multilevel models (6). These incorporate predictors at two different levels. For example, analyses predicting changes in graffiti have a streetblock-level outcome, graffiti in 1994; a streetblock-level predictor, graffiti in 1981; and neighborhood-level predictors from around 1980. These models are appropriate when the units from the lower level of analysis (called Level I) are nested in the higher level of analysis (called Level II). Analyses here examine streetblocks nested within neighborhoods; analyses examining perceived incivilities and reactions to crime (Chapter 6), consider individuals nested within neighborhoods. Multilevel models provide numerous advantages for these types of data situations, as compared to regression models with contextual predictors (4).

Advantages of multilevel models are several. First, multilevel models consider features of the data to generate estimated "true" scores at Level II. For example, multilevel models will generate for each neighborhood the best estimate of the likelihood that graffiti were observed there in 1994, after taking into account the data ranges within and between neighborhoods, the amount of similarity between data points in the same neighborhood, how many cases were supplied by each neighborhood, and where each neighborhood's mean is positioned relative to the mean for all the neighborhoods. Second, multilevel models partition the data, telling us how much of the differences in scores arise from estimated "true" differences between Level II units (e.g., neighborhoods). The contribution of neighborhood differences to item variance is described. Third, the models report whether those Level II differences in outcome scores are significant, that is, are they more than just sampling error? After Level II predictors have been entered, the models also report whether the remaining, or residual, Level II differences in the outcome represent just error or whether significant differences remain. Finally, multilevel models can accommodate analyses where relationships among predictors and outcomes are linear, as well as less restrictive analyses where linear relationships are not presumed. The latter assumptions are sometimes more appropriate with count data, skewed data, or data matching other distributions than the normal one.

Overview of Indicators, Outcomes, and Controls

I approach the question, "Where do the incivilities come from?" in different ways: with different types of indicators, with differing levels of analysis, and with different decades. Since the central concern is changes, where feasible analyses control for prior levels of the incivilities and focus on the remaining outcome variation, that is, the unexpected changes.

Assessment-based outcomes are three and at two levels. For each of sixty-six neighborhoods with streetblocks assessed in 1981, a general, neighborhood-level incivilities index, based mostly on physical features such as graffiti, litter, housing density, and vacant housing was constructed (51).[4] Volume of people on the street also was part of the index.[5]

Since 1981 was the initial assessment for these streetblocks, no directly comparable measure obtained earlier is available as a "control," which would permit focusing solely on changes in incivilities during the 1970s. Nevertheless, several of the indicators in our summary measure refer to housing conditions and abandonment. The percentage of housing units in each neighborhood that had been vacant for six months or more according to the 1970 census was used as a rough proxy measure for earlier physical incivilities. Although this percentage included a number of vacant units that were for sale or for rent, it probably included a sizable number of units that had been abandoned. The correlation between this 1970 proxy for housing deterioration and the 1981 incivilities measure is .435. Using OLS regression and resulting residuals, it was possible to control for 1970 housing deterioration and focus on the *un*predictable portion of the 1981 incivilities, that segment not predictable from the neighborhood's score on the 1970 deterioration indicator.[6] Because of multicollinearity problems, it was necessary to residualize the outcome at each step in the analysis. In other words, the analysis of change focuses on the residuals after predicting 1981 incivilities with 1970 neighborhood housing deterioration. After entering neighborhood structure and structural change, the outcome was again residualized to see how well the crime variables could predict that outcome. This first analysis used regression rather than multilevel models because all the variables are neighborhood level.

TABLE 4.1   Predicting Incivilities: Outcomes, Assessment Dates, and Controls for Prior Level

Outcome	Assessment Date	Control Variable for Prior Level	Period for Predictors
General incivilities index (66 neighborhoods)	1981	1970 % vacant units six months or more	Structure and crime: – 1970 – unexpected change, 1970–1980
Graffiti prevalence (90 blocks in 30 neighborhoods)	1994	Same variable, same block, 1981	Structure and crime: – 1980, – unexpected change, 1980–1990
Abandoned housing incidence (90 blocks in 30 neighborhoods)	1994	Same variable, same block, 1981	Structure and crime: – 1980, – unexpected change, 1980–1990
Perceived neighborhood problems (general index, social index, physical index) Individual level	1994	Same variable, same neighborhood, 1982	Structure and crime: – 1980, – unexpected change, 1980–1990 1994 individual characteristics

At the level of specific streetblocks, analyses examined two changes taking place between 1981 and 1994: the likelihood that both observers on the streetblock would agree graffiti were present (a prevalence measure) and the volume of vacant, abandoned housing (an incidence measure). Raters assessed these features on our ninety sampled blocks in 1994. Other raters had recorded the same block features on eighty-seven of those same blocks in 1981. Consequently, these streetblock analyses control completely for the earlier indicator level when examining change.

The last two outcomes examined are unexpected neighborhood-level changes in perceived social and physical neighborhood problems. Residents' survey responses in 1994 provide the basis for these outcomes, controlling for corresponding perceived problems reported by residents in 1982. In addition to looking at separate social and physical perceived problems indexes, analyses also consider all perceived problems together.

To get at the causes of changing incivilities, after removing the influence of earlier incivilities, neighborhood structure and crime are used as predictors. For stability, the representing variable is the percentage of houses that are owner occupied. For race, it was the percentage of the population that is African-American. Since in Baltimore neighborhoods'

TABLE 4.2   Impacts of Prior Neighborhood Structure and Structural Change on 1970–1981 Changes in Assessed, Neighborhood-Level Incivilities

Predictor	Beta
1970 House value (percentile score)	−.369
Unexpected change, 1970–1980, house value percentile	−.289
1970 % African-American	.249
Unexpected change, 1970–1980, % owner occupied	−.215
Unexpected change, 1970–1980, % African-American	−.197
1970 % owner occupied	−.121 (ns)

NOTE: n=66 neighborhoods.

race and youth composition intertwine, some models include age variables as well. For status, most analyses use percentile house rank based on house values (12). In a few analyses, percentage of households below the poverty line provides stronger results and is thus occasionally employed rather than the house value percentile. For crime, weighted percentile scores either for robbery or assault are used, choosing the one that works best with the outcome in question.

Predictors are separated into two different portions: the scores from a decade earlier and unexpected changes in the predictor between that earlier time and the time the outcome was assessed. Since the latter unexpected changes are residuals, as shown in the example (Figure 4.1), they are orthogonal to the earlier level for the corresponding variable. This separation distinguishes between conditions *causing* later changes in incivilities (the partially longitudinal perspective explained above) and changes in conditions *accompanying* shifts in incivilities (the dynamic perspective explained above). Table 4.1 summarizes the outcomes, prior controls, and predictors.

Incivilities Observed

Changes in Neighborhood Deterioration, 1970–1981

Impacts of Neighborhood Fabric and Changes in the Fabric[7].   The results from an OLS regression model examining 1981 incivilities in sixty-six neighborhoods, after controlling for 1970 vacant housing levels, appear in Table 4.2. The table shows standardized regression coefficients, or betas. These capture the independent (partial) impact of each predictor on the outcome. All the impacts, save the last, are statistically significant, suggesting the connections are not due to chance partial associations. Neighborhood structure, as of 1970, and changes in neighborhood structure from 1970 to 1980 link to incivilities shifts. These six indicators explained a significant 50% of the changes in incivilities.[8] Predictors are listed in order of their decreasing impact on incivility change.[9]

Earlier neighborhood status caused, and contemporaneous changes in status accompanied, incivility shifts. Neighborhoods with higher-priced housing initially or where relative house prices were increasing unexpectedly were locations where incivilities were least likely to increase during the 1970s. These two powerful connections with status underscore both a static and a dynamic connection between neighborhood exchange value and shifting incivilities.

More disturbing is the substantial lagged impact, representing the third largest standardized impact, of 1970 racial composition on increasing deterioration. Controlling for class and stability, neighborhoods where African-American populations predominated in 1970 were at risk of increasing deterioration in the coming decade.

How do we interpret this connection? In the case of Baltimore, McDougall argues, when looking at neighborhoods like Harlem Park, Upton, and Park Heights, that differential service delivery and code enforcement has adversely affected these locations for several decades (see also, 49). Results here may well reflect such discriminatory practices.

Nevertheless, as discussed above, other race-based processes separate from discrimination per se may be relevant as well. How do these other arguments fare?

The expansion of Crutchfield's argument about labor stratification receives some empirical support. Although the expansion offered addressed mostly social incivilities, it also applies to physical deterioration. Shifts from primary to secondary labor market opportunities result in owners having fewer funds to maintain dwellings as well as lower rents, leading to less incentive for landlord upkeep. The drop in manufacturing (blue-collar) employment expected by this argument does appear. Looking at predominantly (over 95%) African-American neighborhoods in 1970, several witnessed substantial drops over the 1970s.[10] These are the some of the same neighborhoods where incivilities increased most dramatically over the decade.

Receiving less support as an interpretation is Wilson's extreme disadvantage argument. The n of neighborhoods with over 40% unemployment in 1970 was just too low.

Massey's focus on the spatial compactness of segregated African-American neighborhoods may be more relevant. The predominantly African-American neighborhoods on the near eastside or near westside are denser neighborhoods, but this is in part because of the time when they were constructed (40). Thus the compactness confounds with the age of the housing stock. It could be that deterioration accelerated in these locations not because of the spatially compact nature of the settlement and the arrangement of adjoining predominantly African-American neighborhoods, but rather because of the more advanced age of the housing.

At the same time, racial change has impacts opposite to those of earlier racial composition. If, during the 1970s, a neighborhood was in the process of *becoming* more African-American, as several were, there was *less* chance of incivilities increasing. Neighborhoods increasing unexpectedly on the proportion African-American also were *less* likely to exhibit increasing deterioration, controlling for the other predictors. The neighborhoods in question were usually located further out from the city center than the neighborhoods already predominantly African-American by 1970. Most of them were in the process of changing from slightly African-American to more integrated during the period (52).

The connection fits with some of the work on neighborhood racial change (16, 41). When a neighborhood begins to become African-American, the leading edge of integration is carried by middle-class, in-migrating households, who often "bid up" prices in the process. Neighborhoods in the early stages of racial integration may have been slightly better looked after, or at least less deteriorated, as part of the process.

Although 1970 stability failed to influence changes in deterioration, in part because homeownership overlapped so strongly with relative house values, changes in homeownership linked to changes in deterioration. As expected by ecological theory, neighborhoods with declining homeownership saw increasing deterioration. As stability wanes, so too does upkeep.

In sum, neighborhood fabric and changes in that fabric explain about half the changes in incivilities at the neighborhood level. The findings support the structural perspective introduced earlier, highlighting most strongly the causal impacts of status and race on later changes in incivilities. In contrast to expectations, initial stability did not help buffer neighborhoods from increasing incivilities. Accompanying deterioration shifts are the expected structural changes (stability, status) and one unexpected one (race).

Impacts of Crime and Changes in Crime. Looking at the impacts of crime percentile scores and unexpected changes in crime percentiles showed that earlier crime levels had no lagged impact on later deterioration changes.[11] But unexpected increases in robbery accompanied unexpected increases in deterioration, explaining a modest amount of additional variance in the outcome.[12] Increasing deterioration is thus accompanied by shifts toward a relatively more dangerous, crime-ridden street environment. As the incivilities thesis of Wilson and Kelling expects, crime and grime spiral upward together; but it is not clear which causes which, and the connection, albeit significant, is not robust.[13]

Results so far have suggested the incivility fluctuations are caused primarily by earlier status and racial composition. Does a different pattern emerge when considering specific incivilities rather than an index and examining changes in a different decade, the 1980s? We turn now to changes in assessed graffiti and abandoned housing during the 1980s on streetblocks in the 1994 sample of thirty neighborhoods. The upcoming analyses not only switch decades, levels of analysis, and outcomes, they also allow more precise change estimates because the same outcome variable is available at both points in time. These analyses use multilevel models.

Streetblock Changes in Graffiti and Housing Abandonment, 1981–1994[14]

The changes of interest are graffiti and boarded-up houses. Overall changes in these measures were noted in Chapter 2. The analysis here examines the reasons behind the differing rates of change in different sites. Clearly, these two attributes represent only a small fraction of physical incivilities of interest. Nonetheless, they are features figuring prominently in the incivilities literature and widely tapped when residents are queried about perceived neighborhood problems.

Averaging across the estimated true scores for each streetblock in each neighborhood yields the probability that both observers agreed graffiti were present on a typical streetblock in each neighborhood. In 1981, these neighborhood prevalence rates ranged from 7.7% to 19.6% (median = 9.5%). In 1994, they ranged from 5.7% to 79.8% (median = 13.8%).[15]

Changes in Graffiti.   With a few exceptions, neighborhoods where graffiti were unlikely to be observed in both 1981 and 1994 were located furthest out from the city center. Several of the low-graffiti locales bordered Baltimore or Anne Arundel County. Perhaps their outer-city location helped buffer them from the changes leading to increased graffiti in other places. Up until recently, they had a reputation as fairly stable places. In these locations, the prevalence of graffiti remained basically unchanged; at both points in time the probability of observing graffiti was around 10%. For the most part, outer-city neighborhoods were more likely to have a predominantly white population in 1980. So 1980 neighborhood racial composition may serve as a predictor of increasing graffiti, given its link with distance from the city center.

Another neighborhood, not bordering one of the adjoining suburban counties but near the former Memorial Stadium site, also remained consistently low on graffiti. This neighborhood was integrated, but predominantly white, in 1980 and also had relatively high homeownership at the time. Also, according to one former local leader, it is a neighborhood with an organization that has worked extremely hard on maintaining neighborhood quality. From the early 1970s up through the early 1990s, robbery there has remained relatively low.

A more heterogeneous batch of neighborhoods showed relatively modest increases in the prevalence of graffiti: middle-class to well-off, predominantly white neighborhoods along or near the York Road corridor in the northern section of the city, as well as a stable white neighborhood in the northeast corner, experienced only modest increases. Several in the outer northwest sector, areas that changed from heavily Jewish to predominantly African-American in the 1960s and 1970s, also increased just slightly on the presence of graffiti. Homeownership has been, and remains, relatively high in this latter group of neighborhoods. In short, an outer-city location, or a "mid"-city location combined with significant stability or middle-class presence, appeared to buffer these neighborhoods from increasing graffiti.

Where did graffiti's presence increase noticeably? It jumped considerably in all of the East Baltimore neighborhoods: from 8% to 30% in one, from about 14% to about 29% in two others, and from 15% to 76% in another. Steve Pardue and I noted local efforts to combat graffiti while driving around this last location, near Patterson Park. In this neighborhood, a few houses south of a main east-west artery, we stopped to admire a newly painted row house wall fronting an alley. The shiny gray was marred by a spray-painted green "tag." On several corners, we saw portions of walls that had been repainted in attempts to cover graffiti.

Ecologically, each of these eastern neighborhoods is quite different. But in all cases, the neighborhood is neither predominantly renters nor predominantly homeowners, but mixed in tenure. In addition, in all these neighborhoods Steve Pardue had some difficulty contacting long-term leaders. Furthermore, most of these eastside neighborhoods were close to problem areas or hosted a lot of nonresidential land uses. One, for example, contains a large maintenance area for city buses. A few blocks west, large-scale drug activity had been targeted in a sweep early in 1994. Another neighborhood is surrounded by industrial land uses and also contains a subsidized housing complex. Two other neighborhoods are close to high-poverty locations. In short, these eastside neighborhoods have several factors working against them: moderate stability at best, lack of uniform residential fabric and accompanying small streets that would facilitate resident oversight of street activity, and proximity to high-poverty locations. Whether these situational factors "cause," or just covary with, leadership and organizational difficulties that also appeared to plague several of these neighborhoods is not clear.

Away from the eastern sector of the city, three different neighborhoods, two on the westside, and one along the York Road corridor, also show marked but not extreme growth in prevalence of graffiti, increasing from about 10% to about 30%. Although in different sections of the city, all were lower or lower middle class socioeconomically, and all had been predominantly, if not almost exclusively, African-American for at least a decade.

Experiencing more sizable increases than the above group of neighborhoods were three neighborhoods that have gentrified or flirted with the process. Not only have these three experienced some gentrification in the recent past, but they also border significantly higher crime, more problem-ridden neighborhoods. The increases in the prevalence of graffiti in these locations may be linked with degentrification or intensifying problems nearby.

Finally, where do we see the most dramatic increases? The largest increases in prevalence show up in two of our highest-crime, most disadvantaged neighborhoods: Both had 1994 prevalence rates of over 75%. In addition, local organizations in both these locales do not have as high a profile as do the leaders and organizations in some other neighborhoods. Both these sites include or are proximate to large-scale, open-air drug markets.

A third neighborhood dramatically increasing on graffiti is a center city neighborhood, with significant numbers of shops and large thoroughfares, not too far from downtown. Graffiti prevalence here went from about 17% to about 80%.

As in the earlier example with 1980 and 1990 house prices, 1994 graffiti prevalence can be separated into two portions: that portion predictable from earlier 1981 levels (expected change) and that portion not predictable from 1981 levels (unexpected change).

How did the neighborhoods sort out on unexpected graffiti change? The ordering is somewhat different from that based simply on the 1994 observed score, particularly at the "high" end. The most dramatic, unexpected upsurges in graffiti appeared in three near-westside neighborhoods that are or are near extremely high crime neighborhoods: In all these neighborhoods the probability of observing graffiti on a typical streetblock in 1994 was about 20% higher than it "should" be. If we look at the reverse end, neighborhoods where observed graffiti were slightly less frequent than expected, we focus on three predominantly white outer-city neighborhoods abutting Anne Arundel or Baltimore Counties.

Summary Thoughts on the Breakdown by Neighborhoods   Dramatic changes in the prevalence of graffiti emerge from a complex mix of forces. For some of these, corresponding quantitative indicators are available. But the neighborhood-by-neighborhood analysis suggests potentially complex interactions of local factors difficult to model with a limited number of cases. In addition to crime and neighborhood structure, a county boundary, proximity to extremely high crime neighborhoods or large open-air drug markets, land use mix within the neighborhood, strength of neighborhood identity, and qualities of local leadership and organizations all appear potentially relevant. Graffiti stayed low in some stable neighborhoods. Graffiti also stayed relatively low in some neighborhoods experiencing sizable racial change. This case-by-case analysis suggests that even though we may be able to capture some of the relevant factors in our models, we may be missing additional, context-specific components of these changes.

Graffiti: Between Versus Within Neighborhoods.   At both points in time, multilevel models reveal that graffiti vary more across neighborhoods than across streetblocks within neighborhoods. In 1981, about 84% of the variance arose from differences between neighborhoods and 16% from pooled differences between streetblocks in the same neighborhood; in 1994 about 94% of the variation arose from neighborhood differences. Graffiti prevalence in 1981 explains about a third of the between-neighborhood differences in graffiti prevalence in 1994. After controlling for the 1981 levels, 64% of the 1994 neighborhood variation remains unexplained. This unexplained variation represents unexpected changes.

Explaining the Unexpected Changes.   Indicators for 1980 neighborhood structure, unexpected changes in neighborhood structure from 1980 to 1990, and 1980 crime levels were used to predict graffiti changes.[16] How well do these predictors work? The total model explains about 63% of the between-neighborhood variation in graffiti, leaving about 36% unexplained. The variation left represents a nonsignificant amount of between-neighborhood differences. In other words, after these predictors are entered, only "chance" differences are left between neighborhoods.

Neighborhood structure has impacts that unfold over time, setting the stage for changes in graffiti over the following decade. Those neighborhoods with higher initial status (gamma = $-.074$; $t = -5.8$; $p < .001$), more homeownership (gamma = $-.035$; $t = -2.28$; $p < .05$), and a higher proportion of African Americans (gamma = $-.048$; $t = -3.77$; $p < .01$) were all *less* likely to experience graffiti upsurges. The status and stability results fit with structurally oriented ecological theory. The race results do not. The race coefficient is probably reflecting the fact that in neighborhoods almost exclusively African-American in 1981, graffiti prevalence was already high, in relative terms, and could not increase as markedly there as it could in neighborhoods with lower initial scores.

The results for robbery (gamma = .079; t=4.17; p < .001) suggest that crime too has effects materializing over time. Controlling for structure, neighborhoods with higher relative robbery scores in 1980–1982 were more likely to later experience more graffiti. Here, in contrast to the sixty-six neighborhoods results using the general incivilities index, crime does lead to later grime.[17]

Incivilities theory predicts that as a neighborhood declines, incivilities should increase. Given that thinking, neighborhoods experiencing unexpected drops in relative house prices should also have witnessed increasing graffiti. *The results here do not support that expectation.* House price changes do not covary with graffiti changes.

In sum, crime and neighborhood structure help predict later increases in graffiti prevalence. Stability, status, and racial composition all have significant impacts, although the race impacts are opposite what would be expected given a structural perspective. Crime plays a role as well, making future deterioration more likely. As seen in the results with changes over the 1970s for the general incivilities index, the strongest predictor is prior neighborhood status.

Changes in Vacant Housing.   The second streetblock-level change in incivilities examined was vacant, boarded-up housing.[18] In 1981, a vacant, boarded-up house was noted by raters on about every third block. On these same blocks, in 1994, a vacant, abandoned unit was seen on about every other block.

In 1981, only one neighborhood, a westside, predominantly African-American neighborhood near Pennsylvania Avenue, had a true score estimate above one vacant house per streetblock. In 1994, slightly less than three vacant houses per streetblock were counted in that neighborhood, based on sampled streetblocks. For all the other neighborhoods, the 1994 rates ranged from a vacant house on three out of every four blocks to a vacant house on one out of every ten blocks.

The 1981 sorting on vacant units shows some similarities to the sorting on 1981 graffiti. The lowest rates appear in predominantly outer-city neighborhoods, touching the city boundary. The highest incidence rates appear in near-westside neighborhoods or near-eastside neighborhoods. But there is far less similarity between graffiti and vacant housing when we look at the change rather than static measures.

Changes in Incidence Rate.   Sorting the neighborhoods on their 1994 vacancy incidence rate, most neighborhoods have about the same place as in the 1981 ordering. There are, however, a few notable exceptions. The two southwest-most neighborhoods, Weldon Pond and Shady Park, each bordering Anne Arundel County, moved from ranks of twenty-sixth and twenty-fifth, respectively, to ranks of eighth and sixth. Odds of finding a vacant, boarded-up house on blocks in these neighborhoods went from one for every eight streetblocks to almost a vacancy per streetblock in Shady Park and a vacancy every third streetblock for Weldon Pond. Both these neighborhoods experienced sizable racial and status change during the intervening period.

Three other neighborhoods changing markedly in their relationship to the other neighborhoods are Midtown, East Parkview, and Elmton. In these neighborhoods, the estimated "true" rate of abandoned units appears to have *de*creased markedly.

For Midtown, the 1980s brought several changes. The proportion of males in the population increased noticeably. The new Meyerhoff Symphony Hall opened nearby. Street cleanup improved due to a privately funded effort. In short, this is a neighborhood that despite its high crime rate has built a niche supporting younger, alternative lifestyles, some professional offices, and major amenities; further, it has garnered a city hall commitment to upkeep. Local building managers play key roles in the maintenance of the location as well, as evidenced in our opening vignette.

East Parkview as well became increasingly attractive to gays during the 1980s. According to the district planner interviewed, East Parkview has become known "up and down the East Coast" as a good place for gays to buy houses. Relative house values increased dramatically in the neighborhood between 1980 and 1990, going from about the thirtieth percentile to about the seventieth percentile, underscoring the increasing desirability of the locale. With the increasing attractiveness of the housing comes fewer abandoned units. At the same time, graffiti also *in*creased markedly in the locale during the 1980s. So we have a locale where one incivilities change indicator dropped dramatically—vacant units—even as another indicator spiraled upward. Figure 4.2 shows the two sides of changes in East Parkview: James Dean's image looks out from one living room window, while a few blocks away waning ethnic identities in the neighborhood leave the Polish Veterans Association of America Post 112 with graffiti and broken windows.

Elmton's case is less easily understood. The neighborhood has strong leadership, but a lot of the small commercial centers in the neighborhood seem to host "fringe" businesses such as tanning salons and beeper sales. Yet there are signs of some city hall commitment here too. We spoke with a carpenter making modifications to a house soon to open as one of two precinct substations, for example. But again, the immediate causes of the improvement are not readily apparent.

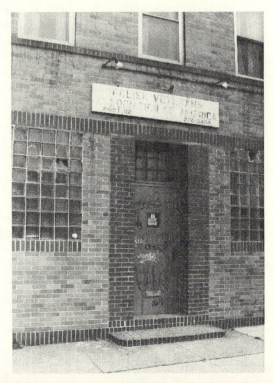

FIGURE 4.2   Two Faces of a Changing East Baltimore Neighborhood:
James Dean and the Polish Veterans Association. Photos by author.

One other point about the changes in the abandonment rate should not be overlooked. The incidence rates in the highest-scoring neighborhoods have gone up, and the rates in the lowest-scoring neighborhoods have gone down. In other words, the between-neighborhood differences are more extreme in 1994 than they were in 1981.[19] This change in the range is partially masked when we look at the citywide averages. If you were to ask in 1981, "Citywide, what are my chances of finding an abandoned unit in a neighborhood in the city?" the answer is one vacant unit on about every third streetblock.[20] In 1994, based on the same streetblocks and extrapolating to all neighborhoods, your citywide chances of finding abandonment are a little above one unit on every other streetblock.[21] This increase in the overall, citywide incidence rate of abandonment, however, is not significant.[22] In other words, it is *not* the case that generally and citywide the abandonment picture is worse than it was in the early 1980s. Yes, there are several neighborhoods, especially those closer to the city center, where abandonment rates have increased noticeably. But there are also some locales where it appears to have decreased somewhat, including at least one center city neighborhood. In many neighborhoods, it has remained relatively constant. In other words, citywide, worsening conditions appear in several locations, but this worsening takes place in a context of stable or even very slightly improving conditions in other locations. Such a pattern agrees well with the results cited in Chapter 2, showing no significant increases in the perceptions of incivilities. It also disagrees, however, with the media coverage of the abandoned housing problem in the 1990s, also described in Chapter 2.

Certainly the most troubling change is this intensification of the problem in several historically African-American, centrally located neighborhoods. Less noticeable, but also causing concern, is the blooming of abandonment on the city's far southern edge (Weldon Pond, Shady Park). These latter two neighborhoods also illustrate, as did East Parkview, discrepant orderings on different incivilities indicators. But here the discrepancy also arises between static indicators. So in ordering communities on incivilities, whether at one point in time or over time, the indicator chosen significantly influences the ordering. At a broader conceptual level, these incongruities fail to lay to rest the important questions about the construct validity of incivilities introduced in Chapter 3. Static and changing incivilities indicators are not tied closely together, suggesting they are *not* driven by an underlying and broader disorder dynamic.

Unexpected Change. After using the 1981 abandonment rate to predict the 1994 abandonment rate on each block, the resulting residuals represent neighborhood-level unexpected change. Looking at the overall list, in eight of the thirty neighborhoods 1994 abandonment rates were higher

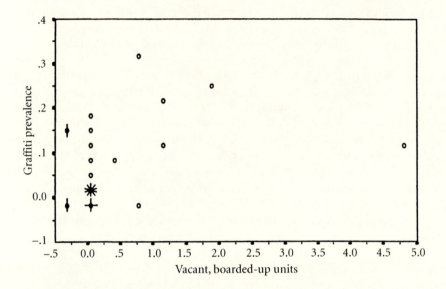

FIGURE 4.3   1981–1994 Unexpected Changes in Graffiti Prevalence and
Incidence of Abandoned Units per Streetblock

than they "should" have been given the 1981 rates and subsequent overall shifts; in twenty-one of the neighborhoods they were lower than they
should have been given the 1981 figures. But the unexpected increases in
several neighborhoods are quite sizable, whereas the unexpected decreases are much more modest.

As expected, the unexpected increases were concentrated in our near-
eastside and near-westside, long-term predominantly African-American
neighborhoods: Olney, West Pine Civic, Sutton-Kent, and Warren. The
first three on this list had at least one more abandoned unit per streetblock than expected; Olney had *four* more per streetblock than expected.
Our two racially changing, far southern neighborhoods, Weldon Pond
and Shady Park, also show more abandonment than expected, as does
Garfield above Patterson Park in East Baltimore.

A racially mixed, gentrifying neighborhood, Jackson, had a much
higher than expected score—one to two abandoned units per streetblock
more than expected—underscoring our conversation with the local
leader there. He emphasized local organization efforts to stabilize housing, cited abandonment as a key neighborhood problem, and lamented
the city's unwillingness to promptly assist on these matters.

Two Unexpected Changes.   Do unexpected neighborhood changes on graffiti agree or disagree with unexpected changes on abandonment? In East

Parkview, as noted above, the two change indicators were moving in opposite directions. What happens for all the neighborhoods? The rank-order correlation between these two change indicators is sizable and significant (.47, $p < .01$; gamma, an alternate ordinal indicator, is .36). Figure 4.3 plots the two sets of scores.

Several neighborhoods are "spread out" on unexpected changes in graffiti, but have roughly the same vacancy score. For these neighborhoods, unexpected graffiti shifts appear to be a more sensitive indicator of increasing incivilities than do the unexpected abandonment shifts.

A smaller group of five neighborhoods shows a roughly monotonic relationship between unexpectedly increasing vacancies and unexpectedly increasing graffiti. In these neighborhoods, both indicators appear about equally sensitive to increasing physical disorder. And one neighborhood has a moderately high unexpected change score on graffiti, combined with an extremely high score on unexpected abandonment change.

In short, considerable and significant overlap exists between the two indicators of unexpected changes in incivilities. But the overlap is not sufficient to convince us that each refers to the same underlying process. Different indicators may be capturing different pathways of decline and disorder or different stages in one process. At the least, questions about the construct validity of incivilities are not safely laid to rest.

Predicting Unexpected Changes in Vacancy. Unexpected changes in incidence of vacant housing were predicted with indicators of 1980 structure; unexpected change in neighborhood structure from 1980 to 1990; and a 1980 crime measure, aggravated assault.[23] After entering these predictors, the remaining between-neighborhood variance on the outcome was not significantly different from zero.[24]

Two structural features strongly predicted later unexpected changes in abandonment rates: poverty in 1980 ($t = 3.5$, $p < .01$) and homeownership in 1980 ($t = 3.7$, $p < .001$). Neighborhoods where more lived below poverty were most likely to see abandonment increasing later. Each additional 10% of the population living below the poverty line in 1980 resulted in 1.4 additional, unanticipated, abandoned houses appearing on a random block in that neighborhood in the next decade. Neighborhoods *already* extremely disadvantaged in 1980, including several near-westside and one near-eastside, predominantly African-American locations, saw their housing problems intensify much more than expected in the following decade. In the 1990s, problems with vacant housing and controversial city-led efforts to restore or clear vacant housing have received attention in several of these same neighborhoods (see Chapter 2). The results here dramatically underscore arguments made (54) about poverty's disintegrative impacts on communities, starkly illustrating how poverty's damaging effects reverberate forward in time.

Somewhat surprisingly, neighborhoods where homeownership was *higher* in 1980 were more likely to see their housing problems worsen. This result was unexpected given our theoretical perspective, but understandable given our sample. Neighborhoods in the sample where the unexpected increases were sizable, and that were predominantly white in 1980, had fairly high homeownership rates in 1980 (e.g., 80%; 65%; 74%). These homeowner rates were higher than the rates (e.g., 50%; 48%) in neighborhoods that did not increase as much on vacancies. In short, we have some neighborhoods, stable in 1980, located close to racially changing locales, or themselves experiencing racial change over the next dozen years, with unexpectedly worsening housing problems. Although some argue in different ways that high stability, reflected in high homeownership rates, is a sine qua non for preventing the emergence of incivilities, it may not be enough. In short, it may be a necessary, but not sufficient, condition, depending on local events or events in nearby neighborhoods.

In addition, the impacts of one dimension of neighborhood structure, such as stability, are linked with how the neighborhood scores on other dimensions, and it is the profile across these dimensions that is important for changing incivilities. Different neighborhood features can support or work against one another. One neighborhood in the sample, Lloyd, experienced significant racial change in the 1980s, but in the context of stable or slightly increasing class status. The locale saw no significant increase in graffiti. Changing racial composition does not necessarily foretell future neighborhood problems, and high stability does not guarantee a problem-free neighborhood future. A broader view of neighborhood composition appears warranted.

Results also revealed two marginally significant impacts. Increasing abandonment was somewhat more likely in neighborhoods where poverty increased unexpectedly during the decade ($t = 1.77$; $p < .10$). So not only does disadvantage spur later deterioration, it also intensifies as that deterioration worsens. Also, increasing abandonment was somewhat more likely in neighborhoods where assault rates were higher in 1980 ($t = 1.91$; $p < .10$). So, again, the suggestion is that crime leads to later grime.

Summary Comments on Changes in Graffiti and Abandoned Housing. The last two series of analyses focus on unexpected changes in on-site features of our study blocks and suggest some general points about changes in observed physical incivilities. As anticipated by the structural, conflict-based perspective articulated by Logan and Molotch and Gottdiener, as well as others, initial neighborhood status shows the strongest and most consistent influence on later changes. Neighborhoods doing poorly, as reflected in lower house prices or higher poverty rates, were more likely to crumble further in the following decade.

The other two structural dimensions proved less consistently relevant. Initial stability helped prevent later graffiti increases, but appeared to facilitate later increases in abandoned units. The latter result appeared linked to some sample idiosyncrasies. Racial composition had an independent impact on graffiti changes opposite to what was expected by the conflict theorists and had no independent impact on later abandonment changes.

Crime appears to facilitate the later emergence of grime. For both outcomes, initial crime levels slightly boosted later deterioration increases.

Intercorrelations across incivilities indicators have raised rather than settled questions about the construct validity of incivilities. Although for both the static and change scenarios, we see moderate, positive correlations appear between graffiti and worn-out housing, several markedly discordant neighborhoods also appear. In one locale, graffiti surged markedly even as the relative housing abandonment rate dropped precipitously. Such divergent changes, across time, in assessed physical incivilities changes have been noticed in other locations, such as Spokane, Washington (17). Researchers there tracked changes in incivilities over a year and found no consistent trend across the different indicators. Each rather was driven by more specific processes.

Three possible explanations may account for the scattered pattern of incivilities changes observed: (1) Changing incivilities may just be more loosely coupled with one another than anticipated. The connections may be sloppy between the underlying decline process and the various observable consequences. (2) Alternatively, increasing disorder in a locale, if it is the broader dynamic driving incivilities shifts, may take place in distinct or at least distinguishable stages; the observable consequences—various assessed incivilities—may "kick in" at different stages. The plot of changes in graffiti against abandonment showed numerous neighborhoods bunched together on abandonment shifts, but spread out on graffiti shifts. Are these neighborhoods at an earlier stage of increasing incivilities than those where both abandonment and graffiti expanded during the 1980s? (3) Finally, increasing incivilities, like neighborhood decline (46), may not be one process, but several. The type of increasing incivilities experienced may depend on historical factors, geographic position in the city, or something else. Neighborhoods may score differently on various incivilities shifts because they are following different pathways toward increasing disorder.

The first and third explanations offered above suggest the disorder construct is far less helpful than researchers and policy analysts had anticipated. Naturally, this raises the question, should the construct be jettisoned altogether? The second explanation noted above intimates the disorder construct may still prove useful, but that it is more time-dependent than had been envisioned.

In the next section, analyses examine residents' changing perceptions of incivilities. Examining the origins of these reports may help clarify which of the above scenarios most appropriately apply.

Incivilities As Perceived by Residents

Numerous investigations into incivilities and their consequences have relied on residents' reports of local conditions (e.g., 27, 36, 44). Studies find both perceived and assessed incivilities contribute to outcomes such as fear of crime (3, 13). Other studies clarified who perceives more neighborhood problems, or the kinds of locations where residents, on average, label their environs as more problem-ridden—poorer, less stable, less predominantly white neighborhoods, for example (e.g., 45). But researchers have yet to examine why, over a long period of time, neighborhoods become viewed as more or less problem-plagued by their residents. That is the focus here.

The perceived incivilities sections in the 1982 and 1994 surveys ask about perceived problems *in the neighborhood*. Those items were introduced in Chapter 2. These analyses will use multilevel models, and the outcome will be perceived problems reported by individual residents in 1994.[25] By controlling for problems perceived in those same neighborhoods in 1982—albeit by different residents—the between-neighborhoods portion of the outcome is transformed into unexpected changes from 1982 to 1994.

What Goes with What?

Studies typically total or average incivilities, focusing on the resulting general index. This is warranted since answers about the severity of different problems usually "hang together" quite well. The same pattern appeared for the 1994 respondents.[26] In addition to predicting such a general index, analyses also predicted two broad types. As described in Chapter 1, social incivilities refer to "people problems," whereas physical incivilities refer to "place problems." Obviously all physical problems are caused by people. Nonetheless, these two foci are different. Separate indexes were constructed for physical and social problems.[27] We can first look at all the problems together, then at the social and physical problems separately, to see if the predictors are different. Separating out the physical and social problems anticipates Chapters 5 and 6, where analyses examine impacts of each type. By looking at physical and social perceived problems separately, we may be able to make more focused policy recommendations and gain added theoretical insight.

Considering all the incivilities together, about one third of the 1994 variation arose from differences between neighborhoods and about two thirds from differences between neighbors. Focusing just on social incivilities, the neighborhood component is a little higher, over 40%. And examining just physical incivilities, a little less than 30% arises from differences between neighborhoods. In all cases, the ecological component is highly significant, suggesting there are marked differences between neighborhoods and not just sampling errors.

Residents' perceptions of problems in their neighborhood in 1994 prove roughly similar to the perceptions of those interviewed in 1982. In all cases, 1982 levels explained well over half of the 1994 between-neighborhood differences and about one fifth to one fourth of the total variation in 1994. The remaining unexpected changes in incivilities across neighborhoods are significant and sizable.[28] Stated differently, between the two surveys, neighborhood views about disorder changed dramatically.

Chapter 2 noted the divergence between assessed and perceived indicators of incivility changes. Particular neighborhoods demonstrate well this divergence. Elmton, along the southern tier of the city, was the neighborhood increasing most strongly on perceived physical problems. But based on on-site assessments, this neighborhood, of the thirty, actually improved the most on both graffiti and vacant housing, generating the lowest residual ranks on both these change measures. Jackson, a gentrifying locale on the westside of town, presented a reverse picture. Residents in 1982 rated their neighborhood as having severe physical and social problems. In 1994, they rated the problems as slightly less severe, leading to an unexpected lessening of perceived problems, that is, a low residual, or unexpected change, score. The neighborhood ranked twenty-seventh on perceived physical change and twenty-ninth on perceived social change. But when we compare on-block conditions in 1994 and 1982 suggest matters have worsened considerably: The neighborhood ranked second on unexpected increases in both vacancies and graffiti. Discrepancies between assessed and perceived change indicators can be found toward the "middle of the pack" as well. West Pine Civic, for example, ranked ninth on perceived change in physical problems but scored noticeably higher, with two third places, for change based on on-site assessments. In other words, for this neighborhood, assessments suggested conditions had deteriorated more significantly than perceptions indicated.

These discrepancies in some instances appear related to recent features of neighborhood history. In the case of Elmwood, the local leader had enlisted local "thugs" (the leader's term) to help keep out dealers and outsiders who did not belong. Residents here did not perceive physical problems worsening, even though on-site assessment suggested a modest increase in deterioration. Elmton's discrepancy, noted above, may have arisen in part from a murder around the time of the 1994 survey and continuing tensions between residents (mostly white) and residents of a nearby public housing community (mostly African-American).

These case histories help better specify the possibility, noted above, that some incivilities indicators may be more labile than others. It appears that perceived indicators may respond better to recent changes than do assessed indicators such as vacancies and graffiti. But another potential explanation deserving attention is the problem of neighborhood exodus. Since the 1982 survey, residents most concerned about local problems may have left, leaving behind less concerned residents. Thus residents interviewed in 1994 may be different from those interviewed in 1982 in ways that depend on 1982 problem perceptions and allied features of neighborhood structure. This differential exodus explanation, however, does not predict the pattern of divergences seen here. The exodus pattern should result in neighborhoods where changes in assessed incivilities outstripped changes in perceived incivilities. *But the pattern of shifts observed is not so simple.* We see some instances where observed increases in deterioration appear to outstrip increasing concern (e.g., Jackson). But we see numerous other instances where the increasing concern seems to outstrip the increasing problems (e.g., Elmton). And which pattern appears is *not* linked to stability in 1980 or 1990. In addition, the differential exodus thesis overlooks divergences within perceptions between shifts in social versus physical incivilities. These crop up in numerous neighborhoods as well. In short, it seems quite unlikely, given the shifts seen here, that the divergences between perceived versus assessed unexpected changes in incivilities emerge simply or mainly from differential exodus patterns.

In addition to cases of divergent changes, several neighborhoods demonstrate convergent patterns of changes, where both perceived and assessed change indicators link tightly together. In these locales, problem increases do indeed seem severe. Neighborhoods worsening most rapidly on both assessed and perceived indicators include several closer to the city center, with lower income and more predominantly African-American populations. These neighborhoods also have, or are near, serious, open-air drug market problems. Furthermore, these neighborhoods are located in the city sectors where, during the 1970s, problems with housing abandonment increased more substantially than they did elsewhere in the city (53). In other words, the locations where we see consistently and markedly worsening incivilities in the 1980s across most indicators appear to be continuing trends toward faster deterioration that appeared in the 1970s.

One final note on divergences between perceived and assessed incivilities shifts. The divergence observed here also appeared in the Spokane, Washington, research project mentioned above. Researchers assessing conditions at the study site documented increasing physical incivilities, such as graffiti, over a one-year time span, even as residents in the project reported perceiving less physical deterioration in the community (17). The divergence seen here between various changing incivility indicators does not appear to be specific to Baltimore.

Predicting Unexpected Changes in Perceived Problems

In this section, hierarchical linear models and hierarchical generalized linear models predict changes in total incivilities. More specific changes in perceived social and perceived physical incivilities are also examined.

Total Incivilities.   Unexpected change in total perceived incivilities reflects 1980 neighborhood makeup. Relative house value, percentage African-American, and percentage of owner-occupied households, after controlling for the earlier level of perceived problems explain the shifts in perception.[29] These variables, along with the earlier level of perceived problems, explain 27% of the total variation in perceived problems in 1994.

In addition to 1982 perceived problems, the other predictors with significant impact are relative house value ($t = -4.1$, $p < .01$) and percent African-American ($t = -2.1$; $p < .05$). Problems were less likely to increase in locations with more expensive housing at the beginning of the 1980s. Problems were less likely to increase in predominantly African-American neighborhoods after controlling for other factors. Impacts of prior stability were negligible ($t < 1$).

The opposite-to-expected race result deserves comment. In 1982, perceived problems were already quite high in many of the predominantly African-American neighborhoods close to the city center. A measurement "ceiling effect" may have prevented these averages from moving much higher. In mixed or predominantly white neighborhoods, worsening conditions took place against a lower starting point. Alternatively, residents in these locations may have become increasingly cognitively adapted to local incivilities as they intensified during the 1980s.[30]

Results do not provide a clear answer to the question of crime impacts. Assault has a marginally significant impact ($p < .06$) on later increasing problems. But this impact appears to be explaining just chance differences between neighborhoods. The remaining between-neighborhood differences in the outcome were already nonsignificant after entering earlier problems and 1980 structure.

Entering only neighborhood structural changes and crime changes, or just prior crime levels and crime changes, shows that neither model "explains away" the between-neighborhood differences in changes in perceived problems. The models most effectively explaining the between-neighborhood differences in changing incivilities are those using 1980 neighborhood structure.

In sum, unexpectedly increasing perceived problems reflect the initially lower relative status and initially lower African-American composition of the neighborhood. The incivility shifts are not explained as clearly by changes in the neighborhood fabric or changes in the crime rate. So, changes in one of the central indicators of disorder in numerous studies, an index of perceived incivilities, largely reflects problems emerging over time from living in lower-status neighborhoods. To a lesser extent, it reflects earlier racial composition, but it links to the latter opposite to the expected direction. It does not reflect ongoing changes in the locale. Consequently, in contrast to expectations from the longitudinal, ecological version of the incivilities thesis, intensifying incivilities are not produced as the neighborhood structurally weakens—owners are replaced by renters and house values drop. Instead, intensifying incivilities emerge later in locations already economically disadvantaged.

Turning to the individual-level portion of perceived problems shows only one significant correlate: education. Those with more education than their neighbors perceive more local problems. Length of residence and presence of friends in the neighborhood have no influence on perceptions. The finding that those with more education perceive more problems agrees with earlier Baltimore neighborhood research (14).

Social Incivilities. As for changing social incivilities, none of the models tried can "explain away" the between-neighborhood differences in ratings of these problems, after controlling for earlier problem levels.[31] The model including 1980 structure and beginning-of-the-decade crime measures appears to be the strongest. The only relevant structural variable with a significant impact is relative house value; in higher-value neighborhoods perceived social problems are less likely to subsequently increase ($t = -3.1$, $p < .01$). Race ($t < 1$), stability ($t < 1$), and assault ($t = 1.3$, ns) are not relevant. Social incivilities were most likely to intensify in neighborhoods with lower initial socioeconomic status.

Looking at individual-level predictors, the only item of significance is length of residence; those who have lived in the neighborhood for a *shorter* time than their neighbors perceive *more* problems in the locale. Again, these results agree with earlier Baltimore neighborhood research and also fit with an adaptation model to local problems (14, 50).

Physical Incivilities.   Between-neighborhood changes in perceived physical incivilities can be "explained away" by 1980 neighborhood structure ($t = -5.4$, $p < .001$ for 1980 house value; $t = -5.01$, $p < .001$ for % African-American; $t = -3.06$, $p < .01$ for stability).[32] Initial crime levels make a contribution as well ($t = -4.3$, $p < 001$). But, again, as with the earlier models, the crime variable may just be explaining "chance" between-neighborhood variation, since 1980 structure alone explained most of the between-neighborhood differences.[33]

In contrast to the changing perceptions of total and social incivilities, changing perceptions of physical incivilities relate more broadly to neighborhood structure; all three dimensions of status, stability, and race appear relevant. Unexpected problems are more likely to increase in neighborhoods with lower value housing, more renters, and *fewer* African Americans. Again, as with total perceived problems, the models including structural change and crime change, or earlier crime and crime change, do not "explain away" the between-neighborhood differences in these perception shifts. The only individual-level variable of relevance (results not shown) was education; those with more education than their neighbors perceived slightly more problems.[34]

Discussion

Table 4.3 summarizes results across different outcomes, concentrating solely on significant or close-to-significant findings and ignoring relative differences in the strength of the findings.[35] The analyses in this chapter have investigated a variety of incivilities indicators, focusing on the causes of and accompaniments to changes on these indicators. The examination spanned both the 1970s and 1980s as the periods of interest, focusing mostly on the latter; indicators relied both on on-site assessments and on residents' reports of neighborhood conditions.

Despite efforts to cast a wide net, assessment-based indicators for disorderly social behavior are lacking. Social incivilities occur at an extremely low base rate in most neighborhoods, and researchers have commented on the difficulties of assessing such (7, 17). It is these behaviors that are of central interest in some current versions of the incivilities thesis (22: 14–15). I was able, however, to gauge changes in perceived social disorder.

The pattern of results obtained here has implications for the different theoretical perspectives introduced at the beginning of the chapter and for how we think about incivilities. The structural perspective anticipates that incivilities will burgeon in economically disadvantaged and politically weak communities within the city. In neighborhoods having less

TABLE 4.3 Summarizing the Causes of Changing Incivilities at the Neighborhood Level

Changes in:	Neighborhood Incivilities (social and physical)	Graffiti	Vacant Housing	Perceived Social Problems	Perceived Physical Problems
Outcome year	1981	1994	1994	1994	1994
Outcome Level	Neighborhood	Block	Block	Individual	Individual
Earlier Structure					
Status	✓	✓	✓	✓	✓
Stability		✓	✓(–)		✓
Race	✓	✓(–)			✓(–)
Change in Structure					
Status	✓		(✓)		
Stability	✓				
Race	✓(–)				
Crime					
Earlier		✓	✓		
Change	✓				
Remaining Level II variation nonsignificant?		Yes	Yes		Yes

NOTE: ✓ = significant; (✓) = marginally significant; (–) = opposite theoretically expected direction.

political pull and lower exchange value for outside interests, investment will lag, code enforcement will be lax, services will go undelivered, and few will want to move in. Which particular feature of the neighborhood is most important in this process depends on the particular author. Wilson and Crutchfield highlight race and economics, McDougall focuses on race per se, Logan and Molotch emphasize exchange value to outside investors, and Bursik and Grasmick focus on public control linked to political pull as well as community stability.

The structural perspective highlighting economic factors receives the strongest support from current results. Neighborhood economic status, usually captured with relative house value, strongly and consistently predicts later shifts in incivilities. The communities with lower initial exchange value experience the most sensational later increases in incivilities—even though problems were serious there initially. The impacts of disadvantaged position cascade forward, intensifying over time. Underclass neighborhoods can become more deeply entrenched over time in this position. The connection appears for survey-based as well as assessment-based indicators and for behavioral as well as environmental quality issues. Prior status proved to be the only predictor of later changes in perceived social problems. Logan and Molotch and Wilson have correctly pinpointed the pivotal elements of structure hastening further community disintegration.

Structural theorists emphasizing the importance of stability to neighborhood viability receive modest support from the results. Stability significantly predicted two of the five outcomes—changes in graffiti and changes in perceived physical incivilities. The outcome was significant but opposite the expected direction for changes in vacant housing. The latter connection suggests residential stability may not serve either as a necessary or a sufficient condition for dampening future problems. In some stable neighborhoods, dynamics in adjoining neighborhoods or other features of the neighborhood itself seeded future problems.

African-American neighborhood composition, pivotal to the race-based perspective, made only one contribution in the expected direction to later disorder change: 1970 racial composition affected growth in the 1970s in assessed incivilities. The only contributions of race as a lagged predictor in the 1980s were opposite the expected direction. The difference between the impact of race on disorder growth in the 1970s and 1980s may be a function of the closer link between economic standing and racial composition in urban locations in the latter decade (54). Furthermore, from 1970 to 1990 we see an increasingly tight connection between racial composition and economic status in Baltimore neighborhoods.[36] Consequently, given the increasingly close coupling, it becomes more difficult for racial composition to demonstrate independent impacts.

Turning to the contributions of race in the unexpected direction to incivilities changes in the 1980s, these may reflect, as noted above, ceiling effects or cognitive adaptation effects in historically and now exclusively African-American neighborhoods located close to the city center.

Earlier crime levels contributed to two assessed shifts, but did not contribute to later changes in perceptions. The two impacts observed contribute further to an already extensive literature on the impacts of crime on communities and expand the outcomes shaped by crime. We now see that crime causes later grime. The impacts, however, are modest, compared to the influence of neighborhood status.

The change periods examined were rather lengthy, about a decade. In this broad a time span, the incivilities theorists suggest that crime should increase in a locale as the grime increases. But these results did not provide consistent evidence to support that position here. In the 1970s, relative crime changes accompanied deterioration changes, but not so for the 1980s, where the analyses control more specifically for the earlier level of incivilities. My inclination is to view the discrepant results between the 1970s and the 1980s as arising from the proxy 1970 measure used for earlier incivilities rather than historical differences. If I put more faith in the results using precisely the same control variable for initial incivilities, it appears that changing incivilities, either perceived or assessed, are more disconnected from crime changes than anticipated. Taub and his colleagues have suggested that there are various pathways to neighborhood decline (46). Consequently, it should not prove surprising to find different pathways to increasing incivilities or different types of shifts in incivilities.

The far-from-unitary shifts on incivility indicators over time proves even more troubling when considered in light of the independence of these shifts from concurrent structural and crime changes. For all incivility changes—perceived and assessed—dynamic changes from 1980–1990 in structure and crime tracked the incivility shifts more poorly than did initial structure and crime. This pattern seems to refute a central proposition of the ecological, longitudinal version of the incivilities thesis, which expects structural decline and waning safety as incivilities intensify. Here the change period of twelve to thirteen years for incivilities is an advantage. The long period makes it harder to argue that the increasing incivilities have not yet had enough time to influence other neighborhood dynamics, or vice versa.

In short, changing incivilities tell us more about how a neighborhood started out than how that neighborhood is changing. Intensifying incivilities appear to emerge largely from initial relative inequalities across neighborhoods. They are the sequelae, unfolding over time, of initial economic and crime differences across neighborhoods. Whether the intensifying incivilities reflect endogenous processes driven solely by those inequalities, exogenous processes as agencies and external stakeholders react to those inequalities, or both, is not clear. In the next two chapters, we turn from changing incivilities to initial incivilities. How do incivilities, as an important component of initial neighborhood fabric, contribute to later changes in neighborhood safety and makeup?

Notes

1. A prevalence rate indicates the proportion of a population with a condition. The population may be individuals, households, or addresses in the example being discussed here.

2. Strictly speaking, the regression shown in Figure 4.1 violates some of the assumptions of ordinary least squares (OLS) regression; more specifically, the residuals appear heteroscedastic, their variance being greater at lower as compared to higher 1980 values. Various procedures can be applied to weight the large residu-

als downward; these result in little substantial movement in the regression line and no substantive differences in the residuals shown.

3. Regression purists will note that in the regressions using information from the entire city, each neighborhood's outcome score, and thus its residual, is likely to be influenced by outcome scores in immediately surrounding neighborhoods and perhaps even more faintly influenced by neighborhoods one neighborhood away. I do *not* control for these spatially autocorrelated impacts in constructing these residuals. Controls for spatial autocorrelation are typically applied when the researcher is concerned about estimating and documenting the strength of a predictor's influence on the outcome for each independent unit and wants outcome scores for each unit untrammeled by dynamics in spatially adjoining locales.

But that is not the purpose here. Rather, recognizing that such autocorrelations are undoubtedly operating, and in that context, the goal is to develop measures of unexpected change. The unexpected change measures exactly reflect what is happening in that neighborhood, given what has been happening in the city overall as well as in adjoining neighborhoods. Whether the sources of that change are purely endogenous is not critical.

4. The outcome used principal components scores, based on a principal components analysis separating assessed features into an incivilities component and a land use mix component. The principal component loadings are shown in Chapter 3, Note 15.

5. The indicator variables here focus largely on *physical* as compared to social incivilities. In repeated assessment efforts, we have found that social disorder occurs too rarely to be meaningfully assessed by block raters. Other studies suggest similar base rate problems. For example, on-site stationary observers in Minneapolis's highest-crime locations recorded only one to two minutes of disorderly behavior an hour, between the hours of 7 P.M. and 3 A.M. (42). Walking observers, during daytime hours, spread out over low-, medium-, and high-crime blocks, are likely to encounter a far lower volume of disorderly behavior.

6. Clearly, 1970 controls for earlier levels of neighborhood incivilities are far from perfect. Therefore this analysis of change needs to be examined in the context of other analyses that provide better controls for earlier incivility levels.

7. To ensure marginally acceptable levels of statistical power, a two-tailed alpha level of .10 was adopted for the analyses with sixty-six neighborhoods.

8. This was equivalent to 40% of the explained variance in *total* incivilities.

9. The regression seen here represents one of several that were run. Alternate indicators for each construct were tried, for example, substituting poverty for relative house rank. No substantial differences were observed from the results discussed here. Multicollinearity and residual diagnostics were also examined to ensure that no cases excessively influenced the results. Outliers were not a problem because the outcome itself, being a principal components score, was already normalized.

10. Looking at neighborhoods that were over 95% African-American in 1970, and more than 3,000 population in 1970, and in inner-city locations, some of the most sizable drops in percentage blue-collar employed from 1970 to 1980 were

the following: 32.5% to 26%; 36.8% to 25.8%; 45.6% to 26.2%; 37.4% to 24%; and 41.3% to 26%.

11. The outcome was again residualized, so that it now represented changes in deterioration after controlling for the predictors discussed above. The progressive residualizing is required because of the strong correlations between crime and neighborhood structure.

12. For unexpected changes in robbery, $b=.006$; beta$=.220$. It explained an additional 4.8% of residualized change in deterioration and 2.9% of total change in deterioration ($F(1,57)=2.91$; $p < .10$).

13. Of course, one can give crime a "better shot" at explaining the outcome by allowing it to predict deterioration changes *before* controlling for neighborhood structure and changes in structure. That analysis shows a lagged impact of assault rate and the same contemporaneous impact of changes in robbery. These two variables together explain about 31% of the variance in deterioration changes. Adding further crime predictors seriously inflates the standard errors of the predictors, suggesting multicollinearity problems. So giving crime and crime change a better chance at explaining changes in incivilities, shows a stronger connection, but crime still explains markedly less than do structure and structural change.

14. In Chapter 2, I reported analyses using eighty-seven blocks that were assessed in *both* 1981 and 1994. The analyses here use all ninety blocks, substituting 1981 neighborhood means for the three blocks lacking 1981 scores.

15. These estimated true scores are different from the observed scores reported in Chapter 2.

16. These analyses used two-level, hierarchical generalized linear models. Level I predictors are group mean centered. Models with uncentered predictors provided comparable results. It was not possible to include additional measures of crime change or structural change. Additional variables produced anomalous results, e.g., residual variances higher than the starting variances. Tests, coefficients, and standard errors are based on population estimates with robust standard errors.

17. Results also show an age connection; unexpected declines in percentage of population aged six to thirteen accompanied increasing graffiti. Areas with lots of preteens in 1980 and fewer a decade later probably also had lots of teens and young adults a decade later.

18. Again, these analyses use generalized hierarchical linear models, given the skewed count variable. Again, Level I is streetblocks, Level II is neighborhoods. Whereas with graffiti the focus is on prevalence, with vacant housing the focus is instead on incidence rates.

19. Consequently, the reliability of the neighborhood true score estimates has increased from .41 in 1981 to .82 in 1994.

20. The Empirical Bayes weighted-population estimate is .348.

21. The Empirical Bayes weighted-population estimate is .586.

22. The confidence interval around the 1994 population rate overlaps the confidence interval around the 1981 population rate.

23. Results are from a generalized linear multilevel model; it assumes a Poisson distribution of the outcome with constant exposure. Predictors have been grand mean centered.

24. $X^2(22) = 33.65; p > .05$.

25. Here Level I = individuals, Level II = neighborhoods.

26. Adding up all the different incivilities produces an index with a reliability, or internal consistency, of .89 by Cronbach's alpha.

27. Details and measurement properties appear in Chapter 3, endnote 22.

28. The two unexpected disorder changes based on on-site assessments of graffiti and vacant housing as our predictor of changes in perceived physical problems explain only an insignificant 9.9% of the outcome in a regression ($F(2,27)$ = 1.48, ns). Neither predictor has a significant regression coefficient.

29. The remaining between-neighborhood variation is nonsignificant ($X^2(25)$ = 33.36; $p > .10$). These two-level HLM models use nonlinear, Poisson estimation. I also examined results from linear models after transforming the outcome, and they were not remarkably different. Throughout, neighborhoods were weighted by population size. Results reported are based on the population-average model with robust standard errors.

30. The dynamics involved here are explained more fully in 50.

31. Between-neighborhood differences in perceived problems account for about 40% of the total variation. The models tested can explain no more than three fifths to three fourths of this between-neighborhood variation. The remaining between-neighborhood variation is always significant. These are hierarchical generalized linear models, assuming a Poisson distribution for the outcome with constant exposure.

32. $X^2(25) = 33.93; p > .10$, for the model with just 1980 structural predictors.

33. These results are from the model with the crime variable in. The only marked change when crime is not in the model is that the impact of stability becomes marginally significant.

34. The crime variable was removed from the model; the model would not converge if Level I predictors are included along with the crime variable.

35. Given the n of thirty neighborhoods, to improve statistical power to marginally acceptable levels, an alpha level of $p < .10$ was used for Level II effects.

36. The *squared* correlations between weighted house value percentile and percentage African-American were as follows:

Year	Linear r^2	Curvilinear R^2
1970	.089	.10
1980	.138	.16
1990	.258	.296

I show the curvilinear correlation, as well as the linear one, to take into account different dynamics affecting integrating neighborhoods in each of the decades.

References

(1) Allison, P. D. (1990) Change scores as dependent variables in regression analysis. *Sociological Methodology* 20, 93–115.

(2) Bohrnstedt, G. W. (1969) Observation on the measurement of change. In *Sociological methodology* (Borgatta, E. F., and Bohrnstedt, G. W., eds), pp. 113–133. Jossey-Bass, San Francisco.

(3) Box, S., Hale, C., and Andrews, S. (1988) Explaining fear of crime. *British Journal of Criminology* 28, 340–356.

(4) Boyd, L. H., and Iversen, G. R. (1979) *Contextual analysis: Concepts and statistical techniques*, Wadsworth, Belmont, CA.

(5) Bryk, A. S., and Raudenbush, S. W. (1987) Application of hierarchical linear models to assessing change. *Psychological Bulletin* 101, 147–158.

(6) Bryk, A. S., and Raudenbush, S. W. (1992) *Hierarchical linear models: Applications and data analysis methods*, Sage, Newbury Park, CA.

(7) Buerger, M. E., Cohn, E. G., and Petrosino, A. J. (1995) Defining the "hot spots of crime": Operationalizing theoretical concepts for field research. In *Crime and place* (Eck, J. E., and Weisburd, D., eds), pp. 237–257. Criminal Justice Press, Monsey, NY.

(8) Bursik, R. J. (1986) Ecological stability and the dynamics of delinquency. In *Communities and crime* (Reiss, A. J., and Tonry, M., eds), pp. 35–66. Chicago: University of Chicago Press.

(9) Bursik, R. J. (1988) Social disorganization and theories of crime and delinquency. *Criminology* 26, 519–551.

(10) Bursik, R. J. (1989) Political decisionmaking and ecological models of delinquency: Conflict and consensus. In *Theoretical integration in the study of deviance and crime: Problems and prospects* (Messner, S. F., and Krohn, M. D., eds), pp. 105–117. Albany: State University of New York Press.

(11) Bursik, R. J., and Grasmick, H. G. (1993) *Neighborhoods and crime: The dimensions of effective social control*, Lexington Books, New York.

(12) Choldin, H. M., Hanson, C., and Bohrer, R. (1980) Suburban status instability. *American Sociological Review* 45, 972–983.

(13) Covington, J., and Taylor, R. B. (1991) Fear of crime in urban residential neighborhoods: Implications of between and within-neighborhood sources for current models. *Sociological Quarterly* 32, 231–249.

(14) Crenson, M. (1983) *Neighborhood politics*, Harvard University Press, Cambridge, MA.

(15) Crutchfield, R. D., and Pitchford, S. R. (1997) Work and crime: The effects of labor stratification. *Social Forces* 68, 489–512.

(16) Galster, G. C. (1990) White flight from racially integrated neighborhoods in the 1970s: The Cleveland experience. *Urban Studies* 27, 385–399.

(17) Giacomazzi, A. L., McGarrell, E. F., and Thurman, Q. C. (1997) *Reducing disorder, fear and crime in public housing: An evaluation of a drug crime elimination program in Spokane, Washington*. Draft Final Report.

(18) Gottdiener, M. (1994) *The new urban sociology*, McGraw Hill, New York.

(19) Gottdiener, M. (1994) *The social production of urban space*, 2nd ed., University of Texas Press, Austin.

(20) Hunter, A. (1985) Private, parochial and public school orders: The problem of crime and civility in urban communities. In *The challenge of social control, citizenship and institution building in modern society* (Suttles, G. D., Zald, M. N., eds.), pp. 230–242. Ablex, Norwood, NJ.

(21) Kasarda, J. D. (1992) The severely distressed in economically transforming cities. In *Drugs, crime and social isolation: Barriers to urban opportunity* (Harrell, A. V., and Peterson, G. E., eds), pp. 45–98. Urban Institute Press, Washington, DC.

(22) Kelling, G. L., and Coles, C. M. (1996) *Fixing broken windows: Restoring order and reducing crime in our communities,* Free Press, New York.

(23) Klinger, D. A. (1997) Negotiating order in police work: An ecological theory of police response to deviance. *Criminology* 35, 277–306.

(24) LaFree, G. (1998) *Losing legitimacy: Street crime and the decline of social institutions in America,* Westview, Boulder.

(25) Land, K. C., and Felson, M. (1976) A general framework for building dynamic macro social indicator models: Including an analysis of changes in crime rates and police expenditures. *American Journal of Sociology* 82, 565–604.

(26) Lane, R. (1986) *Roots of violence in black Philadelphia 1860–1900,* Harvard University Press, Cambridge, MA.

(27) Lewis, D. A., and Maxfield, M. G. (1980) Fear in the neighborhoods: An investigation of the impact of crime. *Journal of Research in Crime and Delinquency* 17, 160–189.

(28) Liebow, E. (1967) *Tally's corner,* Little, Brown, Boston.

(29) Logan, J. R., and Molotch, H. (1987) *Urban fortunes,* University of California Press, Berkeley.

(30) Massey, D., and Denton, S. (1993) *American apartheid: Segregation and the making of the underclass,* Harvard University Press, Cambridge, MA.

(31) Massey, D. S., White, M., and Voon-Chin, P. (1996) The dimensions of segregation revisited. *Sociological Methods and Research* 25, 172–206.

(32) McDougall, H. A. (1993) *Black Baltimore: Toward a new theory of community,* Temple University Press, Philadelphia.

(33) McKenzie, R. D. (1921) The neighborhood. In *On human ecology* (Hawley, A. H., and McKenzie, R. D., eds), pp. 51–93. University of Chicago Press, Chicago.

(34) Miller, E. S. (1981) Crime's threat to land value and neighborhood vitality. In *Environmental criminology* (Brantingham, P. J., and Brantingham, P. L., eds), pp. 111–118. Sage, Beverly Hills, CA.

(35) Olligschlager, A. (1998) *Artificial neural networks and crime mapping.* Unpublished manuscript, John J. Heinz School of Public Policy and Management, Carnegie Mellon University.

(36) Podolefsky, A. (1983) *Case studies in community crime prevention,* Charles C. Thomas, Springfield, IL.

(37) Rogosa, D. (1988) Myths about longitudinal research. In *Methodological issues in aging research* (Schaie, K. W., Campbell, R. T., Meredith, W., and Rawlings, S. C., eds), pp. 171–209. Springer, New York.

(38) Rogosa, D., Brandt, D., and Zimowski, M. (1982) A growth curve approach to the measurement of change. *Psychological Bulletin* 92, 726–748.

(39) Rogosa, D., and Saner, H. (1995) Longitudinal data analysis examples with random coefficient models. *Journal of Educational and Behavioral Statistics* 20, 149–170.

(40) Ryon, R. N. (1993) *West Baltimore neighborhoods: Sketches of their history: 1840–1900,* University of Baltimore, Institute for Publications Design, Baltimore.

(41) Schwirian, K. P. (1983) Models of neighborhood change: A review. *Annual Review of Sociology* 9, 83–102.

(42) Sherman, L. W., & Weisburd, D. (1995) General deterrent effects of police patrol in crime "hot spots": A randomized, controlled trial. *Justice Quarterly* 12, 625–649.

(43) Skogan, W. (1986) Fear of crime and neighborhood change. In *Crime and justice: A Review of research*, Vol. 8: *Communities and crime*, (Reiss, A. J., Jr., and Tonry, M., eds), pp. 203–230. University of Chicago Press, Chicago.

(44) Skogan, W. (1990) *Disorder and decline: Crime and the spiral of decay in American cities*, Free Press, New York.

(45) Skogan, W. G., and Maxfield, M. G. (1981) *Coping with crime*, Sage, Beverly Hills, CA.

(46) Taub, R. P., Taylor, G., and Dunham, J. (1984) *Paths of neighborhood change*, University of Chicago Press, Chicago.

(47) Taylor, R. B. (1995) Impact of crime on communities. *Annals of the American Academy of Political and Social Science* 539, 28–45.

(48) Taylor, R. B. (1997) Social order and disorder of streetblocks and neighborhoods: Ecology, microecology and the systemic model of social disorganization. *Journal of Research in Crime and Delinquency* 33, 113–155.

(49) Taylor, R. B., and Covington, J. (1993) Community structural change and fear of crime. *Social Problems* 40, 374–397.

(50) Taylor, R. B., and Shumaker, S. A. (1990) Local crime as a natural hazard: Implications for understanding the relationship between disorder and fear of crime. *American Journal of Community Psychology* 18, 619–642.

(51) Taylor, R. B., Shumaker, S. A., and Gottfredson, S. D. (1985) Neighborhood-level links between physical features and local sentiments: Deterioration, fear of crime, and confidence. *Journal of Architectural Planning and Research* 2, 261–275.

(52) Taylor, R. B., and Talalay, R. (1981) *Racial change in Baltimore neighborhoods*. Census Note 2, Center for Metropolitan Planning and Research, Johns Hopkins University, Baltimore.

(53) Taylor, R. B., and Webb, T. (1982) *Changes in owner occupancy and vacancy levels in Baltimore census tracts*. Census Note 4, Center for Metropolitan Planning and Research, Johns Hopkins University, Baltimore.

(54) Wilson, W. J. (1996) *When work disappears: The world of the new urban poor*, Knopf, New York.

5

Impacts of Incivilities on Later Crime and Decline

This chapter and the next report on several of the key hypotheses behind the longitudinal, ecological version of the incivilities thesis. The focus here is on two groups of outcomes: changes in crime and changes in neighborhood fabric. The next chapter examines reactions to crime, including fear of crime, avoidance, and moving intentions. As described in Chapter 3, the outcomes examined in this chapter were "added on" to the thesis in its later incarnations, whereas reactions to crime had been of interest for those examining the impacts of incivilities from the beginning. The purpose here is to learn whether either assessed or perceived incivilities, measured in 1981 or 1982, contributed *independently* either to crime changes over the 1980s in the sixty-six neighborhoods or to changes in basic neighborhood makeup.

As was noted in Chapter 3, in his analyses of forty-plus neighborhoods from several cities, Skogan observed an independent impact of incivilities on robbery (34, but cf. 11). But as was pointed out in Chapter 3, those analyses were cross-sectional and did not permit the testing of the *longitudinal* ideas in the ecological version of the incivilities thesis.[1]

The analysis will proceed as follows. To construct unexpected changes in the outcomes, for each crime, the 1990–1992 population-weighted percentiles are regressed on 1980–1982 population-weighted percentiles and the residuals retained. In the case of each structural change, the 1990 scores are regressed on the 1980 scores and the residuals retained. These six residuals will be further collapsed into three independent pathways of change. As discussed in Chapter 4, these unexpected changes capture how much the target neighborhood shifted over the period vis-à-vis other neighborhoods in the city. Results will show the impacts of incivilities, measured either in 1981 (assessed) or 1982 (perceived), on the changes. In addition, to get at the independent impact of the incivilities analyses control for neighborhood structure in 1980.

The rationale for impacts of incivilities was described in Chapter 3. The following section develops more fully how and why fundamental neighborhood features can shape later decline.

A Systemic Perspective

Of interest from a systemic perspective are the lagged impacts of other neighborhood features on changing crime and decline. Ample ideas from urban sociology generally, and the systemic social disorganization model more specifically, help broaden our thinking about causes of changing neighborhood quality and changing neighborhood crime rates. These theorists address one or more of the following four structural features of neighborhoods: status, stability, racial composition, and racial heterogeneity.[2]

Urban theorists concerned with stratification devote considerable attention to links between neighborhood status, reflected, for example, in relative neighborhood house values, and neighborhood outcomes over time (8, 17). Neighborhood house values shape the neighborhood's exchange value for residents and outsiders. The stronger the economic return to house sellers in the neighborhood and to outside entrepreneurial interests, the stronger the commitment of the outside entrepreneurs and local politicians to preserve neighborhood quality. Stated differently, neighborhood decline and increasing crime should both be less likely in higher-status neighborhoods. Not only are they more "protected" to begin with, but strong inside and outside interests work to maintain safety and quality (17: 19, 49). Chapter 8 provides more specific information, from qualitative interviews with experienced community leaders, on some of the processes whereby high-status neighborhoods maintain their relative prestige.

Those concerned with disadvantaged neighborhoods concentrate on the reverse end of the status dimension. In low-income locales, there is little rationale for entrepreneurs or policymakers to stem further decline. Exchange value already has ebbed to too low a point. Of course, such a view overlooks the long-term higher costs to public agencies, and the taxpayers supporting those agencies, for delivering services such as policing and fire protection and subsidizing medical care for indigent households, not to mention the long-term costs for criminal justice processing and the broader community if offending, arrest, and incarceration rates climb in such locations.

Status issues link to racial composition in urban locations, and the two have joined even more tightly in large cities over the past two decades

(42, 43). Consequently, in older cities, because neighborhoods predominantly African-American for a long time, in contrast to predominantly white neighborhoods, are more likely to be economically disadvantaged, for economic reasons alone structural decline and increasing crime are more likely there too. Outside entrepreneurial interests may see little exchange value to preserve in many of these neighborhoods. In Baltimore, public housing siting decisions in the 1950s and 1960s and urban renewal area selections may have contributed to declining status, as well as school problems, in several near-westside, predominantly African-American neighborhoods (19).

Of course, the connection between relative status and race does not deny the existence of a number of middle-class, predominantly African-American neighborhoods in Baltimore; nor does it deny that African-American neighborhoods may sometimes receive treatment based largely on racial rather than economic considerations (19). Neighborhoods may be poorly serviced just because they are occupied by African-American households (18); they also may experience declining quality and increasing crime emerging from the extreme spatial segregation along racial lines that has obtained in many larger cities in the past two decades (23, 30).

Ethnic heterogeneity and instability each may lead to declining neighborhood quality and increasing neighborhood crime through similar processes of weakened informal social control, sparser local social ties, and more reticence to intervene in disorderly or criminal events (5, 29). Declining collective efficacy and increasing social disorganization appear largely reflective of shifting internal dynamics, but external ties, called public control by Bursik and Grasmick, may play a role as well. As internal shifts occur in collective efficacy, or perhaps independently of those shifts, neighborhood ties to external public agencies, external public resources, and external private investment may atrophy as a result of weak or ineffectual neighborhood leadership or representation. Compositional changes in adjoining neighborhoods can prove influential as well (12, 22).

In short, if we turn from the incivilities thesis per se and consider a broader causal net for changing neighborhood quality and crime, each element of a neighborhood's factorial ecology (13)—status, stability, and racial composition—is directly addressed in this broader theoretical framework.[3] Analyses test these predicted impacts at the same time impacts of incivilities are estimated.

Focus

In sum, the suggestion that incivilities make an independent contribution over time to changes in crime and changes in neighborhood quality remains untested. Work to date has used inappropriate indicators, has tested the thesis with just cross-sectional data, or has modeled mediating rather than independent impacts. The focus here is on changes in neighborhood crime rates and changes in neighborhood quality.

Data and Analysis

Analyses use neighborhood-level data for the sixty-six neighborhoods randomly sampled in 1981 from all Baltimore neighborhoods. The analysis here, therefore, will be an ecological one. (For details on the sampling and respondents, see 38.) The resulting sample was 66% female and 37% African-American; median 1981 household income was between $20,000 and $25,000; median education was twelfth grade. (Other urban samples from around the same period using comparable methods also obtained roughly comparable gender ratios; see 7.) The sixty-six neighborhoods themselves included an extremely broad array of setting conditions. Information from the 1980 Census showed that the neighborhoods ranged from 100% African-American to 100% white, with an average of 44% African-American (median = 33%); poverty rates ranged from 1% to 59% (average = 16%; median = 12%); unemployment rates ranged from 0% to 32% (average = 10%; median = 9%); owner occupancy rates ranged from 6% to 89% (mean and median = 55%); proportion with a high school education or better ranged from 13% to 41% (mean = 27%; median = 26%).

The perceived incivilities indicators are based on neighborhood averages from about twenty-five residents per neighborhood, interviewed in 1982. Eight perceived disorder problems were formed into two more general problem indices with acceptable measurement properties (see Chapter 3). One index (alpha = .80) picks up just physical problems: vandalism, vacant houses, vacant lots, people who do not keep property up, and litter. A second index (alpha = .86) focuses on social problems: insults, teens, noise, bad elements moving in, and people fighting. The assessed incivilities indicator was based on a principal components analysis of neighborhood-level data averaged over the blocks in each neighborhood (see Chapter 3, Note 15 or reference 40). It focused mostly on physical features such as vacant housing, litter, and graffiti, but also included two social items, the presence of small groups on the street and the volume of males present.

Results appear here for the four violent Part I crimes. The incivilities thesis has most clearly addressed changes in street crime such as assaults and robberies. Rapes and homicides are examined as well so that the reach of the impacts of incivilities can be established.[4] For each Part I violent crime, the goal was to assess how much each neighborhood's crime rate had gone up or down between the early 1980s and the early 1990s, relative to other neighborhoods.[5] Using average 1980–1982 reported neighborhood crime rates, an average crime rate was constructed for each neighborhood for the period. The same was done for 1990–1992 reported neighborhood crime rates. We then converted the three-year average crime rate for each crime for each period for each neighborhood into a weighted crime percentile score. The 1990–1992 population-weighted percentiles were regressed on the 1980–1982 percentiles and the residuals retained.

These calculations of unexpected crime changes were carried out using all city neighborhoods save the downtown and public housing communities, so that the relative shift of each non-public-housing neighborhood in the overall residential fabric of the city could be gauged. Scatter plots of beginning-of-the-decade and end-of-the-decade crimes, for each crime, showed there were not marked nonlinearities, or outliers, unduly influencing the results.

As a methodological aside, the procedures followed here in constructing change indicators, although widely supported and used (3, 4, 38), are not without their critics, who recommend different approaches, including the use of change scores (1, 27, 28). This debate appears to show no signs of diminishing. The regression residual approach used here best captures overall changes *relative* to other neighborhoods, and thus it is in keeping with an ecological orientation; furthermore, the regression residuals provide indicators by definition independent of initial scores and independent of overall trends affecting all city neighborhoods.

Structural decline was operationalized with six change indicators that most would agree represented worsening conditions: weighted house value percentiles, percentage owner occupied, percentage one-unit structures, percentage with at least some college, poverty, and vacant housing. For the first four items, decreasing scores represent decline; for poverty and vacant housing, increases represent decline. As with the crime data, each of these indicators was operationalized by taking residuals. The 1990 score of each variable was regressed on the 1980 score, residuals retained, and principal components analysis carried out on the residuals. Again, as with the crime changes, these decline indicators reflect *unexpected* decline.

The six indicators were collapsed into three independent dimensions.[6] Changes in homeownership and one-unit structures clustered together to reflect a shift in stability. Changes in vacancy rate and poverty rate joined together to reflect changes in degree of disadvantage. Changes in portion with at least some college education and relative house value together formed a dimension of status change.

Given the lack of bi- and multivariate normal distributions in some instances, analyses were completed three different ways.[7] First, Kendall tau-B nonparametric correlation coefficients linked incivilities with each outcome after partialling parametrically for neighborhood structure. Second, partial Kendall tau-B nonparametric correlation coefficients looked at the same relationship, but partialled nonparametrically (31: 223–229).[8] Finally, multiple regressions via structural equation modeling were carried out, using asymptotically distribution-free estimation procedures for the parameters and their standard errors.[9] These estimation procedures can "accept" data structures lacking multivariate normal distributions.

After presenting the zero-order Kendall tau-B coefficients for descriptive purposes, the results from the structural equation modeling appear, since these permit the most compact presentation of results. A separate model appears for each crime outcome, each structural outcome, and each incivility indicator. Given questions about a broader disorder construct and loose connections between incivility indicators (Chapter 3), it seemed more appropriate to examine how each indicator fared rather than to construct a more general indicator. Furthermore, support for the incivilities thesis will be most convincing if an impact appears not only across different crimes or different structural changes, but also *across different incivilities indicators*. There were no substantial differences in results, except as noted below, between the first approach (nonparametric coefficients after parametrically partialling) and the structural equation results presented here.[10]

Changes on Decline Indicators in the 1980s

Table 5.1 shows how the sample of neighborhoods scored on the six census-based indicators of decline contributing to the three independent pathways of decline described above. The two status indicators show that the percentage of the adult population with at least some college climbed noticeably in the sample. At both points in time, this indicator correlated strongly with house values. And those values increased in the sample, as they did in the city and nationwide during the 1980s. (Figures shown here do not control for inflation.) At both points in time, the sample included neighborhoods at least a full standard deviation below the citywide mean neighborhood house value as well as the highest-priced neighborhoods in the city.

The two disadvantage indicators show a slight worsening of conditions in the sample neighborhoods from 1980 to 1990. The median percentage of households in poverty increased almost 2%; the median percentage of houses abandoned or for sale or rent increased almost 2%. In some of the neighborhoods, poverty rates topped half of the households present in both 1980 and 1990.

TABLE 5.1   Characteristics of Study Neighborhoods on Decline Parameters, 1980 and 1990

	Mean	*Median*	*SD*	*Min*	*Max*
% Residents over 24 with at least some college					
1980	23.8	19.8	16.6	3.0	82.0
1990	36.4	34.1	18.9	0	91.3
Neighborhood average house value					
1980	$33,473	$28,755	$19,417	$11,630	$113,856
1990	$66,748	$52,867	$42,499	$26,895	$281,933
% Households in poverty					
1980	16.5	12.1	13.9	1.3	59.5
1990	17.8	13.9	12.9	0	61.5
% Vacant housing units					
1980	7.1	4.2	7.1	.7	30.8
1990	7.8	6.1	5.0	1.9	22.5
% One-unit structures					
1980	70.3	75.2	18.3	13.6	92.3
1990	69.4	71.3	21.8	4.5	97.8
% Owner-occupied housing units					
1980	54.6	55.2	21.4	5.9	88.8
1990	55.1	53.9	19.5	9.2	90.4

Stability indicators, if we look at the medians, also showed a slight worsening over the decade, with the median percentage of one-unit structures dropping from 75% to 71% and median percentage owner-occupied housing units dropping slightly from 55% to 54%.

Crime Rate Changes

Looking at the bivariate relationships (Kendall tau-B correlation coefficients) between incivilities, structure, and crime changes helps set the stage for the multivariate results to follow. Incivilities show several connections supporting the longitudinal, ecological version of the incivilities thesis. Assessed incivilities linked significantly to later increases in homicide (.238; $p < .01$), rape (.196; $p < .05$), and assault (.17; $p < .10$). Perceived physical and social incivilities both affected later shifts in relative rape (.303, .299, respectively; $ps < .01$) and assault rates (.349, .273, respectively; $ps < .01$). The pattern suggests different types of incivility indicators shape different types of later crime changes.

These bivariate results also showed strong links between 1980 structure and later crime changes. Relative homicide, for example, was more likely to subsequently increase in predominantly African-American neighborhoods (.392; $p < .01$) and in neighborhoods with lower relative house prices (−.176; $p < .05$). Race also linked significantly to changes in rape (.237; $p < .05$) and assault (.186; $p < .05$), with larger increases in more predominantly African-American neighborhoods. More stable neighborhoods were somewhat less likely to experience later increases in assault (−.172; $p < .10$). Before isolating independent impacts, these bivariate results suggest that of the three structural dimensions, status and race appear more influential on later crime changes than stability. And of course, incivilities linked strongly to structure as well, although the connection depends both on the structural dimension and on the type of incivility indicator.

Moving on to multivariate results, regression results via structural equation modeling appear in Table 5.2. To repeat, the estimation procedures used did not require multivariate, normal distributions among the variables. For homicide changes, the only predictor with consistent lagged impacts across all three incivilities indicators was race; homicide was more likely to increase unexpectedly during the 1980s in neighborhoods more predominantly African-American in 1980, after controlling for incivilities, status, and stability. This linkage is deeply disturbing. More important than incivilities, status, or stability in setting the stage for later relative increases in lethal violence was racial makeup. Stated differently, the single feature, of those assessed, that best predicted later relative increases in homicide was initial racial composition, and this connection persisted regardless of the indicator used for incivilities, and after controlling for status and stability. Interpreting this impact of racial composition is difficult. Is it possible that this connection is historically contingent? Open-air drug markets for crack-cocaine expanded sizably in Baltimore and in other large cities, beginning in the latter 1980s. Often, as drug markets were set up, there was competition among rival sellers, often leading to shootings. The geography of where these markets were set up depended on issues of access to customers and access to unsupervised locations like vacant housing (26). Inner-city neighborhoods that had been largely historically African-American, and were usually almost exclusively African-American by 1980, may have witnessed increasing relative levels of lethal violence because of their central-city location, making it easier for customers to get to them, and to the larger volume of older, often worn-out housing stock that could often be found in these locales. The analyses control for housing vacancies with the incivilities indicator.

Of course, if relative lethal violence linked to the drug trade was increasing in these locales, that does not tell us about the locations of victims or perpetrators or how many of each came from within the neighborhood where the crime was located. Offense location, offender location, and victim location are all distinct (2). Homicide case studies in Baltimore from 1988 (32) and an early 1990s ethnography of one West Baltimore drug corner, close to a few of our study neighborhoods, pointed out that in many cases the customers drawn in were from other neighborhoods, and many times they were not African-American (33; see also 9). So the violence taking place in these predominantly African-American communities was increasing over the period and was at least partly related to the drug trade. It is difficult, however, to go much further than this and draw inferences about specific case characteristics. Drawing a direct connection between ecological features and specific cases would be to commit the ecological fallacy (10, 41).[11]

Assessed incivilities demonstrate an independent impact ($p < .10$) on later relative homicide change, contributing to the later increase as hypothesized.[12] The independent impact does *not* appear, however, when either perceived social or perceived physical incivilities, the type of indicator on which most work in the area has relied, are used. In short, the results for this crime are simultaneously encouraging and troubling. They are theoretically encouraging because they show a lagged impact, the expected independent effect of incivilities, on the one violent crime type with the least amount of measurement uncertainty in reporting. They are troubling because the same effect does not appear in the equations with the most widely used type of incivilities indicator.

Worries about the inconsistent pattern of results using different incivilities variables would be lessened if at least one of them proved consistently influential across different crimes. But the results did not show such consistency. Turning to rape, we see that perceptions of social incivilities contributed independently to later relative increases ($p < .10$). In this equation, it was the only significant predictor. In the equation using assessed incivilities, incivilities were not influential on later rape shifts, but neighborhood status was; relative rape rates were less likely to increase in neighborhoods with higher house values ($p < .10$). Assault showed the same pattern as rape: an independent impact of perceived incivilities—physical this time—in one equation, and in another equation a nonsignificant impact of assessed incivilities but an independent impact of house value. Relative assault rates were more likely to increase later in locales where residents had earlier reported more physical incivilities; assault was more likely to increase later in neighborhoods with initially lower status. None of the predictors in the model forecast later relative robbery changes. In the equation with assessed incivilities, higher stability came close to demonstrating a dampening impact on later robbery shifts. So for three different crimes, different incivilities indicators prove

TABLE 5.2   Predicting Later Crime Changes

Crime / Indicator		b	se	b/se	$p <$
Homicide/					
Assessed Incivilities					
(R^2=0.339)	Incivilities	4.084	3.124	1.307	.10
	VALRANK8	0.044	0.091	0.483	
	BLACK80P	0.321	0.066	4.877	.001
	OWN80P	0.096	0.139	0.695	
Perceived Physical Incivilities					
(R^2=0.328)	Incivilities	−0.175	0.826	−0.212	
	VALRANK8	−0.041	0.116	−0.356	
	BLACK80P	0.326	0.068	4.805	.001
	OWN80P	0.002	0.132	0.015	
Perceived Social Incivilities					
(R^2=0.328)	Incivilities	−0.193	0.504	−0.382	
	VALRANK8	−0.053	0.103	−0.514	
	BLACK80P	0.320	0.072	4.414	.001
	OWN80P	−0.004	0.126	−0.035	
Rape/					
Assessed Incivilities					
(R^2=0.157)	Incivilities	−3.515	4.356	−0.807	
	VALRANK8	−0.234	0.137	−1.710	.10
	BLACK80P	0.110	0.087	1.263	
	OWN80P	−0.172	0.163	−1.057	
Perceived Physical Incivilities					
(R^2=0.165)	Incivilities	1.397	1.389	1.005	
	VALRANK8	−0.053	0.142	−0.375	
	BLACK80P	0.110	0.089	1.226	
	OWN80P	−0.029	0.140	−0.205	
Perceived Social Incivilities					
(R^2=0.183)	Incivilities	1.082	0.679	1.594	.10
	VALRANK8	−0.022	0.149	−0.150	
	BLACK80P	0.142	0.095	1.496	
	OWN80P	−0.008	0.135	−0.060	
Robbery/					
Assessed Incivilities					
(R^2=0.078)	Incivilities	−2.818	3.111	−0.906	
	VALRANK8	−0.067	0.120	−0.559	
	BLACK80P	0.047	0.081	0.575	
	OWN80P	−0.246	0.161	−1.532	
Perceived Physical Incivilities					
(R^2=0.078)	Incivilities	0.828	0.866	0.956	
	VALRANK8	0.050	0.140	0.359	
	BLACK80P	0.044	0.083	0.537	
	OWN80P	−0.145	0.135	−1.079	

(continues)

TABLE 5.2   *(continued)*

Crime / Indicator		*b*	*se*	*b/se*	*p <*
Perceived Social Incivilities					
(R^2=0.076)	Incivilities	0.463	0.492	0.942	
	VALRANK8	0.045	0.128	0.355	
	BLACK80P	0.058	0.090	0.645	
	OWN80P	−0.150	0.138	−1.087	
Aggravated Assault/					
Assessed Incivilities					
(R^2=0.124)	Incivilities	−3.105	3.336	−0.931	
	VALRANK8	−0.247	0.096	−2.585	.05
	BLACK80P	−0.014	0.088	−0.159	
	OWN80P	−0.252	0.169	−1.495	
Perceived Physical Incivilities					
(R^2=0.150)	Incivilities	1.826	1.058	1.727	.05
	VALRANK8	−0.040	0.111	−0.362	
	BLACK80P	−0.012	0.086	−0.141	
	OWN80P	−0.092	0.119	−0.776	
Perceived Social Incivilities					
(R^2=0.130)	Incivilities	0.656	0.566	1.160	
	VALRANK8	−0.102	0.100	−1.027	
	BLACK80P	0.005	0.084	0.056	
	OWN80P	−0.130	0.116	−1.127	

NOTE: Probability tests 1 tailed for incivilities, 2 tailed otherwise. Structural equation estimates with asymptotically distribution free estimates.

relevant, and which indicator is used also affects which structural impacts appear.

In sum, the general pattern seen here is one of expected-but-not-consistent lagged incivilities impacts for three violent crime changes. But a few more specific points deserve mention. First, the failure of any incivility indicator to predict robbery changes underscores an important difference between these longitudinal results and Skogan's cross-sectional ones (34: 193, Table A-4-1; but cf. Harcourt 11), where he found an independent impact of disorder on robbery victimization across thirty neighborhoods.[13] Second, race was the only aspect of neighborhood structure to consistently influence a crime change regardless of the incivility indicator used. Race mattered consistently for later shifts in lethal violence. Less consistent across indicators, but relevant to two later crime shifts, was initial status. Higher initial house values significantly dampened later relative increases in assault and rape. But the lagged impact of house values appeared only in the equations with assessed incivilities.

Do the results show support for the incivilities thesis? Yes, but not as consistently as one might hope. For no crime do the results show an independent impact of incivilities regardless of type of indicator. Perceived social incivilities affect assault, perceived physical incivilities affect rape, and assessed incivilities affect homicide. The three incivilities indicators each predicted one crime change in the hypothesized direction. That the predicted impacts emerge is encouraging for the theory; that the impacts are not consistent across different and presumably comparable indicators is worrisome.

Predicting Decline

Again, inspecting the nonparametric bivariate connections (Kendall tau-Bs) sets the stage for the multivariate results. These show that two of the three pathways of structural change were linked to earlier structural conditions. Declining status—unexpected decreases in relative house values and proportion with at least some college—was more likely in predominantly African-American neighborhoods (–.158, $p < .10$).[14] Further, increasing disadvantage was less likely in neighborhoods that were more stable initially (–.268; $p < .01$). No features of initial fabric linked to stability changes. Bivariate results further linked initial incivilities to these same two pathways of decline. Declining status was more likely in neighborhoods where neighbors in 1982 saw more physical incivilities (–.145; $p < .10$) or more social incivilities (–.141; $p < .10$). Finally, increasing disadvantage was more likely in locales where assessed incivilities were more extensive in 1981 (.140; $p < .10$). Initial incivilities did not link to later changes in stability.

The multivariate results, with separate equations for each outcome and for each incivility indicator, appear more consistent than did the crime change equations. What was or was not significant did not fluctuate so markedly from equation to equation or outcome to outcome, but there still were inconsistencies. The general patterns emerging were that incivilities appeared to matter marginally—only for one outcome and only in one equation—whereas race and stability proved consistently important. (See Table 5.3.)

Race affects unexpected changes, relative to other neighborhoods, on status. Initial racial composition predicted status changes in all three models. The race impact was in the direction expected, given generally lower exchange values for predominantly African-American neighborhoods—relative status slipped faster in more predominantly African-American neighborhoods. This probably represents a complex set of external and internal forces in these locales (19). Further exploration of

TABLE 5.3   Predicting Later Decline

Outcome / Indicator		b	se	b/se	p <
Changes in Status/					
Assessed Incivilities					
(R^2=0.069)	Incivilities	−0.022	0.196	<−1	
	VALRANK8	−0.004	0.008	<−1	
	BLACK80P	−0.008	0.005	−1.727	.10
	OWN80P	−0.009	0.007	−1.321	
Perceived Physical Incivilities					
(R^2=0.071)	Incivilities	−0.017	0.102	<−1	
	VALRANK8	−0.002	0.011	<−1	
	BLACK80P	−0.008	0.005	−1.706	.10
	OWN80P	−0.008	0.008	−1.002	
Perceived Social Incivilities					
(R^2=0.073)	Incivilities	−0.015	0.043	<−1	
	VALRANK8	−0.006	0.009	<−1	
	BLACK80P	−0.009	0.005	−1.755	.10
	OWN80P	−0.010	0.006	−1.664	
Changes in Disadvantage/					
Assessed Incivilities					
(R^2=0.234)	Incivilities	0.261	0.116	2.250	.05
	VALRANK8	0.003	0.003	<1	
	BLACK80P	−0.008	0.003	−2.610	.05
	OWN80P	−0.011	0.005	−2.370	.05
Perceived Physical Incivilities					
(R^2=0.206)	Incivilities	−0.040	0.047	<−1	
	VALRANK8	−0.004	0.005	<−1	
	BLACK80P	−0.008	0.003	−2.520	.05
	OWN80P	−0.018	0.007	−3.200	.01
Perceived Social Incivilities					
(R^2=0.197)	Incivilities	−0.004	0.013	<−1	
	VALRANK8	−0.002	0.004	<−1	
	BLACK80P	−0.008	0.003	−2.440	.05
	OWN80P	−0.017	0.005	−3.200	.01
Changes in Stability/					
Assessed Incivilities					
(R^2=0.024)	Incivilities	−0.112	0.187	<−1	
	VALRANK8	−0.001	0.004	<−1	
	BLACK80P	0.003	0.003	<1	
	OWN80P	−0.002	0.007	<−1	
Perceived Physical Incivilities					
(R^2=0.016)	Incivilities	0.005	0.057	<1	
	VALRANK8	0.001	0.007	<1	
	BLACK80P	0.003	0.003	<1	
	OWN80P	0.001	0.005	<1	

(continues)

TABLE 5.3   *(continued)*

Outcome / Indicator		*b*	*se*	*b/se*	*p <*
Perceived Social Incivilities					
($R^2=0.016$)	Incivilities	-0.001	0.028	<-1	
	VALRANK8	0.0001	0.006	<1	
	BLACK80P	0.003	0.004	<1	
	OWN80P	0.0001	0.005	<1	

NOTE: 1-tailed test for incivilities; 2-tailed test for other predictors. Structural equation results with asymptotically distribution free estimates.

some bivariate relationships suggested the impact was limited to neighborhoods in the sample already predominantly African-American (70% or over) in 1980. Neighborhoods with this makeup drifted down more than did predominantly white neighborhoods, and especially more so than a smaller group of initially integrated neighborhoods in the sample (40% to 70% African-American in 1980). In the sample, predominantly African-American neighborhoods lost relative housing value faster than other sample neighborhoods. This dynamic operating over time helps explain how the connection between race and lower exchange value, seen cross-sectionally, replicates and reinforces itself, becoming tighter and tighter over successive decades (16, 43).

Notable in their absence were impacts of incivilities; in none of the equations for status change did a significant one appear. The failure of any indicator to influence later status changes contradicts the longitudinal incivilities theorists. It does *not* appear to be the case that incivilities on their own cause later softening of the housing market or decreasing attractiveness to moderately educated residents or potential in-migrants. In short, grime does *not* lead to later status decline.[15]

Turning to changes in disadvantage, incivilities theorists receive some support. Incivilities showed expected lagged impacts in one of the three models. Neighborhoods where more extensive incivilities were recorded by raters in 1981 increased faster on vacancies and poverty in the 1980s ($p < .05$), relative to other neighborhoods, controlling for 1980 structure. Incivilities based on residents' assessments did not show the expected impacts. So, again, as with the crime results, the pattern for this outcome is both encouraging—because an expected effect emerged—and troubling—because the influential indicator is not the one widely used in the literature, and the widely used ones did not work out.

As with the earlier pathway of decline, race was significant in all models. But here the results were *opposite* the direction anticipated. Disadvan-

tage increased *less* in more predominantly African-American neighborhoods. Close examination of a number of scatter plots showed why. The
neighborhoods exclusively or almost exclusively African-American at
the beginning of the period already demonstrated moderate levels of vacancy and poverty. Although matters there worsened (median unexpected poverty change = −.14%, n=23), they worsened more dramatically
in neighborhoods starting out the decade relatively integrated (median
unexpected poverty change = −2.8%, n=11).

More expected were the homeownership impacts. Greater stability in
1980 helped prevent increasing disadvantage over the following decade.
This connection appeared in all three models. This lagged impact
strongly confirms ecological theorists who expound the virtues of stable
neighborhoods (e.g., 20).

In contrast to the relative predictability of the first two pathways,
changes in stability were not predicted by any of the variables in our
model.

In sum, incivilities proved relevant to one pathway of decline, increasing disadvantage. As with the crime changes, however, the impact only
showed up for one type of incivility indicator. Viewing this result with
more confidence than may be warranted, and in the context of nil impacts
of incivilities on status shifts, it appears that actual deterioration spawns
more deterioration when the deterioration betokens a neighborhood already in an underclass position relative to other neighborhoods. This supports Skogan's suggestion that incivilities may have some self-propagat-
ing qualities (34). If the housing and economic situation in a
neighborhood is already so bad that the neighborhood abounds with graffiti, abandoned houses, and lots of people hanging out, those problems
will worsen, as shown by more empty units and more poverty, in the
years to come. For the 1970s, Jeanette Covington and I documented how
already-disadvantaged neighborhoods in Baltimore in 1970 became more
deeply entrenched in this status as the decade progressed (38). That
process appears to be continuing into the 1980s. In Chapter 4, I reviewed
the neighborhoods where abandoned housing was increasing in the
1980s; it was growing particularly in low-income, predominantly African-
American near-westside and, to a lesser extent, near-eastside neighborhoods. If we knew how much deterioration was evident on the street in
1981, we could help predict how much worse the degree of disadvantage
would become, as reflected in vacancies and poverty. Nonetheless, it is
not clear how we should interpret such an incivilities impact since it did
not appear when we relied on residents' views about incivilities.

The results control for status and race, two factors with a major influence on how outsiders gauge the exchange value of the locale. So it is

probably not just a lack of outside investor interest spurring faster decline. Here are some possibilities: (1) For some reason, these locales with high assessed incivilities in 1981 were already underserved by the public agencies concerned with the physical environment (sanitation, fire, housing); they also may have been underserved by police as well, because officers' responsiveness may have been lower in these more disorderly contexts (15). That spatial differentiation continued forward in time, deepening the differences between less deteriorated and more deteriorated locales. The information supplied by some neighborhood leaders about deterioration issues and connections with outside agencies (Chapters 7, 8) would seem to support this idea. The poverty increased because, as Shaw and McKay pointed out, it is only in the deteriorated locales that extremely low income households can find affordable lodgings. (2) Neighborhoods with extensive assessed incivilities in 1981 were more likely than other neighborhoods to have established criminal subcultures, given the larger numbers of people on the street and the greater number of available places without supervision, such as abandoned houses, to carry on criminal activities (36). Those subcultures grew and became more dominant over the decade, especially after the crack cocaine invasion circa 1987, thereby deepening deterioration. (3) Residents and perhaps especially leaders in the locales with high incivilities in 1981 may have lacked strong public control and were unable to secure external resources and services (5). This ineffectiveness, in ways separate from the service differentials first mentioned, may have shaped residents' and leaders' neighborhood maintenance efforts over the following decade.

The above-described processes are speculative only; with details lacking about the dynamics in each neighborhood, it is difficult to decide in favor of one set of processes over another. In Chapters 7 and 8, however, comments from neighborhood leaders provide some insight into the relationships between neighborhoods and outside agencies and resources.

Discussion

Both incivilities and basic neighborhood composition have demonstrated impacts on crime changes; at least one incivilities indicator demonstrated an independent impact on three of the four later violent crime changes examined. Furthermore, at least one feature of neighborhood fabric demonstrated lagged impacts on three of the four violent crime changes. But neither structural nor incivility impacts, except the impacts of race on changing homicide, proved consistent across the equations using different indicators of incivilities. The lack of consistency across different indicators does not appear to be solely an artifact of different-strength connections between incivilities and structure. Rather the different indicators themselves connect in various ways to each outcome.

The crime results also underscored a continuing spatial stratification of local crime rates along socioeconomic lines, showing how these differentials persist and move forward in time. Relative status buffered neighborhoods against later unexpected increases in rape and assault in at least one equation for each outcome. Higher-status neighborhoods were better at protecting themselves from these two violent crime *changes* in the 1980s. Work on community crime prevention might suggest this protection emerges largely from different police-community relations in high- versus medium- versus low-status locales (24, 25). But the qualitative material to be reviewed in Chapters 7 and 8 shows the sources of relative protection differences are several, involving a wide array of actors and factors, including public control, history, and fundamental differences not only in resources but also in strategic planning approaches. That qualitative material suggests the buffering effects of higher initial status are "real," and beneath the simple coefficients presented here lie complex processes both internal to and external to the neighborhoods in question.

Turning to the structural decline outcomes, incivilities revealed an even weaker pattern of lagged impacts—significant in only one of the nine equations. Assessed deterioration, controlling for initial structure, did facilitate later relative growth in poverty and vacant housing. As seen when looking at the crime outcomes, the impact here on disadvantage change did not hold up across various indicators of incivilities. In short, we are *unable* to make a strong case that grime leads to later structural decline.

When the outcome switched from crime changes to structural changes, not only did impacts of incivilities weaken, lagged impacts of structure emerged more consistently. Race, consistently relevant to only one crime change, proves consistently relevant here for two pathways of structural change—status and disadvantage. Stability likewise proved consistently relevant to changing disadvantage. Changes in structure link to initial structure (e.g., 13, 14). Results here suggest these links are stronger than the links of structure to later crime change.

But the connections were sometimes not as expected in the case of race. In keeping with McDougall's arguments, more heavily African-American neighborhoods dropped faster on status, relative to the other neighborhoods. This finding may be evidence of discrimination, although other factors also could be at work. But when we switched to looking at another pathway of change, disadvantage, initial African-American composition *protected* the neighborhood against further erosion. As noted above, this connection emerged from differences between initially integrated and initially African-American neighborhoods.

More consistent than race, and fully in keeping with ecological theory on this topic, were the impacts of stability. Higher levels of initial stability consistently protected against later increases in disadvantage.

The longitudinal results shown here provide weaker support for the latest versions of the incivilities thesis than other cross-sectional examinations (11, 34) have done. It is often the case that when researchers shift from cross-sectional to longitudinal analyses, support for an idea weakens. This is true especially in the work on communities and crime (21: 136–138). This seems to be the case with the longitudinal, ecological version of the incivilities thesis. In the one test most closely comparable to the cross-sectional, neighborhood-level, decline and disorder work, with robbery as the outcome, a highly significant cross-sectional relationship seen in other work appeared as nonsignificant in a longitudinal framework (but cf. Harcourt's comments on the initial robbery analysis [11]).

Certainly there is some support for the ecological and longitudinal version of the incivilities thesis. The longitudinal impact of assessed incivilities on later homicide shifts may be the strongest case in point. But that support seems slightly stronger for crime change as compared to structural decline, and it is not as robust as the cross-sectional work has suggested.

Evidence reviewed in Chapter 3 revealed that different types of indicators, for either static or changing incivilities, often failed to link tightly together. Chapter 4 commented on these divergences in the context of some specific neighborhoods. This lack of convergent validity appears even more troubling when considered in light of some of the results seen here: It appears that lagged impacts on later crime or structural changes are *not* general across different incivility indicators; to some extent each type of incivility indicator is linked with disparate lagged outcomes. Just as there can be different pathways of neighborhood change or neighborhood decline (35), there may not be one level of incivilities or incivilities change in a locale. Instead we may have a loosely linked set of neighborhood issues—housing vacancies, uncivil neighbors, rowdy teens, or poor housing maintenance—each amplifying the other issues less than anticipated and each deserving separate recognition and separate remedies.

Turning to community structure, results here show more consistent lagged impacts for structure than for incivilities. These results are fully in accord with the political economy perspective on neighborhood shifts (17: 123). When all is said and done, initial racial composition, stability, and status appear more important for predicting later neighborhood decline than incivilities, and status and race appear at least as important as incivilities for predicting crime changes.

Certainly the current work has numerous limitations. First, some may argue that the change period examined here is too lengthy. For researchers relying on decennial census data, however, there are no alternatives for gauging community structure without funding for very sizable community surveys. Second, results here are limited to one city and one decade of change. External validity, however, as must be the case, is an empirical question and cannot be gauged a priori. Third, some may argue that the pathways of structural decline were too "thinly" defined, with only two variables for each pathway. Certainly different results with different structural variables are possible. But the focus here was on changes in fabric that all would agree are either desirable or undesirable. One hopes that the six variables used meet that standard. Fourth, some may argue that the equations should have included interaction terms, so that incivilities could have stronger or weaker impacts under varying conditions and thus have a stronger overall impact. I find this a reasonable suggestion, but the purpose here was to test the longitudinal, ecological version of the incivilities thesis. That thesis does not concern itself with interaction terms, but rather with "main effects" of incivilities after controlling for structure. Finally, some may have wished for crime variables to be included in the structural change equations. They were excluded in fairness to the incivilities thesis. To have included crime would have made it even more difficult for incivilities to demonstrate an independent impact. Offsetting these concerns, of course, are the numerous advantages of the current investigation. They include the use of multiple types of indicators for incivilities; analyses prepared to accommodate non-normally distributed data; and, most important, a longitudinal analytic design capturing outcome shifts over time, the very shifts of central interest to the incivilities thesis.

This chapter has gauged two of the three outcome areas where incivilities were expected to change neighborhood life: shifts in fabric and violence. The thesis has not fared as well as expected, proving of minimal relevance to structural changes and moderate relevance to crime changes. The next chapter turns attention to the outcomes that initially drew the attention of incivilities theorists: fear, local commitments, and other reactions to crime. Perhaps the thesis will fare better with these outcomes, which have been of interest for longer.

Notes

1. Harcourt (11) has reanalyzed Skogan's data, playing closer attention to outliers and how they may have influenced results. He also has redone other features of the analysis. His reexamination leads to some markedly different conclusions. He also has provided an extensive theoretical critique of the decline and disorder thesis.

2. Analyses do not include initial relative crime rates as predictors of structural change. Analyses first sought to learn whether incivilities showed a lagged impact on structural changes. To look for this impact after controlling for crime rather than before would be to make an even more stringent test of the incivilities thesis.

3. In Baltimore, during the time period examined the two major racial groups present were African Americans and whites. Given the lack of large proportions of other racial groups, it was not possible to simultaneously examine impacts of ethnic heterogeneity and racial composition.

4. Harcourt (11) has criticized Skogan's 1990 (34) neighborhood analysis for focusing just on robbery results and has shown different results with different crimes.

5. Of the four violent crimes, skepticism about measurement issues is likely to be strongest for rape and weakest for homicide. Therefore, results that appear only for rape should probably be viewed with considerable caution.

6. The principal components analysis yielded three eigenvalues greater than 1.0: 1.91, 1.38, 1.16. These three explained a cumulative 74% of the variance in the items before rotation. The varimax rotated solution provided an extremely clean component matrix. Percent owner occupied loaded .91 and percent one unit structures loaded .90 on Component I (Changes in Stability). Percent vacant units loaded .83 and percent households in poverty loaded .83 on Component II (Changes in Disadvantage). Percent with at least some college education loaded .83, and house value percentile loaded .83 on Component III (Changes in Status). All variables, again, represented unexpected change between 1980 and 1990. The principal components analysis was carried out for all neighborhoods in the city (n=262), excluding only the downtown and public housing communities.

A parallel analysis was completed using the percent of the adult population with a high school degree but no better. That variable, however, produced a muddier principal components solution. I will report, however, on the places where the results differed depending on which education variable was used.

Some might argue that the loss of households with at least some college might *not* represent neighborhood decline. It is true that a neighborhood can be destabilized by the influx of large numbers of professional households who bid up house prices beyond the reach of long-term residents. But those households often have completed college or have gone beyond to complete additional professional degrees. The variable here focuses rather on at least some college or more, not college completion or professional degree.

The principal components solution here uses only two variables to define each component. Ideally, each component would be defined by more variables. But expanding the number of variables runs the risk of including some variables that people would not agree represent decline. All six variables included here represent changes that almost all would agree are deleterious for a neighborhood.

7. See 37: Figures 7-A–1 through 7-A–13 in chapter 7, Appendix A.

8. Unfortunately, this procedure allows for partialling only one variable at a time, and the procedures to determine the statistical significance of the partials have not been specified.

9. AMOS version 3.6 was used to obtain these estimates.

10. To obtain an acceptable level of statistical power, an alpha level of .10 (one-tailed) was adopted for the incivilities and .10 (two-tailed) for features of neighborhood composition. The direction of expected incivility impacts was clear, leading to the one-tailed tests, whereas for lagged impacts of structure, effects opposite to those predicted were of substantial interest, leading to two-tailed tests. Power analyses for closely related models suggested that regression results should yield

power of about 87% for the impacts of incivilities and 78% for the impacts of features of neighborhood structure, given a medium effect size. The generous alpha level used here was not shrunk to control for multiple correlated outcomes in the case of the four violent crime rate changes. Some might argue the level should be Bonferroni-adjusted. The regression results shown here treat all the variables as observed and all predictors as correlated and presume error in the outcomes.

11. To commit the ecological fallacy is to presume that relationships observed at one level of analysis (e.g., neighborhood-level, ecological connections) apply at a smaller level, e.g., to individuals or incidents. Such presumptions are not warranted because the relationships may operate differently at different levels of analysis.

12. This is one result that depended on the analysis approach. If structure is parametrically partialled from assessed incivilities and then nonparametrically correlated with homicide change, the result was nonsignificant.

13. Of course, in addition to the cross-sectional vs. longitudinal approach, the outcome in his study was based on self-report whereas analyses here use reported crime data. With the latter, it is not possible to separate out robberies of residents from robberies of nonresidents.

14. If the status change component used an education variable that was percent who had completed high school education and gone no further, status change also linked to initial status. Status was less likely to drop in neighborhoods with initially higher house values ($.17; p < .05$).

15. This result does not contradict the substantial literature linking crime and related dynamics to house values—see Chapter 4. It is quite conceivable that crime but not incivilities would independently influence house prices.

References

(1) Allison, P. D. (1990) Change scores as dependent variables in regression analysis. *Sociological Methodology* 20, 93–115.

(2) Baldwin, J., and Bottoms, A. E. (1976) *The urban criminal,* Tavistock, London.

(3) Bohrnstedt, G. W. (1969) Observation on the measurement of change. In *Sociological methodology* (Borgatta, E. F., and Bohrnstedt, G. W., eds), pp. 113–133. San Francisco: Jossey-Bass.

(4) Bursik, R. J., and Webb, J. (1982) Community change and patterns of delinquency. *American Journal of Sociology* 88, 24–42.

(5) Bursik, R. J., and Grasmick, H. G. (1993) *Neighborhoods and crime: The dimensions of effective social control,* Lexington Books, New York.

(6) Covington, J. C., and Taylor, R. B. (1989) Gentrification and crime: Robbery and larceny changes in appreciating Baltimore neighborhoods in the 1970's. *Urban Affairs Quarterly* 25, 142–172.

(7) Crutchfield, R., Geerken, M. R., and Gove, W. (1982) Crime rates and social integration: The impact of metropolitan mobility. *Criminology* 20, 467–478.

(8) Gottdiener, M. (1994) *The social production of urban space* 2nd ed., University of Texas Press, Austin.

(9) Hagedorn, J. M. (1994) Neighborhoods, markets, and drug gang organization. *Journal of Research in Crime and Delinquency* 31, 264–294.

(10) Hannan, M. T. (1971) *Aggregation and disaggregation in sociology,* Lexington Books, Lexington, MA.

(11) Harcourt, B. E. (1998) Reflecting on the subject: A critique of the social influence conception of deterrence, the broken windows theory, and order-maintenance policing New York style. *Michigan Law Review* 97, 291–372.

(12) Heitgard, J., and Bursik, R. (1987) Extracommunity dynamics and the ecology of delinquency. *American Journal of Sociology* 92, 775–787.

(13) Hunter, A. (1971) The ecology of Chicago: Persistence and change, 1930–1960. *American Journal of Sociology* 77, 425–443.

(14) Hunter, A. (1974) Community change: A stochastic analysis of Chicago's local communities, 1930–1960. *American Journal of Sociology* 79, 923–947.

(15) Klinger, D. A. (1997) Negotiating order in police work: An ecological theory of police response to deviance. *Criminology* 35, 277–306.

(16) Liska, A. E., and Bellair, P. E. (1995) Violent crime rates and racial composition: Convergence over time. *American Journal of Sociology* 101, 578.

(17) Logan, J. R., and Molotch, H. (1987) *Urban fortunes,* University of California Press, Berkeley.

(18) Massey, D., and Denton, S. (1993) *American apartheid: Segregation and the making of the underclass,* Harvard University Press, Cambridge, MA.

(19) McDougall, H. A. (1993) *Black Baltimore: A new theory of community,* Temple University Press, Philadelphia.

(20) McKenzie, R. D. (1921) The neighborhood. In *On human ecology* (Hawley, A. H., and McKenzie, R. D., eds), pp. 51–93. University of Chicago Press, Chicago.

(21) Miethe, T. D., and Meier, R. F. (1994) *Crime and its social context,* State University of New York Press, Albany.

(22) Morenoff, J. D., and Sampson, R. J. (1997) Violent crime and the spatial dynamics of neighborhood transition: Chicago, 1970–1990. *Social Forces* 76, 31–64.

(23) Pattillo, M. E. (1998) Sweet mothers and gangbangers: Managing crime in a black middle-class neighborhood. *Social Forces* 76, 747–774.

(24) Podolefsky, A. (1983) *Case studies in community crime prevention,* Charles C. Thomas, Springfield, IL.

(25) Podolefsky, A., and Dubow, F. (1981) *Strategies for community crime prevention: Collective responses to crime in urban America,* Charles C. Thomas, Springfield, IL.

(26) Rengert, G. (1996) *The geography of illegal drug markets,* Westview, Boulder.

(27) Rogosa, D. (1988) Myths about longitudinal research. In *Methodological issues in aging research* (Schaie, K. W., Campbell, R. T., Meredith, W., and Rawlings, S. C., eds), pp. 171–209. Springer, New York.

(28) Rogosa, D., Brandt, D., and Zimowski, M. (1982) A growth curve approach to the measurement of change. *Psychological Bulletin* 92, 726–748.

(29) Sampson, R. J., Raudenbush, S. W., and Earls, F. (1997) Neighborhoods and violent crime: A multi-level study of collective efficacy. *Science* 277, 918–924.

(30) Shihadeh, E. S., and Flynn, N. (1996) Segregation and crime: The effect of black social isolation on the rates of urban black violence. *Social Forces* 74, 1325–1352.

(31) Siegel, S. (1956) *Nonparametric statistics for the behavioral sciences*, McGraw-Hill, New York.

(32) Simon, D. (1991) *Homicide: A year on the Killing Streets*, Ballantine, New York.

(33) Simon, D., and Burns, E. (1997) *The corner: A year in the life of an inner-city neighborhood*, Broadway Books, New York.

(34) Skogan, W. (1990) *Disorder and decline: Crime and the spiral of decay in American cities*, Free Press, New York.

(35) Taub, R. P., Taylor, D. G., and Dunham, J. D. (1981) Neighborhoods and safety. In *Reactions to crime* (Lewis, D. A., ed), pp. 103–119. Sage, Beverly Hills, CA.

(36) Taylor, R. B. (1987) Toward an environmental psychology of disorder. In *Handbook of environmental psychology* (Stokols, D., and Altman, I., eds), pp. 951–986. New York: Wiley.

(37) Taylor, R. B. (1996) *Crime and grime over two decades: Stability, decline, and spatial inequality in charm city neighborhoods*. Unpublished final report (Grant No.: 93-IJ-CX-0022), Temple University, Philadelphia. (Available online: http://www.ncjrs.org, NCJ number 171628)

(38) Taylor, R. B., and Covington, J. (1988) Neighborhood changes in ecology and violence. *Criminology* 26, 553–589.

(39) Taylor, R. B., and Covington, J. (1993) Community structural change and fear of crime. *Social Problems* 40, 374–397.

(40) Taylor, R. B., Shumaker, S. A., and Gottfredson, S. D. (1985) Neighborhood-level links between physical features and local sentiments: Deterioration, fear of crime, and confidence. *Journal of Architectural Planning and Research* 2, 261–275.

(41) Thorndike, E. L. (1939) On the fallacy of imputing the correlations found for groups to the individuals in smaller groups composing them. *American Journal of Psychology* 52, 122–124.

(42) Wilson, W. J. (1996) *When work disappears: The world of the new urban poor*, Knopf, New York.

(43) Wilson, W. J., and Aponte, R. (1985) Urban poverty. *Annual Review of Sociology* 11, 231–258.

6

Longitudinal Impacts of Incivilities on Reactions to Crime and Local Commitment

Understanding why some people are more afraid of crime than others and why such fears are higher in some locations than others has been of continuing interest to researchers and policymakers alike for well over a quarter century. Incivilities theorists have contributed to that discussion, describing how disorderly local social conditions (called social incivilities) and deteriorated local physical conditions (called physical incivilities) contribute to fear and other reactions to crime. As described in Chapter 3, these outcomes have been of central interest since the earliest versions of the incivilities theory. But as also noted in that chapter, the nature of the connection between incivilities and reactions to crime such as fear has shifted. The early theorists argued at the individual level: Those who were surrounded by more deteriorated or disorderly conditions— usually operationalized as those who perceived themselves to be so— were more fearful.

The connection has been well documented, even though it is not yet clear which causes which. Later theorists such as Wilson and Kelling added additional arguments either at the small group or streetblock level or, as did Skogan, at the neighborhood level. That neighborhood-level, longitudinal connection has not been documented and is the focus of this chapter. More specifically, the longitudinal, ecological version of the thesis posits lagged neighborhood-level impacts of incivilities on fear. In neighborhoods where incivilities are more widespread, over time residents should become more fearful, see the surround as more dangerous, and become more desirous of leaving. Using evidence from the thirty neighborhoods where residents were interviewed in 1994, do we see evidence of these suggested impacts?

Before turning to the main evidence, however, a broader background for work on reactions to crime is provided. The following section looks beyond concerns about incivilities per se and reviews the predictors of fear, avoidance, and mobility intentions.

Reactions to Crime

Much has been written on reactions to crime, such as fear of crime, avoiding dangerous places, taking steps to protect person or property, or joining with neighbors to collectively combat crime. (For reviews see 6, 9, 24, 30, 60.)

Fear

Well-documented since the mid-1970s have been the demographic correlates of safety concerns. Expressing more fear are women; African Americans and other minorities; and, in most studies, older persons. Various interpretations arise to explain each of these differentials.

Gender. Several researchers ascribe gender differences to fear of sexual assault (29, 43, 58). Warr suggests this results from women's greater fear of dark, nighttime scenes (59). Ferraro shows this concern is especially high among younger women (12: 97). Young women, he argues, are more vulnerable to sexual assault because they may move often and be involved in family transitions.

Others argue from a markedly different approach, suggesting that women's fear of crime is different from men's throughout the life course. For example, Stanko argues that women from an early age learn to fear men and remember this lesson. Women may have as much to fear from known males, such as ex-lovers or ex-husbands, husbands, or employers, as they do from strange men. Their fears are not just about rape, but about "hey honey" hassles and a wide array of possible other intrusions from males. "Early lessons in danger become part of a lifetime of negotiating danger, inside and outside the home" (43: 49).

Race. Race differences receive various interpretations as well. Skogan and Maxfield suggested that race differences in fear reflect the more disorderly ecological context in which African Americans are likely to find themselves, at least as compared to whites in the same urban settings (40). Because of where they live, African Americans experience higher ecological vulnerability. But one study found that race differences persisted even after controlling for disorder and crime in the surrounding neighborhood (5), raising questions about the relevance of ecological vulnerability as an interpretation of race differences.

Impacts of race, and gender too, may interact with age in shaping fear (26). It is not clear from the work to date if these interactions dramatically outweigh the main effects of each attribute.

Turning to neighborhood racial context, at least one study fails to find independent impacts of racial composition on fear after controlling for neighborhood status and stability (46). Discrepant findings for net impacts of neighborhood racial composition across studies may reflect differing study contexts (e.g., statewide telephone surveys with census data attached vs. clustered, urban neighborhood samples), varying controls applied (e.g., some control for neighborhood crime rate but others do not), or different definitions of "neighborhood."

The racial heterogeneity of the locale may influence fear (23, 34, 35), as may the discrepancy between an individual's race and the overall neighborhood makeup (5). Merry's thesis linking intercultural distance positively to fear provides a clear-cut theoretical interpretation for impacts of community racial diversity (23).

To sum up on race, the following points are suggested. African Americans, compared to whites, routinely report higher fear levels. Even after controlling for features of the neighborhood, including crime and incivilities, these differences persist. Race impacts can be moderated by gender or age. Less often examined are fear differences between whites and other racial groups, such as Asians or Hispanics. Even less work has been completed on fear differences within racial groups, for example, contrasting Chicano, Puerto Ricano, and Cuban Hispanics. At the neighborhood level, racial composition may not be influential after controlling for other features of the neighborhood with which it may closely link, including crime, stability, status, and disorder, but the racial diversity of the neighborhood does appear relevant. As racial heterogeneity increases, it may become increasingly difficult for residents to interpret the street behavior of those belonging to dissimilar cultural or ethnic groups.

Age. Although individual-level gender and race differentials on fear are beyond dispute, age impacts are not. Most studies find increasing fear with age (12: 67–69). But not all. Ferraro's (1994) results with a national telephone sample conducted in 1990 asking people about fears of specific crimes showed slightly lower fear among older respondents. Rountree and Land, analyzing a Seattle community survey also completed in 1990, find a slight negative impact of age on perceptions of neighborhood safety (34: Table 3; see also 35: Table 4). Ferraro suggests discrepant findings may emerge given measurement, analytical, and time differences across studies.

Not only are there questions about age's solo impact on fear, but several studies suggest age's impact on fear may be conditional on other features of the person or context. Ortega and Myles suggest interactions between age, gender, and race (26). Maxfield finds age effects stronger in higher-crime neighborhoods, suggesting in those locales the elderly feel particularly at risk (20). He suggests the vulnerability arises not from the person characteristics, but rather from links between person and setting characteristics. And Liska and colleagues have added a different wrinkle, proposing that the connection between fear and other reactions to crime, such as constrained behavior, gets stronger the older the respondent (18).

Knowing if there is an age-fear link has important policy implications (4). If there is a strong positive linkage, as "boomers" become elderly in larger numbers, nationwide, fear of crime should increase. This general fear increase has not yet surfaced (24).

Status.   Typically, higher-status respondents, measured through education or income, report lower fear levels. Work suggests this relationship holds at the neighborhood (46), streetblock (52), and individual levels (5). At the neighborhood level, the connection may be carried by how attached residents are to their neighborhood and how socially involved they are there (46), as well as by urban service differentials (19). At the streetblock level, the connection is mediated by physical features that support territorial functioning, such as real and symbolic barriers (52), and by land use characteristics (16). The presence of some territorial and land use factors covaries with status. For example, mixed land use blocks are less likely in higher-status neighborhoods. At the individual level, the connection may be mediated by territorial cognitions, such as how responsible people feel for locations immediately adjoining their residence (45, 52).

Local Crime and Victimization.   Studies routinely find weak-to-moderate correlations between local crime rates and fear levels (9, 53). A recent study by Rountree, however, observed a stronger linkage than has been typically observed by using victimization data and separating out different types of fears and different types of victimization (33). Despite this last study, important questions remain about why the connection is not stronger.

One reason may be how fear is distributed. Most of the variation in fear reflects differences between neighbors, not differences between neighborhoods (27). In short, these contextual connections have only a relatively small portion of the fear variable with which to work. Another possibility is that fear might cause "protective action and decreased exposure to risky and vulnerable situations, which in turn, results in lower risks of victimization" (24: 14). We do not know in systematic detail the behavioral adaptations people are making to living in locales with high crime or high victimization rates and how those connect to fear over time. One study linked protective behaviors with later *in*creases in fear, suggesting that steps people take to cope with crime may make them more rather than less concerned over time (55). Some quasi-experimental work on community crime prevention initiatives also points toward a similar dynamic (31, 32).

Individual victimization experience connects more consistently to fear of crime, with victims reporting more fear (e.g., 40). It appears that indirect victimization—hearing about local crime events from neighbors—also fuels fear (53).

As researchers—with a few exceptions—have failed to unearth exceedingly strong connections between fear and local crime or victimization rates, they have turned toward a broader array of neighborhood conditions to perhaps explain the sources of fear.

Social Dynamics. Local social dynamics prove relevant. Those who are surrounded by similar, as compared to dissimilar, others; who recognize more of the people living nearby; or who have stronger local social ties, report less fear (36, 37, 52).

Territorial Functioning. Also relevant is residents' territorial functioning (45, 47, 49, 51). Stronger territorial functioning—having more say about who does what where in outdoor spaces nearby—dampens fear. The impacts emerge at the streetblock level, and they also explain fear differences between individuals on the same blocks (52).

The impacts of incivilities are described in detail below, following a discussion of other outcomes and the theoretical evolution of the incivilities thesis.

Avoidance, Behavioral Restriction, Constrained Behavior

Individual behavioral responses to crime or the possibility of victimization can include avoiding places seen as dangerous, either all the time or at certain times, and more generally restricting one's behavioral orbit. For the latter, one may, for example, no longer go out at night or may only go out in the evening only if accompanied by others.

Researchers often join avoidance of specific places and behavioral constraint. For example, for his index of constrained behavior Ferraro used three items: "Do you generally avoid unsafe areas during the day because of crime?" "Do you avoid unsafe areas during the night because of crime?" and "Within the past year, have you limited or changed your daily activities because of crime?" (12: 56)

Has avoidance been increasing? Available national indicators include items such as, "Is there any area near where you live—that is, within a mile—where you would be afraid to walk alone at night?"[1] Gallup polls conducted since the mid-1960s show the proportion of U.S. residents saying yes to this question has varied from 31% to 45% (41: Table 2.32). These data suggest avoidance was higher in the 1970s and 1980s than it was in the 1960s, but may have come down slightly in the mid-1990s. This latest, slight downturn may shadow the national violent crime drop witnessed from about 1992–1993 through—at least—the first half of 1998. It is intriguing that these data show a noticeable jump in the early 1970s, when fear also moved up.

Going beyond these national results for this one item, we see that the amount of avoidance varies somewhat depending on the question. Looking at results up through the late 1970s, DuBow and his colleagues noted that 42% to 52% of respondents would mention specific places they avoided going, whereas closer to two thirds would say they avoided someplace in the city (9: Table 1). "It is reasonable to assume from these studies that a clear majority of urban residents in the late 1970s avoided particular places within their city because of crime" (24: 22).

Who is more likely to avoid dangerous places? Nationally, in 1996, those who were more likely to say there was a nearby fear-inspiring place to avoid were women, African Americans, or nonwhites; had less education; and lived in urban as opposed to suburban or rural areas (41: Table 2.0016) Ferraro's national telephone survey in 1990 confirmed some of these connections (12). After controlling for the impacts of incivilities and perceived risk on constrained behavior, he found the latter higher among women; urban residents; and, up to a point, older respondents.

What are the kinds of dangerous places that people avoid? In a 1995 national survey, adults reported avoiding particular locations in their neighborhood (29%), public parks or recreation areas (28%), and the nearest mall or shopping center (21%) (22: 155).

Avoidance, constrained behavior, and fear link together in complex ways, especially for women, whose behavioral orbits are most restricted as a result (14, 28). As mentioned above, Liska's work suggests a tightening of the positive fear-avoidance link as age increases. By contrast, Miethe suggests that as people protect themselves more by avoiding dangerous places and constraining behavior, fear might decline.

Two main ways questions on this topic have differed are in the spatial scope and the specificity required. Spatial scope has varied from anywhere in the city, to within a mile of home, to within the neighborhood. Given decreasing territorial control as one moves away from home and decreasing recognition of others, we would expect that the chances of people saying they avoid someplace would increase with increasing distance encompassed (49). Sometimes questions ask for specific place nominations; sometimes they ask the respondent to say yes or no to a specific type of place, such as a shopping center; and sometimes they just ask the respondent if there is "anyplace" he or she avoids because it makes him or her feel unsafe. It seems likely that as specificity decreases, more respondents would say there are places they avoid.

In sum, one third to two thirds of respondents appear to avoid dangerous places. Avoidance does not appear to have increased nationally since the early 1970s. Avoidance is clearly more of an issue for urban residents and for women. People appear to avoid a wide array of public locations, including some that are likely to be high-crime locations. The amount of avoidance reported probably depends in part on how the question is asked, although we have had no firm tests of this notion.

Intending to Move

A few studies link perceptions of crime problems with an intent to move. One research project from the late 1960s used perceptions of crime and violence as predictors. More than 1,400 households in forty-three metropolitan areas were interviewed at two points in time. Researchers found that perceptions of disorder in the neighborhood were strongly linked to a desire to move. The connection appeared stronger for central city as compared to suburban residents (8). Similarly, in his decline and disorder data set of forty-plus neighborhoods from six cities, Skogan found both robbery victimization and perceptions of crime-related problems in the neighborhood correlating cross-sectionally with a desire to move out (38).

Intending to move, however, is not synonymous with actually moving. Mobility is not as clearly influenced by neighborhood crime or perceptions of neighborhood problems as is the intent to move. Studies spanning the mid-1960s through the late 1970s do *not* find individual-level connections between perceptions of crime and mobility or suburban flight (17, 25, 42, 57). One author concluded, for example, "This study's findings . . . refute the commonly accepted belief that many urban families move because of poor schools, the lack of police protection, or for other deficiencies in public service" (57: 193). The relationship fails to appear even when African Americans and whites are modeled separately (42). Demographic factors such as race and income, stage of life cycle, and location of employment represent the strongest factors influencing actual moves.

Numerous studies have relied on the Census Bureau's Annual Housing Survey (AHS), now completed every other year and called the American Housing Survey. Unfortunately, this data source provides only a small number of neighborhood indicators linked to crime (7).[2] The AHS does include interviewer reports about neighborhood conditions that might be linked to crime or related problems, but these are available only for respondents living in multiunit structures. The characteristics include each of the following within 300 feet of the target household: at least one abandoned building, at least one building with bars on the window, major repair of road needed, major accumulation of trash/litter. A more recent study, using National Crime Victimization data *did* suggest that some types of victimization may lead to later mobility (10).

In sum, relatively recent aggregate-level connections between perceived neighborhood problems and moving intention have surfaced, and some studies link intention to move and perceived crime problems; some suggest, however, the impact may be obviated by other local features (44). But connections between local crime, or incivilities, and residents' actual mobility are rarely seen, probably for a variety of reasons. One recent study with victimization data, however, does suggest impacts of victimization on later mobility.

Focus

Some questions about incivilities and fear persist. First, do incivilities at the neighborhood level have impacts over time on residents' reactions to crime, such as fear, avoidance, and local commitment, as predicted by the decline and disorder version of the thesis? Of particular interest are independent ecological impacts, net of neighborhood structure and crime, on *shifts* in the outcomes. In the current investigation, by controlling for earlier fear, avoidance, and commitment at the neighborhood level, the ecological focus is exclusively on *changes* in the neighborhood portion of the outcome; these shifts are the focus of the longitudinal versions of the thesis. Extant deterioration or shared perceptions of local deterioration, over time, should inspire more concern and weaken commitment. The particular dynamics carrying the connection may be those originally suggested by Hunter; faced with local deterioration, residents conclude that indigenous leaders are ineffective and external political leaders uncaring (15), thereby heightening feelings of vulnerability. Alternatively, the dynamics may center on weakening local attachment or commitment in the face of high incivilities, although cross-sectional results would argue against this pathway (46).

Indicators used to address the above question include both perceived and assessed incivilities. Research has relied extensively on residents' perceptions of incivilities at the individual level or aggregated to the neighborhood level. If residents in a locale agree with one another about the extent of incivilities, incivilities aggregated to the neighborhood level reflect a social fact, the views held in common by residents about these neighborhood qualities. Alternatively, assessed conditions, as revealed by how raters score neighborhood conditions, come closer to the policy targets of community policing initiatives, local associations' cleanup and beautification efforts, or efforts to combat vacant housing. From a policy perspective, it is the latter type of incivility—assessed—that suggests the most direct program goals.

The specific focus described so far is on longitudinal impacts. Unfortunately, both the broken windows version and the decline and disorder version of the thesis are silent about the timing of these impacts. How long does it take for the process to work over time? The lag in this study is a twelve-year span.

In addition to the longitudinal issues of central interest here, this investigation also addresses the cross-sectional, individual-level version of the incivilities thesis. Although we know that those individuals who perceive more problems are more afraid, we do not know which type of incivility is more fear inspiring. Studies generally use an index combining different physical and social incivilities. Here the two types are separated. Rowdy street behavior by unsupervised teen groups or others has always been a focus of social disorganization theory. One of the contributions of incivilities theorizing has been its attention to physical neighborhood conditions. But at the individual level, do these perceptions of physical problems contribute independently to outcomes such as fear, after we have controlled for perceived social incivilities and other demographics?

Data and Analysis[3]

In 1981, my colleagues and I assessed physical and social features on over 800 blocks in sixty-six randomly selected Baltimore neighborhoods. In 1982, we interviewed twenty-five household heads or their spouses in each of those neighborhoods (total n=1,622). In 1994, in thirty neighborhoods sampled from the sixty-six, we again interviewed household heads or their spouses. Most of the 1982 surveys were completed by phone; some were completed in the field. Contact procedures were the same in the two survey modes. For the 1994 survey, all the interviews were completed by phone. Computer assisted telephone interviewing (CATI) began in September 1994 and concluded in early November 1994. Selected households received a preapproach, signed letter. The response rate for the 1982 survey was 73%. The response rate for the 1994 survey was at least 51%. But if we exclude from the response rate calculations the numbers not used because the sample was complete in a neighborhood, the neighborhood quota having been reached (n=569), the response rate for the 1994 survey was 76.3%.

Because Steve Pardue took slides of a random subsample of sampled addresses on each block in the summer of 1994, we were able to complete a more detailed analysis than is usually done comparing respondent and nonrespondent addresses. The slides were coded by trained raters on features related to upkeep, territorial functioning, and defensible space. On four of the six scales, there were no differences between addresses producing a completed interview and those not producing a completed interview; on two scales there were significant differences.

The resulting 1994 sample was 33% African-American, slightly underrepresenting the 1990 African-American population in these same neighborhoods (average = 41.5%; median = 23.9%). The sample slightly overrepresented owners (75% compared to 56% average and 51% median across the thirty neighborhoods in 1990) and women (60%). Some of these discrepancies—and we cannot say how much—may have been due to neighborhood shifts from 1990 to 1994. But perhaps more important, the 1994 sample was excellently representative of the 1990 neighborhoods on racial composition and at least adequately representative on the two other ecological dimensions of factorial ecology.[4] The characteristics of the 1994 sample appear in Table 6.1.

Outcomes

I investigated six outcomes. The first four, described in Chapter 2, were standard National Crime Survey (NCS) fear of crime items, except they referred specifically either to the resident's streetblock or to elsewhere in the neighborhood. Early in the interview protocol, questions appeared about the respondent's neighborhood, its name, and its qualities, and streetblock was defined. Therefore the arenas were specified.

The avoidance item asked, "Are there any specific places in your neighborhood that many people try to avoid because they think these places might be dangerous?" The question emphasizes that the places are within the already-defined neighborhood and that many people avoid them, not just the respondent. Residents nominated a wide range of locations. The types of places expected to "generate" crime, such as bars and schools, were mentioned with moderate frequency. Residents also noted nonresidential land uses not likely to have legitimate nighttime users: playgrounds, cemeteries, and parks, for example. Respondents made numerous mentions of specific locations, corners, or streets that were trouble spots. In some predominantly African-American neighborhoods, residents would sometimes assert with confidence "drugs are sold there" when naming specific locations. Busy nonresidential land uses also inspired concern. Numerous mentions were made of convenience stores or

TABLE 6.1   Characteristics of 1994 Sample

	Mean	*SD*	*Median*	*Minimum*	*Maximum*
Age	51.6	16.6	50	20	94
Length of Residence	18.8	16.2	14	0	85

		N	*%*	*Missing/refused*
Sex	Men	275	39.1	
	Women	429	60.1	
Tenure	Owner	529	75.1	
	Renter	175	24.9	
Race	African-American	231	32.8	15 (2.2%)
	White	425	60.4	
	Other	33	4.7	
Education	LT High School	121	17.2	13 (1.8%)
	High School Only	226	32.1	
	Some College	134	19.0	
	BA / BS Only	115	16.3	
	Graduate Degree	95	13.5	
Household Size	1	184	26.1	2 (.3%)
	2	236	33.5	
	3 and up	282	40.1	
Marital Status	Married	364	51.7	
	Single, widowed, divorced, never married	340	48.3	

main thoroughfares with a number of stores. Shopping centers, 7-11s, even food stores and pharmacies merited several mentions.

The moving intention item asked: "Have you ever *seriously* considered moving out of your neighborhood?" (No (1) / Yes). IF YES: "Have you considered moving very often (4), now and then (3), or very rarely (2)?"

The marginal distributions for all outcomes for both the 1982 and 1994 surveys appear in Table 6.2. I examined bivariate scatter plots of neighborhood means for 1982 versus 1994 to ensure that no particular 1982 means had undue influence on the respective 1994 outcome means.

Previous work has shown that incivilities link in different ways even to different reactions to crime, such as daytime versus nighttime fear (50). I opted, therefore, to examine outcomes separately rather than creating broader indices. Hierarchical linear models or hierarchical generalized linear models were applied to each of the six outcomes. Level I was individuals; Level II was neighborhoods. For each outcome, at least four sets of models were run.

TABLE 6.2   Distributions of Outcome Scores

			Fear Items					
Arena		*Block*				*Neighborhood*		
Time of Day	*Day*		*Night*			*Day*		*Night*	
Year	1982	1994	1982	1994	1982	1994	1982	1994
Very safe (1)	602	538	332	217	517	400	194	93
	(81.9)	(76.4)	(45.2)	(30.8)	(70.3)	(56.8)	(26.4)	(13.2)
Somewhat safe (2)	114	139	229	285	160	230	244	267
	(15.5)	(19.7)	(31.2)	(40.5)	(21.8)	(32.7)	(33.2)	(37.9)
Somewhat unsafe (3)	15	17	98	116	43	50	160	161
	(2.0)	(2.4)	(13.3)	(16.5)	(5.9)	(7.1)	(21.8)	(22.9)
Very unsafe (4)	4	7	69	79	11	19	124	174
	(.5)	(1.0)	(9.4)	(11.2)	(1.5)	(2.7)	(16.9)	(24.7)
Don't know		3	7	7	4	5	13	9
		(.4)	(1.0)	(1.0)	(.5)	(.7)	(1.8)	(1.3)
Mean	1.212	1.277	1.868	2.082	1.382	1.554	2.296	2.599
SD	.491	.556	.977	.962	.667	.744	1.044	1.005

Avoidance Item

Are there any specific places in your neighborhood that many people try to avoid because they think these places might be dangerous?	*1982*		*1994*	
	n	*%*	*n*	*%*
No (0)	376	51.20%	363	51.56%
Yes (1)	280	38.10%	295	41.90%
Don't know	79	10.70%	46	6.53%

Moving Intention

Have you ever seriously considered moving out of your neighborhood?		*1982*		*1994*	
		n	*%*	*n*	*%*
No	1	435	59.20%	323	45.90%
Yes: very rarely	2	86	11.70%	71	10.10%
Yes: now and then	3	123	16.70%	145	20.60%
Yes: very often	4	85	11.60%	159	22.60%
Missing		2	0.30%	6	0.80%

NOTE: 1982 n = 735; 1994 n = 704. Data are from the same 30 neighborhoods at both points in time.

Model 1.   First, initial random effects ANOVAs via HLM established whether significant between-neighborhood variation on each outcome existed. If significant between-neighborhood variance did not exist, there would be no point adding neighborhood-level variables to the model to predict that between-neighborhood variation. At the bottom of Table 6.3, the line for Model 1 reports the percentage of the outcome variance that arises from between-neighborhood differences.

Model 2.   The second set of models entered for each outcome its Time 1 (1982), neighborhood mean as a predictor. This set of models accomplished two purposes. It reports whether significant variation remained on the outcome, from neighborhood to neighborhood, after controlling for the earlier outcome level. If the remaining between-neighborhood variation was not significant, there would be no point trying to add additional, neighborhood-level predictors to the model. In addition, it transformed the neighborhood portion of the outcome into an indicator of neighborhood change from 1982 to 1994. At the bottom of Table 6.3, the line for Model 2 reports how much total variance has been explained by adding in the outcome at Time 1 as a predictor. Since the predictor is a Level II (neighborhood) predictor, the amount explained cannot exceed the percentage shown in the line for Model 1.

Model 3.   The third set of models kept the same predictor from Model 2 and also added all other predictors *save* the incivilities indicators: demographic predictors (1994) at Level I and demographic (1980) and crime predictors (1980–1982) at Level II. Level I demographics were length of residence, gender, and education.[5]

It was not possible to enter either race or homeownership as control variables at Level I, because in several neighborhoods all respondents were of one race or one tenure status. Entering the variable at Level I would have meant dropping those neighborhoods from the analysis. Added at Level II were percentage African-American, percentage homeowners, population-weighted house value percentile (3), and a robbery population-weighted crime percentile, all based on beginning-of-the-decade (circa 1980) scores.[6] At the bottom of Table 6.3, the line for Model 3 shows the percentage of total outcome variance explained by all these predictors.

Model 4.   The final set of models uses all the predictors previously entered and adds incivilities.[7] At the neighborhood level, either perceived or assessed incivilities from 1982 or 1981 (respectively), or both, were included. Impacts linked to these predictors tested the hypothesized longitudinal impacts from the decline and disorder version of the incivilities thesis. Available indicators included a summary index of perceived incivilities (Cronbach's alpha = .87) or on-site assessments either of prevalence of graffiti or abandoned housing in the neighborhood.[8] These models also added current perceived incivilities at the individual level. These last predictors tested the hypothesized impacts for the individual-level, cross-sectional version of the incivilities thesis, as described by Garofalo and Laub and others. At the individual level, both indices for perceived social incivilities (groups of teenagers hanging out, noise, people who say insulting things or bother people as they walk down the street, fighting or arguing; Cronbach's alpha = .82) and physical incivilities (vacant housing, vacant lots, litter and trash, people who do not keep up their property or yards; Cronbach's alpha = .80) were entered. At the bottom of Table 6.3, the figure for Model 4 represents the percentage of total outcome variance explained after entering all these predictors.

Variance Analysis

I first discuss the distribution of variance and the percentages of variance explained by each model. I then turn to a discussion of individual predictors.

How Sizable Are Differences Between Neighborhoods?   All six outcomes contained significant between-neighborhood differences (all $p < .01$). The variation ranged from 15.1% to 3.6% of the total variance (mean = 7.2%, median = 6.2%). See the row for Model 1 at the bottom of Table 6.3.

Are these results typical of what we might see in other cities? An investigation of surveys on reactions to crime in four other cities suggest they were (54).[9] Results from these other surveys using relatively comparable outcomes found amounts of neighborhood-to-neighborhood variation quite closely comparable to the portions seen here.

How Much Can We Explain?   Adding in the 1982 neighborhood mean for the outcome explained, on average, a little over 2% of the total outcome variation (median = .9%), ranging from a low of 0.1% for block fear at night to 7.4% for avoid. See the row for Model 2 at the bottom of Table 6.3. Although these numbers are modest, they are low in large part because the between-neighborhood variation averaged only 7% of the total variance.[10] Focusing only on this between-neighborhood portion of the variance, the pattern is more impressive (results not shown). On average, 1982 outcome scores explained 25% (median = 17%) of the 1994 between-neighborhood differences on the outcomes.

With the addition of lagged demographics at the neighborhood level, current demographics at the individual level, and earlier crime, the explained total variance increased about 7% to 8.9% (median = 9.1%); total explained variance ranged from a low of 6% to a high of 12%. See the row for Model 3 at the bottom of Table 6.3.

After controlling for neighborhood outcome means at Time 1 and earlier neighborhood structure and crime, significant between-neighborhood differences remain to be explained for moving plans ($p < .001$), avoidance ($p < .01$), block fear at night ($p < .01$), and block fear during the day ($p < .05$). But *no* significant between-neighborhood differences remained to be explained for neighborhood fear during the day or at night (both $p > .05$).[11] In short, once people move off their immediate streetblock, ecological changes in safety concerns while abroad in the neighborhood have been "explained away" by beginning-of-the-period neighborhood fabric and crime. Earlier incivilities were not relevant to these ecological shifts because there was nothing left to explain beyond chance between-neighborhood variation.

Results for the last set of models appear at the bottom of Table 6.3 (Model 4), showing total explained variance. These models added in both earlier incivilities at the neighborhood level (if warranted) and current incivilities at the individual level. For all six outcomes, the total explained variance jumped considerably, from around 9% for Model 3 to 17% (median total explained = 16.7%); the total explained variance in Model 4 ranged from 11.1% to 24.1%. Clearly, given this jump, incivilities contributed substantially to the outcomes in question.

For the two neighborhood fear items, the contribution of incivilities was solely at the individual level. But for the other four outcomes, how much of the impact of incivilities was based on individual, Level I differences, reflecting impacts of current (1994) perceived incivilities on the outcomes, and how much reflected neighborhood-level, lagged, causal impacts? A set of submodels addressed this question (results not shown). These contrasted the contributions of individual-level demographics and individual-level perceived incivilities to see how much total variation on the outcome was explained using just individual-level predictors. Looking at all the outcomes, adding perceived, individual-level incivilities increased the explained total variation to an average of 12.4% (median = 14.1%); this was a substantial increase from 4.5% (median = 5%) of the total variation explained when only using individual-level demographic predictors for these six outcomes. The increase in total explained variation was most substantial for moving intentions and neighborhood daytime fear. The only outcome for which perceived incivilities appeared *irrelevant* was avoidance.

In accord with Garofalo and Laub's version of the incivilities thesis, then, current perceived problems contributed substantially both to concerns about personal safety and to neighborhood commitment. If residents saw more problems than their neighbors, they were more afraid than their neighbors and more serious about moving out of the neighborhood. They were not, however, more likely to nominate nearby dangerous locations.

Another set of submodels (results not shown) examined the contribution of incivilities at the neighborhood level and their hypothesized lagged impact, looking just at the explained neighborhood-level variation rather than the explained total variation. Controlling for earlier neighborhood structure and crime made the most substantial contribution; the explained between-neighborhood variation increased from an average of 25% (median = 17.3%) to an average of 58% (median = 59.2%).

By contrast, prior neighborhood-level assessed or perceived incivilities made a far more modest contribution.[12] For block fear at night and during the day and for avoidance, incivilities failed to increase explained between-neighborhood outcome variation at all. For only one outcome, moving intentions, was the contribution noticeable; neighborhood-level explained outcome variation went from 48.9% to 59.1%.[13] In short, for only one of the six outcomes did the hypothesized lagged impact of incivilities on ecological changes emerge as sizable.

Examination of these between-neighborhood contributions of earlier incivilities in the context of total outcome variation shows much more modest results, since the between-neighborhood differences are such a modest part of outcomes. The biggest neighborhood contribution of prior incivilities, as noted above, increased the explained neighborhood-level variance for moving intentions from 49% to 59%. Looking at the contribution in terms of the total variance, we went from 3.9% of the total variation explained to 4.7% explained. This was a modest impact by most practical standards, although a program with a significant, moderate-sized impact could still dramatically affect a variance component of around 1%, which is the difference we are seeing here (11).

To sum up so far: Results have controlled for neighborhood structure and crime in the early 1980s and for early 1980s outcome level, so that at the neighborhood level the outcomes captured changes. Assessed incivilities and perceived incivilities from the early 1980s were allowed to predict shifting responses to crime and neighborhood commitment evident by the early 1990s. For two outcomes there were no significant neighborhood changes to explain. For three other outcomes, prior incivilities made no sizable contribution. For one outcome, intention to move, prior incivilities explained about 10% of the neighborhood change in the outcome over the period. Over a significant time frame, such as the twelve-year period elapsing between the first and second surveys in these neighborhoods, neither 1981 assessed incivilities nor average 1982 perceived incivilities contributed as substantially to changing reactions to crime and neighborhood commitment as had been anticipated by the longitudinal version of the incivilities thesis.

To sum up on the individual-level incivility connections: In a cross-sectional framework, strong support appears for Garofalo and Laub's version of the thesis. In 1994, those who, compared to their neighbors, were more afraid, were more likely to say there were dangerous places nearby, and were more likely to hope to move also perceived more physical and social problems nearby than did their neighbors. Perceived problems accompanied heightened safety concerns and weakened neighborhood commitment. Depending on the outcome, incivilities appeared as important as or more important than demographics in explaining these outcomes.

Impacts of Specific Predictors

Table 6.3 shows the results for individual predictors across the six outcomes. For each outcome, the table displays two sets of models. In the first set of models, sociodemographic controls were applied at the individual level; at the community level, controls included the prior level of the outcome from the 1982 survey, a 1980–1982 crime measure, percentage African-American, house value percentile, and percentage owner occupancy, each of the last three from the 1980 census. These were the Model 3 results. The second set of models, shown further to the right under the columns "+ Incivilities," added current perceived incivilities (Time 2, 1994) at the individual level and earlier (Time 1: 1981 or 1982) incivilities at the neighborhood level. These were the Model 4 results. For HGLMs, separate columns also show exponentiated coefficients (e^b).

Daytime Fear on the Streetblock

Those more concerned than their neighbors about safety on their home streetblock during the day were more likely to be women and to have less education than their neighbors. Women's fear score for this item was about 1.08 times the men's fear score. Each additional year of education a respondent had more than his or her neighbors reduced his or her fear score about 2%. Both of these connections with fear remained significant after adding in incivilities.

At the neighborhood level, before we add incivilities, daytime fear on the home streetblock was somewhat ($p < .10$) *less* likely to increase from 1982 to 1994 in predominantly African-American neighborhoods. This unexpected marginal impact of racial composition disappeared, however, after adding in neighborhood-level incivilities.

By contrast, the impact of earlier neighborhood status on fear change remained significant after adding the incivilities measures. Neighborhoods with more expensive housing initially were *less* likely to experience increasing fear from 1982 to 1994. The top-priced neighborhood (100th percentile) had a fear score about one-fifth of the score (.2) of the lowest-priced neighborhood (1st percentile).

Perceived incivilities strongly influenced daytime fear on the streetblock. Those perceiving more social and more physical problems in the

TABLE 6.3 Hierarchical Models Predicting Reactors to Crime and Local Commitment

Outcome	Day Block Fear[ab]				Night Block Fear[ab]			
Model	Prior, Controls		+Incivilities		Prior, Controls		+Incivilities	
	b / se	e(b)	b / se	e(b)	b / se	e(b)	b / se	e(b)
Level I: Individual								
Gender	0.0760* / 0.0320	1.0790	0.0729* / 0.0333	1.0756	0.2112*** / 0.0331	1.2352	0.2047*** / 0.0325	1.2271
Education	−0.0180* / 0.0080	0.9822	−0.0227*** / 0.0077	0.9776	−0.0185+ / 0.0100	0.9816	−0.0234* / 0.0094	0.9769
Length of Residence	−0.0002 / 0.0015	0.9998	−0.0001 / 0.0015	0.9999	0.0025* / 0.0010	1.0025	0.0025** / 0.0009	1.0025
Perceived Social Incivilities	—		0.1271* / 0.0562	1.1356	—		0.1243*** / 0.0262	1.1323
Perceived Physical Incivilities	—		0.1089* / 0.0476	1.1151	—		0.1556** / 0.0461	1.1683
Married	—		—		—		—	
Level II: Neighborhood								
1982 Outcome Level	0.2040 / 0.1390	1.2263	0.1487 / 0.1611	1.1603	0.0707 / 0.0927	1.0733	0.0413 / 0.0950	1.0421
1980 % African-American	−0.0013+ / 0.0006	0.9987	−0.0010 / 0.0007	0.9990	−0.0011+ / 0.0005	0.9989	−0.0008 / 0.0005	0.9992
1980 House Value Rank	−0.0020** / 0.0007	0.99	−0.0015* / 0.0006	0.9985	−0.0009 / 0.0008	0.9991	−0.0002 / 0.0009	0.9998
1980 % Homeowned	−0.0003 / 0.0007	0.9997	0.0002 / 0.0007	1.0002	−0.0000 / 0.0010	1.0000	0.0007 / 0.0010	1.0007
1980 Robbery Percentile	0.0009 / 0.0007	1.0009	0.0006 / 0.0006	1.0006	0.0021* / 0.0010	1.0021	0.0017+ / 0.0009	1.0017

(table continued from previous page)

	Day Neighborhood Fear^ab						Night Neighborhood Fear				
	Prior, Controls b	se	e(b)	+Incivilities b	se	e(b)	Prior, Controls b	se	+Incivilities^c b	se	e(b)
1981 Graffiti	—			0.1340	0.0960	1.1433	—		0.1966*	0.0894	1.2173
1982 Perceived Incivilities	—			—			—		—		

	Day	Night
Model 1: Percent variation at Level II	4.5	3.6
Model 2: Percent total variance explained	0.69	0.1
Model 3: Percent total variance explained	6.4	8.8
Model 4: Percent total variance explained	14.6	15.3

Outcome	Day Neighborhood Fear^ab						Night Neighborhood Fear				
Model	Prior, Controls b	se	e(b)	+Incivilities b	se	e(b)	Prior, Controls b	se	+Incivilities^c b	se	e(b)
Level I Individual											
Gender	0.1282***	0.0288	1.1368	0.1256**	0.0312	1.1339	0.4352***	0.0730	0.4273***	0.0693	
Education	-0.0174+	0.0087	0.9828	-0.0237**	0.0079	0.9766	-0.0345*	0.0130	-0.0474**	0.0124	
Length of Residence	0.0029**	0.0010	1.0029	0.0033**	0.0009	1.0033	0.0047*	0.0022	0.0052*	0.0021	
Perceived Social Incivilities	—			0.2381***	0.0422	1.2688	—		0.4500***	0.0862	
Perceived Physical Incivilities	—			0.1005*	0.0479	1.1057	—		0.3025**	0.0983	
Married	—			—			—		—		
Level II: Neighborhood											
1982 Outcome Level	0.4434***	0.0921	1.5580	0.4398***	0.0910	1.5524	0.1502	0.1548	0.1533	0.1523	
1980 % African-American	-0.0017*	0.0006	0.9983	-0.0016*	0.0006	0.9984	-0.0031*	0.0013	-0.0031*	0.0013	

(continues)

222

(continued)

Outcome	*Avoidade*				*Moving*	
Model	Prior, Controls b / se	e(b)	+Incivilities b / se	e(b)	Prior, Controls b / se	+Incivilities b / se
1980 House Value Rank	-0.0020**	0.9980	-0.0019*	0.9981	-0.0041**	-0.0040**
	0.0007		0.0007		0.0014	0.0014
1980 % Homeowned	-0.0002	0.9998	-0.0001	0.9999	-0.0005	-0.0005
	0.0008		0.0008		0.0020	0.0020
1980 Robbery Percentile	0.0002	1.0002	0.0001	1.0001	0.0056**	0.0056*
	0.0006		0.0006		0.0018	0.0018
1981 Graffiti	—		—		—	—
1982 Perceived Incivilities	—		—		—	—
Model 1: Percent variation at Level II	8.5				3.8	
Model 2: Percent total variance explained	4.5				0.72	
Model 3: Percent total variance explained	12.2		24.1		9.5	
Model 4: Percent total variance explained						18.8

Outcome	*Avoidade*				*Moving*	
Model	Prior, Controls b / se	e(b)	+Incivilities b / se	e(b)	Prior, Controls b / se	+Incivilities b / se
Level I Individual						
Gender	-0.1701	0.8436	-0.1928	0.8246	-0.0050	-0.0078
	0.1703		0.1769		0.0931	0.0870
Education	0.0329	1.0334	0.0135	1.0136	0.0313+	0.0154
	0.0305		0.0357		0.0164	0.0154
Length of Residence	-0.0034	0.9966	-0.0022	0.9979	-0.0054+	-0.0042
	0.0052		0.0064		0.0028	0.0027
Perceived Social Incivilities	—		0.9438***	2.5698	—	0.7828***
			0.2105			0.1070

Perceived Physical Incivilities	—		0.3116+ / 0.1730	1.3656	—	0.1807 / 0.1219
Married	0.1194 / 0.1800	1.1268	0.0624 / 0.2275	1.0644	0.1859+ / 0.0980	0.1350 / 0.0916
Level II: Neighborhood						
1982 Outcome Level	2.2598 / 1.0728	9.5810	3.3195*** / 0.7132	27.6469	-0.0911 / 0.3318	-0.6263 / 0.3879
1980 % African-American	-0.0087 / 0.0047	0.9914	-0.0139* / 0.0037	0.9862	-0.0048+ / 0.0023	-0.0048* / 0.0023
1980 House Value Rank	-0.0125* / 0.0054	0.9876	-0.0208*** / 0.0052	0.9794	-0.0047+ / 0.0026	-0.0033 / 0.0032
1980 % Homeowned	0.0003 / 0.0064	1.0003	-0.0063 / 0.0048	0.9937	-0.0074* / 0.0035	-0.0107* / 0.0039
1980 Robbery Percentile	0.0125+ / 0.0069	1.0125	0.0122+ / 0.0065	1.0122	0.0050 / 0.0031	0.0041 / 0.0033
1981 Graffiti	—		-0.7810 / 0.5136	0.4579	—	-0.6864 / 0.4397
1982 Perceived Incivilities	—		-1.3053 / 0.8498	0.2711	—	1.2066+ / 0.6032
Model 1: Percent variation at Level II	15.1		11.1		7.9	18.2
Model 2: Percent total variance explained	7.45				0.98	
Model 3: Percent total variance explained	10.9				5.9	
Model 4: Percent total variance explained						

+ = p < .10, two tailed
* = p < .05, two tailed
** = p < .01, two tailed
*** = p < .001, two tailed

a. Population average model with robust standard errors.
b. HGLM model with poisson distribution with overdispersion.
c. No incivilities entered at Level II because no significant Level II variation remaining.
d. HGLM model with Bernoulli distribution.
e. Aggravated Assault percentiles are used rather than robbery percentiles.

locale than their neighbors expressed more concern. Each unit increase in perceived social incivilities increased respondents' fear score by about 14%; each unit increase in perceived physical problems increased the score by about 11%.[14] At the neighborhood level, however, indicators of earlier incivilities, assessed graffiti in this case, had no significant influence on neighborhood-level fear changes.

Nighttime Fear on the Streetblock

Three individual-level demographic factors proved important with regard to nighttime fear on the streetblock. Gender again influenced the outcome, but more strongly than for the prior outcome. Women reported a nighttime fear score about 23% (or 1.23 times) higher than men's. This larger impact for gender with the nighttime as compared to daytime item underscored Warr's suggestion that women, as compared to men, find dark scenes more concern-inducing (58, 61). Education again has a significant impact, of around the same magnitude and in the same direction as seen for the last outcome; those more educated than their neighbors expressed less concern. But one item not significant before at the individual level, and significant here, is length of residence. Those living longer in the neighborhood than their neighbors expressed *more* safety concern. Each additional decade of greater-than-average residence increased the fear score by about 2%.[15]

Contrasts with the results for daytime streetblock fear also appeared with the community predictors. The results with earlier graffiti included show only graffiti had a significant impact ($p < .05$); earlier robbery level had a marginally significant ($p < .10$) influence on shifts in fear. With graffiti, nighttime streetblock fear was about 22% higher in neighborhoods where graffiti was seen on every streetblock by raters, as compared to neighborhoods where it was seen in none of the streetblocks. And fear was about 17% higher in the highest robbery neighborhoods, compared to the lowest robbery neighborhoods. Neither race, nor status, nor stability proved relevant. Race's earlier impact, as with the daytime streetblock item, was rendered nonsignificant after adding incivilities.

For nighttime streetblock fear, the shift in neighborhood means from 1982 to 1994 was explained solely by earlier crime and earlier graffiti. For this one outcome, crime and grime did lead to later fear.

Perceived incivilities contributed as well at the individual level to nighttime streetblock fear. Each unit of additional perceived social incivilities increased the fear score about 13%; each additional unit of perceived physical problems increased it about 17%. So, as with the other streetblock outcome, both contemporary social and physical perceived incivilities contributed independently to fear.

Neighborhood Fear

Two fear items addressed the neighborhood beyond the streetblock. For both these items, all three sociodemographic predictors proved relevant. For being abroad during the day in the neighborhood, women's fear score was about 13% higher than men's. For nighttime fear, women scored .43 units higher on the four-point scale than did the men.

Increasing education, as before, linked to lower fear. For both outcomes, each year of schooling more than one's average neighbor lowered the fear score about 2% for the daytime item and about .05 outcome units for the nighttime item.

Again, as with the streetblock items, living longer in the neighborhood resulted in more neighborhood fear. Each decade respondents had lived in the neighborhood longer than their average neighbor boosted daytime fear about 3% and the nighttime fear score about .05 outcome units.

Differences between neighbors on both perceived incivilities indices linked to higher fear. Social incivilities appeared more influential. Each unit increase on this index—relative to the neighborhood average—boosted daytime neighborhood fear about 27%, compared to an 11% boost from each perceived physical incivilities index unit increase. For nighttime fear, each additional unit of perceived social incivilities increased the outcome score by .45 units, compared to .3 units for the physical problems.

Turning to lagged community impacts, both initial status and racial composition influenced fear changes, and, for each, the impacts were stronger for nighttime fear. For race, the difference between all-white and all–African-American neighborhoods in 1980 was 20% for daytime fear and .3 units for nighttime fear. Fear was *less* likely to increase in predominantly African-American neighborhoods.

Earlier status impacts were about comparable with the race impacts. Neighborhoods with the most expensive housing in town in 1980 were about 20% lower for the daytime item, as compared to locations with the least expensive housing; for the nighttime item the difference was .4 outcome units.

In short, neighborhood fear was less likely to increase in locales that at the beginning of the period had more expensive housing or were populated by predominantly African-American households.[16] These lagged structural impacts appeared slightly stronger for the nighttime outcome.

As remarked earlier, no lagged neighborhood-level incivilities indicators for these two neighborhood fear outcomes merited entry because between-neighborhood outcome variation was already explained by prior outcome scores, crime, and structure.

Avoidance

For dangerous places to avoid, no significant impacts of individual characteristics appeared; neither gender, nor education, nor length of residence influenced the outcome. The only significant coefficients were those linked to current perceived incivilities. Of the two, social incivilities had a much larger effect. For each additional unit on the social incivilities index above the neighborhood average, chances of reporting dangerous nearby places increased 156%. By contrast, for each additional unit on physical problems perceived, the chances of reporting a nearby place to avoid increased only about 37%. Perceiving more unruly nearby behavior than their neighbors led residents to conclude there were dangerous places to avoid in the neighborhood. They presumed that these are places their neighbors would recognize too.

Turning to neighborhood predictors, earlier race and status played significant roles. Those living in the most expensive neighborhoods were about 2.1 times less likely to agree there were dangerous places to avoid compared to those in the least expensive neighborhoods. For race, those living in completely African-American neighborhoods were about 1.4 times less likely to agree there were dangerous places to avoid compared to those living in completely white neighborhoods. As with the other outcomes, the Level II results reflected changes from 1982 to 1994, since we have controlled for the earlier level of the outcome.

These two structural results each reflected different dynamics. The house value impact demonstrated the protection afforded by living in a higher-status neighborhood.[17] These protective effects may emerge from actions taken through a local improvement organization or relationships maintained with city agencies, including the police, to help the neighborhood manage fluctuations in order versus disorder taking place in and around the locale (19). Fieldwork completed in several of these locations, including meetings attended and leaders interviewed, confirmed the power advantage wielded by higher-income neighborhoods. See Chapters 7 and 8 for more details.

The racial impact, opposite the expected direction, proved to have an interesting source. In 1982, high proportions of residents in several neighborhoods racially mixed at the time (30% to 70% African-American in 1980) reported dangerous places to avoid; 35% to 88% of respondents did so at the time. All of these neighborhoods, save one, experienced unexpected increases between 1980 and 1990 in the African-American portion of the population, even though in none of them the 1990 percentage African-American exceeded 70%. As these neighborhoods continued to integrate or resegregate, the portion later reporting one or more dangerous places to avoid *decreased* for most of these neighborhoods. Furthermore, the proportion also decreased in two neighborhoods between 70% and 95% African-American in 1980.

In other words, the negative impact of earlier African-American racial composition emerged from neighborhoods somewhat African-American in 1980 and becoming increasingly African-American between 1980 and 1990. Residents in those sites, on average, were less likely to nominate nearby dangerous places in 1994 as compared to 1982. As the locales moved beyond an initial racially mixed composition, dangerous place nominations decreased, as also happened in neighborhoods almost exclusively African-American at the beginning of the period.[18]

The model shown in Table 6.3 includes two earlier neighborhood incivilities indicators: graffiti and residents' average perceptions. Neither contributed significantly to changes in dangerous place nominations.[19] Neither did earlier assault levels.

Intention to Move

The prospect of moving was weakly linked to three demographics; it was contemplated somewhat more often by those who were married, were better educated, and had lived there a shorter time (all $p < .10$). But entering perceived local problems weakened all those impacts. Those who thought more often about moving than their neighbors were those seeing more disorderly social behavior in the locale than their neighbors. For each unit increase on the social incivilities index, scores on the four-point outcome increased almost .8 units.[20]

At the neighborhood level, race, stability, and perceived incivilities all influenced shifts in intentions. Residents were more likely to be looking for exit in 1994, as compared to 1982, in neighborhoods with more perceived problems, fewer homeowners, and fewer African-American households at the beginning of the period. All-white neighborhoods in 1980 were about .5 units higher on the four-point outcome than were all–African-American neighborhoods. Neighborhoods composed solely of renters in 1980 scored about 1.1 units higher on the outcome than did neighborhoods with only homeowners. And finally, seeing more incivilities at Time 1 in the locale increased residents' desire to leave in the following decade. Each unit increase in average perceived problems resulted in a 1.2-point increase in the four-point outcome. This represents an important piece of support for the longitudinal incivilities thesis.

These Level II results for homeownership and incivilities are as we would expect. But how about the race results? How do we explain predominantly African-American neighborhoods being *less* likely to increase in moving intention?

A couple of different, but perhaps overlapping dynamics may be responsible. During the period, deterioration intensified markedly in several of these almost exclusively African-American neighborhoods. These shifts would not have been fully captured by our incivilities indicators from the beginning of the period. Whether through declining city services and inspections, simple aging of the housing stock, or other processes, housing quality eroded markedly. (See Chapter 2.) At the same time, the gap between house prices in these locations and the prices in feasible outer-city destinations increased as well. In short, following the constrained rationality model of mobility, residents may have increasingly recognized how limited their options were (13). Alternatively, a different argument could focus on increasing community building in these locales. Local community development initiatives supported and assisted by local institutions of faith and community development corporations may have helped strengthen local commitment and sense of community (21).

Closing Thoughts

Two questions motivated the current investigations. First, did incivilities influence ecological changes in fear, avoidance, and local commitment, over time, after neighborhood structure and crime are controlled for? These impacts were hypothesized by both the broken windows and decline and disorder versions of the incivilities thesis, but had not yet been tested with sizable, longitudinal data sets. Using measures based on both residents' shared perceptions and on-site assessments of graffiti and abandoned housing, the hypothesized lagged impacts proved significant at the adopted significance level, for two outcomes: block, nighttime fear and moving intentions. For two other outcomes, the hypothesized impacts were nonsignificant (block fear during the day, dangerous places to avoid). For another two outcomes, the ecological impacts of incivilities were irrelevant because the between-neighborhood outcome differences remaining represented only chance variation after the outcome at Time 1, earlier structure, and earlier crime were entered. In terms of explained variance, only for the moving intention outcome was the amount of total explained variance for the hypothesized lagged impact at all sizable, approaching 1%. Although this last finding represents an important piece of support for the longitudinal thesis, it needs to be considered in the overall pattern of results. Lagged impacts of incivilities were neither as consistent nor as sizable as had been anticipated, given the theorizing to date.[21]

These analyses also attempted to better specify the cross-sectional contributions of individual-level incivilities. If the incivilities thesis is no more than a psychological version of social disorganization theory, impacts of perceived physical incivilities after controlling for perceived social incivilities would be nonsignificant, since only the latter reflect social disorganization. Results showed that for the four fear outcomes, *both* perceived social and perceived physical incivilities influenced fear significantly. For dangerous places to avoid and moving intentions, however, only perceived social incivilities were significant. Thus, for the fear outcomes, but not for the other two, it appears that the incivilities thesis specifies a contribution that goes beyond a psychological version of social disorganization processes. This hardy connection provides solid support for Garofalo and Laub's version of the incivilities thesis. And it clearly portrays this thesis as an individual-level dynamic. Since the linkage operates at the *individual* level, it is not so much that residents in some neighborhoods are surrounded by a lot more problems than residents in other neighborhoods; rather, different residents living in the same neighborhood see varying amounts of local turmoil and strife, and these variations shape differential concerns about safety and differential neighborhood commitment.

But an important question remains about the Garofalo and Laub incivilities thesis, even though the results here do establish an independent contribution of perceived physical incivilities to fear of crime. It is not certain the causal ordering is correct. Data on perceived individual-level incivilities were gathered at the same time as the outcome information. It also seems plausible that residents start to feel more concerned for their safety, and those concerns affect their cognitions about local neighborhood conditions. Social psychologists have a long tradition of showing the different ways that affect can shape cognition. That could be happening here as well. Alternatively, both perceived local problems and fear could be spuriously correlated, both driven by a third variable, such as anxiety or depression. Thus, there are still some points needing further clarification on this version of the thesis.

The results here also may help explain why assessed incivilities have such a weak impact on neighborhood changes in fear and commitment. Residents are most troubled by uncivil behaviors. Yet because these behaviors seem to occur rarely—at least when raters are around—it is extremely difficult to find enough of these to rate them reliably. One study posted observers in the highest-crime spots in Minneapolis from mid-evening until midnight or so and found less than 1–2 minutes of disorderly behavior per hour (2). The incivilities most troublesome to residents are the hardest to reliably assess.

Turning to other predictors, results show multilevel impacts of status. Those who were more educated than their neighbors were less fearful, but not more likely to have nominated dangerous places nearby or thought about moving. The individual-level fear impacts are consistent with prior works. At the neighborhood level, and in accord with current theorizing about urban political economies, higher-status neighborhoods benefited over time from their privileged status (19). Here we saw decreasing fear (three of four indicators) and decreasing perception of dangerous places in higher-status locations. In Chapter 8, open-ended information from interviewed neighborhood leaders provides details on specific strategies employed in high-status locales to maintain use value in the form of relative neighborhood safety. The results of those strategies may be partially reflected in the lagged impacts of neighborhood status seen here.

Proving consistently important for almost all outcomes was gender; at the individual level, next to perceived social incivilities, this was the most consistent predictor. This connection fits well with previous work showing strong links between fear and gender (24, 43). But the importance of gender did not extend to the nonfear outcomes; women were not more likely to intend to move, nor were they more likely to nominate dangerous places to avoid. The reach of gender across a range of reactions to crime has not yet been clearly bounded.

Proving more surprising were the impacts of ecological racial composition, linked significantly to both neighborhood fear items, places to avoid, and moving intentions. In all cases, the outcomes were unlikely to increase in neighborhoods almost exclusively African-American at the beginning of the period. Different dynamics appeared to undergird this unexpected racial connection for different outcomes. This opposite-from-expected connection between race and the outcomes could well be highly contingent on and driven largely by the particular changes in racial composition taking place in the decade of change examined.

Turning to crime, results revealed lagged impacts at the specified alpha level for three outcomes: nighttime streetblock fear; neighborhood nighttime fear; and dangerous places to avoid. More reported crime, net of structure, and net of disorder, results in increasing safety concerns evident a dozen years later. Although these lagged crime-fear links might not be as robust as some would hope (33), the lag in question is sizable, about a dozen years. Lagged impacts on changing fear might have proved stronger had a shorter lag been used. The fact that relative reported crime rates shape changing reactions to crime for such an extended period seems noteworthy. How do the lagged crime impacts compare to the lagged impacts of incivilities? The latter significantly affected changes in two outcomes—moving intentions and nighttime streetblock fear—contrasted with crime's impact on three outcomes. It seems fair to say that crime is at least as important as grime in shaping the future safety concerns and commitments of a neighborhood's residents.

Support for Longitudinal Impacts of Incivilities

This chapter brings to a close the strictly quantitative assessment of impacts of neighborhood incivilities over time. This and the preceding chapter include lagged impacts of neighborhood incivilities on changes in:

- Two out of six reactions to crime
- One pathway of neighborhood structural decline, increasing disadvantage
- Three out of four changes in relative, reported violent crime rates

These results certainly provide partial support for the longitudinal incivilities thesis. Incivilities do affect some later changes in crime rates, in neighborhood fabric, and in reactions to crime. But that support is qualified in two important respects.

First, the pattern of results has not proved robust across indicators or outcomes. In the chapter examining crime and structural impacts, for no single outcome was a significant impact of incivilities observed that persisted across different indicators for incivilities. The lack of consistency across indicators, coupled with a failure (Chapter 3) of the different indicators to correlate closely with one another, leaves open important questions about the validity of a broad construct of disorder. The lack of consistency across outcomes suggests that the reach of the longitudinal, ecological version of the incivilities thesis may have been overestimated.

In addition, the pattern of impacts supporting the ecological incivilities thesis must be considered in the context of other, more consistent findings, especially for initial status and initial racial composition. Initial status influenced two later crime changes: relative rape and relative assault levels. It also influenced later changes in daytime streetblock fear; both neighborhood day and nighttime fear; and nominations of dangerous places to avoid. The far-reaching impacts of relative neighborhood standing speak to the power of neighborhood exchange value. Once a relatively privileged position has been obtained in the urban community status hierarchy, a range of social and political processes are set into motion (see Chapters 7 and 8) that help protect those advantages. The result is that crime and fear both grow less in these locales than in others.

Notes

1. Some researchers have criticized the Gallup poll item for asking about areas within a mile of home. In an urban area, traveling a mile may take you through

several distinct neighborhoods, and it may be difficult for the respondent to gauge that distance.

2. A recent report by DeFrances and Smith (7) uses the AHS to get at residents' perceptions of crime problems in their neighborhood. The indicator used was the respondent saying "crime" when asked, "Is there anything about the neighborhood that bothers you?" In a phone conversation (September 1998), the first author reported that she had concluded this was the best way to use the AHS to get at crime as a neighborhood problem.

3. Further details on sampling, analysis, and indicators are available in an online technical appendix available at http://www.rbtaylor.net/technical.htm.

4. We used Pearson's *r* and Mu2 (a coefficient reflecting the strength of a monotonic relationship) to gauge how representative the 1994 sampled households were of the 1990 populations, as reported by the census, in each of the thirty neighborhoods where we interviewed residents in 1994. The number of completed interviews per neighborhood averaged 23.4 in 1994 and 24.6 in 1982. The correlations for 1994 were as follows:

	Pearson's *r*	Mu2
Percent African-American	.96	.99
Percent with at least high school education	.43	.80
Percent owner-occupied housing units	.56	.77

The monotonic relationships for education and ownership are higher than the linear relationship for the following reason. In the case of education there was a curvilinearity to the relationship, with the proportion of high school educated respondents "flattening out" at the higher percentages of proportion high school educated in the neighborhood. In the case of homeownership, there were three neighborhoods where the survey-census relationship departed somewhat from the strong linear relationship at all levels of the census variable. Because the departures from representativeness on both these variables was not systematic, but limited to a small number of neighborhoods, we opted not to try and reweight the entire sample. Furthermore, weighting was not possible with our models using hierarchical generalized linear models for binary and markedly skewed outcomes.

5. Gender was coded 0 = male, 1 = female; length of residence and education were both in years. Length of residence and years of education were always group mean centered, so the length variable reflects how much longer or shorter the resident had lived in the neighborhood compared to the average of his or her neighbors, and the education reflects years of schooling the respondent had more or less than his or her average neighbor. Results in the table for avoid and moving intention include married vs. unmarried respondents. Additional analyses completed (results not shown) showed that its exclusion made no difference. The variable also was added (results not shown) to the four fear outcome models where it is not shown in the table, and its inclusion had no significant impact on the coefficients for the other variables.

For all models save dangerous places to avoid, the 1980 robbery percentile was the earlier crime indicator. For the avoid outcome, the 1980 aggravated assault percentile was the crime indicator. The models were repeated, substituting robbery for aggravated assault (results not shown). Results were comparable, except the explained Level II variance was less; no shifts in predictor significance were observed.

For the neighborhood nighttime fear outcome, models used standard linear estimation. The outcome was quite normally distributed. The other three fear items had skewed outcomes—many more people felt safe than unsafe—and the distribution assumptions most closely approximating these outcomes were for a Poisson model with overdispersion, requiring hierarchical generalized linear models (HGLM), with that distribution, for those outcomes.

Our "dangerous places to avoid" item was, of course, a binary outcome, also requiring HGLM with a Bernoulli distribution. The moving intention outcome also was not normally distributed, with so many scoring in the lowest category, but its distribution was much flatter than those for the daytime fear items and the block nighttime fear items. Nonetheless, the analyses for moving intention were repeated using HGLM with a Poisson distribution with overdispersion. The following differences from those reported in Table 6.3 surfaced. In the analysis controlling for demographics, earlier structure and prior outcome levels, the 1980 percentage owner occupied became slightly less significant ($p < .10$) than it was in the linear model ($p < .05$). At Level I, the coefficient for length of residence became slightly more significant ($p < .10$ in linear model, $p < .05$ in Poisson model). In the last analysis, adding in incivilities, at Level II racial composition remained slightly less significant ($p < .10$) than it was in the linear model ($p < .05$). At Level I, length of residence, nonsignificant in the linear model, was slightly significant ($p < .10$) in the Poisson model. No differences were observed between the linear and Poisson models in significance of remaining Level II residual variance.

6. Which specific crime indicator was used at Level II (robbery or assault) and which specific Level II incivility indicators were used was based on the models generating the lowest residual Level II variance.

7. At Level II, we had several possible incivilities that could enter: average perceived neighborhood incivilities in 1982; assessed graffiti in the neighborhood in 1981; and counts of vacant, boarded-up residential housing in 1981. Most of the models shown include only the earlier graffiti measure. Some also include the earlier perceived incivilities measure. Although these three measures did not correlate substantially with one another, their correlations with other structural variables ranged from weak to relatively strong. Models for each of the outcomes with different combinations of incivilities were attempted. The models shown here were the ones resulting in the highest levels of explained variance. Including additional incivilities usually did not affect the significance or nonsignificance of other structural predictors.

8. For assessed incivilities, scores were averaged across the two raters on each block and then results were aggregated to the neighborhood level. For information on interrater reliabilities see (56).

9. The four other cities were Seattle, Minneapolis–St. Paul, Atlanta, and Chicago. Contact the author for more details.

10. The 1982 neighborhood mean can only explain neighborhood-level variation in the 1994 outcome.

11. For neighborhood daytime fear, 70% of the between-neighborhood differences have been explained; for neighborhood nighttime fear, 98% of the between-neighborhood differences have been explained by prior outcome level, structure, and prior crime level.

12. Of course, incivilities were not added for the two neighborhood fear outcomes, since no significant neighborhood differences on the outcomes remained to be explained.

13. Prior neighborhood incivilities were added to models in different ways. First, I tried adding in all three items together: 1982 neighborhood average on perceived incivilities; 1981 assessed graffiti; and 1981 assessed vacant housing. I also tried each predictor separately. Results reported are those producing the most explained variance.

14. Each incivilities index averaged scores across items where the initial items each had three response categories: not a problem, somewhat of a problem, and a big problem.

15. Length of residence and age correlate strongly in the sample ($r = .702$).

16. The negative connection between fear change and prior racial composition proved to have an interesting basis. Essentially, neighborhoods somewhat African-American in 1980, between about 15% and 55%, showed much higher 1994 fear levels than they did in 1982. By contrast, in the almost exclusively (over 85%) African-American neighborhoods in 1980, the increase in fear was more modest. The different ranged fear "jumps" between the slightly to moderately African-American vs. almost exclusively African-American neighborhoods in 1980 may reflect some cognitive adaptation processes in extremely low income, predominantly African-American neighborhoods (55). Some of the most deteriorated neighborhoods in our sample are predominantly African-American and have been that way since at least 1970. They score over a standard deviation higher on assessed deterioration than all-white neighborhoods in the sample (50). A curvilinear relationship exists between assessed deterioration and nighttime fear (55). Thus if fear, already relatively high, was not rising substantially in these high-deterioration, historically African-American neighborhoods, but was rising elsewhere, as it was in the moderately African-American neighborhoods in 1980, we can understand the impact of racial composition seen here.

17. The data showed that dangerous place nominations were most likely to decrease in neighborhoods where the 1980 house value rank was above the fifty-fifth to sixtieth percentile. Some of the decreases in prevalence were marked (e.g., from around 90% to around 40%, or from around 40% to around 15%). All of the sizable drops appeared in the neighborhoods with more expensive housing. By contrast, in neighborhoods with the less expensive housing, the fraction of respondents nominating dangerous places to avoid was likely to increase a small-to-moderate amount. In short, a protective effect emerges of higher status working forward in time.

18. Results here focus on the proportion of residents nominating one or more dangerous places known to residents. Results might be quite different if we looked not at the prevalence of dangerous place nominations, but the incidence, and counted how many places were nominated by respondents.

19. As noted earlier, different combinations of neighborhood-level incivilities indicators, including each indicator on its own, were also analyzed (results not shown). In those other models, Level II incivility impacts also were not significant. Results shown here provided the lowest residual Level II variance.

20. For comparison between these results and those using a Poisson model with overdispersion, see above.

21. Two possible reasons for weak lagged incivilities impacts that focus on study limitations are the change period used and sample sizes that are too small at the neighborhood level. With regard to the first issue, the longitudinal incivilities thesis is generally silent on how long the impact cycles *should* be. So we cannot know if the twelve- to thirteen-year period used here has been theoretically appropriate. In another investigation, however, with a more focused spatial arena, the block, and only one year passing between the two assessments, we also have been unable to uncover sizable lagged incivilities impacts (48). An earlier study used a change period of five to seven years, but failed to operationalize the outcome as a change variable or to control for earlier structure (39). Although it could be that the twelve-year period used here is too long, and one year might be too short, until we have multiwave investigations in a range of contexts or a more grounded, detailed description of the operative social psychological and ecological processes themselves, the appropriate time frame will remain unclear.

The second potential limitation is addressed by the operations of, or the information provided by, the hierarchical models themselves. First, on the outcome side, HLMs consider sample size, how much residents in each neighborhood agree with each other, and how far the specific neighborhood mean is from the grand mean, making Empirical Bayes adjustments of neighborhood means toward the grand mean as sample sizes shrink, as the specific neighborhood mean is further from the grand mean, and as residents in the same neighborhood disagree more with one another. The analysis uses these Empirical Bayes estimates when gauging ecological impacts. On the predictor side, HLM reports average neighborhood reliabilities, i.e., interneighbor agreement, across the neighborhoods in the sample. These represent the precision of the neighborhood-level estimates (1: 43, 57) If the reliabilities are low for the outcomes at Time 1, there is a danger that the ecological partialling to create neighborhood mean outcome change score residuals at Time 2 will be too inexact. If the reliabilities are low for perceived incivilities at Time 1, the key lagged predictor will have too much measurement error. To address these questions on the predictor side, I calculated the reliabilities of all the neighborhood means for the outcomes at Time 1 and for perceived incivilities at Time 1. The more residents in each neighborhood agree with one another on an item, the higher the reliability. Reliability of neighborhood means for perceived incivilities at Time 1 was excellent: .85. Reliabilities for the outcomes at Time 1 were acceptable, .60 or better, for the two day fear items (.74, neighborhood-day; .75, block-day) and avoidance (.69). They were marginally acceptable, .50 to .60, for the two night fear items (.59, neighborhood-night; .55, block-night) and moving intentions (.50).

The implications are as follows. The lagged predictor for perceived incivilities had excellent measurement properties and was not adversely affected by having only twenty-four respondents per neighborhood. For the assessed incivilities, graffiti and abandoned housing, we looked at a different type of reliability: inter-rater. For vacant houses, it was .78 at the streetblock level (Cronbach's alpha); graffiti had a reliability coefficient of .78 (kappa). So the lack of significant impacts for perceived incivilities cannot be attributed to too few respondents per neighborhood in 1982, and for assessed incivilities it also cannot be attributed to poor measurement.

In addition, for the outcomes at Time 1 only three outcomes have reliabilities below .60. For one of those outcomes (neighborhood, nighttime fear), incivilities did not have a chance to enter because structure and crime left nothing beyond sampling error to explain at the neighborhood level. For the second outcome, moving intentions, we *did* see the significant expected lagged impact of perceived incivilities. For the third outcome, block fear at night, we also saw the significant expected lagged impact of assessed incivilities. Thus, the low n per neighborhood at Time 1, resulting in less than satisfactory reliabilities of the neighborhood means, cannot be used to explain away the lack of results for these outcomes, because in two of the three low-reliability outcomes we did get the expected result and with the third outcome only chance between-neighborhood variation remained after controlling for the outcome at Time 1, structure, and crime.

References

(1)   Bryk, A. S., and Raudenbush, S. W. (1992) *Hierarchical linear models: Applications and data analysis methods*, Sage, Newbury Park, CA.

(2)   Buerger, M. E., Cohn, E. G., and Petrosino, A. J. (1995) Defining the "hot spots of crime": Operationalizing theoretical concepts for field research. In *Crime and place* (Eck, J. E., and Weisburd, D., eds), pp. 237–257. Criminal Justice Press, Monsey, NY.

(3)   Choldin, H. M., Hanson, C., and Bohrer, R. (1980) Suburban status instability. *American Sociological Review* 45, 972–983.

(4)   Cook, F. L., and Skogan, W. G. (1984) Evaluating the changing definition of a policy issue in Congress: Crime against the elderly. In *Public policy and social institutions* (Rodgers, H. R., Jr., ed), pp. 287–332. JAI, Greenwich, CT.

(5)   Covington, J., and Taylor, R. B. (1991) Fear of crime in urban residential neighborhoods: Implications of between and within-neighborhood sources for current models. *Sociological Quarterly* 32, 231–249.

(6)   Cuba, L., and Hummon, D. (1993) A place to call home: Identification with dwelling, community, and region. *Sociological Quarterly* 34, 111–131.

(7)   DeFrances, C. J., and Smith, S. (1998) *Perceptions of neighborhood crime, 1995*. Bureau of Justice Statistics Special Report, NCJ–165811, U.S. Department of Justice, Washington, DC.

(8)   Droettboom, T., McAllister, R. J., Kaiser, E. J., and Butler, E. W. (1971) Urban violence and residential mobility. *Journal of the American Institute of Planners* 37, 319–325.

(9)   Dubow, F., McCabe, F., and Kaplan, G. (1979) *Reactions to crime: A critical review of the literature*, Government Printing Office, Washington, DC.

(10)   Dugan, L. (1999) The effect of criminal victimization on a household's moving decision. *Criminology* 37, 903–930.

(11)   Duncan, G. J., and Raudenbush, S. W. (1999) Assessing the effects of context in studies of child and youth development. *Educational Psychologist* 34, 29–41

(12)   Ferraro, K. F. (1994) *Fear of crime: Interpreting victimization risk*, State University of New York Press, Albany.

(13)   Fischer, C. S. (1977) Comments on the history and study of "community." In *Networks and places: Social relations in the urban setting* (Fischer, C. S., et al., eds). Free Press, New York.

(14)   Gordon, M. T., and Riger, S. (1979) Fear and avoidance: A link between attitudes and behavior. *Victimology* 4, 395–402.

(15)   Hunter, A. (1978) Symbols of incivility. Paper presented at the Annual Meeting of the American Society of Criminology, Dallas, Texas, November.

(16)   Kurtz, E., Koons, B., and Taylor, R. B. (1998) Land use, physical deterioration, resident-based control and calls for service on urban streetblocks. *Justice Quarterly* 15, 121–149.

(17)   Landale, N. S., and Guest, A. M. (1985) Constraints, satisfaction and residential mobility: Speare's model reconsidered. *Demography* 22, 199–222.

(18)   Liska, A. E., Sanchirico, A., and Reed, M. D. (1988) Fear of crime and constrained behavior: Specifying and estimating a reciprocal effects model. *Social Forces* 66, 827–837.

(19)   Logan, J. R., and Molotch, H. (1987) *Urban fortunes*, University of California Press, Berkeley.

(20)   Maxfield, M. G. (1984) The limits of vulnerability in explaining fear of crime: A comparative neighborhood analysis. *Journal of Research in Crime and Delinquency* 21, 233–250.

(21)   McDougall, H. A. (1993) *Black Baltimore: A new theory of community*, Temple University Press, Philadelphia.

(22)   Mcguire, K., ed. (1995) *Sourcebook of criminal justice statistics 1995*, Bureau of Justice Statistics, Washington, DC.

(23)   Merry, S. E. (1981) Defensible space undefended: Social factors in crime control through environmental design. *Urban Affairs Quarterly* 16, 397–422.

(24)   Miethe, T. (1995) Fear and withdrawal from urban life. *Annals of the American Academy of Political and Social Science* 539, 14–27.

(25)   Newman, S., and Duncan, G. J. (1979) Residential problems, dissatisfaction, and mobility. *Journal of the American Planning Association* 45, 154–166.

(26)   Ortega, S. L., and Myles, J. L. (1987) Race and gender effects on the fear of crime: An interactive model with age. *Criminology* 25, 133–152.

(27)   Perkins, D., and Taylor, R. B. (1996) Ecological assessments of disorder: Their relationship to fear of crime and theoretical implications. *American Journal of Community Psychology* 24, 63–107.

(28)   Riger, S., and Gordon, M. T. (1978) Women's fear of crime: From blaming to restricting the victim. *Victimology* 3, 274–284.

(29)   Riger, S., and Gordon, M. T. (1981) The fear of rape. *Journal of Social Issues* 37, 71–92.

(30) Rosenbaum, D. P. (1988) Community crime prevention: A review and synthesis of the literature. *Justice Quarterly* 5, 323–395.

(31) Rosenbaum, D. (1988) A critical eye on neighborhood watch: Does it reduce crime and fear? In *Communities and crime reduction* (Hope, T., and Shaw, M., eds), pp. 126–145. Her Majesty's Stationary Office, London.

(32) Rosenbaum, D., Lewis, D., and Szoc, J. (1986) Neighborhood-based crime prevention: Assessing the efficacy of community organizing in Chicago. In *Community crime prevention: Does it work?* (Rosenbaum, D., ed), pp. 109–136. Sage, Beverly Hills, CA.

(33) Rountree, P. W. (1998) A re-examination of the crime-fear linkage. *Journal of Research in Crime and Delinquency* 35, 341–372.

(34) Rountree, P. W., and Land, K. C. (1996) Burglary victimization, perceptions of crime risk, and routine activities: A multilevel analysis across Seattle neighborhoods and census tracts. *Journal of Research in Crime and Delinquency* 33, 147–180.

(35) Rountree, P. W., and Land, K. C. (1996) Perceived risk versus fear of crime: Empirical evidence of conceptually distinct reactions in survey data. *Social Forces* 74, 1353–1376.

(36) Silverman, R. A., and Kennedy, L. W. (1985) Age, perception of social diversity and fear of crime. *Environment and Behavior* 17, 275–.

(37) Silverman, R. A., and Kennedy, L. W. (1985) Loneliness, satisfaction and fear of crime: A test for non-recursive effects. *Canadian Journal of Criminology* 27, 1–13.

(38) Skogan, W. (1990) *Disorder and decline: Crime and the spiral of decay in American cities,* Free Press, New York.

(39) Skogan, W., and Lurigio, A. J. (1992) The correlates of community anti-drug activism. *Crime & Delinquency* 38, 510–521.

(40) Skogan, W. G., and Maxfield, M. G. (1981) *Coping with crime,* Sage, Beverly Hills, CA.

(41) Bureau of Justice Statistics (2000). *Sourcebook of criminal justice statistics online* (on-line: http://www.albany.edu/treetops/docs.sourcebook. Retrieved: July 11, 2000).

(42) South, S. J., and Deane, G. D. (1993) Race and residential mobility: Individual determinants and structural constraints. *Social Forces* 72, 147–167.

(43) Stanko, E. A. (1995) Women, crime, and fear. *Annals of the American Academy of Political and Social Science* 539, 46–58.

(44) Taub, R. P., Taylor, G., and Dunham, J. (1984) *Paths of neighborhood change,* University of Chicago Press, Chicago.

(45) Taylor, R. B. (1988) *Human territorial functioning,* Cambridge University Press, Cambridge, UK.

(46) Taylor, R. B. (1996) Neighborhood responses to disorder and local attachments: The systemic model of attachment, and neighborhood use value. *Sociological Forum* 11, 41–74.

(47) Taylor, R. B. (1997) Social order and disorder of streetblocks and neighborhoods: Ecology, microecology and the systemic model of social disorganization. *Journal of Research in Crime and Delinquency* 33, 113–155.

(48) Taylor, R. B. (1998) Crime, grime, fear and decline: A longitudinal look at the impacts of incivilities. Paper presented at the annual meetings of the American Society of Criminology, Washington, DC, November.

(49) Taylor, R. B., and Brower, S. (1985) Home and near-home territories. In *Human behavior and environment: Current theory and research*, Vol. 8: *Home environments* (Altman, I., and Werner, C., eds). New York: Plenum.

(50) Taylor, R. B., and Covington, J. (1993) Community structural change and fear of crime. *Social Problems* 40, 374–397.

(51) Taylor, R. B., Gottfredson, S. D., and Brower, S. (1981) Territorial cognitions and social climate in urban neighborhoods. *Basic and Applied Social Psychology* 2, 289–303.

(52) Taylor, R. B., Gottfredson, S. D., and Brower, S. (1984) Block crime and fear: Local social ties and territorial functioning. *Journal of Research in Crime and Delinquency* 21, 303–331.

(53) Taylor, R. B., and Hale, M. (1986) Testing alternative models of fear of crime. *Journal of Criminal Law and Criminology* 77, 151–189.

(54) Taylor, R. B., and Kurtz, E. (1997) Reactions to crime and specific incivilities in five cities. Paper presented at the annual meetings of the American Society of Criminology, San Diego, CA, November.

(55) Taylor, R. B., and Shumaker, S. A. (1990) Local crime as a natural hazard: Implications for understanding the relationship between disorder and fear of crime. *American Journal of Community Psychology* 18, 619–642.

(56) Taylor, R. B., Shumaker, S. A., and Gottfredson, S. D. (1985) Neighborhood level links between physical features and local sentiments, fear of crime, and confidence. *Journal of Architectural Planning and Research* 2, 261–275.

(57) Varady, D. P. (1983) Determinants of residential mobility decisions: The role of government services in relation to other factors. *Journal of the American Planning Association* 49, 184–199.

(58) Warr, M. (1984) Fear of victimization: Why are women and the elderly more afraid? *Social Science Quarterly* 65, 681–702.

(59) Warr, M. (1990) Dangerous situations: Social context and fear of victimization. *Social Forces* 68, 891–907.

(60) Warr, M. (1994) Public perceptions and reactions to violent offending and victimization. In *Understanding and preventing violence: Consequences and control*, Vol. 4 (Reiss, A. J., Jr., and Roth, J. A., eds), pp. 1–67. National Academy Press, Washington, DC.

(61) Warr, M., and Stafford, M. (1983) Fear of victimization: A look at proximate causes. *Social Forces* 61, 1033–1043.

PART THREE

Qualitative Evidence from Community Leaders

7

The Community Perspective: Views About Incivilities and Responses to Incivilities in the Context of Collective Crime Prevention Initiatives

This chapter considers incivilities from the community perspective. The empirical evidence examined so far has concentrated on the origins and impacts of incivilities. The material here enables an examination of what local groups are doing about incivilities. What steps are they taking to cope with social or physical incivilities? What types of incivilities are of interest in different locales? Do leaders attack a range of incivilities at once, seeking to reduce "disorder," or do they sponsor more targeted efforts? What factors influence their targeting? How are they thinking about incivilities and their remediation? Closed- and open-ended information from experienced community leaders is used to answer these questions. The focus is not just on "grime fighting" on its own, but in the context of other collective community crime prevention initiatives.

The broader context of other collective crime prevention initiatives is critical given the results of the last two chapters showing varying impacts of incivilities on long-term changes. In general, that pattern of observed impacts has proven more modest than expected. Therefore, from a community perspective, it is important to learn how many "eggs" local leaders are putting into the incivilities "basket." In response to the press and policymaker attention devoted to incivilities reduction, have they narrowed their efforts? Or are they continuing to pursue the range of initiatives documented in earlier studies of community crime prevention efforts?

For the purposes of this chapter, I follow Podolefsky's definition of community crime prevention: any activities the community pursues because it thinks these activities will "do something" about crime or related problems (29: 18). Bringing this broader context into view raises an additional set of questions. When leaders seek to reduce specific incivilities, how are their goals similar to or different from the goals behind their other collective crime prevention efforts? In what ways does incivility reduction complement other initiatives? Are there instances where other collective crime prevention initiatives may shoulder aside concerns about incivility reduction?

In addition to linking various crime prevention efforts and rationales, the current chapter sketches in the broader context to see how the links between efforts and rationales depend on the community structure and the nature of the local crime problem. Do the leaders of prevention efforts view the threats posed by incivilities and the possible cures in different ways across various community and crime contexts? And if so, what shapes this variation? How do these differences in their views about incivilities coincide with views about other crime-related problems and solutions? Stated differently, underneath differences in how leaders think about and respond to incivilities, are there common themes in their prevention thinking, and how do the variations on those themes play out in different settings? Focusing on these two sets of broader issues—how incivility reduction responses link to other collective crime prevention initiatives, and how community context affects the broader range of prevention efforts—provides an initial framework within which to understand incivilities, their impacts, and the collective responses, from the community's vantage point.

In the same way that the origins and impacts of incivilities can be profitably viewed within the broader social disorganization and urban political economy perspectives, responses to incivilities may be most readily understood if placed in the context of what we already know about collective crime prevention efforts. Such an initial grounding supplies ready-made suggestions about different ways community leaders might respond to incivilities and the factors that might influence those variations.

The model chosen to theoretically ground this portion of the investigation was initially developed by Podolefsky in the mid-1970s, based on surveys and qualitative fieldwork in ten different communities in three different cities (Philadelphia, Chicago, San Francisco) (13, 29, 30). Podolefsky's model linked community structure, local views of crime and related problems, and the types of collective responses chosen. He suggested two general types of collective efforts: victimization prevention and social problem reduction. More details about these two types of approaches appear below. Using grounded theory techniques (16), he developed a model linking the type of initiative adopted with the demographic fabric of the community and the community's beliefs about crime and related problems. This model was developed in collaboration with other researchers working on the Northwestern University Reactions to Crime research project (1975–1980) just as those colleagues (Fred DuBow, Al Hunter, Dan Lewis, Michael Maxfield, and Wes Skogan) were beginning to address incivilities and their impacts on citizens. Advantages of using this framework include its broad and high-quality evidentiary basis as well as its consideration of incivilities.

Nonetheless, Podolefsky's model presents one significant disadvantage, at least in the eyes of undergraduate students in my community crime prevention classes over the years. His data sources date from the mid to late 1970s, thus predating the crack invasion experienced in many urban communities by about the middle or end of the 1980s (29: 66). And as my students remind me constantly, "Crack changed everything." According to their syllogism, Podolefsky's model can no longer apply to urban communities in the wake of the crack cocaine invasion and can no longer help us understand what leaders are doing to collectively prevent crime.

There is certainly no question that the crack invasion dramatically changed the crime problems confronting many urban communities. It spurred violent crime increases (31: 202). It changed the political economy of drug dealing for local gangs (15). It ravaged countless urban neighborhoods (35). In addition, in the communities most severely afflicted by the invasion, drug sales and the problems attendant with those sales and with the involved customers far outstripped many other crime-related concerns.

Data from a nationally representative sample of hospital emergency departments provide some details about increasing drug and cocaine problems in the 1980s and 1990s. From 1978 to 1994 total "drug-related episodes rose by 60 percent . . . from 323,100 to 518,500" (26: 5). Of course, during this time people were going to emergency rooms more frequently anyway, but overall visits increased only 26 percent from 71.3 million to 89.7 million (26: 5). The increase in cocaine-related episodes was dramatic: "From 1978 to 1994, cocaine-related episodes rose from 3,400 to 142,900" (26: 9). Much of this increase was concentrated in the late 1980s; cocaine-related episodes increased from 28,000 to 110,000 between 1985 and 1989, an increase of 280%. By 1994 cocaine-related episodes accounted for about one out of every four drug-related episodes in emergency departments, and from 1985 through 1992, it was the cocaine-related episodes that were driving up the total drug-related episodes (26: 9). See Figure 7.1.

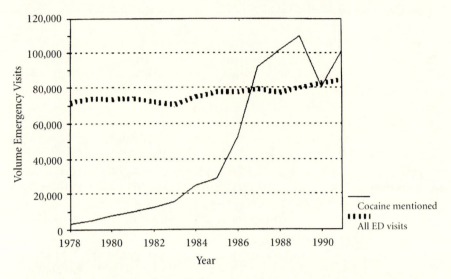

FIGURE 7.1   National Estimates Volume Emergency Department Visits: Cocaine, and All Visits (All in thousands).

These national changes notwithstanding, Baltimore has a reputation among many as predominantly a "heroin" town (25). If it is, then is it possible the crack-cocaine epidemic did *not* hit Baltimore hard?

The emergency department data suggest it hit *very* hard, with cocaine-linked visits increasing markedly in the late 1980s. Figure 7.2 shows the Baltimore area estimated emergency department visit rates per 100,000 population for 1988 through 1993, for heroin or morphine; cocaine, including crack and powder; and marijuana or hashish. The cocaine rate went from around 100 visits per 100,000 population to about 380 per 100,000 population. The heroin rate increased as well, going from around 50 visits per 100,000 population to around 250 per 100,000 population. But at all points in time, the cocaine-related visit rate appears markedly higher than the heroin-related visit rate. Heroin incidents increased, but by the end of the period the visit rate for crack cocaine was 52% higher than the heroin rate.

Given the trends seen nationally as well as in Baltimore, it is no surprise that much of the recent work on community crime prevention has focused specifically on collective responses to dealers, dealing, and drug markets (e.g., 11, 20). An exclusive focus on drugs and related problems implies two points: first, that drug activities represent a problem for local crime

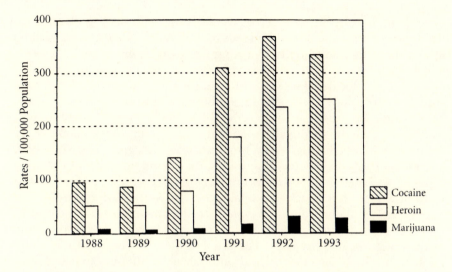

FIGURE 7.2   Baltimore Area Emergency Department Episode Rates: Cocaine,
Heroin/Morphine, Marijuana/Hashish, 1988–1993.

prevention leaders qualitatively different from previous issues; and second, that the associated levels of violence pose an unprecedented threat to
communities. By extension, researchers advocating new drug-centered
models for understanding collective responses imply that theoretical
models for collective responses based on information prior to the crack
era are outdated and irrelevant. Case studies highlighting collective confrontations with drug dealers and emphasizing how communities have
been forced to adopt "new" tactics (e.g., 45) underscore how precrack collective responses, and our models to understand them, are inadequate.

Certainly, in some ways the problems caused by crack represented
qualitatively new challenges; in response, groups have adopted new
strategies such as direct confrontation, nuisance abatement laws, and
community prosecution (3, 18, 45). But has the landscape for community
leaders shifted completely? Are there no points of contact with how they
tackled similar issues in the precrack era? The current scholarly focus on
"new" approaches, by uncoupling the framework used to understand
these initiatives from earlier theoretical work, makes it extremely difficult
to accurately gauge the amount of change in collective responses.

Such a view about current collective antidrug initiatives overlooks
three points. First, prior to the crack invasion, neighborhood leaders,

even going back to the late 1970s, were coping with drug problems. Indeed, drug problems in the late 1980s and early 1990s were more serious in just those neighborhoods reporting drug problems in the late 1970s and early 1980s (36). The problem was not completely new for leaders in many affected locales. Furthermore, what is not clear from current case studies is the relative reliance of neighborhood groups on "new" versus "old" collective strategies. It may be the case that many neighborhood leaders, despite the media attention and concomitant sensationalizing of confrontational tactics, rely on a broad mix of strategies, many of which are not completely new. If communities are relying on many of the same types of activities that they drew on previously, it would be of interest to learn how big a role confrontational tactics, as well as incivilities-related issues, play in the broader mix. Finally, the factors influencing how communities respond collectively to crime may *not* have shifted in the wake of the crack cocaine invasion. Factors that make a neighborhood more likely to follow one strategy versus another may still be connected similarly to those choices.

This chapter examines whether *variations* in how communities collectively respond to drugs and crime follow the same pattern seen in the precrack era. The emergence of this "new" crime problem, its impact on other crime and nuisance problems, and the accompanying "novel" collective responses raise potentially serious questions about Podolefsky's model. Does community structure influence how local leaders think about drugs and related problems in the mid-1990s in the same way that it influenced how they thought about nondrug crime problems in the late 1970s? And do these views link to the type of collective action mounted to "cope" with these drug problems or crime problems linked to drug issues? In short, has the emergence of crack so altered how communities think about and approach crime prevention that none of our previous understandings apply? If Podolefsky's model, which links community structure, perceptions of crime problems, and responses to crime, has generality, it should apply even after the crack invasion arrived in urban communities.

The answers have practical as well as theoretical import; they can clarify what collective reactions are favored in different community settings. Such information can be used to more effectively support community-based initiatives. Agents outside the neighborhood, whether they be local police personnel or activists in broader umbrella associations, can more effectively promote anticrime programs with such understanding. Too often, outside agents "push" one type of program, in accordance with an "implant hypothesis" (e.g., 33): Any program can take root anywhere. If programs are pushed that do not fit with the local perspective on the crime problem, they are unlikely to take root and be widely adopted. Organizers can avoid squandering energy if they understand links between neighborhood fabric and locals' views of the crime and drug problems.

Turning back specifically to incivilities, certainly their prevalence in some neighborhoods has increased, in part because of the emergence of the crack cocaine markets. Chapter 2 reviewed some of those changes on the study blocks. It is hard to know how much of the increase in abandoned housing relates to drug markets. Tax delinquencies and later housing abandonment may grow in the shadow of expanding open-air drug markets (32). Open-air drug markets by themselves create numerous social irritants for residents: noise, fighting, gunfire, and public urination, among others (2). Indoor drug markets can create similar problems on a smaller and perhaps less obtrusive scale. Therefore, in neighborhoods where drug activity is taking place, we might expect local leaders are quite preoccupied with incivility reduction. How they define and respond to these concerns and how those definitions and responses dovetail with other initiatives will be of interest.

Organization of the Chapter and Questions Addressed

The following section summarizes Podolefsky's model, describing two types of collective responses and how those responses emerge from the community fabric by way of community views about crime and related social problems. An overview of the sampling and interview procedures for gathering the current data appears next. The following sections detail collective responses in different types of neighborhoods. Neighborhoods are reviewed in the following order: those adopting almost exclusively a victimization prevention strategy; those where victimization prevention predominates, but social problem reduction strategies also play a role; those adopting almost exclusively a social problem reduction approach; and finally, those with a mixed approach, but where a social problem reduction orientation predominates. The key questions for Podolefsky's theory are as follows:

- Do the different collective community responses to crime continue to cluster into the types described by Podolefsky?
- Are the community-level demographic correlates of these different types of collective responses similar to those seen earlier?
- Do community views about drugs, crime, and crime-related problems continue to emerge from community makeup and also predict the type of community response adopted?

As the focus shifts from locales following purely victimization prevention approaches to locales pursuing purely social problem initiatives, leaders' views on and responses to incivilities, as well as variations in both, are described. How do leaders' anti-incivility initiatives relate to their crime prevention activities? What types of incivilities do they choose to address and why?

A closing section examines whether, and if so in what ways, the original model addresses some new features of collective responses. Can these new features be easily folded in? Or do they suggest model modifications? To put it another way, if we view the information gathered here as input to another round of grounded theorizing rather than as just a test of the external validity of the model, what changes are suggested by the information gathered?

In broad terms, this chapter connects to the previous ones in two ways. First, the focus helps us understand more about how leaders view incivilities. What significance do leaders attribute to them? Which specific ones are of interest? Do interpretations about incivilities and their impacts vary across locales? In addition, by hearing about broader collective crime prevention efforts, we can gauge the relative emphasis leaders put on incivilities versus other concerns. This too might vary across locales. Are there some locales focusing exclusively on incivility reduction efforts and other locales where incivilities do not even come up on the radar screen?

What Influences the Type of Collective Strategies Adopted? Podolefsky's Model

Podolefsky (29) asked how do residents' views of the crime problem influence the type of collective response to crime adopted? He found two features of residents' perceptions that predisposed them to adopt one particular type of collective response to crime or another.

- Did residents believe the crime problem originated outside the neighborhood and was perpetrated largely by outsiders coming into their neighborhood? Or did they believe that the crime problem involved local residents and local youth?
- Did residents believe that the crime problem emerged from and was driven by other local social problems, such as unemployment or lack of educational, housing, or recreational opportunities? Or did they believe crime problems were relatively *independent* of these other crime problems and *not* driven by them?

Podolefsky's data and model suggested that if residents believed crime and related problems emerged from *outside* the neighborhood, and such problems were largely *un*related to other social problems, leaders and residents would be predisposed to adopt *victimization prevention* (VP)

TABLE 7.1   Selection of Collective Crime-Prevention Meta-Strategies in Podolefsky's Model

	In residents' view: *Where does the crime problem come from?*	
In residents' view:	*Inside Neighborhood*	*Outside Neighborhood*
Crime linked with other social ills	Social Problem Reduction approach likely to be adopted	
Crime not linked with other social ills		Victimization Prevention approach likely to be adopted

strategies in their collective crime prevention efforts. By contrast, according to Podolefsky's model and data, if residents believed crime and related problems arose mostly from perpetrators living *inside* the neighborhood and that crime events were largely *driven by* other problems simultaneously afflicting the community, they would be predisposed to adopt *social problem reduction* (SPR) strategies.[1] Podolefsky's labels refer to meta-strategies, or clusters of strategies. The two types represent end points on a continuum, with variation along the continuum possible. In the current lexicon, the second (SPR) orients toward root causes, the first (VP) toward crime control (see Table 7.1).

Social problem reduction (SPR) strategies seek to reduce social problems that, in the minds of residents and leaders, are substantially responsible for local crime and related problems. Podolefsky identified two groups of strategies within this approach: positive, youth-oriented efforts; and physical, social, and economic environmental improvement efforts.

The youth focus encompasses after-school programs, special educational programs, job training for teens, counseling or mentoring programs for troubled youth, and recreational programs. Local leaders and residents hope such efforts would remove youth from potentially criminogenic situations on the street, provide them with skills and opportunities making criminal or delinquent activities less attractive, and equip them with skills to resist criminal or delinquent involvement. "These positive youth-oriented programs involving recreation, employment, counseling, and education, are responses to what citizens perceive as problems of excess leisure time, the lack of effective socialization of youth (both in the home and community), and related problems such as drug and alcohol abuse" (29: 32).

Environmental improvements refer to a broad swath of physical, social, and economic initiatives. These would include bringing jobs into the community, making physical improvements such as rehabbing housing, attracting new housing, general cleanup and beautification efforts, making physical changes to keep troublemakers out, and closing up spots spawning crime such as troublesome bars or abandoned houses. Social activities furthering community development and strengthening local social ties or residents' commitment to the locale also fall in this category. All of these activities seek to firm up community fabric, strengthen residents' informal control over their locale, and make the mix of legitimate versus illegitimate activities more conducive to residential satisfaction and positive youth development. These are

> efforts to (a) alter the physical and social conditions so as to draw people more closely together and form a more tightly knit community, (b) alter these conditions which are more directly seen to produce a criminogenic environment such as getting rid of drug pushers in the community, (c) reduce access to the community, (d) make physical changes which will facilitate the use of other approaches, and (e) improve the economic conditions of the neighborhood, particularly so as to reduce unemployment. . . . Cleaning up streets, alleys, parks, vacant lots and business and residential areas are intended to increase the pride in community felt by local residents. Residents often view lack of community pride and concern as related to crime and "uncivil" behavior of residents. (29: 33)

The last section of the above quote highlights thinking at the time about responding to minor physical incivilities. Residents reasoned that cleanup and beautification efforts would simultaneously stimulate civic pride and curb some uncivil behavior of residents.[2] These assumptions are well supported by over two decades of empirical work on human territorial functioning. Neatness and territorial markers such as flowers signal residents who care more about their locale, are more watchful, and are more likely to intervene should uncivil behavior take place (4, 40, 41). Leaders in effect with their beautification and cleanup efforts were hoping to activate or strengthen local residents' willingness to exercise control over the behaviors taking place in the public spaces around their home and over who has access to those spaces. At the same time, leaders hope the signage would encourage outsiders to behave more "civilly" there because they recognize they are being surveilled (39). "Real world" examples suggest these efforts can prove highly successful (40: chap. 8). In short, the issue is stimulating residents' localized informal social control via the removal of minor physical incivilities; removal of minor incivilities is a means to the end of enhanced residential territorial functioning, not an end in itself.

This view contrasts with current views, some twenty years later, where, as can be seen from Chapter 3, incivility removal has emerged as an end in itself. This shift has taken place for a number of reasons, including a shift in outcome focus, on the part of both residents and leaders as well as researchers and policymakers, from "community pride" to less fear and crime; and higher crime rates in many of these locales. The material below describes how current leaders view incivilities, the connections between incivilities and outcomes, and how views of those connections vary across locales.

It also is worthwhile considering how attitudes toward other problems and their resolution have shifted over twenty years and vary across locales. Drug sales, even in the mid-1970s, were a concern for some of the leaders Podolefsky interviewed at that time. Of course, as will be seen, in our mid-1990s interviews getting rid of drug sales was a major concern in many neighborhoods. But despite the current salience of drug issues, there are still variations in how leaders approached the issue. In some of the locations with the most serious drug problems, leaders adopted a personal approach, helping with the recovery of those they knew. In one locale with a large number of active drug market locations, efforts to push out dealers, even from one street for part of a day for a local fair with uniformed police nearby, proved fruitless. In still another location, the leader simultaneously enlisted local dealers to help keep intruders out and warned them against dealing within the neighborhood or corrupting local youth. And in several locations, leaders were convinced the problem had external origins. But the connecting thread in these various initiatives against drug sales, and for all the environmental improvement efforts as well, were hopes to build or restore the social or physical capital in the neighborhood with a view toward enhancing the *long-term* ability of the neighborhood to resist crime and delinquency.

Podolefsky does mention drug and alcohol counseling. These activities were viewed at the time not as crime prevention initiatives, but rather as strategies to prevent delinquency and future criminality among residents. As we will see later, when drug treatment is mentioned by leaders in the current context, they point out *both* the personal benefits for the addicted individuals and the broader benefits to the community.

In contrast to social problem reduction, *victimization prevention* (VP) efforts focus almost exclusively on preventing victimization of neighborhood residents. Three clusters of strategies appear in this approach: protective, surveillance, and criminal justice oriented.

In the surveillance category, we find "traditional" community crime prevention programs such as Block Watch, Neighborhood Watch, and Citizens on Patrol (COP). These seek to reduce victimization of neighborhood residents by letting potential offenders know they are being watched and by contributing information leading to the arrest of offenders. Programs geared to enhancing the protection of persons, such as street safety tips, or the protection of property, such as Operation Identifi-

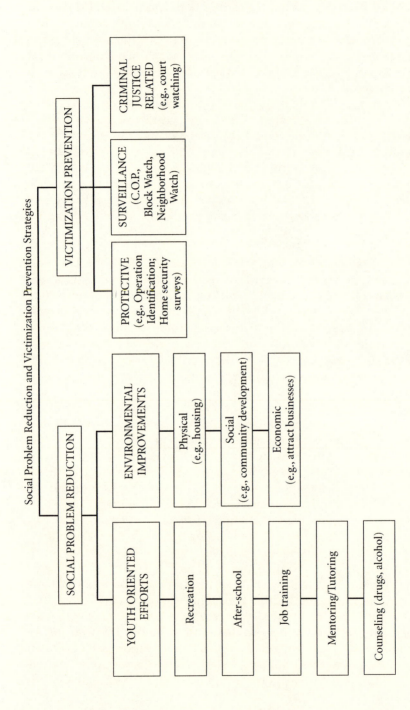

FIGURE 7.3 Two Classes of Collective Crime Prevention Strategies. Adapted from A. Podolefsky (1983) *Case Studies in Community Crime Prevention*, Springfield, IL: Charles C. Thomas. Adapted with the permission of Charles C. Thomas, publisher.

cation or house security surveys, are part of the protective approach as well. Here the hope is to reduce either the chances of immediate victimization or the costs of victimization events should they occur.

Environmental efforts designed to keep offenders out, such as blocking off streets, may reflect victimization prevention as well if the focus is on keeping out offenders who would victimize residents. (For a recent example, see 12.) Podolefsky notes (29: 27) that a few anticrime activities, such as street lighting, do not fall neatly into either group. Street closures and destruction of abandoned housing may both be examples of other activities that are similarly dual purpose, promoting long-term community viability and deterring proximate offenders.

Criminal justice approaches include court watching and police watchdog efforts. Such activities prod agents in the criminal justice system to help prevent crime by pursuing criminals and locking up those arrested for a long time.

In some cases, neighborhoods may pursue strategies representing "pure" crime control or "pure" attacks on root causes. In other cases, neighborhoods may adopt mixed strategies. But the more important point suggested by Podolefsky's model is that it is unlikely neighborhoods will pursue both SPR and VP with equal vigor; neighborhoods will favor one or the other, even if some outside observers might think the community would benefit by vigorously pursuing both strategies. Furthermore, which category of strategies a neighborhood favors depends largely on the overall structure of the locale. The two general types of strategies have been described earlier (see Figure 7.3), and the following section briefly describes the processes underlying the links between neighborhood fabric, perceptions of the crime problem, and types of collective strategies adopted.

Podolefsky's model not only linked collective crime perceptions with the type of prevention strategy pursued; it also suggested those perceptions arose, in part, from the demographic characteristics of the neighborhood itself. In short, the basic neighborhood fabric—its ecological structure—shaped how residents thought about crime and related problems and their causes and cures. In other words,

Community Fabric → Views About Crime Problems → Type of Collective
Strategy Adopted

Podolefsky focused attention on three standard dimensions of neighborhood ecology: ethnic composition, socioeconomic status, and stability. Some of the relevant dynamics underlying these connections are described below in abbreviated form. (For more detail on the processes underlying these connections, see 29: 43–48.)

Ethnicity links to how extensive local social problems are. In predominantly African-American communities, local social problems such as unemployment, poor housing, and lack of recreational and employment opportunities for youth are likely to be more widespread. For example, in the 1982 sample of sixty-six Baltimore neighborhoods, neighborhoods almost exclusively African-American were more than one standard deviation higher than all-white communities on assessed deterioration (42). As discussed earlier (Chapter 4), the causes of these higher levels of dilapidation in predominantly African-American communities are multiple, extremely difficult to pin down, and subject to controversy.

Because such social problems are often more widespread in predominantly African-American communities, and crime may be higher in those communities as well, residents there are more likely to see the crime problem as part of a larger constellation of social ills, not as a separate entity meriting separate treatment. In their eyes, the crime problem emerges from other problems. To quote the longtime Baltimore neighborhood leader and activist Lena Boone, in this view, "The first criminal is the landlord."

All else being equal, African-American communities are likely to have higher densities of released offenders or offenders under supervision than are predominantly white communities (17). The volume of released or supervised offenders may be extremely high in some low-income African-American communities (27: 558). Given such variations in released offender densities, all else being equal, it is harder for residents in low-income African-American communities to argue that offenders are coming into their neighborhoods only from the outside. Although in-migration of offenders may occur, that in-migration may take place in the context of higher released or supervised offender populations.

One final point about released offender density merits mention. In neighborhoods where residents know they are surrounded by large numbers of offenders or potential offenders, some protection may be provided residents if they are part of a group being protected by a local gang or gang leader. Local gangs may even resource residents to help buy their "silence" when police arrive (43). In such settings, residents are understandably reluctant to cooperate with or call on the police, as required by some community crime prevention programs, especially if residents have long-term ties to some gang members (28).

In short, in predominantly African-American communities, residents may more readily see local social problems as the cause of crime and, at the same time, may be more willing to acknowledge that some of the offenders connected with the local criminal activity, now and in future, may come from inside the neighborhood.[3] Such views predispose residents and leaders in these neighborhoods to adopt social problem reduction rather than victimization prevention collective crime prevention strategies. Social problem reduction strategies try to assist offenders as well as nonoffenders and delinquents as well as nondelinquents.

For predominantly Hispanic or African-American neighborhoods, another dynamic also orients them away from victimization prevention. In these communities, views of police are likely to be more negative (19). Such views originate, in part, from the less courteous treatment these populations receive at the hands of the police (37). Given historically difficult relations between many police departments and many urban African-American communities, leaders in these communities are unlikely to adopt crime prevention programs depending substantially on police-community cooperation for their success (35: 147–153; 19). "Traditional" victimization prevention programs such as COP, Neighborhood Watch, or Block Watch presume such cooperation.

The social class of the neighborhood influences views on the crime problem. In higher-class neighborhoods, visible social problems are generally less frequent. Housing is likely to be better maintained, local schools and job opportunities for youth are both likely to be better, and there are likely to be fewer problems with "nuisance" land uses. These advantages accrue because of a complex mix of factors that undoubtedly include the stronger political clout of such neighborhoods, the preferential treatment they may receive from local officials and agencies, and the stronger control that local leaders may exercise over residents (23: 49). The control may be enhanced by informal ties, background homogeneity on education and income levels, or formal covenants or incorporated neighborhood associations. (For a fuller discussion of these issues, see Chapter 8.)

Whatever the origins of the visible social problems that do arise in such higher-income neighborhoods, the important point is that their rates are lower. So when a crime problem does occur there, local residents are less likely to link it to *visible* local social problems, given the latter are less prevalent in the higher-income locales. Therefore the crime problem is more likely to be seen as a relatively separate issue. Acting on those views, residents will be more likely to favor collective approaches directly addressing the crime problem—a victimization prevention strategy—rather than more indirect approaches geared to improving local social and physical conditions.

Furthermore, in these higher-income neighborhoods, relations with the police have probably been more amicable (37). Therefore residents are generally more willing to cooperate with the police in mounting local surveillance or property identification efforts. They do not expect that cooperation will create risks for them.

The last ecological dimension is *stability*, called family orientation by Podolefsky, perhaps the most complex ecological dimension. More stable neighborhoods might have more homeowners, more households with children, more married couple households, households that have lived there longer, more one-unit as opposed to multiunit structures, and fewer single-parent households.

Podolefsky generally predicts that in more stable communities, concern for local youth is higher. Thus residents are predisposed to adopt crime prevention programs focusing on long-term prevention. Long-term stability in a locale means that residents know each other better and, presumably, become more concerned about the welfare of their neighbors. Given this higher level of concern, residents in more stable contexts seek to prevent delinquent involvement of local youth and thus favor long-term prevention, that is, SPR-focused strategies, such as enhancing recreational and job-training opportunities. Podolefsky (29: 47) suggests that stability may be the most important ecological dimension of the three.

But it is not unusual to find stable neighborhoods with few children and large numbers of aging homeowners or ones with sizable youth populations but few married or home-owning households. Podolefsky's model does not directly address what we would expect to happen in these communities with mixed scores on stability. With this ecological dimension, more than the others, discrepant scores on relevant indicators seem likely. Presumably, if the suggested indicators did not all point toward high stability, we would expect a predisposition away from SPR strategies and toward VP strategies.

Data Sources

To better address the questions raised above, my colleagues and I sampled an additional forty-two neighborhoods beyond our already-selected thirty.[4] In this chapter, I use pseudonyms for all participating neighborhoods to protect the anonymity of their leaders. Toward that end, I also have changed some street names and other geographical features. Furthermore, in reporting comments from individual leaders, I have *sometimes* changed the respondent's gender or other features of his or her background. In one (and only one) instance, I have changed geographic references in a quote to better mask a neighborhood's identity. The additional neighborhoods were stratified on neighborhood population, so that we would include small, medium-sized, and large neighborhoods. We successfully completed semi–open-ended interviews with twenty-seven leaders in our original thirty neighborhoods and thirty-two leaders in the additionally sampled forty-two neighborhoods. One additional leader refused to be interviewed, but returned a written response when provided with a list of key questions (total = 60; 58 complete enough to be usable). We sought neighborhood leaders who had lived in the locale for at least seven years, so they could provide us with insight into changes in the neighborhood's name and population that might have taken place (see Chapter 8). They were not necessarily current leaders.

Information from the closed-ended portion of the protocol suggests we were relatively successful in contacting experienced local leaders. On average, the leaders had lived in the neighborhood for about a quarter century (median year moved in = 1970). Over 75% of respondents had lived in the neighborhood for at least a decade. Those moving in more recently either had had relatives living there previously or had had prior contact with the neighborhood and its organization. For example, one person had been involved with the neighborhood for a time, but reported "moving in" only recently because he had been living on his boat. Two others had had relatives living in the neighborhood and had spent time there when younger.

The leaders in general were not only experienced with the locale, but heavily involved as well. On average, at the time of the interview they reported being involved with two community groups; almost 60% were involved with two or more groups at the time of the interview. At the time of the interview, only five (9%) reported no local organizational involvements. When asked about previous organizational involvement, almost 70% reported affiliation with one or more local groups.

Before leaving the discussion of data sources, the appropriateness of our site location deserves mention. Podolefsky (29: 53) acknowledges that city context influences collective responses to crime and how those responses connect with community dimensions. These data come from one city (Baltimore). I have already noted that the rate of cocaine-related emergency room episodes outstripped the rate for heroin-related ones. Nonetheless, one might argue that had we completed interviews in a city where the crack epidemic had been even more sizable than was the case in Baltimore, our conclusions about the continued applicability of Podolefsky's model could be different. That may be true. There may be other cities where "crack changed everything" to a greater extent than in Baltimore. On the other hand, although our data are limited to one city, that city was *not* one of the three used by Podolefsky in his original grounded theorizing. In addition, it appears that the crack epidemic did at least register dramatically in Baltimore (see Figure 7.2). In addition, the on-site evidence of crack dealing reported by our field workers in the summer of 1994 was extensive. David Simon and Ed Burns's ethnography of a West Baltimore drug corner, done about the same time as our data collection, amply documents the prevalence of crack dealing and the accompanying neighborhood devastation (35).

Finally, the leaders' responses underscored the increasingly serious nature of drug problems. Of the fifty-eight leaders providing usable closed-ended responses (of sixty total providing some information), thirty-seven (64%) rated drug problems in their neighborhood as serious (18) or very serious (19). Seventy-seven percent agreed that drug problems were worse in their neighborhood compared to ten years earlier. In short, the crack epidemic hit Baltimore hard, as shown both by emergency department visits and leaders' comments. Although other cities may have been hit harder, there is no reason to suspect that our study site's history and character make it especially likely we would or would not find a continuing applicability of Podolefsky's model.

Of course, these data, although spanning a sizable number of neighborhoods, are too limited to provide a detailed, definitive view of collective responses to crime in any one particular neighborhood. In contrast to Podolefsky's original study, for example, resident interviews in each neighborhood are not available, nor are extensive field observations of local organization meetings. But the purpose here is not to provide a detailed picture of each community, but to examine connections between community contexts, problem views, and problem responses.

Responses to Drug Sales and Use and Related Crime Problems

According to Podolefsky's model, when examining different community responses to drugs we should find the "purest" victimization prevention approaches in the highest-status, predominantly white communities, particularly if there are few children in these locations. We should find the "purest" social problem reduction approaches in predominantly African-American, lower-status communities, particularly if these host sizable youth populations. In neighborhoods where the demographic makeup does not match either of these two profiles—that is, higher-status African-American communities or poorer predominantly white communities—we should find a blended approach, with elements of both strategies.

Exclusively Victimization Prevention

The leaders in several predominantly white, middle- to upper-income neighborhoods reported, as predicted, strategies centered on victimization prevention. **Oakwell** provided one of the clearest examples of a "pure" victimization prevention approach. The northern section of the city of Baltimore contains several neighborhoods that went up in the first quarter of the twentieth century as planned, high-income communities, developed by a single development corporation, with incorporated community associations and accompanying legal powers. These neighborhoods included Elm Park, Oakmont, Original Birchwood, Pineland, and Oakwell.

Oakwell had some of the highest-priced housing in the city and had been similarly positioned for the past twenty years. It was over 90% white, and the nonwhites living there were located mostly in less expensive housing along the neighborhood's eastern border. As the interviewer, Steve Pardue, wrote in his field notes, "It is characterized by very large, sumptuous homes, many dating from early in the century, by large and beautifully landscaped lawns, and by narrow, slowly winding streets. Many of these streets are one-way, making it quite difficult for the uninitiated to get around in the area without a map."

Nearby are some neighborhoods that are economically much worse off than Oakwell and are predominantly African-American. Only a few blocks from Oakwell, one finds an X-rated video store in a commercial center clustered around an intersection. Shopping around the intersection has declined considerably in the past two decades, as stores geared more toward moderate-income households have been replaced by video stores, drugstores, and the like.

The Oakwell leader interviewed had lived in the neighborhood for at least a couple decades at the time of the interview (December 1994) and had held several positions on the community association. This leader reported that the main initiatives pursued by the association were encouraging improved home security, obtaining better street lighting, and the funding of a private security patrol.

The origin of the private security patrol was as follows. The leader noted that Oakwell had always had a burglary problem. Its burglary percentile scores were 39, 76, and 98 over the past three decades, suggesting an intensifying rather than steady burglary problem over the long term. In 1992, according to the leader, three murders took place.[5] A robbery also took place in the neighborhood, and an older couple was assaulted by a burglar.[6] In response to this incident, citizens gathered and decided to put up money to pay for private patrolling in the neighborhood. Initially the program used off-duty Baltimore city police personnel, but it no longer does so. Eight security officers patrolled the neighborhood. About one third of the neighborhood's residents contribute to the security effort. The Baltimore Police Department was initially "resistant and uncooperative" about the effort.

In the mind of our interviewee, the program has proven effective. He suggested the presence of the patrol has "reduced criminal activity" and "gives peace of mind to residents"; he thought that "overall crime is down, although [last year's] murders caused a sense of increasing crime in the area, and had the effect of increasing participation in the security patrol program." The respondent suggested that the success of the patrol was due to "very dogged organizers, who stayed with it."

Residents believing in a victimization prevention approach tend to see the crime problem as coming from "outside." Oakwell's leader strongly endorsed this view, and it was probably substantially correct, given the attractive targets in the neighborhood to draw in potential offenders. Oakwell had paid a nationally known security expert to visit the neighborhood and make security suggestions. She recommended closing off some neighborhood entrances to make it more difficult to get in. Reduced entrances, she suggested, combined with the confusing pattern of one-way streets already present in the neighborhood, should reduce offender in-migration.

At the time of our leader interview, the neighborhood was leaning *against* petitioning the city for street closures. The neighborhood leader had proved politically astute in the past, as evidenced by one incident he shared. He thought pushing for the closures might be too politically sensitive. But his view notwithstanding, the following year (1995) the city sponsored a planning workshop to discuss the street closures that Oakwell sought. One member of our research team attended. At that meeting, white representatives of Oakwell met with African-American leaders from three neighborhoods adjoining or close to Oakwell, to discuss the impacts of the proposed closures on the adjoining neighborhoods. Leaders from those adjoining locales expressed concern about the proposed closings, fearing the action would drive traffic volume in their own neighborhoods even higher. Tempers flared at the workshop as participants discussed each of the proposed closures, but by the time our observer left the meeting, some of the proposed closings already had been acceded to by leaders from the adjoining locations. We heard several reports that ultimately all of the proposed closures were put into place; later trips through the locale seemed to bear this out.

Apparently, Oakwell was willing to be "politically incorrect" and pursue boundary-enhancing traffic pattern changes recommended as a crime prevention measure by an internationally renowned expert. The process was clearly part of the neighborhood's overall community crime prevention plan and, Oakwell leaders hoped, would have an impact on crime in the neighborhood.

For Oakwell's leader, drugs caused people to come into the neighborhood and burgle and rob. The neighborhood's response was to keep them out as best as possible and to keep close watch over intruders through private patrol services. Given this neighborhood's high status, physical incivilities were essentially unknown in all but one small section of the neighborhood. The only social incivilities causing concern were would-be offenders passing through on foot or by car. Closures and private security were aimed directly at reducing these social incivilities and thus reducing street attacks and burglaries. The connection between social incivilities and crime was direct in the minds of residents.

In **Sherman Heights,** in contrast to Oakwell, we find major, heavily traveled north-south arteries coursing through the neighborhood. On the main streets, one finds moderate-to-upscale row houses, two to four stories high, and a few large apartment buildings. On the cross streets and the north-south streets away from the main arterials, housing is smaller, usually only two stories high, and more modest. The area experienced considerable gentrification and revitalization in the 1970s and 1980s. Housing went from the nineteenth percentile in price in 1970 to the sixty-second percentile in 1980 and the seventy-ninth percentile in 1990. Renovators in the 1970s were younger, low- to moderate-income households, self-dubbed by one as "weekend warriors," sometimes with children. By the early and mid-1980s, the original rehabbers were selling to buyers who were lawyers, doctors, or other high-income professionals.

The 1979 neighborhood mapping of city neighborhoods (see Chapter 8) showed distinct sections of Sherman Heights. The heart of Sherman Heights, labeled Sherman Heights 2, is predominantly white, with a modest African-American population that has remained at about 15% to 20% since 1970. Despite the gentrification of the 1970s and early 1980s, homeownership has stayed steady at 20% to 25% for the period. The latter is not surprising given the large student population and the large apartment buildings in the locale. The preteen population aged six to thirteen years declined from about 9% in 1970 to about 6% in 1990.

Sherman Heights 2, given its extensive student population, and the late-night, perhaps incautious lifestyles often followed by this group, has always had a relatively high level of street crime. The figures show the *relative* level, in the case of robbery, drifting down somewhat over the past twenty years, from the ninety-third percentile in 1970–1972 to about the eighty-third percentile in 1990–1992. On the other hand, burglary has become more problematic, relative to other city neighborhoods, as Sherman Heights 2 has gone from the sixty-first to the ninety-ninth percentile since 1970. The increased burglary problem may be partially explained by the increasing volume of available targets in the locale accompanying the partial gentrification (7). Since the increase seems to predate the crack invasion, it is probably not due to higher volumes of offenders seeking to support their habits and traveling in from adjoining locales.

Near Sherman Heights is **Spruce,** also predominantly white, but without the large apartment buildings of Sherman Heights. Housing is almost completely row houses, although they are smaller than in the heart of Sherman Heights, mostly two stories in height. Many students rent there, but homeownership has climbed from more than one third pregentrification to about one half postgentrification. Situated closer to high-crime locations to its east, Spruce has had a more serious robbery problem than Sherman Heights, as reflected in higher robbery percentile scores. Burglary is a serious problem there as well, but has been serious for longer as compared to Sherman Heights. On the day of our interview with the Spruce leader, her husband was downtown testifying against a man he had seen attempting to break into a car across the street from their home.

Both Sherman Heights and Spruce respondents linked the crime problems in their locales to addicted offenders seeking support for their habits, even though the serious crime problems in both locales predated the crack epidemic. Both leaders viewed the drug problem as originating outside the neighborhood. The Spruce leader remarked, "A drug dealer wouldn't last five minutes here. He'd stand out in a second. There aren't any vacant buildings—this neighborhood is relaxed, but alert." The leader apparently viewed vacant buildings as the only type of home base from which dealers operated unobserved, concluding that since there were no unoccupied buildings, the dealers would be immediately spotted. In her mind, following the incivilities theory, abandoned housing necessarily provided drug-dealing bases and, the neighborhood lacking vacant units, drug dealing was therefore excluded. Again, as with the social incivilities discussed in Oakwell, we see a direct incivilities-crime connection in a leader's thinking.

Perhaps the biggest community crime prevention initiative being mounted around the time of our leader interviews was a special fund. (See Chapter 8 for a more detailed discussion of this initiative.) Residents would be levied a special tax or assessment that would go to local improvements. Our two leaders were split in their reactions to the initiative.

The Spruce leader reported having differences of opinion with the umbrella organization. This organization, representing a number of adjoining neighborhoods, was one of the sponsors of the special district initiative. She reported that plans called for extra funds to be spent on hiring private security, along the lines of the Oakwell model, and providing additional sanitation patrols. Again, with the sanitation patrols, we see the axiomatic connection of "crime and grime" surfacing. But in her mind, there were doubts about these connections; she considered the proposals unwise because the area to be covered was too large for the security patrols to operate effectively, and the sanitation patrols would be little more than "glorified pooper scoopers." Nonetheless, despite this one leader's concerns, the special legislation had passed just a couple weeks before our interview and was implemented in the months following.

Our Sherman Heights respondent, who worked more closely than the Spruce leader with the umbrella organization, expressed more confidence in the potential benefits from the forthcoming funds, although he did not comment on specific initiatives. In his mind, it had not yet been determined how the funds were to be spent; that would be done at later meetings of local community organization representatives. But it was clear from both newspaper accounts and the leaders' comments that significant portions of the funds would be spent on community crime prevention in the form of victimization prevention activities. The Sherman Heights leader viewed the entire district initiative as a reaction to crime and geared primarily to preventing victimization. He reported how the idea first surfaced in a series of large community meetings following the mugging and murdering of an architect in 1993, a subsequent rape, a kidnapping, armed holdups, and several shootings.

Because both neighborhoods are close to an elementary school where local parents in past years helped shape curriculum, there was some youth work ongoing in these neighborhoods. But the leaders did not connect these initiatives with crime prevention, and efforts related to the school were listed as lower priority by these organizations. Youth work and housing improvements were not major features of their crime prevention strategies. Along these lines, the Spruce leader detailed one story surrounding a small vest pocket park nearby, used for football by local youth. The organization got the city to buy it in the early 1980s, and the organization agreed to maintain it. Ball playing was prohibited there because it tore up the turf, as a sign we saw there in 1995 confirmed. Although not stated, the prohibition may have had as a purpose keeping older teens out of the neighborhood. In short, except for education initiatives geared to younger children at a local school and seen as education rather than crime issues, the organization's approach to crime lacked a youth component. Given the low-to-moderate scores on stability in the locale, these views are not surprising.

In keeping with a victimization prevention strategy, both neighborhood leaders supported formal surveillance activities such as Citizens on Patrol and Neighborhood Watch. Since both neighborhoods were predominantly white and moderately high status, the requisite functional police-community ties can be presumed.

In Spruce, the organization sponsored organized resident walks through the neighborhood in the evening hours. The leader was not sure whether Neighborhood Watch or COP was more effective: "It's hard to say which is the more effective, only the police would know that [based on crime statistics]. I don't think there has been more or less crime because of these activities, but they do make people feel better . . . they're more willing to go outside."

In Spruce, COP was conducted by neighbors who walked around the community with a cellular telephone. It was organized "two or three years ago" by the then-president of the Spruce organization. "She single-handedly recruited people and started the program." The telephone was obtained through a grant. At the time of the interview, the COP was not operational because the telephone had broken, and "people think it's useless to go out if they can't communicate." About thirty people were involved in the program at first, but that number had dropped considerably by the time the telephone broke, "because people figured out that it [the program] goes on and on." Apparently, for motivational and equipment reasons, COP proved difficult to maintain.

The Sherman Heights leader reported similar walking surveillance activities in that neighborhood, but suggested that the activities might actually be preventing crime as well as fostering perceptions of a safer neighborhood. The program there, called the Strollers, had been in existence for about three years at the time of the interview. Apparently the effort in Sherman Heights was not hampered by the equipment problems that surfaced in Spruce. Perhaps Sherman Heights's somewhat wealthier residents could supply their own phones. The leader was hoping to complement it with an organized porch-sitting program, where people would agree to sit out on their porches for 1–2 hours on designated evenings.

Whereas the Spruce leader saw COP and Neighborhood Watch as relatively interchangeable programs, the more discerning Sherman Heights leader was less enthusiastic about Neighborhood or Block Watch, complaining it was "too bureaucratic." According to the leader, the city police department required about 60% participation on individual blocks before issuing the code number for a resident to use when reporting a crime or suspicious activity.

In sum, in both these neighborhoods leaders viewed the crime problem as coming in from outside the area because the drug dealing—in their view—was taking place outside the neighborhood; these leaders relied heavily on formal surveillance programs to promote actual or perceived neighborhood safety and reported plans to begin private patrolling with future funds from a special plan. Reduction of minor physical incivilities would be accomplished through sanitation patrols to be funded by the special fund, but one leader thought the activities of these patrols were a waste of time. In both locales, major physical incivilities, in the form of abandoned housing, for example, were not present. That absence reassured one leader that the locale was thus safe from drug dealing—dealers had no base and would stick out too much. Responding to minor physical incivilities was seen in both neighborhoods as secondary to patrol activities directly enhancing residents' safety.

Groveland is another relatively high status, predominantly white neighborhood positioned further northeast in the city from the three neighborhoods discussed so far. Its housing stock is relatively high priced, ranking about the seventy-fifth percentile in both 1980 and 1990. It remains almost exclusively white, being less than 5% African-American from 1970 through 1990. It is also an extremely stable neighborhood, with two thirds to three fourths of the households being home owners through the three censuses. There are substantial numbers of elderly and near-elderly households, and the preteen population has dropped from about one in eight in 1970 to about one in twelve in 1990. Substantial racial change has taken place in some of the adjoining neighborhoods.

Groveland has been experiencing a decreasing relative crime rate, going from a robbery percentile score of about 30 in 1970 to 12 in 1990; the burglary percentile score had declined from 44 to 5 over the period. This fits with the leader's depiction of the locale as a relatively low crime area with few muggings. The elderly leader we interviewed there reported that the neighborhood's main anticrime activities were prevention oriented, including having police in to give prevention and household security talks and keeping a Block Watch going. According to the leader, about 100 residents were involved with the Block Watch program. He felt the program served a purpose because it "keeps people aware that problems do exist." The program began in the mid-1980s at the instigation of the Baltimore Police Department. Again, following Podolefsky's model, the relatively high status and predominantly white makeup of the neighborhood made it more likely that good police-community relations—prerequisite to mounting standard community anticrime prevention programs like COP and Block Watch—were present.

The neighborhood, as might be expected given its relatively high status and high homeownership rate, appeared relatively incivility-free when we walked through it. In the leader interview, no mention was made of either social or physical incivilities meriting attention. Outside the neighborhood's boundaries, however, the leader admitted there were a few problems "around the edges" that the residents were keeping an eye on. The organization had been involved in monitoring conditions around a used car lot on the neighborhood's boundary—the owner had parked vehicles on the street—and in scaling back development plans at a local nursing home.

In all four of these neighborhoods—Oakwell, Sherman Heights, Spruce, and Groveland—leaders saw the crime and drug problems as occurring outside the neighborhood. Incivilities were either minor, in the cases of Spruce and Sherman Heights, and to be dealt with by sanitation patrols, or nonexistent, in the cases of Oakwell and Groveland. Major incivilities, such abandoned housing, were not even "on the radar screen" in these communities because they were almost unknown at the time. In the Spruce leader's mind, the lack of vacant housing helped exclude dealers. In Oakwell, the neighborhood was taking steps to close off the neighborhood and keep out social incivilities. In Groveland, the leader spoke of problems "around the edges." This "out there" mentality about crime fits with and helps drive victimization prevention strategies. In the next neighborhood considered, although it is predominantly white and has an economic status only somewhat lower than Spruce and Sherman Heights, housing patterns brought drug-selling problems right to the neighborhood edge.

Further north and west in the city from Groveland is **Maplecroft**. Just south of the Baltimore County line, it is a neighborhood of tree-lined streets, with well-kept row houses and detached houses. The neighborhood looks moderate-to-upper income, given the housing stock. Immediately adjoining neighborhoods are sometimes more impressive, as in the case of Pineland, which is almost all detached homes, and sometimes less impressive. Maplecroft itself includes or abuts a small number of apartment complexes that seem to be almost "tucked away" in the neighborhood. There is one south of the main artery running east-west through the neighborhood, and another north of it. Driving around the neighborhood, one sees few children. Our interviewee here noted with apparent satisfaction that there are few if any children on his block, and that when children are noticed, the police are often called because the children are thought to be either dangerously far from home or having the potential to disrupt the neighborhood—the categorization seemed to depend on the age of the particular children. Given the neighborhood's predominantly white, moderate to moderately high status residents and the paucity of children—all factors favoring a VP approach—it was not surprising when the leader reported on efforts to stop drug dealing in an area near his home.

The leader routinely walked his dog past an apartment complex around the corner from his house. The complex is technically outside the neighborhood boundaries. According to the leader, the complex contains over a hundred units, with about one third of the units designated for Section 8 assisted housing. During frequent dog-walking trips past the apartments, he made note of the particular apartments that seemed to be harboring drug-dealing activities. He spent some time talking with children from that area about what went on in various locations within the complex. In addition, he also recorded license plate numbers and went on a police ride-along, during which the officer concurred that drug trafficking indeed was going on.

After gathering information for a few months, he worked through his neighborhood association to put pressure on the landlord to do something about the problem and on the police for an increased presence. The association contacted the owner of the apartments and requested help in controlling the residents there. Reportedly, the owner refused to engage in any monitoring activities or take any action. Subsequently, the vigilant resident approached the Baltimore Police Department, through the Maplecroft Community Association, and requested action. He gave the police *specific* information, including the apartment numbers of suspects and their names. Soon thereafter, the police conducted raids and made arrests. The apartment complex has since been sold, and the leader reported some improvements at the site.

Unfortunately, he also reported a "cost" for his crime prevention initiative. Since the raids and arrests, he does not walk his dog near the complex, concerned he will be recognized as someone involved with the police action. The costs of surveillance-related victimization prevention initiatives, and how residents seek to minimize them, will be explored in more detail when I examine the predominantly white but lower-status neighborhoods in south and southwest Baltimore and predominantly African-American communities.

But before examining such communities, I want to consider one variant of white neighborhood much rarer when Podolefsky did his original study: gentrifying neighborhoods (7).[7] In these locales, one is likely to find a substantial volume of high-priced, renovated housing, the amount depending in part on the stage of gentrification. But in these locales, gentrification is likely to remain spotty, with significant portions of the neighborhood remaining unimproved, resulting in neighborhoods where residents may vary considerably on status (22, 24, 34).[8]

We completed interviews with leaders of three gentrifying neighborhoods: **Sycamore, Midtown,** and **Jackson.** Sycamore is close to the new downtown baseball stadium and not far from a high-rise public housing site recently vacated at the time of the interview and since torn down. Midtown is not too many blocks from the central business district. Jackson is surrounded by neighborhoods with severe economic problems and not too far away one can find large open-air drug markets. Its housing was among the lowest priced in 1970; by 1980 it had reached the sixtieth percentile in neighborhood house prices, and by 1990 the seventy-seventh percentile. Homeownership had increased from 24% to 39% over the same period. During this time of increasing house values and stability, the neighborhood also became more integrated, with the African-American population growing from less than 13% to over 40% during this twenty-year period.

Given Jackson's location proximate to increasingly distressed neighborhoods, it was not surprising to see, paralleling these ecological shifts, that its crime problems had worsened. The relative robbery percentile went from 89 in 1970 to 98 in 1990; the relative burglary score climbed from the forty-second percentile in 1970 to the ninety-ninth in 1990. The leader candidly admitted that crime was a serious problem in the neighborhood and had increased in severity. "It's gotten more personal. It's one thing to come home and find your stuff stolen, but a gun in your face leaves more of an impression. Armed robberies and muggings are happening more."

Jackson's leader reported local participation in both Block Watch and COP. Block Watch had been active for about five years at the time of the interview, COP about three to four. The leader felt that COP was the more effective of the two. In this program, about "fifty or sixty" residents patrol the locale nightly, equipped with cellular phones. They patrol on foot and in cars.

In describing the motivation for residents' participation in organized prevention programs, the leader connected local property values and crime. She recognized concern about crime had

> obviously affected the ability [of the neighborhood] to attract people in to renovate homes. There has also been some population loss. People finally get to the point where it doesn't work for them anymore and they move; if you feel that your personal safety is in jeopardy, no amount of low-interest loans is going to attract you. Even renters and some students are discouraged from living here. Concern about crime tends to put a certain amount of stress on the whole neighborhood . . . we're not as likely to wander . . . down the street to see someone. Ten years ago you'd be worried about someone breaking into your house while you were gone, now you're wondering if you'll make it back . . . .This is not a perceptual problem, it's very real.

In the leader's eyes, the problem emerged from outside the neighborhood; the metaphors she used suggested a siege mentality, "and we don't see any reinforcements coming over the hill." She also recognized the economic distress affecting those adjoining neighborhoods and cited the large companies that had left the area. The leader well appreciated the severity of problems in those nearby neighborhoods.

In contrast to the previous batch of neighborhoods, in Jackson major physical incivilities in the form of abandoned housing were of concern. The local organization had taken steps to prevent further deterioration of these units (see Chapter 8). Minor physical incivilities and social incivilities were not of concern. The extremely serious crime situation there appeared to leave scant organizational energy for minor incivilities, especially since the neighborhood was surrounded by extremely distressed locales.

Sycamore, located close to the downtown, confronted problems similar to those afflicting Jackson. Like Jackson, Sycamore was close to severely distressed neighborhoods in the form of high-rise public housing. The neighborhood also had gentrified significantly, but local politics had played a greater role in the renewal. Sycamore had been targeted under Mayor Schaefer as a site for the city's "dollar houses" program in the 1970s (see Chapter 2). As a result of this initiative, large numbers of vacant housing had been rehabbed and large numbers of new residents had moved in.

Before the renewal, housing in Sycamore had been among the lowest priced in the city; by 1980 the housing ranked in the ninetieth percentile, and it remained at about the same level in 1990. Homeownership increased from 16% to 41% from 1970 to 1980, but had dropped slightly to 38% by 1990. So the renewal had increased both stability and house values over a twenty-year span. In the course of the transition, racial composition had shifted from 82% African-American in 1970 to 38% African-American in 1990. Driving down the streets of the neighborhood, one sees renovated brick housing with exterior brass fixtures. Some of the streets are short or narrow or both, giving the neighborhood an "old town" feel. Occasional for sale signs—about one or two on a long block—were in evidence.[9]

The renewal process, however, failed to reduce the neighborhood's robbery problem, which shifted between the seventy-second and ninety-first percentile relative to other neighborhoods during the period 1970 to 1992. Unfortunately, burglary problems worsened, as the locale went from one of the lowest burglary neighborhoods in the city in 1970 (third percentile) to one of the highest (ninety-ninth percentile in 1980, eighty-eighth percentile in 1990). Given that houses either empty or with few valuables had been replaced by moderate-income homes, and given the proximity of nearby offenders, such an increase in property crime is certainly understandable (7).

In keeping with these numbers, the leader reported repeated break-ins at his business, and he thought that robberies and break-ins were a serious problem in the neighborhood. He related some serious crime incidents "off the record" and expressed concern that should the media get access to these stories they would blow them out of proportion. In short, our respondent, who operated a business in the neighborhood, recognized that crime was serious in the locale but also expressed concern that giving too much attention to the problem raised the danger of tarnishing the neighborhood's public image.

The specific type of crime of concern to residents, beyond break-ins and muggings, arose from extensive crack dealing in and around the neighborhood. The leader suggested that residents' most likely response to suspicious people or evidence of drug activity was to "call [the] Narcotics [division of the police department]." Block Watch had previously been active but was no longer so. Given the large numbers of younger student, rental households in the locale, problems with maintaining a program like this are not surprising; comparable lack of interest was also seen in Midtown, which also has a significant student population.

In contrast to the incivility concerns mentioned in the neighborhoods so far, the worries in Sycamore centered on minor social incivilities. Given nearby low-income communities, nearby drug markets, and some bars and liquor stores, the leader was familiar with drunks urinating on his wall and addicts throwing up on his front steps when he came to work in the morning. He cited these as serious public order problems and related the story of a white-collar professional neighbor, living in the neighborhood and working in Washington, D.C., who had recently come by to announce he was moving out. The departing resident mentioned these types of incidents as contributing to his upcoming relocation. The leader did not mention, however, specific initiatives mounted by the neighborhood to address these minor social incivilities. By contrast, concerns about serious crime, and media enlargement of such events, appeared more important to the Sycamore leader. In short, although the types of incivilities of concern in Sycamore as compared to Jackson differed, in both locales concerns about serious crime far outstripped worries about incivilities.

Midtown is gentrified like Sycamore, although the process did not involve the city "dollar houses" program. Housing there went from among the lowest priced in the city to the ninety-third percentile in 1980, dropping back a bit to the eighty-seventh percentile in 1990. Homeownership, however, remains very low, around 10%. In his field notes, Steve Pardue described the neighborhood as follows:

> Midtown is an irregularly shaped area of perhaps fifteen or twenty blocks. . . . It is comprised almost completely of multi-story attached structures, and is home to a wide range of businesses as well as educational and several cultural enterprises. . . . Several major streets run through and around the neighborhood. . . . Most structures in the area are three or four stories high, and are backed by alleys. There is nearly always considerable traffic in the area, including large trucks; it is often noisy.

More than Sycamore, Midtown has a substantial "alternative lifestyle" population (see beginning of Chapter 4). Given such a heterogeneous locale, we might expect a fairly high tolerance for unusual street behavior and less willingness than in Jackson or Sycamore to label some behavior as a public order problem. And indeed, social incivilities were not mentioned by Midtown's leader. Serious crime merited far more attention, as it had in the interviews with the leaders of the two other gentrifying neighborhoods. Crime was as serious in Midtown as it was in the other two gentrified neighborhoods. Its robbery and burglary crime percentile scores were both in the upper 90s.

The neighborhood, like Sycamore, has been unable to mount a consistent collective crime prevention effort. According to the Midtown leader, COP was started three or four years ago, but had become inactive. Given the high rental and student populations, this is not surprising. The neighborhood had sought status as an improvement district, but this initiative had not been finalized by the time of our interview (December 1994). The leader suggested, "Nothing has had much of an effect on crime . . . for whatever reasons people are going to have to learn how to protect themselves."

At the same time, the leader recognized the significant costs crime was having for the community, as people drove short distances they would have walked in the past and stayed in more at night. She asked, "People aren't going out at night; what's the point of living in the city if you can't go out at night?"

All three of our gentrified neighborhood leaders recognized the significant toll crime was having on their areas and acknowledged the connections between the crime problem and long-term neighborhood viability. But in only one locale, Jackson, were significant collective efforts to prevent crime reported. The form taken, as predicted by Podolefsky, is crime control rather than long-term social problem reduction. But in the other two neighborhoods, no collective efforts appeared that were maintained over time. Stability in both these locales is extremely low, and heterogeneity is high; both these features probably impede collective efforts, such as attempts at surveillance programs.

The significant and almost overwhelming concern about serious crime in each of these gentrifying neighborhoods, more serious than in Spruce and Sherman Heights, effectively relegated incivility-linked concerns to the background. There was no point in worrying about incivilities now to prevent worse crime later; crime was already worse. But beyond the common backgrounding of concerns about incivilities, marked differences in the profile of incivilities across these three neighborhoods surfaced. In Jackson, consternation focused on major physical issues, such as abandoned housing. In Sycamore, the leader cited minor social incivilities on the street caused by drunks and addicts. And in Midtown, heterogeneous demographics and an "alternate" lifestyle ambience precluded labeling as uncivil a wide variety of street behavior. Such marked variety in leaders' views about incivilities, despite the relative structural similarity of the locales, recalls the discussion in Chapter 3 on the divergence of incivility indicators. I suggested there that different incivility indicators may not reflect a common underlying problem such as disorder but may reflect different and perhaps only loosely related dynamics. The different concerns described by these three leaders appear to support that idea. Although incivilities were far less important to the three leaders than serious crime, the incivilities they did (or did not, in Midtown's case) worry about were highly specific to the local context and issues linked to that context. They did not see disorder; they saw a housing market problem or a drunks and addicts problem. To sweep up their concerns into a broader disorder bundle would be to abstract too much; to risk losing the focus of their concerns; and to blur the connections between their long-term goals for the neighborhood, their prevention efforts, and local dynamics.

Predominantly Victimization Prevention, Some Social Problem Reduction

In southwest Baltimore, and further south in the southernmost section of the city, we interviewed leaders in six predominantly white neighborhoods of varying statuses (West Pine Civic, West Pine Community Council (WPCC), Teaberry, Elmton, Weldon Pond, and Shady Park). These neighborhoods have lower economic status than the white neighborhoods discussed so far. Given their makeup, according to Podolefsky's model these locales should adopt an approach combining social problem reduction efforts with victimization prevention efforts. Of course, if neighborhood racial composition has more influence on the type of strategy adopted than class does, these neighborhoods would exhibit predominantly victimization prevention strategies. Podolefsky did not clarify the relative influence that different ecological factors would have on the type of collective strategies adopted.

In three of these neighborhoods, residents report significant, sizable, and dangerous drug dealing operations: **West Pine Civic, West Pine Community Council (WPCC),** and **Teaberry**. Basic neighborhood fabric in these locales was as follows. The African-American population in these neighborhoods ranged from 22% in WPCC to 3% in Teaberry. The two West Pine neighborhoods had extremely low priced housing, relative to other neighborhoods, as has historically been true there. In 1990, in WPCC the housing ranked in the twentieth percentile on price; in West Pine Civic, the twelfth percentile. Teaberry's housing, priced similarly in 1970, had risen to the sixty-first percentile by 1990. Despite the variation in house prices, all three neighborhoods were at least moderately stable. Homeownership ranged from 44% in West Pine Civic to 72% in Teaberry in 1990.

As predicted by the model, in some of these neighborhoods we see a "mixed" approach to the drug problem, one that encompasses short-term crime control and longer-term prevention. But in some other neighborhoods in this group, we see an approach focused largely on short-term crime control. West Pine Civic and Teaberry, especially the first, both adopted mixed approaches.

West Pine Civic is a distressed neighborhood. In our surveys, residents on some of these blocks reported the highest fear levels of all our 1994 telephone respondents. Housing stock is varied and burned-out or boarded-up housing is a common sight. The avenue marking the eastern boundary is an active drug-trafficking area. As Steve Pardue commented in his field notes:

> It is a working class community, with straight streets fronted by two-story rowhouses, with many formstone facades. There are many beatup American-made cars along the streets, and few trees. The general level of maintenance is low. There is trash in most street gutters, and crack vials can be found on many sidewalks. Many businesses are now boarded up and vandalized to some extent, especially with graffiti. Except in very cold weather, there are many people on the streets.

As one might expect from the street conditions, West Pine Civic is moderate to high on reported crime (fifty-eighth percentile on robbery in 1990; eighty-seventh percentile on burglary in 1990).

The leader interviewed reported both control and prevention efforts to reduce drug problems. On the control side, he said residents call police whenever they see drug activity taking place. The effectiveness of these calls is not clear. Block Watch had been active in the community "for years" and COP efforts were just beginning at the time of our interview. Particularly liked by residents was the anonymous reporting provided by Block Watch. When an officer arrives on the scene, he or she need not go to the complainant's address; thus the community need not know who made the initial report. This feature of Block Watch is highly touted in predominantly African-American communities, as we will see below.

Also on the control side, the organization notifies a landlord if at least two complaints are received about drug dealing by tenants. The organization offers assistance in screening potential tenants. Some owners have followed up and sought assistance; others have not. At the time of our interview, the organization had just been developing procedures based on nuisance abatement laws, with assistance from the Community Law Center, to take direct action on houses being used for drug dealing.

Finally on the control side, the organization had sought active foot patrolling in their locale. Residents had decided to hold a street festival to emphasize their request. They sought to close part of Jefferson Street, an active drug sale area, so that the festival could be held there. Local dealers, who have "considered Jefferson their territory for years" told residents the party could not take place there. The residents persisted, and the event took place in early November 1994.

Unfortunately, more than good food was sold at the fair. Local dealers rented a table and sold hot dogs as a cover for drug transactions, which they carried out at the same time. Buyers approached the table to buy food and got a packet slipped to them under the hot dog. This activity was spotted after a time, and the extra police assigned to the event "moved the dealers around from corner to corner" during the festival.

The "kielbasa with crack" story underscores the unwittingly close relationship between local dealers and local residents in the locale; we will encounter other communities where this same closeness also obtains and causes substantial concern among residents. Simon and Burns's yearlong ethnography completed on a drug corner not far from West Pine Civic provides ample evidence of how those engaged in legitimate activities are intertwined with those engaged in illegitimate ones (35). Recent ethnographies in other drug-plagued neighborhoods in other cities report similar connections, sometimes even in middle-class African-American communities (e.g., 28).

On the long-term prevention side, the organization sponsored fundraising events for tot lots and helped local addicts obtain assistance in recovering. In support of the latter goal, the local leader reported his organization assisted a drug information and recovery center and also coordinated with another organization assisting parolees. The association, in collaboration with other local organizations, has sponsored children's festivals for the past two years.

The closeness between residents and local dealers has reached a much more threatening level in two other neighborhoods in this group. West Pine Community Council (WPCC) is located just southeast of West Pine Civic. The leader there reported he was unable to recommend Block Watch, Neighborhood Watch, or COP, because participation would be too dangerous. He reported two to three drug houses on each block in the neighborhood, with the houses used either as sales or as rest areas by the dealers. On a mid-July (1998) drive through one section of the neighborhood, we saw lookouts on one streetblock where there was a large volume of people on the street call out distinctively when we turned into the streetblock, notifying dealers of potential surveillance. An interview with district police personnel in December 1997 suggested at least three very active drug-dealing locations in one corner of the neighborhood, and our follow-up observations suggested those nominations were accurate. In short, our observations supported the leader's suggestion of extremely intense drug sales activities in this neighborhood.

According to the leader, the neighborhood dealers support both local users and "people [who] come into town to buy their drugs." It is a big business. He related an incident where a resident complained of dealing near a tot lot close to her home. After that complaint, a dealer came up to her on the street and displayed a gym bag of empty shell casings. If he wanted to intimidate her, he succeeded.

In response, the organization went "underground" with its surveillance activities. The group, in collaboration with other agencies the leader was reluctant to name, had organized a secret drug watch. Using detailed reporting forms they believe will hold up in court, they monitor drug activities and use the evidence to get sellers prosecuted.

Like West Pine Civic, WPCC also reported youth-related, long-term prevention initiatives, being particularly proud of spearheading an effort to reopen a local recreation center. So here too we see a mixed response, in accord with what Podolefsky's schema leads us to expect.

Teaberry's leader reported activities focused largely around crime control and admitted there were few youth-related initiatives. But the lack of longer-term prevention programs may arise in part from the admitted tilt of the organization toward upper-income residents. The leader conceded that even though the upper-income segment is in the minority in the community, the organization better reflects that segment. The leader wondered about the factors responsible for the tilt. Did the organization try harder to recruit the higher-income residents who had more influential local jobs? Did the higher-income residents have more of a volunteer ethic or more time to become involved? The reasons are not clear, but the more important point for us here is that the tilt may help explain the lack of long-term, prevention-focused community initiatives sponsored by the organization.

In the Teaberry leader's view, drugs in the neighborhood were omnipresent. He saw the drug-trafficking problem as "unsolvable" and "common knowledge." He suggested that shipments come in daily in cars and vans and are unloaded in the streets or alleys. "You see cars and dealers come by and fill their cars with stuff." Teaberry's location, the leader recognized, made it ideal as a major distribution area. I forgo describing those geographic factors.

The main citizen-based crime control initiative reported in Teaberry used COP as a base. But given the large numbers of dealers in the locale and concerns about possible retaliation, Teaberry has moved toward a partially clandestine patrolling arrangement, with perhaps fifty residents involved.

The Teaberry COP effort was started about three years prior to our interview. A long-time local leader spearheaded mobilizing and maintaining the effort. The police department also provided support. The effort has both an "aboveground" and an "underground" component. Patrolling is done on two weekend nights and a randomly chosen weeknight. Patrollers receive membership cards.

The aboveground portion uses cars with conspicuous flashing lights. The visible effort reassures residents that something is being done. The underground portion patrols in unmarked cars or on foot. In some cases, patrollers wear disguises to avoid recognition. If they have cell phones, they keep them out of sight. The leader acknowledged that although the privacy of the underground approach made it safer for patrollers, it also failed to boost residents' morale in the way the aboveground patrol did.

Dealers have tried to infiltrate patrolling efforts, encouraging their cronies to volunteer. These intrusion attempts have forced the organization to screen program applicants.

When asked about patrol impacts, the leader guessed that crime prevention activities have probably helped deter some crime, simultaneously uplifting some residents' morale. Participants benefit too, the leader thought; they feel "they are making the neighborhood better by doing something."

These last three neighborhoods, by some accounts, appear to face an almost overwhelming drug problem. The response from these low- to mid-status communities has been primarily crime control oriented, but significant long-term prevention activities also have been pursued in two of them. The only "pure" crime control response to the drug problem comes from Teaberry, where the organization admittedly caters to the higher-status portion of its resident base.

In these three neighborhoods, serious crime problems drive concerns about incivilities into the background, as also happened in the three gentrifying neighborhoods. In two of them, WPCC and West Pine Civic, serious physical incivilities in the form of abandoned housing were widespread. In these two locales, it seemed that given the pressing and serious crime problem and the extensiveness of the abandoned housing, the owners of which many times were beyond community reach, there was no point in worrying about reducing physical incivilities.[10]

On the edge of the city, we had three predominantly white neighborhoods bordering suburban counties, each with moderately priced housing in the fortieth to sixtieth house value percentile range in 1990: **Weldon Pond, Shady Park,** and **Elmton**. In the first two, as expected given high homeownership levels of over 60%, we saw a mixed prevention approach, but one that mostly favored crime control. Shady Park had begun to integrate racially over the past decade; by 1990 it was about 20% African-American.

Shady Park and Weldon Pond create an interesting contrast. In Shady Park, the local organization, with encouragement and assistance from district police personnel, aggressively pursued funding for COP. Approaching a local bank, residents obtained funds for vests and cell phones. According to the leader, about thirty people patrol on Thursdays through Saturdays, both on foot and in cars. Even though the local organization got direction from police district personnel in setting up COP, the leader emphasized that police could not listen in on the radios used by COP. Whether this heightened their sense of autonomy, protected them from some police they had suspicions about, or both was not clear.

Initiatives taken against large-scale dealing underscored the organization's autonomy. The leader identified two types of dealing problems: teens dealing on the street and more organized distribution activities housed in an apartment complex, not unlike the situation described earlier in Maplecroft. For the first problem, patrolling citizens report teens out past curfew and pressure police to come and send teens home. For the second problem, organization personnel took the initiative in documenting the problem; they recorded over 1,000 license plate numbers at a particularly troublesome complex and turned those in to the police. Police drove around with citizens to better understand the situation, and according to the leader the police eventually came in and "broke up the ring." Given easy access from the site to a nearby interstate, such a ring seems plausible.

In Weldon Pond, next door, conditions vary markedly by block. Some tidy streetblocks of row houses with neat yards and clean glass storm doors are followed by other streetblocks with less well kept detached housing and *Starsky and Hutch*–vintage vehicles shading weeds in backyards. Weldon Pond, in contrast to Shady Park, reported little victimization prevention activity of an organized nature. The leader we interviewed there reported that COP had been started about eight years earlier, but was now dead. Block Watch had "fizzled out." Why the different response, in comparison to Shady Park?

Many factors could be responsible, but I am inclined to pay most attention to land use differences. Touring the neighborhood highlights how it is broken up by large chunks of industrial land uses, isolating residents in different parts of the neighborhood from one another. We encounter this problem again in Sutton-Kent, much closer to the center of town. The leader in Weldon Pond reported extensive problems at a storage facility, for example. These barriers to socializing and travel probably make it difficult for residents to develop a broader concern about neighborhood-wide problems.

The leader reported initiatives against specific locations to remedy public order problems. For example, public urination and trash problems outside a bar had led the organization to contact the state liquor board; in response the bar installed bouncers. Thus both neighborhoods reported initiatives against teen or young adult incivilities. In contrast to what Podolefsky's model predicts, despite relatively high homeownership levels, the groups did not seem to focus on long-term prevention for teens or young adults. This is probably because for both social incivilities mentioned, teens out late and purportedly dealing and uncivil bar patrons, the youth in question were—in the leaders' eyes—not from the area.

Elmton is one of Baltimore's most populous neighborhoods. It is a predominantly white, blue-collar community. Housing is mostly two-story brick row houses of small-to-moderate size. Some feel the neighborhood has a "tough" quality. Here too the leader recounted organization efforts focused on controlling industrial land uses. Subsequent coverage in a *Baltimore Sun* series on the industrial land-use problem she was fighting confirmed her concerns (for examples of problems similar but not necessarily identical to the ones addressed by the leader, see 6, 14, 21). She also recounted efforts to monitor a nearby medical waste facility at Hawkins Point, where she documented and complained about waste from out of state.

The leader reported no organized crime prevention activities, describing how hard it was to get residents out to meetings: "No one is interested, television is a priority here." In addition to residents' viewing habits, local attitudes toward the police also may play a role. Although police attend local organization meetings and provide crime updates, the leader expressed frustration at the police department's ineffectiveness in addressing local problems such as drugs and prostitution. She summed up residents' perspective by observing, "Citizens won't get involved with the police because you can't get police involved anyhow." In short, a perceived symmetric lack of interest exists.

How active *are* police in the area? When we were touring the neighborhood in early 1995, we witnessed a row house being converted to a police mini-station. The worker there reported another mini-station also under construction at the same time. During a December 1997 conversation with district police personnel, it appeared that the police department and the neighborhood had different views about how extensively these mini-stations should be staffed, with the neighborhood looking for a more round-the-clock presence than the police felt equipped to resource.

Is crime in Elmton serious enough to warrant a high police profile? Our leader interview occurred soon after a grisly murder, allegedly carried out by a resident from public housing nearby. But in this neighborhood, robbery, relative to other city neighborhoods, has historically been low and stayed low, in the tenth percentile or lower. Its burglary rate placed it in the sixty-seventh percentile in 1970, and although it had dropped by 1980, by 1990 it was back to the 1970 level.

The main social incivility of concern to the organization was prostitution, which the leader reported was a problem in the area. (Not too far west of Elmton, along a major artery, early one spring afternoon in 1995 we spotted both an African-American and a white hooker, literally working different sides of the street.) In response, the leader reported, groups of about thirty residents would get together in the summer months and walk the streets where the activity was heaviest to "move the trade along." Although the activity is not sponsored by the local improvement association, some of the leaders often take part.

To sum up: In these three predominantly white, low- to moderate-status, moderate-stability neighborhoods there are several common features of the collective responses. In each locale, there is a focus on specific social incivilities: teens gathering and allegedly dealing in one location, unruly tavern goers in another, and prostitution in a third. Incivility reduction efforts generally seemed geographically focused and targeted to the specific issues. Collective crime prevention efforts followed victimization prevention strategies; in one locale the effort appeared viable, whereas in the other two it had faltered. In one locale where the effort had "fizzled," comments suggested residents viewed the police as unhelpful. In the second location where collective initiatives had waned, land use features fragmenting the neighborhood may have played a role.

So far, our examples have focused on the impacts of racial composition and economic status. Is stability unimportant? One example from predominantly white **Mantua** underscores the importance of stability, as reflected in the prevalence of married couple households and young children. Mantua, in the northeast section of the city, is an enclave of detached housing east of a major artery, bordering a large nonresidential land use along one side. The houses are relatively high priced, in the eighty-seventh price percentile in 1990, and well maintained. Crime is low, with robbery and burglary percentiles both below 10. Many of the residents there attend the same local parish. Neighborhood ties are strong, which is not surprising given the racial and religious homogeneity. Toys, trikes, and scooters litter front yards. A story related by the leader interviewed here demonstrates how this strong family orientation influenced reactions to a drug problem. A resident's teen began selling drugs out of the house. People brought this to the attention of the organization, the parents were contacted, and the problem was resolved quietly. Again, this fits Podolefsky's model, with the high degree of familism, as evidenced by many households with children, suggesting a long-term, youth-oriented, rather than a punitive response.

The contrasts seen so far suggest the following pattern. The predominantly white and moderately high to upper income locations favored collective crime prevention approaches focused almost exclusively on victimization prevention strategies for crime, drugs, and related problems. In low- and moderate-income, predominantly white locales, strategies mix victimization prevention with social problem reduction, but still favor the former. Features of the locale, such as large nonresidential land uses "splitting up" a neighborhood or antipathy toward police, probably dampened collective activity in different sites. But in general, the split between "pure" victimization prevention approaches and those largely favoring victimization prevention is along race and economic lines, as Podolefsky would have predicted. In the predominantly white, upper-middle- to high-status locations, whether they be stable or unstable, the crime problem is viewed as an imported one, also as Podolefsky predicted. Leaders tend to see the problems linked to drug selling, using, and the associated criminal activities as crime problems, rather than problems linked to addiction. When asked in open-ended questions to characterize the major issues coming to the attention of their neighborhoods, when dealing and using are mentioned the leaders describe these as *crime* rather than *drug* problems. We will see a different description when we get to predominantly African-American neighborhoods.

In sum, we do see the "pure" victimization prevention approach in the type of neighborhoods expected—predominantly white and middle to upper-middle class. People in these neighborhoods viewed crime as mostly outside their locale and did not identify a separate drug problem. As we shifted to white low-to-moderate-income and moderate-income locations, victimization prevention approaches still predominated, but we saw some social problem reduction activity. Most leaders, although there were some exceptions (e.g., Jackson), did not view the crime problems as linked to a lack of employment, educational, or recreational opportunities. Stability appears less relevant than race and economic status, although in one highly family oriented and homogeneous neighborhood we did hear of a social problem approach to one drug-dealing incident.

Approaches to incivilities and definitions of problematic incivilities varied as well, but the variation appeared less straightforwardly linked to ecological structure than did definitions of and responses to the crime problems. Rather, views of and responses to incivilities depended on the extent of the serious crime problem and highly specific local features. If serious crime was high, leaders devoted their attention to that, sometimes bypassing consideration of serious incivilities that coexisted with the high crime rates, such as abandoned housing. Attention to more minor incivilities, either social or physical, seemed more likely if the crime problem was lower. But the specificity of leaders' views about and responses to incivilities underscores the suggestion in Chapter 3 that incivilities may *not* be the various manifestations of a common underlying quality, such as disorder, social disorganization, lack of collective efficacy, or lack of public control. Instead they are distinct issues the appearance of which and the amount of concern inspired both depend on specific local features and the specific agendas of local leaders.

Granted, it appears that some locales are overwhelmed by all variety of minor and major physical and social incivilities (see, e.g., 35). In such neighborhoods, dealers hawk drugs from the steps of shuttered stores on several corners, abandoned houses seem to mar almost every block with their fire-blackened eyebrows above busted-out second-story windows, and groups of people seem to be fighting and arguing or talking loudly in front of every other house. But such a profile of incivilities, often found in extremely disadvantaged neighborhoods, is as atypical and misleading as the opposite incivility profile: well-tended yards and well-maintained houses at every address, little foot traffic at any time of night or day, few people socializing loudly outside, and nary an abandoned let alone old model car to be seen. Such extreme cases give the impression that incivilities are an "all or nothing" phenomenon, driven by some single, darker dynamic. But the extreme cases are rare, in the same way that extremely high or extremely low income neighborhoods are rare. Far more typical are locales that have one or more specific problems—late night teens on corners, as in the Fourth District in Philadelphia; prostitution; or abandoned housing. To focus on the extreme "all or nothing" incivility sites is to miss the different dynamics playing out across a much larger number of neighborhoods, dynamics that depend on local geography, local culture, neighborhood fabric, and the hopes of local organizations and local leaders.

Almost Exclusively Social Problem Reduction

I turn now to predominantly African-American neighborhoods that also are lower-income locations. Podolefsky predicted that collective efforts oriented toward social problem reduction will predominate in these locations. And they do. But accompanying and perhaps justifying this strategy, I also find a particular view on the drug problem. I see more of a distinction drawn between the drug dealers and the drug users in these locations. As in the white lower- to moderate-income neighborhoods, leaders in many of these neighborhoods express strong concerns about personal safety from the dealers. (When we get to neighborhoods with mixed approaches, we will discuss one neighborhood where the leader enlisted local dealers.) But for several leaders, preventing drug use or rehabilitating drug users was a highly personal issue. In several instances, this resulted in a focus on long-term prevention initiatives.

The drug problem was seen as *more* than a crime problem by several leaders. Leaders in **Davis** and **Avon Neighbors** related efforts to rehabilitate addicted family members, with the support of close neighbors and relatives. Both of these neighborhoods are predominantly African-American, with relatively low priced housing and moderate to high relative crime rates. Davis was less stable than Avon, being about three fourths rather than one half rental.

In a third neighborhood, **Osage,** a small neighborhood of neat row houses along a main artery on the westside of town, sociodemographically similar to Avon Neighbors, the leader interviewed also reported a personal rehabilitation approach to drug problems. Members of the community association paid $1.50 per month in dues, and the funds helped pay drug rehabilitation costs for addicts in the neighborhood. The leader "uses the organization as support rather than hide the problem." "Drug addicts" are invited to community association meetings, and the organization works to get them into rehabilitation so they "don't need to thieve." "We need to give them something to instill a sense of self-value." In all three of these neighborhoods, helping those affected by drugs was a personal matter.

Concerns about rehabilitating addicts probably helped fuel efforts against dealing. The Osage leader reported crusading until a vacant house and potential drug-selling or crack den site was boarded up. The Avon leader reported keeping a close eye on dealers in the locale; ones he knew he would approach and ask to stop selling. He also would call the federal Drug Enforcement Administration (DEA), apparently thinking the local police untrustworthy, if the dealing activity nearby got too intense.

Given Podolefsky's model, and previous work, views toward local police in these locations were not expected to be warm. The leaders' comments revealed views ranging from cautiously approving to decidedly negative. On the relatively positive end of the spectrum, in Davis our interview took place soon after a major police department drug sweep and cleanup had taken place in the area. (For more context on these major sweeps, see Chapter 2.) The leader and the interviewer, Mary Hyde, who had previously lived nearby for a time, both noted lower than usual levels of street-dealing activity. But the leader stressed it would make matters better just for a time, and the operation would probably need to be repeated.

Illustrating more negative views toward police, the leader in Avon reported calling high-level officials when he noticed that local officers were spending too much time at the 7-11 convenience store buying coffee rather than patrolling. He also related a story of calling the police to inspect evidence of a break-in, police arriving and labeling it vandalism, and people going into the house to find it had been emptied. These negative views of the police, in combination with the high level of local perceived threat, help explain residents' reluctance to support standard community crime prevention programs requiring cooperation with the police, such as COP or Neighborhood Watch.

Even though Neighborhood Watch required some police cooperation, leaders in several African-American neighborhoods touted its anonymous reporting as the big selling point. But police action can sometimes cancel out that advantage. One leader told of an incident where a person had called in using a Neighborhood Watch number, but the police had come to the reporting house anyway. Needless to say, such action effectively erased much of the support for the program in that neighborhood.

The extremely high levels of perceived threat in these neighborhoods, coupled with views of the police as ineffective at best and dangerously incompetent at worst, effectively precludes widespread participation in collective crime prevention surveillance strategies oriented toward victimization prevention. The leader interviewed in Richard Heights admitted that local efforts to get COP up and running had failed because everyone was too afraid to get involved. The leader in Sutton-Kent reported residents were reluctant to serve on local community boards, largely because of their concerns about being targeted by local dealers.

In one neighborhood, **Morgan,** we found a personal approach to reducing drug involvement, focusing largely on youth initiatives. A small neighborhood on the eastside of town, Morgan's streets are generally neat and the row houses well kept. Morgan's leader had recently moved back to the neighborhood and taken over the reins of the local improvement association, having spent time there as a child when his grandparents lived there. He fondly recalled the ambience of the neighborhood when he was a small boy, and he contrasted it with current conditions. He reported at the time of our interview that dealing was serious and widespread and also took place in shops.

The leader's main strategy for keeping teens off the street was to sponsor basketball leagues, being an avid player himself. Other youth initiatives reported by Morgan's leader included efforts to establish a scholarship program for local youth and a resurgence of the Clean Block contest. Sponsored by the local African-American newspaper, streetblocks sign up for the contest, get official colors, and spruce up their streetblock for an annual judging (40: chap. 8). The virtue of this environmental improvement effort, in the leader's view, was that it got youth involved in constructive activities. He recounted that twenty-five local youth had recently signed up to participate in the effort.

The leader cited flaws with some standard approaches for community crime prevention. He did not think programs telling residents how to protect themselves were needed, since so many of the residents were heavily armed. He expressed strong skepticism about bringing in motivational speakers to encourage teens to stay off drugs. He suggested outside speakers were pointless; either they cannot relate to neighborhood youth, or, if they are former felons, local youth think they were stupid to get caught. Outsiders in his view just mouthed a lot of "insincere bull . . . "

Winteroak, a predominantly African-American community on the westside of town, of about the same economic level as Morgan, had a leader who responded to us in writing. Again, we saw an emphasis on youth activity. Their "history" flyer, for example, indicated that a "modern, well-equipped playground was built at the instigation of the organization for the place of the neighborhood youth."

In sum, in this group of locales social problem reduction approaches predominate, as Podolefsky's model predicts based on the racial and class fabric in these settings. Concerns center on youth socialization and addict rehabilitation. Generally negative views of the police, coupled with personal relationships with some users and dealers, effectively preclude victimization prevention strategies relying on police-community cooperation and surveillance. The leaders' comments revealed a personal approach to the drug issue. The problem confronting these communities was not so much that drug sales and use were crimes, but rather that these were destroying the lives of neighbors, relatives, and friends. The leaders' goals were to impede that destruction or repair damage that had already occurred. Concerns about incivilities did not even surface as serious topics in the interviews, except as conditions that would facilitate drug use or sales. An abandoned house in Jackson was a problem because leaders and residents wanted to keep house prices up. In Osage, an abandoned house was a problem because drug activities might start up there and pull in and harm people the leader knew. Serious drug problems, their antecedents, and their ensuing wreckage consumed much of leaders' attention in this last group of neighborhoods.

Predominantly Social Problem Reduction, Some Victimization Prevention

In predominantly African-American communities of lower-middle, moderate, and upper-middle economic status, Podolefsky's model predicts a mix of short-term VP approaches and longer-range SPR initiatives. The strategies reported in these locations generally fit that expectation. I generally find, with one exception, a mix of long-term prevention and immediate crime control efforts, with the former dominating. These neighborhoods, generally economically better off than the group just described, include **Smithton II, Wilbur, Elmwood, Lloyd, Northwest Golfview,** and others.

Perhaps the most interesting approach surfaced in Elmwood. Elmwood is a moderate-crime, moderate-status, moderately stable predominantly African-American neighborhood. Housing consists mostly of small to moderate-sized row houses, although there is a section of apartments in one portion. At a nearby elementary school at midday, we found well-dressed mothers, fathers, and grandparents either walking children home or collecting them in new Pontiacs or Ford Explorers. Backed by nonresidential land use, the neighborhood is somewhat more physically isolated than adjoining neighborhoods. The leader used its relative inaccessibility and his local contacts to create a defended neighborhood (38). In a defended neighborhood, local youth play roles in keeping outsiders out of the neighborhood, monitoring them when they enter and generally keeping an eye on things.

Elmwood's leader reported several activities that would fit with a SPR approach. He fought a range of development issues. He defeated a planned siting for a juvenile home. He enticed a developer into building low- and moderate-income units on a large parcel, giving residents first choice at the sites. He also worked on maintenance at a playground and kept up with those helping to sponsor related youth activities there. All of these efforts were geared to providing a neighborhood that would be stable for a long period and that would be supportive of child-rearing efforts. A crime control effort, described below, also sought to make the neighborhood safe for its children.

About four years prior to our interview, the leader developed a "neighborhood-wide agreement about intruders" employing local "thugs" (his word) to monitor intruders. The immediate stimulus was the mugging of a local retarded girl. Probably contributing as well was (in the eyes of the leader) less-than-adequate police services. Under this agreement, all residents would ask intruders their business. The leader went door-to-door soliciting support for the initiative, and issues were aired at community meetings. The leader's comments suggested that local teens and young adult males involved in drug crews contributed substantially to this monitoring. During the 1994 gubernatorial campaign, Glendening's workers were repeatedly stopped by locals. During Steve Pardue's trips into the area, he was stopped twice; in one instance he was questioned at length about his activities and asked to provide a business card and phone numbers.

The leader used his "home thugs" to find who had mugged the retarded girl and turned that name in to the police. He protects these locals who may be involved in dealing from the police, but at the same time asks that they refrain from dealing in the neighborhood itself. "We tell the home thugs that Elmwood is their home, and that they're always safe here. We don't ever turn in thugs. The police don't even ask any more. They know it's hopeless." But if the thugs do deal in the neighborhood, the leader will not protect them. "For example, if they're caught in a drug raid here, they'll be taken in like anyone else." He also used the "thug grapevine" to recover a stolen vehicle.

Collaborating with gangs to provide informal neighborhood control is an inherently risky business. Nonetheless, some criminologists have advocated using gangs to help protect neighborhoods (5). Our information does not permit us to learn whether the arrangement in Elmwood resulted in less neighborhood crime. It is clear, however, that the leader feels the neighborhood is better protected with these people assisting. Recent ethnographies in other cities also point out that gangs can help keep the neighborhood peace (e.g., 43).

In a Chicago neighborhood, Pattillo describes a similar situation in a middle-class, African-American neighborhood (28). She argues that these neighborhoods are likely to be home to some drug dealers, in part because they are close to poorer African-American neighborhoods where drug market activity takes place. The relative stability of such a middle-class, African-American community means that dense local ties are likely to develop. Such local networks mix up those pursuing solely legitimate activities with those pursuing illegitimate activities. It is interesting how the Elmwood leader attempted to separate that intertwining of illegitimate and legitimate, essentially warning those involved in dealing that it would not be tolerated in the neighborhood.

Also along the lines of a VP approach, Block Watch membership was widespread in Elmwood. The leader reported that people had cut their hedges and put up floodlights to reduce crime. In sum, Elmwood presents a complex mix of both VP-oriented and SPR-oriented initiatives.

Lloyd, not as predominantly African-American as Elmwood, is similar in many ways to Elmwood. Housing is priced similarly, stability is relatively high, there is an elementary school nearby, and at the end of the school day the scene outside school with parents and grandparents picking up their kids looks similar. Again, in Lloyd as in Elmwood, we saw from our leader interviews a blended approach. On the SPR side, the leader reported several environmental initiatives, including a semi-annual dumpster cleanup and alley cleanups, the latter because lots of kids play in the alleys. For the cleanup, the organization arranges with the city for a large dumpster to be on-site for a weekend so households and yards can be cleared out. The organization also worked to get a halfway house for retarded people moved out of the neighborhood. They complained to the state since they felt it was housing too many residents, and after two months of work they got the license revoked and the facility closed.

Beyond the alley cleanups for children playing, concerns for youth surfaced in other ways as well. The organization helped straighten out after-school care problems. The organization interceded in an effort to get an improperly run day care center thrown out. The leader also reported heavy involvement in a school mentoring program for fourth and fifth graders and holding a car wash twice a year to help underwrite the program.

At the same time, the leader reported standard VP activities such as Block Watch and Town Watch Night Out. The Block Watch was started by the local umbrella group, but for both that and the "night out" activity he reported widespread participation. No specific numbers were provided.

In Lloyd, it appears the SPR approaches receive most attention, although overall a mix of the two types of approaches is clearly present. Given the high stability, school presence, moderate or better income level, and high youth population, this tilt is not surprising. Youth issues were salient in this neighborhood.

How do the two leaders in Elmwood and Lloyd frame incivility issues? Physical incivilities per se failed to emerge as a dominant issue in either interview. The only specific mention was the household and alley cleanup support in Lloyd. Physical incivilities probably generated little concern because both neighborhoods boasted large numbers of homeowners. Homeownership was 74% in Lloyd in 1990 and 51% in Elmwood. Organization spurs to maintenance were probably not widely required. Social incivilities were a dominant concern in Elmwood if we define "intruders" as a social incivility. It was interesting that the intruder alert originated in a concern to protect neighborhood children. The problem of intruders and the problem of child safety were joined, fused in the minds of residents and leaders alike by the attack on the retarded girl. With his helpers, the leader there was able to mount and sustain challenges to all intruders. It also proved revealing that the leader was able to expand the "duties" of the local protectors to help solve other types of crimes as well, such as car theft. The solution to a specific social incivility proved more generally useful. Also noteworthy was that for this social incivility reduction approach to work, the leader had to completely rebuff contacts with the police. In Elmwood, as seen earlier in predominantly white neighborhoods, the incivilities of interest proved highly specific and grounded in local context, history, and goals. In Lloyd, social incivilities failed to crop up in the interviews.

Where Is the Confrontation?

As mentioned earlier, much of the new literature on collective crime prevention focuses on confrontational tactics used against drug dealers. From the interviews, evidence appeared of community leaders and organizations, often working with the police, trying to oust dealers. The neighborhoods where this occurred were often white or predominantly white lower-middle to middle-income locations near African-American or racially changing neighborhoods. Maplecroft and Weldon Pond, in the very southern edge of the city, both reported substantial efforts, in collaboration with the police and the local organization, to remove active dealers. A southwest neighborhood reported similar activities, but would not inform us of details, because of fear of retaliation. Although these actions were adversarial, they were not confrontational. From the interviews, especially the Maplecroft one, it appears that leaders generally took numerous steps to avoid identification or confrontation, opting rather to collect information surreptitiously and pass it along to police or other agencies. The leaders' concerns about threats appeared well-founded. One threatened resident was already mentioned; other leaders not discussed so far also mentioned threats. In predominantly African-American neighborhoods, confrontation was not reported. Again, recall from Pattillo's work in Chicago, that in moderate-income African-American communities strong local friend and family ties intertwine those pursuing illegitimate activities with those pursuing legitimate ones. Such connections make confrontations unworkable. Instead, leaders either focused on working with the dealers to buttress community safety, as in Elmwood, or worked one-on-one to turn around those whose lives were adversely affected by drugs.

Neighborhood Fabric and Responses to Crime and Drug Sales and Use

Podolefsky's Model Appears Applicable

The results presented here, in general terms, confirm that the connections observed by Podolefsky still apply, despite the dramatically different crime problems confronting many urban community leaders in the 1990s as compared to twenty years earlier. In high-status and predominantly white neighborhoods, leaders view drug and crime problems as coming from outside, unrelated to other local social problems, and adopt victimization prevention approaches. As we move toward middle- to lower-income predominantly white neighborhoods, victimization approaches are still favored, but communities also mix in social problem reduction initiatives such as youth-oriented activities. Low-income predominantly African-American communities report little interest in victimization prevention approaches such as citizen patrolling, but strong concerns about youth initiatives and drug rehabilitation. Drugs are not viewed as crime problems but as personal problems. In middle-income predominantly African-American communities, more enthusiasm surfaces for victimization prevention, although social problem reduction approaches still predominate. All of these connections are in accord with Podolefsky's original theory. In short, although the level and type of crime problem has shifted, connections arise between community fabric, crime views, and between-community differences in collective responses that have been largely unaffected by the crack invasion. Crack has changed a lot, but it has not changed everything.

Are There Current Issues Podolefsky's Model Fails to Address?

Although the connections observed are generally what the model has predicted, there are three issues where one might argue the model is not up to date: the broader application of environmental improvement strategies, the failure of the model to address collective confrontations, and drug rehabilitation. I consider each of these issues in turn.

Environmental improvements, such as housing rehabilitation, evicting nuisance tenants, or cleanup and beautification activities, are omnipresent and no longer appear to be exclusively associated with social problem reduction strategies. There are several reasons behind this increase. The prevalence of deterioration has increased, making it so much more widespread than previously (8, 9, 10). Grime reduction is also more closely linked in leaders' and residents' eyes with crime reduction. Many are more convinced than they were previously that attacking grime is "doing something about crime." Finally, abandoned housing creates locations where drug use and drug sales can occur. In many neighborhoods, taking care of abandoned housing dramatically reduces opportunities for these activities. Of course, this does not mean, as some leaders think, that neighborhoods without any vacant housing will be free of all drug activity.

It may help to distinguish between two types of environmental improvements: those geared toward creating long-term infrastructure in a neighborhood, such as rehabbing housing for low-income families, and environmental improvements geared toward reducing crime, such as closing down crack houses. The first type of effort represents a long-term strategy to maintain neighborhood viability; the second type of effort is focused on short-term crime control.

In short, the crack invasion and widespread drug activity has given rise to a new set of environmental strategies focused more on immediate crime reduction than the environmental strategies seen previously. Consequently, one modification we might make to the model is to separate environmental improvements into these two types, short versus long term, aligning each with the appropriate broader strategy, respectively CP versus SPR initiatives.

The above point can be expanded given the concern in this chapter with how leaders think about and respond to incivilities. The type of incivility identified, what its presumed impacts would be, whether it was targeted for action, and if so what type, all turned out to be matters highly dependent not only on neighborhood makeup but also on local history, geography, culture, and leaders' goals. Leaders acted on specific incivilities that drew attention for very particular reasons. In a partially gentrified neighborhood heavily populated with professionals who bought houses after the initial price surge, general cleanup via funded sanitation patrols were of interest. This would keep up the neighborhood image and house prices as well. In another partially gentrified locale near severely distressed neighborhoods, the leader hoped to keep abandoned houses in good enough shape for resale, thereby supporting the house prices there. Needs for minor cleanup were probably stronger there than in the neighborhood with the sanitation patrols but did not merit attention, in part because surrounding neighborhoods were so much worse off and the more major incivilities presented graver long-term threats to viability of the local housing market. In yet another neighborhood with extensive abandoned housing, the leader was conscious of biting off more than she could chew, and recognizing the volume of it, seemed to think not much of a dent could be put in the problem. In short, neighborhoods did not confront physical incivilities; rather they faced specific social and physical problems grounded in a specific context. Figuring out of which problems to address and which to overlook was part of a complex "dance." Leaders wanted to address serious issues influencing neighborhood life, but also wanted to be able to show progress achieved on a front once it was targeted for action. In making these decisions, they were acting strategically, in accord with specific goals; but they also were responding to local interpretations of what specific incivilities "meant." These meanings arose from the neighborhood's local history, culture, and geography.

The second issue deserving consideration in the context of Podolefsky's model is confrontation with dealers. Much has been made of this "new" strategy (44, 45). It has received extensive press attention as newspapers chronicle local leaders, such as the late Reverend Wrice of Mantua Against Drugs, in Philadelphia, bursting into crack houses (1).

But on closer examination, this confrontation may not be so new. It really represents three sets of activities: active surveillance of drug sellers and buyers, often letting them know they are being watched; direct attempts to push sellers and users out of certain public locations by occupying those sites at prime business hours, a strategy used in the past with prostitution; and attacking crack dens. In interviews, the first type of activity appears to be far more prevalent than the latter two. The frequency of antidrug marches and occupations and crack den invasions may be overestimated because of their attention-getting properties, compared to less media-worthy actions.

In the confrontation through active surveillance, residents let dealers know they are being watched. For example, one leader interviewed reported that she would call neighbors on the block when she saw dealing, trying to get everyone out on their porch, and would shout at dealers to let them know they were being watched. The dealers did retaliate against her, she reported, digging up her garden. This was the *only* case of *active and confrontational* surveillance appearing in our interviews.

More often, as mentioned earlier, organizers sought nonconfrontational surveillance. Residents felt threatened and reported that dealers did threaten them. Residents or leaders might clandestinely survey local drug activity and call in activities to local police or DEA or the narcotics squad, but at the same time try not to involve themselves. Especially in the African-American neighborhoods, the strongest selling point of

Neighborhood Watch was that you could use your special number and not have police show up at the reporting household, leaving neighbors guessing about who did the reporting.

A couple of leaders reported approaching sellers asking them why they did what they did, but only if they knew the sellers personally. These were efforts at personal dialogue, not collective confrontation.

When the threat of confrontation escalated, as it did in West Pine Community Council, local members responded by "going underground" and making their surveillance even more clandestine. Teaberry also reported clandestine surveillance programs.

One leader recognized an irony accompanying the latter approach. One intended effect of the surveillance programs is to make residents feel safer and increase, à la Jane Jacobs, the eyes on the street. But the clandestine mode of operation, required because of the potential danger to watchers, had none of these beneficial externalities, because it was covert.

In short, it appears that locals avoid collective confrontation rather than seek it, directly and personally approaching only those they know and carrying out collective surveillance in a way that minimizes potential harm to themselves. Case studies and media coverage spotlighting community-dealer confrontations (45) are problematic because they provide a distorted view of broader surveillance efforts, suggesting the clashes occur far more frequently than they probably do. In addition, recent ethnographies explaining how dealers not only support neighborhood functioning but are also closely intertwined with legitimate residents through dense local social networks clarify why such confrontations probably are so rare (28, 35, 43).

To sum up this point, collective confrontation with drug dealers and users, garnering extensive media attention, clearly represents a "new" form of collective crime prevention, and one that has not been included in Podolefsky's model. Among our neighborhoods however, despite serious crack problems in several of them, such confrontations rarely occurred. The coping tactic employed far more frequently by leaders, and included in Podolefsky's model, was surveillance in various forms. At this time, we have no way of knowing the relative frequency of collective confrontations, nor their relative importance to local crime prevention leaders. Until we have such information, it may be premature to conclude that the failure of Podolefsky's model to include collective confrontations represents a serious flaw, especially when we have clear-cut evidence explaining how social and structural factors inhibit such confrontations in the most drug-plagued neighborhoods.

Finally, the reports we have heard speak to the emerging importance of drug rehabilitation in those neighborhoods with numerous addicts. We heard from more than one leader of personal efforts to rehabilitate drug-addicted neighbors, friends, or relatives. At least two leaders also reported systematic efforts, through the local improvement association, to provide or support programmatic rehabilitation assistance. How do we incorporate these collectively sponsored drug rehabilitation efforts into Podolefsky's model?

Podolefsky's model did include education and counseling efforts, including alcohol abuse counseling, as part of a social problem reduction approach. Getting off drugs can be seen as a prerequisite to participating in these efforts. Getting into scarce drug rehab slots, however, can be a lengthy process (e.g., 35: 241–242). In addition, these programs are likely to be administered by a state or city agency, in contrast to education programs, such as after-school tutoring, or employment counseling, where the local organization can enlist nearby resources. In short, although local leaders in some neighborhoods recognize the importance of drug rehabilitation and in some cases attempt to support those efforts, the program is far less "local" than the other education or counseling efforts. These are not programs that local organizations can shape, even though they can support them. In this way, they are different from other collective efforts.

Closing Comments

Neighborhood leaders provided us with information about their activities against crime, drugs, decay, and related problems. This information helped illuminate connections between different types of collective initiatives, views about the crime problem, and neighborhood demographic structure. In large part these connections replicated those observed by Podolefsky in the late 1970s in three other cities. Although Baltimore's crack invasion, arriving in the mid to late 1980s, has changed the crime problems confronting many communities and has fundamentally altered the fabric of those communities, local leaders still rely heavily on techniques similar to those described in the previous work. Further, between-neighborhood differences in types of strategies pursued link in the same way to views about crime and community fabric. Apparently, although the arrival of large-scale drug trade changed many things in urban neighborhoods, it has not changed everything.

For incivilities, the present interviews suggest that leaders really do not think about them as incivilities per se. Rather, they view them as highly local and separable issues that may or may not demand attention depending on a broad range of local factors and leader-identified strategic priorities. Some neighborhoods overwhelmed with a particular type of incivility pay it no mind, either because it is too extensive or too intransigent or they are focusing attention elsewhere, usually on a serious crime problem. Although the types of incivilities present depended somewhat on neighborhood makeup, it appeared that leaders' responses depended on a broader set of issues and were less sociodemographically linked than the choice of responses to crime problems. Leaders' selective attention toward incivilities, contextualized interpretations, and widely varying responses to incivilities support the data pattern seen in Chapter 3. That pattern intimated incivilities are just a wide range of issues, loosely related at best, tightly linked at only the highest and lowest ends of the status continuum. The measurement information suggested incivilities are not clustered symptoms of a broader, underlying neighborhood deficit; interviews in this chapter showed leaders do not respond to them as such.

Finally, the results seen here, confirming the wide array of initiatives pursued, proves comforting in one respect. Local leaders have not flocked to collective strategies focused solely on incivilities reduction, abandoning other approaches in the process. They continue to pursue an exceedingly broad range of approaches and strategies to preventing crime, as they have in the past. Incivilities of one type or another are usually part of that mix, but concern about these social and physical features of neighborhood life do not necessarily dominate leaders' agendas.

Appendix

Sample Selection Procedures and Contact Attempts

Sampling Neighborhoods

Our overall goal was to add to the already sampled 30 neighborhoods about 40 additional neighborhoods, stratified both on population size and on whether blocks had been added or taken away, or boundaries had remained the same, when the city's Department of Planning remapped the neighborhoods in 1990. (The reason for our interest in neighborhood boundaries is discussed in the next chapter.) We used the following procedure to accomplish this goal.

1. A comprehensive list of areal changes, for the period 1979 to 1990, was developed for all neighborhoods in the city of Baltimore. A list was created by comparing the City of Baltimore Planning Department map from 1990 with the map generated in 1979. The list contained the names of the neighborhoods; whether changes in area occurred in the neighborhoods; and if change occurred, whether the neighborhood got larger or smaller. The list also noted whether changes were primarily residential or nonresidential and gave a brief description of the changes. The descriptions were usually confined to noting how many residential blocks were included, or, in the case of nonresidential areas, what kind of land uses (e.g., institutional, industrial, park) were included, if this could be determined using only maps.

2. All city neighborhoods were sorted on 1980 population.

3. Each neighborhood was assigned "+" (blocks added), "−"(blocks taken away), or "n"(no blocks added or taken away), to indicate whether it had grown, become smaller, or not changed in the period 1979–1990.

4. Because we thought neighborhood size might be related in important ways to issues of neighborhood redefinition and therefore wanted to stratify on neighborhood population, we segmented the population-ordered list of neighborhoods into groups of 12 neighborhoods each, thus creating segments with neighborhoods of roughly equal population within them. Population size ranged from 3 residents in "Unorganized Public Housing 3" to 16,559 residents in Belair-Edison.

5. In each of the list segments, we sampled three neighborhoods. Our goal was to randomly sample one neighborhood with increasing size, one with decreasing size, and one with no change. Neighborhoods within each change status were sequentially numbered and then selected using a random number sequence.

In each segment, if one of our originally sampled 30 study neighborhoods appeared, it was automatically sampled, regardless of the change status ("+," "–," or "n"). If one of the 30 neighborhoods was included in the segment, no other neighborhoods were randomly sampled with the same change status (but for an exception, see below).

If the segment contained no neighborhoods within a specific status group, e.g., no "–" neighborhood in a group of 12, a neighborhood from another status group (e.g., "+") was substituted. Initially, the status group selected for the substitution was randomly chosen. But as we proceeded through the segments, we kept a running tally of substitutions by status group and counterbalanced as needed in the immediately following segments. For example, if in a given segment of 12 neighborhoods there was no neighborhood that lost area between 1979 and 1990, one that had gained area in that period might be selected in place of the missing "–" neighborhood. In the next segment of 12 neighborhoods, an extra "–" neighborhood would be taken, in addition to the usual "+," "–," and "n" selections in the group. If the deficit for a change group was more than one, which it often was for the "–" group—meaning that several sequential 12-neighborhood segments were lacking even one "–" neighborhood, and the deficit could not be made up by taking extras—as many neighborhoods as needed in the required change category would be taken as soon as possible in the sequential process. Because of this scheme, in a small number of cases three or more "+" or "–" neighborhoods were sometimes sampled from a single group of 12. In all cases, a random number selection process was used when there was more than one possible choice of neighborhoods. In addition to the original 30 neighborhoods in the primary study, 42 additional neighborhoods were chosen using the method outlined above.

Selecting, Contacting, and Interviewing Leaders

Since we were interested not only in current community crime prevention attempts, as described in this chapter, but also in the history behind recent changes in neighborhood names and boundaries, as described in the next chapter, we wanted to talk to leaders who had been in the neighborhood for a time, preferably at least seven years. Thus respondents were not necessarily current neighborhood leaders.

In a couple of instances, we relaxed our criterion on length of residence when we found leaders who had moved into the neighborhood recently but had lived in the neighborhood for a significant period of time previous to that. Often these leaders were able to provide insightful comments about how the neighborhood had changed since they had lived there last.

Using contacts in the Department of Planning and in other local community organizations, we developed a list of longtime leaders in each of the sampled locations. Letters were sent to the leaders, with follow-up phone calls. In cases where local community organization presidents referred us to other local leaders with a longer memory, we then attempted to contact the newly recommended leader.

We tried hard to contact these leaders or former leaders. In some cases, attempts to interview a leader went on for almost a year. The process of contacting leaders began in late 1994 and continued until early fall 1995. In most cases, between three and a dozen contact attempts, usually by phone, were required before we could complete the interview. In one case, a leader refused to complete the interview but offered to respond in writing to questions that we posed to her in writing. We accepted the offer.

We developed an interview protocol that included both closed- and open-ended questions. The protocol, if strictly followed, resulted in an interview lasting 45 to 90 minutes. Often, however, leaders diverged from the interview to tell us stories or amplify details. In a couple of instances, leaders refused to follow the interview at all, but rather insisted on telling us what they felt it was important that we know about their neighborhood. We listened.

The bulk of the interviews with the leaders of the original 30 neighborhoods were completed by Steve Pardue, with a few completed by Mary Hyde. The bulk of interviews from the additional set of leaders were completed by Mary Hyde. In addition, several students in a graduate seminar at the University of Maryland completed several interviews each. The student interviewers double-teamed, with one interviewer asking the questions and one interviewer observing.

All interviewers were encouraged to write up their open-ended notes about the interview, preferably within 24 hours of the interview itself. In most cases, they complied, generating a detailed set of field notes for each interview. In project meetings, we reviewed these field notes for the first several interviews, providing feedback and asking questions, hoping to help the interviewers write more detailed and concise narratives. In cases where two interviewers were present, they were instructed to each write up their notes separately, thus providing us with independent sources of information on the interview itself.

Notes

1. The theory suggests the two questions under consideration are independent but linked. Thus, if residents see the crime problem as coming from outside, they are more likely to see it as separate from rather than tied to other social ills. Given this expected linkage between the two different issues, it is not clear what collective responses would be adopted when the two views about crime did not converge as expected.

2. At the end of the 1970s, according to comments from Podolefsky (personal communication), the views of the researchers on the Reactions to Crime project were perhaps beginning to diverge from residents' and leaders' views. Whereas the latter were thinking about incivility removal as a stimulus to community

pride and a well-ordered street life, researchers were elaborating impacts of incivilities on fear and weakened local commitment.

3. The same views may operate in minority neighborhoods of different ethnicity, such as predominantly Hispanic neighborhoods, but the information here does not address that.

4. Details on the sampling for the additional neighborhoods and our contact procedures, appear in the chapter appendix. More discussion of the rationale for the sampling of the additional forty-two neighborhoods also appears in Chapter 8, as do details about our neighborhood mapping procedures.

5. Reallocated reported crime counts showed no murders in 1990 and 1992, and a half a murder allocated to the neighborhood in 1991. Oakwell is a neighborhood where the imprecision of our crime allocation creates problems, because it is relatively close to substantial and crime-prone commercial establishments.

6. The raw reported crime, reallocated to neighborhoods, shows about thirty-five to forty robberies per year in and around Oakwell. The robbery percentile scores show robbery being a steadily increasing problem in Oakwell, with percentile scores going from 23 to 55 to 63 over the past three decades.

7. Gentrified African-American neighborhoods exist in Baltimore as well, such as Madison Park. We just did not have any of them in our samples of neighborhoods.

8. Sherman Heights, despite its increased relative house values, did not represent a typical gentrifying neighborhood.

9. This was as of early spring 1995.

10. In one of these neighborhoods, however, a foot patrol focusing on reducing *social* incivilities was mounted in late 1997.

References

(1) Anonymous (1988) Anti-drug protest turns to demolition. *Philadelphia Inquirer* August 4, (Article ID: 8802180674; http://www.phillynews.com/newslibrary).

(2) Boccella, K. (1996) Police cracking down on street-corner gatherings. *Philadelphia Inquirer* May 5, B1, B3.

(3) Boland, B. (1997) The Manhattan experiment: Community prosecution. In *Crime and place: Plenary papers of the 1997 Conference on Criminal Justice Research and Evaluation*, pp. 51–68. National Institute of Justice, Washington, DC.

(4) Brower, S., Dockett, K., and Taylor, R. B. (1983) Resident's perceptions of site-level features. *Environment and Behavior* 15, 419–437.

(5) Bursik, R. J., Jr., and Grasmick, H. G. (1993) *Neighborhoods and crime: The dimensions of effective social control*, Lexington Books, New York.

(6) Cohn, G., and Englund, W. (1997) Milkuski criticizes Navy shipbreaking. *Baltimore Sun* December 12, 1A.

(7) Covington, J. C., and Taylor, R. B. (1989) Gentrification and crime: Robbery and larceny changes in appreciating Baltimore neighborhoods in the 1970's. *Urban Affairs Quarterly* 25, 142–172.

(8) Daemmrich, J. (1995) Baltimore again backs house sales: In third auction try, city will help buyers in six neighborhoods. *Baltimore Sun* April 15, 1A, 8A.

(9) Daemmrich, J. (1995) City sale of vacant homes ends "beautifully" for pair. *Baltimore Sun* March 12, B1, B2.

(10) Daemmrich, J., and West, N. (1994) Neighbors welcome city plan to demolish abandoned, tumbledown houses. *Baltimore Sun* October 9, B2.

(11) Davis, R. C., Lurigio, A. J., and Rosenbaum, D. P. (1993) Introduction. In *Drugs and the community: Involving community residents in combatting the sale of illegal drugs* (Davis, R. C., Lurigio, A. J., and Rosenbaum, D. P., eds), pp. xi—xviii. Charles C. Thomas, Springfield, IL.

(12) Donnelly, P. G., and Majka, T. J. (1998) Residents' efforts at neighborhood stabilization: Facing the challenges of inner-city neighborhoods. *Sociological Forum* 13, 189–214.

(13) DuBow, F., and Podolefsky, A. (1982) Citizen participation in community crime prevention. *Human Organization* 41, 307–314.

(14) Englund, W., and Cohn, G. (1997) Scrapping ships, sacrificing men. *Baltimore Sun* December 7, 1A.

(15) Fagan, J. (1993) The political economy of drug dealing among urban gangs. In *Drugs and the community: Involving community residents in combatting the sale of illegal drugs* (Davis, R. C., Lurigio, A. J., and Rosenbaum, D. P., eds), pp. 19–54. Charles C. Thomas, Springfield, IL.

(16) Glaser, B. G., and Strauss, A. L. (1967) *The discovery of grounded theory: Strategies for qualitative research*, Aldine, Chicago.

(17) Gottfredson, S. D., and Taylor, R. B. (1988) Community contexts and criminal offenders. In *Crime and community context* (Hope, T., and Shaw, M., eds), pp. 62–82. Her Majesty's Stationary Office, London.

(18) Green, L. (1996) *Policing places with drug problems*, Sage, Thousand Oaks, CA.

(19) Hagan, J., and Albonetti, C. (1982) Race, class and perception of criminal injustice in America. *American Journal of Sociology* 88, 329–355.

(20) Hillenbrand, S. W., and Davis, R. C. (1993) Residents' perception of drug activity, crime and neighborhood satisfaction. In *Drugs and the community: Involving community residents in combatting the sale of illegal drugs* (Davis, R. C., Lurigio, A. J., and Rosenbaum, D. P., eds), pp. 5–18. Charles C. Thomas, Springfield, IL.

(21) Klingaman, M. (1995) Coral Sea, One hard ship to dismantle. *Baltimore Sun* June 4, C1, C3.

(22) Lee, B. A., and Mergenhagen, P. M. (1984) Is revitalization detectable? Evidence from five Nashville neighborhoods. *Urban Affairs Quarterly* 19, 511–538.

(23) Logan, J. R., and Molotch, H. (1987) *Urban fortunes*, University of California Press, Berkeley.

(24) London, B., Lee, B. A., and Lipton, A. G. (1986) The determinants of gentrification in the United States: A city-level analysis. *Urban Affairs Quarterly* 21, 369–387.

(25) Nurco, D. N., Kinlock, T. W., O'Grady, K. E., and Hanlon, T. E. (1996) Progression of criminal activity prior to addiction for narcotic addicts and two

nonaddicted control groups. Paper presented at the annual meetings of the American Society of Criminology, Chicago, November.

(26) Office of Applied Statistics, Substance Abuse and Mental Health Statistics (SAMHSA), U.S. Department of Health and Human Services (1996) 1978–94 Historical estimates from DAWN (Advance Report Number 16, DHHS Publication No. (SMA) 96-3105, published 8/1996). Available on-line: http://www.samhsa.gov/oas/p0000018.htm#EDcomp, retrieved July 4, 2000.

(27) Olson, S. H. (1997) *Baltimore: The building of an American city,* Revised and expanded bicentennial ed., Johns Hopkins University Press, Baltimore.

(28) Pattillo, M. E. (1998) Sweet mothers and gangbangers: Managing crime in a black middle-class neighborhood. *Social Forces* 76, 747–774.

(29) Podolefsky, A. (1983) *Case studies in community crime prevention,* Charles C. Thomas, Springfield, IL.

(30) Podolefsky, A., and Dubow, F. (1981) *Strategies for community crime prevention: Collective responses to crime in urban America,* Charles C. Thomas, Springfield, IL.

(31) Reiss, A. J., and Roth, J., eds. (1993) *Understanding and preventing violence,* Vol. 1, National Academy Press, Washington, DC.

(32) Rengert, G. (1996) *The geography of illegal drugs,* Westview, Boulder.

(33) Rosenbaum, D. P. (1987) The theory and research behind neighborhood watch: Is it a sound fear and crime reduction strategy? *Crime & Delinquency* 33, 103–134.

(34) Silverman, R. A., and Kennedy, L. W. (1985) Age, perception of social diversity and fear of crime. *Environment and Behavior* 17.

(35) Simon, D., and Burns, E. (1997) *The corner: A year in the life of an inner-city neighborhood,* Broadway Books, New York.

(36) Skogan, W., and Lurigio, A. J. (1992) The correlates of community anti-drug activism. *Crime & Delinquency* 38, 510–521.

(37) Smith, D. A. (1986) The neighborhood context of police behavior. In *Crime and justice: A Review of research,* Vol. 8: *Communities and crime* (Reiss, A. J., Jr., and Tonry, M., eds), pp. 313–342. University of Chicago Press, Chicago.

(38) Suttles, G. D. (1972) *The social construction of communities,* University of Chicago Press, Chicago.

(39) Taylor, R. B. (1987) Toward an environmental psychology of disorder. In *Handbook of environmental psychology* (Stokols, D., and Altman, I., eds), pp. 951–986. Wiley, New York.

(40) Taylor, R. B. (1988) *Human territorial functioning,* Cambridge University Press, Cambridge, UK.

(41) Taylor, R. B., Brower, S., and Stough, R. (1976) User generated visual features as signs in the urban residential environment. In *The behavioral basis of design: Book 1* (Ward, L. M., et al., eds). Dowden, Hutchinson, and Ross, Stroudsburg, PA.

(42) Taylor, R. B., and Covington, J. (1993) Community structural change and fear of crime. *Social Problems* 40, 374–397.

(43) Venkatesh, S. (1997) The social organization of street gang activity in an urban ghetto. *American Journal of Sociology* 103, 82–111.

(44) Weingart, S. N. (1993) A typology of community responses to drugs. In *Drugs and the community: Involving community residents in combatting the sale of illegal drugs* (Davis, R. C., Lurigio, A. J., and Rosenbaum, D. P., eds), pp. 85–105. Charles C. Thomas, Springfield, IL.

(45) Weingart, S. N., Hartmann, F. X., and Osborne, D. (1994) *Case studies in community anti-drug efforts (National Institute of Justice Research in Brief)*, Government Printing Office, Washington, DC.

8

Place Power and Implications for Coproduced Safety: Changes and Stability in Neighborhood Names, Boundaries, and Organizations

Neighborhood status proved a powerful predictor in models examining both the origins and the outcomes of incivilities. Such connections testify to the wide-ranging impacts of stratification by place. Status produces benefits flowing steadily over time. This chapter attempts to dig deeper into this relationship. The particular focus is on changes versus stability in neighborhood names, boundaries, and organizations. Why do we have stable names or boundaries in some locations and not others? And how do shifts or the lack thereof relate to what neighborhood organizations try to accomplish? Earlier work in this area suggests that the processes of naming and bounding a neighborhood play important roles in crafting the community image and preserving neighborhood status. Comments from the leader interviews described in the last chapter provide insight into how naming and bounding link to status; race; organizational initiatives; and other more specific local concerns, including incivilities and safety. The dynamics described can fill in some of the specifics on why neighborhood status is so influential for the outcomes of interest in this volume.

In a related vein, a second purpose is to explore the *types* of changes taking place in neighborhood names and boundaries. I group the changes into eight types of changes; each type goes beyond just whether land area was added to or subtracted from a neighborhood and describes the dynamics surrounding these shifts. Both the comments from the leaders on their goals, in cases where the change was internally initiated, and the theoretical literature on place-based stratification and symbolic communities, provide insight into the functions served by these shifts. The different types of changes appear to reflect both concerns about symbolic communities and leaders' specific goals. The symbolic image of the community has implications for the neighborhood's exchange value, and leaders' specific goals relate to maximizing neighborhood use value for residents in particular arenas of neighborhood life.

There is a third purpose as well to the current chapter, when attention turns to public agencies rather than just community actors: What are the implications of these place-based dynamics for coproduced public safety? As long as there has been community policing, there has been the question, "Where is the community?" (18). This question means different things to different people, but one interpretation is, how do police identify stable community partners? The process of identifying stable partners is, I suggest, building on Klinger's work (32), a question of organizational frameworks. Do you try to make the police administrative unit match the service delivery organizations in the community? Or do you try to shoehorn the relevant community organizations into the appropriate police administrative unit, such as the beat? The way police work is administered spatially does not coincide with the spatial structure of the partners in coproduction, the community organizations. This mismatch and the ways in which it is addressed have significant implications for the success of community policing efforts. The dynamics described here have implications for building effective partnerships in community policing.

Curiously enough, this branch of the current investigation started with an unexpected finding. In 1979, Sidney Brower, Whit Drain, and I produced a map of Baltimore neighborhoods. The 1990 map of neighborhoods produced by the Department of Planning showed more changes than anticipated, and they seemed to be patterned in an interesting way. I describe below, briefly, the neighborhood mapping processes. I then detail the prior work in neighborhood naming and bounding. I follow that with a brief set of comments on organizations and community policing. I move next to describing the observed changes in mapping, reporting on several different types of neighborhood boundary changes and issues of name changes (see Table 8.2 later in the chapter). What seemed to be the factors behind these shifts? The implications of the results for sociological understandings of neighborhood dynamics and for community policing initiatives are then explored. With regard to the latter, one of the most central questions is, can police work be organized around the neighborhood unit? This query leads to a brief discussion of neighborhood governance.

One final introductory point: After a lot of struggle, the conclusion was reached *not* to use real neighborhood names in this chapter. Pseudonyms are supplied, as in the previous chapter, although sometimes they are different pseudonyms for the same neighborhoods. This conclusion was reached with considerable difficulty because it dramatically reduces the clarity of some patterns observed here and perhaps the utility of the work performed. But the promise to neighborhood leaders not to identify individual neighborhoods outweighed other concerns. Further, in some cases minor details are switched to preclude local experts from being able to identify particular locales.

Neighborhood Mapping and Current Data Sources

In 1979, Sidney Brower, Whit Drain, and I used input from local community organizations and, where needed, other local experts to map Baltimore's neighborhoods (58). We started with a listing of all city community associations and their boundaries. To ensure that neither the organizations nor their presumed extent were fictitious, we consulted extensively with district planners. At that time, Baltimore was divided into six planning districts, each with a planner and assistant planner. In most parts of the city, neighborhood organizations are served by larger organizations, either umbrella groups or community development corporations (CDCs). We consulted with them as well. In a small number of cases, we relied on either planners or umbrella personnel to allocate land to one organization if it was claimed by two competing organizations. If land was not claimed by any organization, it was left outside of a neighborhood. If that unclaimed land was residential, it was called an "unorganized" area, meaning not that it was disorganized, but rather that it was not yet organized or claimed. The unorganized areas (n=26) were small in extent and population (range = 3–6,734 in 1970 population; median 1970 population = 1,063). Unclaimed nonresidential land included campuses, parks, large institutions, cemeteries, large industrial land uses, and streams. We carried out a series of checks using our main informants, the district and assistant district planners. The planners agreed with each other on their categorizations of the status and stability of the locales using a sorting technique. And their data correlated well with census data. These checks suggest our main informants knew these locales relatively well. To our knowledge at that time, no one had yet attempted such a comprehensive mapping for the city.

It is possible to conduct such a neighborhood mapping and not deny "the embeddedness of local neighborhoods in larger vertical structures" (28: 283). People reside in nested groupings of residential structures, ranging from the streetblock to an entire area of the city (27, 55). In mapping these neighborhoods, the hope was to highlight one level of residential groupings. The mapping does not deny the existence or importance of other groupings at higher or lower levels or the ways in which those other levels might shape neighborhood features. Indeed, given the embedded conceptual framework suggested by Hunter, it was not surprising to find that neighborhood leaders often described how neighborhood dynamics were influenced by structures embedded at lower levels and at higher levels.

In 1980, and again in 1990, as part of the prerequisites for participating in the Bureau of the Census Neighborhood Statistics Program, the Baltimore City Department of Planning also completed an exhaustive mapping of the city's neighborhoods.[1] The 1980 "official" neighborhood map was based heavily on our map, with modifications as required to qualify for the Census Neighborhood Statistics Program. Although the planners used slightly different guidelines from ours, when we began the current project we did not anticipate that the 1990 mapping would differ in many ways from our 1979 effort. For example, we knew that every nonresidential block had to be part of a neighborhood. We were surprised nonetheless when we found many changes had taken place on the 1990 map in boundary or name or both. We decided to investigate. We sampled forty-two additional neighborhoods beyond our original thirty and sought experienced neighborhood leaders to interview.[2] We wanted to understand the reasons for the changes in names and boundaries and how these neighborhoods contrasted with those where the names and boundaries had stayed the same. We were particularly interested in how these changes might be related to a neighborhood's population size, so we stratified by population size and type of neighborhood boundary change when selecting additional neighborhoods. We successfully completed interviews with fifty-nine leaders (plus one interview with written responses to our questions) in the sampled seventy-two neighborhoods. The interviews included showing the leaders a detailed map of the neighborhood and its 1979 boundaries and, where different, a map of the neighborhood's 1990 boundaries, asking them to comment on both maps and to outline where they thought the neighborhood boundaries "should" be. The information they provided was complemented with relevant census and crime information for the current chapter.[3]

Clearly, the information base described is too thin to provide a detailed picture of the dynamics in any one particular site. In almost every neighborhood, only one leader from one organization was interviewed. Although we tried to locate long-standing leaders with enough local history to interpret recent changes—and the backgrounds of our leader interviewees (Chapter 7) suggests we were successful—other leaders from the same organization may have provided markedly different pictures. In addition, in some of the locations, more than one improvement association was operative. But we did not go to those other groups. Consequently, the cases described here should not be viewed as definitive commentaries on events taking place in one neighborhood or within one organization. Rather, these data are used to illustrate more general processes and trends.

The information presented here contrasts in several ways with Hunter's data sources for his study of neighborhoods in Chicago (27). Whereas he investigated neighborhood name changes after a fifty-year gap, the gap here is only fifteen years. He focused on resident perceptions; the focus here is on local leaders. Finally, whereas the seventy-five natural areas in Chicago had roughly comparable populations at the time of their initial definition, the neighborhoods mapped in Baltimore varied widely in size, from less than 100 households to over 4,000. Consequently, differences between Hunter's analysis of neighborhood change in Chicago and the current effort seem likely. On the other hand, common findings, given the different data sources, would prove striking.

Organization

The following section provides a brief review of the concepts of natural areas, defended neighborhoods, and symbolic communities. These core socioecological concepts guide how sociologists and others have thought about urban communities. Some of the empirical work on neighborhood naming and bounding is reviewed. The work by Hunter, carefully examining name and boundary changes over a fifty-year span, highlights the influences of class-linked stratification concerns, and racial dynamics, on processes of neighborhood naming and bounding.[4]

Moving into the evidence produced in the investigation, the overall volume of change is described. A group of high-status neighborhoods, and one much poorer one, where names and boundaries did not change, receive detailed attention, and the sources of such stability are considered. The different *types* of changes in naming and bounding are examined. These changes are grouped into several categories (see Table 8.2 later in the chapter). The dynamics surrounding these changes in name or boundary or both are described.

A closing section extends the discussion of stability and changes to concerns about neighborhood mobilization, effective community organizations, and community policing. Organizing, visibility-maintaining, coordinating, and maintenance difficulties bedevil organizations representing areas with unstable names and boundaries. Other researchers, like Hunter, have pointed up the utility of informally driven processes of neighborhood naming and bounding, focusing on how they allow residents to respond, albeit slowly, to changes in the surround. The stability of the naming and bounding process, he suggests, might slow these changes down as well. But from a leader perspective, these alterations through time create enormous difficulties. It might make sense to consider citywide, sanctioned *and empowered* names and boundaries. Moving into the specific policy arena of citizen-police coproduced improvements in neighborhood quality and safety, some of the pros and cons linked with officially sanctioned neighborhood governments are briefly considered.

Naming and Bounding

Neighborhood, Natural Areas, and Levels of Community:
The Conceptual Underpinnings

Neighborhood and community are notoriously slippery concepts (1; 20; 26; 27: 19–26; 55). To better understand some types and purposes of neighborhoods and communities, sociologists have developed the ideas of *natural areas, defended neighborhoods,* and *symbolic communities.* Each of these, reviewed below, highlights different aspects of neighborhoods. These terms, and the psychological, sociological, and ecological processes linked to their operation, provide a broader theoretical framework within which to consider stability and shifts in names and boundaries.

Chicago sociologists early in the twentieth century labeled their city's separate communities. Borrowing from the ecological concept of niche, these community "natural areas" of roughly comparable size represented the largest level of community within the city at the time of their research (27: 72). Residents and researchers alike recognized at the time that smaller levels of community existed within these seventy-five natural areas covering the city of Chicago. The researchers may have attempted to roughly standardize the different areas on size.

The areas were "natural" in three senses. First, "the urban residential groups were not the planned or artificial contrivance of anyone but grew out of many independent personal decisions based on moral, political, ecological, and economic considerations" (55: 7–8). They represented settlement patterns, not centralized planning decisions. Second, their boundaries often were natural, in that they were at least convenient and relied on salient natural features:

> By "natural boundaries" Burgess primarily meant broad avenues or expressways, rivers, large plots of vacant land, and wide swaths of industry or railway yards. These represent barriers to communication, interaction, and functional integration. From another perspective, if boundaries are needed, these perhaps represent the most "convenient" and unambiguous ones available. (27: 81)

Finally, within these boundaries, a natural area's population was often—but not necessarily—relatively homogeneous along ethnic, racial, or class lines (e.g., 14, 15). Such homogeneity would permit easy recognition of outsiders (54), and may lead to defended neighborhoods (55: 21). At the ecological level, ethnic heterogeneity links both cross-sectionally and longitudinally with crime shifts (41).

In such defended locales, outsiders are viewed with suspicion, and local residents may resist in-migration of dissimilar others (25). "The residential group which seals itself off through the efforts of delinquent gangs, by restrictive covenants, by sharp boundaries or by a forbidding reputation" is a defended neighborhood (55: 21). Ironically, however, such defended neighborhoods may persist through periods of ethnic succession or ethnic diversity; ecological features and local history may influence community identification independently of population features (see also 13).

Despite such persistence in some locations, the defended neighborhood is not "a single bounded unit persisting through time. The defended neighborhood can expand or contract boundaries; its activation is episodic" (55: 37). In short, the defended neighborhood is not just a set location, but a site the bounds and character of which may shift over time, as may the actions locals undertake to sustain it. Thus, although preserving the ecological focus of natural areas, the concept of defended neighborhood also incorporates a sensitivity to local political, social, and population dynamics. This sensitivity suggests more changes over time in these units than does the focus on natural areas.

Hunter's concept of symbolic communities highlights the social interactionist aspects—features emerging as participants mutually interpret the actions of one another—of both natural areas and defended neighborhoods. Names and boundaries, although they may help urban residents carry out everyday tasks, also cognitively organize how residents, individually and collectively, map the urban social world (27: 88; 38). Names and boundaries are "often only the symbolic representation of significant social divisions and distinctions" (27: 88). The extensiveness of residents' local social involvement influences whether residents see their neighborhood in primarily social or physical terms (20).

Geographers' work on cognitive mapping makes some similar points (10, 38). Consequently, even more than the defended neighborhood concept, the symbolic communities concept anticipates greater fluidity over time in neighborhood naming and bounding.

Local boundaries are often ambiguous. . . . The . . . informal character of these boundaries allows greater change and freewheeling in the system than might be permitted by a more rigidly fixed and widely shared set of administrative boundaries. Of course there are potential costs to such ambiguity,

such as confusion about collective identity and loss of commitment and responsibility at the local level. . . . we should not lose sight of the symbolic
character of community boundaries. As symbols, they are on the one hand
subject to manipulation and conscious redefinition, and on the other hand
are subject to reality testing and thereby provide a relatively quick psychic
and collective readjustment to the rapid changes occurring in today's urban
milieu. . . . they are also a conservative constraint. To the degree that they
are contained within a strong local culture they preserve and maintain the
historical continuity of an area, thereby shielding residents from the consequences of social and ecological change. In short, the names and boundaries
of local areas may be subject to a "symbol lag" which adjusts more quickly
than formal lags and yet provides a cushion and a barrier to rapid urban
change. (27: 88)

To summarize, defended neighborhoods and symbolic communities,
emerging in natural areas or in communities embedded at lower levels of
spatial aggregation, capture the connections between local ecology, politics, population, and broader sociocultural dynamics. The symbolic communities idea also emphasizes how local actors interpret these connections. The symbolic communities idea, being social constructionist in
flavor, recognizes that "varying conceptions of neighborhood have an
underlying rationality in the social and physical position of residents
within urban society" (20: 53), but also sees that rationality as relatively
fluid in response to local changes.

What are the implications of these connections for changes over time?
The ideas of both defended neighborhoods and symbolic communities
anticipate significant changes in neighborhood bounding and naming
taking place quickly. The defended neighborhoods view frames the
changes in relationship to local ethnic, cultural, and political dynamics.
The symbolic communities view interprets the changes as residents' ac-
commodation, within a constrained ecological context, to the changes
taking place around them, that is, the local historical forces at work. Such
shifts take place within a broader vertical array of levels of community.

Neighborhoods and communities represent two of several levels of sociocultural integration within a broader array of spatial units. The array
refers to different-sized geographic units, nested within one another, providing different functional benefits and patterns of attachment. Suttles
(55: 55–60) describes these different levels. The face block—what is called
the streetblock here—is the "smallest discrete areal unit" (55: 55), providing a significant physical and social container for urban life (see also 56).
Beyond the face block is the defended neighborhood, where residents
feel relatively secure from "risks of insult or injury" (55: 57; see also 57).
Beyond this, the community of limited liability may draw on residents

and other stakeholders who define local interests in opposition to exter-nal agents and invest in local issues up to a point (29). Beyond that arena is the expanded community of limited liability where the sphere of concern is even broader but influence is weaker.[5]

In this array of nested units, different writers draw distinctions between neighborhood and community in different ways. Hunter, in his discussion of neighborhood and community, suggests that the latter has a functional base, including not only one's residential area but also local amenities and institutions (27). For him, the neighborhood refers to the solely residential area with which one identifies. Brower highlights the contributions of local amenities to neighborhood identity (1). Guest and Lee find that institutions are mentioned only about 10% of the time when people define their neighborhoods. But those who use institutional definitions usually envision larger neighborhoods (20).

Neighborhood Naming

A neighborhood needs a name if it is to be collectively represented to those living there and elsewhere (27: 68; 48). "Above all, the neighborhood has a name" (32: 65; 19). Researchers have investigated both the kinds of places where residents more easily provide a common name and the kinds of residents who can supply a neighborhood name.

Some residential locations are more distinctive and "nameable" than others (19, 49). Residents more readily name higher-status locations and places with more distinctive topography, land use, or history. Such features may contribute to the distinctiveness of the neighborhood as a "district" in locals' cognitive maps (38). Past and present neighborhood features help form images of locale varying in clarity.

Although some specific names for some locations can be more persistent over time, the variation in this persistence opens the question, how stable are these labels? Interviewing Chicago residents in the early 1970s, Hunter found that 42% of his sample provided the same natural area names Burgess had used a half century earlier. He concluded "that not only is there persistence in the names of such areas; but these names are part of a shared local culture that is fairly widely known" (27: 77). (For information on Seattle changes, see 21).

In Baltimore, over a *much shorter* period, persistence comparable to Chicago appeared. In the 1994 survey of *residents* in thirty neighborhoods, 44.2% of respondents provided the same name for their locale as had been used by the local community organization fifteen years earlier. About the same portion of residents interviewed in the 1982 sample of sixty-six neighborhoods—36.6% of respondents—provided the same names used in the 1979 neighborhood mapping. In both the 1982 and

1994 Baltimore resident samples, about 76%–77% of respondents agreed that their neighborhood did have a name. Of those agreeing that the neighborhood did have a name, in 1982, 41%; and in 1994, 47% agreed that they had heard the area referred to by its 1979 name.

It is difficult to know how much to make of the closely comparable persistence levels in naming in the two cities, Hunter's 42% over fifty years and our 44% over fifteen years. The change periods differ in length, the decades are different, and survey modes and sampling procedures are not comparable. Does this mean that researchers in Chicago surveying fifteen years after Burgess's mapping would also have found about 42%–44% supplying the official names? Does it mean that thirty years from now Baltimore researchers will find 42%–44% of respondents supplying the 1979 names? We do not know. All that we can safely assert is that in both cities neighborhood names are widely shared and a significant and persistent feature of the local culture.[6] Guest also agrees that salience of neighborhood identification failed to decline in Seattle from the 1920s to the 1970s and may have increased slightly (21).

What were the determinants of the persistence of the 1979 names in the 1994 resident surveys?[7] Across the thirty neighborhoods, the proportion correctly recalling the designated name ranged from none to all. In the Baltimore sample of neighborhoods, as in other neighborhoods in other cities, some neighborhoods have much more salient profiles (19, 21). A brief comment on prior work on neighborhood nameability is in order before describing current results.

Resident and neighborhood characteristics have both been linked to nameability (19). Regrettably, research has not always pointed to the same features. Residents can more readily supply the accepted neighborhood name if they are more educated and have lived in the locale longer (7, 19, 27). Most studies find stronger local involvement, either in organizations or in local acquaintanceship and friendship networks, helps residents name the area (7, 27). But some studies do not find this connection (19). Ties between local involvement and naming have been shown to operate at both the streetblock and individual level (59). Controlling for status, naming may be less frequent in more predominantly African-American neighborhoods (55, 59). In short, considering the three dimensions of community structure discussed in this volume—status, ethnicity, and stability—status makes the clearest, most consistent contribution. Race appears relevant in some studies but not others; likewise for stability variables such as length of residence and homeownership.

Guest and Lee's work in Seattle suggests that consensus on neighborhood names is also influenced by site features: "the physical design of streets and proximity to parks, a major type of landmark which can serve as an integrating factor in many areas" (19: 388).[8] In another study, Guest and Lee found that distance from the central business district contributes to stability in naming (21). The Seattle work points to important contextual features, net of macro-sociological parameters, influencing the recognizability or durability of a neighborhood identity.

Hierarchical generalized linear models allow examining both the "who" and the "where" portions of neighborhood naming. To predict name persistence, a range of individual and neighborhood factors were entered: demographics, crime, local social involvement, and perceived problems. Among the 1994 interviewees, one strong correlate of 1979 name persistence emerged at the individual level: Those reporting more years of schooling than their neighbors were more likely to supply the designated 1979 name. At the neighborhood level, only one sturdy correlate emerged: In more predominantly African-American neighborhoods, a lower portion of residents supplied the designated name. Considerable variation in nameability remained to be explained at the neighborhood level, confirming the point made earlier by Guest and Lee that local history and sometimes relatively idiosyncratic features may influence the salience of locale. Both of the connections with nameability seen here—education at the individual level and racial composition at the neighborhood level—agree with earlier work.

Bounding the Neighborhood

The neighborhood boundary, like the name, serves a wide range of psychological, social, cultural, and political purposes. For individuals, groups, and organizations, it marks where one community ends and another begins. Early work in this area investigated whether consensus existed among residents on boundaries (24, 30, 36, 49). Mixed results surfaced, in part because researchers used different numbers of neighborhoods and different definitions of consensus. Later work on boundaries has recognized that significant and potentially dangerous "gaps" can exist between neighborhoods. Boundaries between communities may be deep enough to become their own regions. These are potentially dangerous "no man's lands," zones of nonresidential land uses where no one watches out (54; 55: 53).

Where available, residents may use as boundaries major nonresidential features that might make a no-man's land. The zone helps anchor and highlight differences between communities. These sizable gaps between where people live provide ready-made but also enduring partitions in the residential fabric. Such sizable gaps, like magnets attracting metal filings, tend to draw the neighborhood boundaries to themselves.

But overlaid on top of such social, ecological processes are political processes. Later researchers also have recognized that boundaries are subject to considerable manipulation, both by insiders and outsiders, for specific purposes (27: 71).

> Sometimes "boundary work" is more informal; a realtor may advertise a property as located within a certain prestigious area when it is actually "just outside." Repetitions of such incorrect designations may eventually alter perceived boundaries to include the parcels involved. . . . Residents also may strive to manipulate boundaries in order to improve their standing in the larger social world, laying claim to participating in the prestigious surround that corresponds to a given community. (37: 44)

Logan and Molotoch's quote highlights the status-linked purposes of bounding locations. People seek to include their location in higher-prestige regions. Therefore, on the one hand static land use features—major land use shifts, no man's lands, or big housing differences—draw in boundaries, given the convenience and salience of such edges; on the other hand, status dynamics among residents or outside agents tend to pull boundaries off such features if that manipulation serves specific purposes.

Since neighborhood boundaries are informal, they can shift not only in response to manipulators but in response to changing ecological conditions as well (27: 77). Hunter argues that important purposes served by neighborhood boundaries are to maintain relative status (27: 82–83) and racial (27: 85–86) distinctions. When separating communities, his respondents mentioned class factors most often and racial or ethnic factors secondarily. The bounding process, he argues, like the naming process, serves to simultaneously recognize ongoing reconfigurations in the residential environment and to slow down class- and race-linked community changes.

Hunter illustrates status issues with two types of examples: lower-status communities attempting to fuse with higher-status adjoining communities and higher-status communities attempting to differentiate themselves from surrounding lower-status communities. He suggests these asymmetries in the bounding process are similar to the asymmetries observed in the broader stratification literature (27: 78).

Left unexplored by research to date are questions of boundary *types*. Although we have some information on the physical features that may help make a particular boundary widely recognized and agreed on, the overall clarity versus fuzziness of boundaries remains relatively unexamined.

Granted, some physical features can better symbolize major neighborhood boundaries than others. Larger nonresidential land uses; bigger differences in housing quality, size, and lot size; or more traffic carried on a major artery all result in more secure differentiation between adjoining neighborhoods, clearer boundaries, and more well known boundaries by both outsiders and residents. But the idea of "boundary work" points to additional dynamics affecting both the salience of a boundary and where it is actually placed. Placement and salience are related but conceptually distinct concerns. For example, the common boundary between two neighborhoods with different household income levels may be placed similarly by residents of both neighborhoods, but residents from the higher-income locale may demonstrate firmer agreement about the boundary's location. Furthermore, the neighborhood organization in the higher-income locale may do more to increase the clarity of the boundary. Below, examples are provided of this and other types of more typical boundary work, where the issue is placement. One major purpose of the investigation is to learn more about such boundary work. Why do organizations undertake it? What do they hope to accomplish? How salient are concerns about highlighting race and class differences to enhance symbolic community, as compared to other motivations? How do these objectives link to crime or incivilities?

Considering Local Context

Undoubtedly, processes of boundary maintenance or boundary shifting may deny, hasten, or recognize distinctions based on relative status or ethnicity. Nevertheless, features of local context also drive these processes. To lose sight of these other shaping influences may result in truncated understanding. The influence of context on boundary work may result in boundaries being moved, but not necessarily in the same direction we would expect based on class or ethnic differentials.

Especially important features of local context are the goals local leaders hope to achieve. Following a social constructionist perspective, leaders' rationales for their actions deserve consideration. What specifically did they hope to accomplish? What parties did they think might be affected? Sometimes these rationales may reflect concerns based on place-based stratification, that is, symbolic community image. For example, leaders may talk about steps required to maintain property values in the neighborhood. But other times, concerns expressed may not touch on status or race; instead leaders may seek outcomes to enhance specific aspects of neighborhood functionality. At the risk of oversimplifying, I argue that the macro-sociological perspective on symbolic communities and boundary work highlights efforts to maintain neighborhood exchange value, whereas leaders' concerns may center on making the neighborhood a better place for its residents, that is, enhancing neighborhood use value. These two sets of concerns may point in the same policy direction for a leader or they may point in opposite directions.

In short, despite the extensive work on both ecological and macro-sociological factors shaping neighborhood names and boundaries, the explanatory scope should remain broad. By talking to leaders with significant local history and listening to their explanations of changes and maintenance of boundaries and names, we may find they pursue strategies opposite those expected based on macro-sociological processes such as stratification. To put the point even more strongly, the functional concerns of leaders may lead to boundary work opposite from that expected, given a class- and race-based perspective.

Service Delivery Issues and Community Policing

A final piece of conceptual background briefly considers community or problem-oriented policing (17). What are the implications of stability and shifts in neighborhood naming and bounding for delivery of community policing services and the coproduction of public safety (45)?

Police-Community Collaboration in Community Policing

Collaboration with local organizations represents a core feature of community policing. Typically, outside police organizations "find" extant communities via the community organizations representing residents and other local interests. This aspect of community policing is captured in most definitions of the process. For example, Skogan and Hartnett offer four principles of community policing. These include the following comments about collaboration:

> Community policing relies on organization decentralization and a reorientation of patrol in order to facilitate communication between police and the public . . . [It] requires that police respond to the public when they set priorities and develop their tactics . . . effective community policing requires responsiveness to citizen input concerning both the needs of the community and the best ways police can meet those needs . . . [It] *implies a commitment to helping neighborhoods solve crime problems on their own, through community organizations.* (52: 6, 7, 8, emphasis added)

The above features of community policing processes are most easily satisfied if community policing officers can locate local organizations and their leaders and work directly with them in a meaningful partnership. But officers can interact and collaborate with those communities in many different ways. They can organize the partnership along the lines of the extant community units. Or alternately, they can organize the partnership around police administrative units, such as police beats or districts.

Community Policing Organized Around Police Work Groups

Policing is done through territorially organized work groups, with officers sharing corporate responsibility for individual beats. In larger departments, these beats are organized into precincts, sectors, or divisions (31: 280–282). Community policing initiatives can be "tacked onto" the way police do their work anyway, so that the efforts are closely aligned with how these groups work.

Such a model was followed in the recent Chicago Alternative Policing Strategy (CAPS) community policing initiative (2, 3, 4, 52). There, beat meetings represented the central mechanism for drawing together police and residents. Local organizations were asked to support the beat meeting process and did so to varying degrees (52: 147). Attendance at beat meetings in many locations continued to be unacceptably low in the minds of many beat commanders (4: 54). Evaluators report the police using a variety of strategies geared to increase attendance at beat meetings. Some of these strategies involved creating neighborhood organizational structures, such as beat facilitators, at the beat level.

Such an arrangement for community contacts fits well with how police work is organized. Advantages accrue from such congruence. Within the police department itself, officers are clear on who is responsible for what locations, because the boundaries are the same as the beats. The police-citizen communication process benefits too, because both sides know who is the responsible contact person in the police department, for example, the beat commander.

But there are disadvantages as well in a process centered on the police organization. It does not fit with how communities are organized. Police beat and district boundaries do not coincide neatly with community boundaries. Furthermore, the beat meeting process, such as in the Chicago CAPS project, occurs outside of the normal activities of local community organizations. Since the process takes place *outside* of ongoing neighborhood organization–based initiatives, it is not something those organizations are already mandated to do; rather it is an external process, run by the police, to which the organizations are asked to contribute. Although successful organizations appear capable of contributing substantively to the process, the police-community partnering in the Chicago CAPS program was not closely tied to the endogenous organizations.

Not only was the process not endogenous to the local community groups, the boundaries of the police administrative units, the beat, cut across community organizational boundaries, creating collaboration difficulties between very different organizations in the same beat (52: 151). The difficulties of partnering with community leaders is compounded in such situations. Such extreme mixing would probably be less likely if the endogenous community groups are used as the organizing unit.

It appears that in the CAPS project the differential success of organizing using the beat administrative structure exactly matches the differential pattern that would have been obtained had endogenous organizations been used. As will be shown shortly, boundary stability and organization longevity and effectiveness in the Baltimore data generally follow class and race lines, being highest among high-income, predominantly white locations. The CAPS program found the same differential pattern in beat organizing and partnering. The patterning is what would be predicted given the tilt, discussed in Chapter 7, of white, higher-income locations toward victimization prevention agendas. "We found the effects of race and class on involvement in CAPS were strong ones, but that they were indirect . . . race and class were linked to the kinds of organizations that people were involved in. . . . Organizations that served largely white constituencies were the kinds of organizations that were particularly likely to be heavily involved in CAPS" (52: 146, 147). In other words, problems of differential involvement of endogenous community organizations persisted despite the organization around police beats rather than local organizations.

It seems plausible that if the CAPS process were located firmly within particular organizations, the leaders of those organizations might commit themselves more wholeheartedly to it, interorganizational collaboration problems might be minimized, and the process might enjoy wider support and longer-term viability. Making it endogenous to each organization attaches the citizen responsibility for it, and the political advantages of success, to each association and its leadership. Astute local leaders are likely to readily see these advantages.

Furthermore, if citizen-police coproduction were to be nested within extant organizations, the message communicated to police about what citizens expect them to address is likely to be clearer. What each neighborhood wants from the partnership should be clearer. A community-organization–centered coproduction model is considered after reviewing changes and stability in neighborhood names and boundaries. Does that information help explicitly anticipate the advantages and disadvantages of organizing community policing efforts using neighborhood administrative units?

Stability and Changes

The focus here is on the information provided about neighborhood names and boundaries, why they may have shifted or remained the same, and ongoing boundary work. The overall volume of changes is described. Some neighborhoods that stayed stable in terms of names and

TABLE 8.1   Number of Changes in Neighborhood Boundaries

Gained nonresidential land	94
Lost nonresidential land	72
Gained residential blocks	78
Lost residential blocks	101

boundaries are then examined. Several different types of changes, roughly sorted by scale, ranging from more to less substantial, are then reviewed.

Background: How Much Change?

The 1979 map, as mentioned earlier, contained 277 exhaustive and nonoverlapping units, including the downtown, 20 public housing communities, and 26 unorganized areas. The 1990 map was produced by the city's Department of Planning to conform with the requirements of the 1990 Census Neighborhood Statistics Program. A neighborhood, if its boundaries changed, could experience four specific changes: it could gain or lose nonresidential land or it could gain or lose residential blocks. Many neighborhoods experienced each change. The numbers, leaving out unorganized areas, the downtown, and public housing communities, are shown in Table 8.1.

These different gains and losses could combine in different ways. A neighborhood could simultaneously lose and gain nonresidential land; similarly with residential blocks. The total number of neighborhoods experiencing a gain or a loss of nonresidential land or both was 127 out of 230 (55%). The total number of neighborhoods experiencing a gain or a loss of residential blocks or both was 138 out of 230 (60%). The changes in residential blocks are most meaningful here, since the allocation of nonresidential sites to neighborhoods was driven by the formal parameters of the 1990 mapping process—all census blocks in the city had to be covered.

What determined whether a neighborhood's residential makeup would be altered in the 1990 remapping? Would a neighborhood be left alone? Or would it have blocks added or subtracted? Following Logan and Molotch's suggestion that the least powerful neighborhoods are most easily manipulated by outside interests, adding or subtracting residential blocks could be considered a form of manipulation by outsiders. (For the moment, ignore the possibility that a neighborhood may have wanted its boundary changed, which did occur sometimes.) Their argument suggests that smaller, lower-income, less stable, more predominantly African-American neighborhoods would be more likely to have their residential makeup altered. These alterations represent "manipulation" if they do not reflect residents' and local leaders' views.

Extensive analyses using both probit and logit models showed that only 1990 racial makeup was significantly linked to the addition or subtraction of residential blocks ($p < .05$). Neighborhoods not experiencing a change in their residential blocks averaged 47% African-American in 1990; neighborhoods experiencing a change averaged 58% African-American. In 1980, the racial difference between the two groups was marginally significant ($p < .10$); neighborhoods to be changed averaged 53% African-American; those not to be changed averaged 43% African-American.[9] None of the other indicators for status or stability were significantly connected with shifting residential makeup. Neither crime nor neighborhood size influenced change versus stability in residential boundaries.

In sum, a modest connection appears between racial makeup and stability of the residential neighborhood boundary. As the conflict theorists would predict, public agencies were more likely to alter the residential configuration of predominantly African-American neighborhoods. But this relationship is a modest one, albeit significant. Other features of neighborhood fabric do not relate to residential boundary redrawing. The lack of strong connections between structure and rebounding suggests that local features of context may have a strong influence. The 1994 sample of neighborhoods and the interviews with the leaders in those locations provide insight into these important local features.

Sources of Stability

Among the seventy-two sampled neighborhoods were many in which the boundaries and names did not shift from the initial mapping in 1979 to the 1990 mapping by the Department of Planning. The stability appeared greatest at the highest and lowest ends of the socioeconomic spectrum. At the two different ends, the sources of the stability were vastly different.

At the upper socioeconomic end, Baltimore contains several early-twentieth-century neighborhoods toward the outer edge of the city, originally planned as solid, upscale developments. The Roland Park Company was involved in many of them. (For details on Roland Park, the Roland Park Company, Oakwell, and restrictive covenants, see 11: 32–33.) These developments contain sizable houses on moderate-to-sizable lots and streets laid out in anything but a grid pattern. McDougall also claims that the developers in these sites sought to exclude African-Americans and other nonwhite racial groups and that those segregationist sentiments helped drive the imposition of restrictive covenants for these areas (40). In several of these neighborhoods, the local improvement organization was vested by the original developer with legal powers over local residents. We interviewed leaders in three of these neighborhoods.

The power vested in the local community associations by the original developer allowed them to closely monitor local conditions and act quickly if needed. In Pineland, organization leaders inspect the entire neighborhood yearly for properties and lots in need of physical repairs, issuing requests as needed to owners for remediation. Should cited occupants not comply speedily with a request, the organization can take them directly to court; outside agencies need not be brought in as enforcers. As a result, in all of these neighborhoods the original relatively high standards of upkeep have been evenly maintained, for the most part, throughout each area. Even though housing styles vary a bit throughout each area, levels of upkeep appear uniformly high. This consistency helps prevent any one section of the neighborhood from following a markedly different path of house pricing.

The local organization can badger, even to the point of legal proceedings, those who are not keeping up to the preferred standard. In addition to the stabilizing effect of such vigilance, it is also notable that the original developer's boundaries were legally sanctified when the original covenants were put into place. The local organization is vested with particular legal powers over a *specific* area.

Also contributing to the stability in these locations, aside from uniform development, firmly fixed boundaries, and legally empowered organizations, is the political clout that goes with being an upscale neighborhood. These Roland Park Company neighborhoods have some of the consistently highest priced housing in the city, and they are populated by many of the politically connected. One neighborhood's experiences in getting the city to put in "designer" lighting and to transfer a disagreeable city employee represent small cases in point.

Organizations in higher-status neighborhoods can also use their clout to "beef up" their boundaries. One of these neighborhoods succeeded in closing off five traffic entrances into the neighborhood, for example (see Chapter 7). In the early 1970s, one of the Roland Park Company neighborhoods put bollards down the middle of a street connecting the neighborhood to a much lower status, adjoining neighborhood. In effect, the neighborhood cut off traffic and marked its boundaries. In these two examples of boundary reinforcement, leaders undertook the actions for one specific, functional reason: to reduce neighborhood through traffic, thereby enhancing neighborhood safety. In the case of the entrance closings, leaders of the higher-status neighborhood were adamant in the city-sponsored workshop we attended about the functional benefits they sought. But, as or perhaps more important, and on a more symbolic level, the actions also shored up the line dividing the neighborhood from adjoining, markedly less well off neighborhoods.

Suttles would argue these acts of boundary reinforcement are undertaken by defended neighborhoods whose members perceive a threat. The leaders of the high-status neighborhood sought to render the locale less permeable in the face of a potential danger to their neighborhood quality. From a complementary perspective, that of territorial functioning, these are "bulwarking" actions (57). Residents experience progressively increasing threat as they move farther from home. If they are confronted with a threat greater than expected, given that distance from home, they may seek to block off the threat.

But boundary stability is not limited just to the highest-status neighborhoods. Moving from these outer-city, predominantly white settings to some core, predominantly African-American neighborhoods, one instance surfaced where boundary and name stability emerged from a markedly different source: designation as an urban renewal area. McDougall (40) describes the conditions and leaders in the near-westside neighborhoods of Park Heights, Harlem Park, Upton, and Druid Heights in some detail. Two of these were designated as urban renewal areas in the 1960s. When asked about neighborhood boundaries, the accomplished, politically connected, and successful long-term leader in one of these two neighborhoods for over three decades refers always to the urban renewal boundaries laid down decades ago. The naming came about as part of the same process. There is no discussion.

The neighborhood is extremely disadvantaged. As Steve Pardue described it in his field notes:

> Nearly all of the housing . . . is apartments and rowhouses. Most of the units are brick; they vary in size from wide three and four-story dwellings to fairly narrow two-story ones. Although some of the units are in good shape, many throughout the area are run down or boarded up, stenciled with the ubiquitous "No Trespassing—If animal is trapped inside call . . . ." There is traffic on most of the area roads during most times of the day, and there is heavy pedestrian traffic and loitering in the commercial areas, particularly along . . . [two major] avenues.

In marked contrast to the stable, high-income, outer-city locations described above, where one official organization speaks for the residents, in these neighborhoods organizational density is extremely high. The long-term leader sees her group, the Olney planning committee, as an umbrella group having, as Pardue put it (interview notes), "some degree of oversight over the twenty one groups working in the area at the time of the interview." At the time of the interview (October 1994), thirty-two named groups existed in the neighborhood, with twenty-one labeled as "active."[10] The other urban renewal neighborhood similarly hosts several community groups, and the leaders of many of them claim to speak "for the community." These high levels of organizational density replicate recent five-city findings showing high levels of participation in predominantly African-American neighborhoods (47).[11]

In the case of the sampled neighborhood, the local leader's eminence and her steady adherence through the years to the urban renewal boundaries simplify the process of locating the community and its leader. But when she is succeeded, for she can never be replaced, there are questions whether that one voice can be maintained. In the interview, she did mention that she was hoping to groom a successor, and she expressed concern about the age of the members of the planning committee, whose oldest member was ninety-two. The leader interviewed was the youngest member.

Lloyd represents another interesting case of stable boundaries and name. It is an outer-city neighborhood with clusters of two-story brick row houses set back twenty to thirty feet from the streets, some of which curve or end in a cul de sac. Except when the elementary school is opening or closing, traffic, vehicular and pedestrian, is light in the neighborhood.

Racial composition has changed dramatically in Lloyd. It went from 7% (1970) to 22% (1980) to 60% (1990) African-American. Given this substantial racial change and the dramatic disappearance of some racially changing neighborhoods in the same section of town (see below), one might expect to see Lloyd's name or boundaries change. But neither did. The key here may be twofold. The locale is clearly middle class, with a substantial professional population and high homeownership levels. In addition to a solid status, the neighborhood's boundaries are all major arteries. These natural features undoubtedly help stabilize the neighborhood configuration.

The implications of continuity in name and boundary for police-community partnerships are substantial. In this sample of neighborhoods, stability was most likely in high-status locales. Boundaries remained the same over time, and a single, legally empowered and long-standing organization represented the locale. Clear differences between these and adjoining neighborhoods in housing quality and lot size were readily apparent. The representing organizations took steps to reinforce their boundaries as needed, in two cases making them less permeable to vehicular traffic. Instances also appeared of one extremely disadvantaged neighborhood and one moderate to moderately high status neighborhood where both boundaries and names remained constant across the two mappings, albeit for different reasons. But the general trend was sta-

tus providing stability in naming and bounding. The result is that each
high-status neighborhood represents a clearly defined service area, and
police can readily identify the responsible local organization with which
they can build a partnership. These also are locales where in general
views toward the police are more positive. Thus, in these higher-status
locations, (1) the service area is delineated, (2) a stable community partner is identified, and (3) residents are in general more willing to work
with police in joint efforts. In short, these high-status locations share
three specific ingredients for partnership success; the likelihood of finding those ingredients in lower-status neighborhoods is less.

If and as the following conditions hold, these dynamics may help explain the impacts of status on changes in crime and reactions to crime:
The three identified ingredients contributed to more successful police-
community partnerships; those partnerships played a role in density and
types of police coverage and police-community information sharing; and
that coverage and sharing contributed to the shifts in crime rates and
shifts in reaction to crime noted in Chapters 5 and 6. Going against this
suggestion was one high-status neighborhood's willingness to give up
on the Baltimore Police Department and hire private security patrols. But
despite that one counterexample, the dynamics described here still may
apply to the other high-status neighborhoods in the sample. Simply put,
the place-based dynamics around boundaries, names, and organizational
power, and the implications for coproduced safety, may help unpack the
strong and diverse impacts of status on the outcomes of central interest
to the incivilities thesis.

Types of Changes

This section examines the different types of changes in boundaries and
naming that occurred. The types of changes are defined in Table 8.2,
listed, roughly, from the most to the least dramatic. Examples of each and
the reasons and dynamics surrounding each type of change are described. At this time the generality or exhaustiveness of the types discussed here is not known. Other types of changes may take place in other
locations, and other types of changes may have been taking place here
that were missed or misclassified. The connections between the types of
shifts and locational characteristics also might be different elsewhere.

Ex Nihilo. Neighborhoods can be created out of nothing, with the creation sponsored largely by external, public agencies. Usually, significant
amounts of building or rebuilding are involved. Most familiar in this regard are clustered public housing communities, of the high- or low- rise

TABLE 8.2 Types of Changes in Neighborhood Boundaries and Names

Ex nihilo	A neighborhood is created out of "nothing." Usually significant physical building or renovation is involved. Distinct from an unorganized area becoming organized.
Into a black hole	A large, well-known neighborhood name disappears; changes in surrounding neighborhoods not as substantial as in etch-a-sketch.
Etch-a-sketch	In a section of town, neighborhood boundaries are redrawn and names are changed for several neighborhoods at the same time.
Morphing to fit	A neighborhood, to achieve current goals, substantively reconfigures its boundaries; name remains the same.
Resisting add-ons	A neighborhood is reluctant to include areas previously labeled as adjoining, but merged with the target neighborhood in the most recent mapping.
Splinters take root	A portion of a neighborhood splits off and becomes a neighborhood with a separate identity.
Coming of age	Areas previously mapped as unorganized develop their own neighborhood identity and association.
Minor fiddles	Leaders want, or do not want, adjoining nonresidential land that has been merged into the neighborhood.

variety. But in the 1970s, Baltimore witnessed the creation of several "new" neighborhoods in inner-city locations targeted for gentrification (see Chapter 2). Housing stock here was largely worn out, and vacancy rates high. Ridgely's Delight, Barre Circle, and Otterbein were cases in point.

One leader in such a neighborhood disagreed his neighborhood was "new." It was, he insisted, an "original neighborhood," having life before the central city, "dollar houses" renovation initiatives of the 1970s. That may be so, but before this intervention the neighborhood had housing worth next to nothing, was 80% African-American, and had high vacancy rates. By 1990, the white to African-American household ratio was roughly 2:1. The original neighborhood, as a social unit with a widely recognized identity, was largely replaced by the gentrification of the 1970s.

Such new or reborn neighborhoods present difficulties for the delivery of policing services. Three dynamics are probably relevant. The leaders there, after the renovation, demand higher levels of city services, policing among them. The leader we interviewed in a renovated neighborhood believed the city had made a promise to his locale; part of keeping that promise was delivering improvements and services. Thus demand was high, even though the neighborhood might already be getting more than its "fair share" of city resources, compared to adjoining locales. Further-

TABLE 8.3   African-American Population of Several Northeastern Neighborhoods

Neighborhood / % African-American	1970	1980	1990
Cedonia 1	2	32	59
Cedonia 2	7	72	87
Furley	0	1	17
Smithton 1	1	1	10
Smithton 2	0	30	36

more, the demand for protection is driven not only by a sense of what is owed; lower levels of safety may fuel it as well. The economic contrasts between a revitalizing neighborhood and the surrounding locales, all else being equal, probably increases the number of offenders moving into the gentrifying areas (5). Nearby offenders may be drawn to the area by the relatively high density of "high-quality" targets for crimes such as street robbery or larceny. Gentrification in Baltimore in the 1970s does appear to be linked with reported crime rates higher than they "should" be for these crimes (6). Third, gentrifying neighborhoods typically remain highly mixed on tenure, with significant amounts of renters (8, 35). Renters of course, compared to owners, prove harder to draw into collective crime prevention efforts (34). In sum, feeling both that they are owed and at risk, such locales may make unappeasable claims for protection services; at the same time mixed tenure profiles may impede widespread citizen-based collective prevention efforts. So more will be demanded from police at the same time that the community side of the partnership is weak.

Into a Black Hole.   Even sizable neighborhoods with recognized names can disappear off the map without a trace, the cause of their disappearance as much a mystery to the leaders who still run their "lost" neighborhoods as it was to us.

Smithton is situated in the northeast section of the city. In 1979, two distinct sections were identified: a lower, smaller section, and a second, larger section further north. A small neighborhood of just a few blocks was situated in between the two Smithtons. The smaller and larger sections were home, respectively, to 2,700 and 4,800 people in 1990.

The racial change dynamics in this section of town look complex. Running to the east of these two neighborhoods and continuing to the city boundary are Cedonia 1 (further north) and Cedonia 2. The percentages African-American in these five neighborhoods over the past three censuses are shown in Table 8.3. The table shows that the two sections of Smithton have been integrating at different rates, with the smaller section, Smithton 2, closer to the city center, integrating faster than the larger section, Smithton 1. In 1990, Smithton 1 remained predominantly white, whereas nearby neighborhoods Cedonia 1 and 2 were either integrated or had resegregated as African-American. The 1990 official neighborhood mapping relabels all of these neighborhoods, save Cedonia 1, as Frankford. Frankford's racial composition looks less heavily African-American in 1990 (54% according to Department of Planning neighborhood statistics) than did some of the constituent neighborhoods (Cedonia 2). Smithton has disappeared.

These changes represent an example of boundary work carried out by outside agencies. A staunch conflict theorist would suggest the goal was to increase exchange value in these neighborhoods by masking the amount of racial change that had taken place there. Since I was not privy to the discussions around these redefinitions and know neither which groups were contacted nor what the groups wanted, I cannot say whether the shifts should be thought of as outside manipulation. Some of the community groups may have wanted the change, or the change may have corresponded with organizational dynamics and boundaries far different from those in place in 1979. As I do not know, manipulation should not be presumed. Nonetheless, these changes appear from an outsider's perspective to be classic examples of boundary work in which outside agencies were involved; furthermore, even if unintended, the net effect is to mask the more extreme racial changes taking place in one of these involved neighborhoods (Cedonia 2). The African-American neighborhood leader we spoke with from the subsumed group in Smithton professed concern and confusion about what had happened.

Driving through the area in 1994 on a winter afternoon after school had let out, we saw a mix of pedestrians around the major stores along Belair Road that appeared to be predominantly African-American, with whites present but in the minority. In the morning when children are at school bus stops, the racial mix looks about the same. The area has probably continued to integrate since 1990. As the population has changed, so too have some of the local institutions serving them. In the mid-1990s, for example, on Belair Road not too far from Smithton 2, a Caribbean/African food market appeared and later closed.

The Smithton leader we interviewed distinguished the racial composition of her organization, the Smithton Neighborhood Association, "the second black younger association coming up now and still here," from the longer-lived Cedonia and Frankford associations, which were predominantly "white." As already noted, on the official 1990 neighborhood map these two organizations had captured the areas formerly represented by Furley, Cedonia 2, and Smithton 1 and 2. Perhaps this leader's organization had not been active at the time of the 1990 official neighbor-

hood mapping, since in 1994 she reported her group as being active "going on five years." Because of some difficulties surrounding the interview
due to a recent incident affecting the organization, the interviewer was
not able to learn more about the neighborhood name and boundary
changes. All that is clear is that in a racially changing part of town a historical neighborhood name disappeared; a recent organization using that
name and run by African-Americans was not recognized, perhaps because it was not active at the time of the remapping; and the area was renamed to align with another organization, run by whites, that was probably in existence at the time of the remapping effort. This remapping may
be an example of the process, mentioned by Hunter, where definitions of
symbolic communities are used to retard—or at least not recognize—ongoing ecological changes.

Etch-a-Sketch.   In a few small sections of town, neighborhood boundaries proved extremely fluid in the 1980s, resulting in an almost complete
remapping by 1990. This wholesale reconfiguring of neighborhood
boundaries seems to have taken place in locations where two or more of
the following conditions obtained: the local population composition had
changed extremely rapidly in the recent past, local planners carved out a
new urban renewal site in the location, or housing and land use were extremely mixed.

Southwest Neighbors (SWN).   One area remapped in entirety in 1990 is
the southwest section of town. In this area in 1979, in addition to two unorganized areas (10, 11) we had mapped three neighborhoods with
"southwest" in the name, two neighborhoods named after the Mount
Clare machine shop of the old Baltimore & Ohio (B&O) railroad, and two
gentrified neighborhoods. Around the Tyler Market itself was Tyler Park
and, to the east, Tyler Hill. Except for the two gentrified neighborhoods
and a greatly expanded Tyler Park, *none of the other neighborhood names
survived.*

Interviews with three different leaders in this part of town shed some
light on the processes underlying these changes. But the story appears to
be a tangled one. Different interviewees partially filled in sections of the
puzzle; there are undoubtedly still some missing pieces.

The leader we interviewed from Southwest Neighbors (SWN) told the
following tale of name and boundary shifts. SWN was originally a political action committee "chartered"—by whom is not clear—in 1973 to
cover the area that roughly agrees with the 1979 mapped boundaries. In
the mid-1970s, a gentrifying neighborhood was carved out of the upper
northeast edge of the neighborhood as part of the "dollar house" program of the time. In 1985, Garfield Heights, close to a gentrifying neigh-

borhood and the site of some Section 8 (public assistance) housing, was created as an urban renewal area. A major artery was also built nearby.

The *name* most widely known, especially among the older, working-class residents, was Yard, after the stockyards that had been located there historically. (This name, for years considered unfashionable outside of the area, seemed to be gaining some in popularity, especially among the younger crowd drawn to the revitalized bar/music scene in the locale.) One group of older, blue-collar residents in the area calls itself the "Hearts of the Yard," and, again according to our interviewee, "are no longer accepting members." Younger, more educated residents refer to the locale as Garfield Heights, the name for the area officially sanctioned on the 1990 neighborhood map.

Ironically, even though SWN was no longer used inside the neighborhood and did not appear on the official map, the leader expressed confidence that well more than half of the professionals outside the locale would recognize the name. If the name was widely used outside the area, why not inside? Apparently it became tainted, which, Hunter suggests, can be a reason for dropping a neighborhood name. Allegations of political scandal(s) tarnished the name. Following a fire in 1976, SWN received funds either to compensate victims or to be used for rebuilding; it was not clear which. Some amount of the money allegedly disappeared, and people pointed fingers at SWN. In addition, in a local election circa 1990 there were rumors that SWN had played a role in helping "rig" the outcome.

In short, we see several threads in the account of this leader. External intervention occurred in the original selection of a "dollar house" neighborhood to renovate. Later, the city's need to designate a specific area to receive funding for Section 8 housing led it to carve out Garfield Heights. Sentiment in the neighborhood about the neighborhood name has split along age and class lines. Older, blue-collar residents favor the historical Yard; younger, white-collar ones favor instead Garfield Heights, perhaps hoping to repeat the uptown success of Sherman Heights.[12] The leader reported some ongoing gentrification, with dilapidated units being bought by developers and sold at prices too high for longer-term residents to afford. And finally, scandals or rumors of scandals have tainted the name we mapped in 1979, so it was not used by locals even though it was well recognized by professionals outside.

Tyler Hill. A bit further north of these neighborhoods, we heard a slightly less convoluted account from a leader in Tyler Hill. His story is one of consolidation in the hopes of political advantage. In his view, "historically" there were three distinct subneighborhoods in the area: Tyler Hill, Tyler Park, and Little Lithuania. In the 1970s, a "little old lady" who ran one of the Tylers decided the two Tylers should merge so they could have more clout. They consolidated to become Tyler Park. The two groups also agreed, perhaps with the consent of Little Lithuania, that they should represent the latter area as well. They viewed Little Lithuania as a "political heavyweight" at the time. Later, in the 1980s, for reasons not clear, the entire group decided to affiliate itself with Poppleton, a lower-income, predominantly African-American neighborhood just to the north, since, according to the leader, the latter had recently been declared an urban renewal area. Apparently, after a few years the leadership grew inactive. After a bit more time, a new coalition of neighborhoods arose—the Roundhouse Coalition, named after the eminently recognizable building in the B&O Railroad Museum. Locals decided to go with this coalition as their "last, best hope." The leader noted that when this newly named group met, you saw "the same players, but different uniforms."

In our interviewee's eyes, the arrival of the empowerment zone initiative in Baltimore in early 1995 changed the political landscape yet again, reducing the political clout of the new neighborhood organization. According to the leader, empowerment zone decisions were being made by Citizens Organized to Improve Life (COIL), an umbrella group operating in this part of town for quite some time. He reported frequent conflicts between COIL and the local neighborhood leaders. Thus the neighborhood, in our leader's eyes, had lost clout again as the planning process had moved to a higher level, squeezing out community input. In his mind, the empowerment zone represents "more of an implant than empowerment." In short, the narrative provided by this leader is of shifting alliances in pursuit of "political clout," frustrated by a lack of effective local leadership, difficulties forming effective coalitions, and disempowering outside initiatives.

Southwest Citizens.   In the western edge of this district, we interviewed a person affiliated with an up-and-coming community association with a coverage that more or less matches the area designated as Southwest Citizens in 1979. Our attempts to contact the groups listed on the 1990 map for this area produced no results.

The interviewee, whose organization roughly matches that of the old Southwest Citizens, expressed confusion about why his organization did not appear on the map: "I don't know why they wouldn't have put us on the map. Chris [Ryer, the sixth district planner at the time] knows us." It could have been that the organization was not formed in time for that mapping.

The interviewee expected that few of the local residents and none of the leaders from adjoining areas would recognize the Southwest Citizens name, although most of both groups would recognize the name of his current group, Harrison Improvement. Even though this is the third name for the locale in fifteen years, he expressed confidence in recognition of the name.

When asked why he did not extend his eastern boundary to the east of Adams Street, an area labeled in 1979 as Unorganized BB, he said he felt that to do so would be trying to do too much and would make the area unmanageable. The area covered is "manageable in terms of the number of people and the area it takes in. When the community was established, that's why we didn't take in any area on the other [east] side of Adams Street; that would be taking in too much, with the problems there."

His assessment is on target. Violent crime does seem to be higher in the unorganized areas just to the north (Unorganized AA) and east (Unorganized BB) of Southwest Citizens. According to the 1990–1992 reported crime data, Unorganized BB had a percentile homicide score 24 points higher than Southwest Citizens, and Unorganized AA had a homicide score 50 percentile points higher. In the case of robbery for the same period, Unorganized BB was 10 percentile points higher, and Unorganized AA was 41 percentile points higher. Apparently recognizing these problematic locations and his group's slim chances of organizing successfully there, the leader elected not to incorporate them. He made a strategic decision, opting not to append a more problem-ridden section to his organization's already difficult-to-manage domain.

At the same time, the strategic decision does possess the sociological overtones expected from a symbolic communities, place stratification perspective. Race differences exist between Southwest Citizens and the two unorganized areas in question. In 1990, Southwest Citizens was still a predominantly white neighborhood (5% African-American). By contrast, Unorganized AA was 68% African-American, and Unorganized BB was 27% African-American. In addition, a slight status difference between Southwest Citizens and Unorganized BB was apparent in 1990, with the latter's house value percentile score about 5 points lower. From Hunter's perspective, by refusing to "take in" either or both of these adjoining areas, Southwest Citizens maintained a distinction between itself and adjoining locations that were racially and economically different.

In spite of such relevant stratification-related issues, these matters ought not overshadow the leader's pragmatic concerns. He recognized that the higher crime rates in the unorganized areas signaled conditions against which his organization could make scant headway. He prudently opted not to overburden his organization's capabilities. To concentrate solely on the dynamics linked to stratification is to obtain only an obstructed, partial view of the bounding process.

Walking Southwest Citizens, one finds variations in both land use and housing. Nonresidential land uses, many backing on a right-of-way, pepper the southern section. Although most of the housing is two-story, on some streets there are no porches and housing is not set back, whereas others include both porches and setbacks. Some blocks have uniform formstone fronts, others do not. Formstone is a gray cladding that looks like stone and is often found on East Baltimore rowhouses. These contrasts probably impede the emergence of a coherent neighborhood image.

Such contrasts, coupled with a lack of large-scale "natural" boundaries, except along the southern perimeter, effectively blur the edges of the neighborhood. Crossing the neighborhood boundaries on the north, east, or west, one does not see marked shifts in house values, styles, or the incidence of abandoned or burned-out buildings. In the future, given such ingredients, the boundaries and identity of the neighborhood will probably continue to fluctuate.

Edmondson Village.   Another section of the city exemplifying almost comparable volatility is the Edmondson Village area, near the western boundary of the city, straddling U.S. Route 40. Although the overall community boundaries of Edmondson Village remained in place, fixed in several instances by large-scale nonresidential land uses, within that frame several boundaries shifted between 1979 and 1990.

The continued turbulence in neighborhood naming and bounding may stem from the massive and rapid racial change experienced in the 1960s and 1970s (42, 44). As in Southwest Citizens, internal variation in housing and layout probably also contributed to confusion about where particular neighborhoods begin and end in the Edmondson Village area. We did not interview sufficient leaders in this part of town to fully understand the changes from 1979 to 1990. But at least in the eyes of the one leader interviewed, they were several.

In 1979, to the west of Hilton Avenue, we mapped two neighborhoods with "Edmondson" in the name: Edmondson IA and, to its west, Concerned Citizens for Edmondson Village, both straddling the major east-west artery, U.S. Route 40. North of these two was Unorganized 3; to the south of Edmondson IA was the smaller Unorganized 7. To the southwest was Unorganized 12.

In 1990, the entire area north of U.S. 40 from Hilton Avenue to Rognel Heights was designated Edmondson. The area south of U.S. 40 was labeled Allendale in the easternmost portion, then West Mulberry to its west. The area previously labeled Unorganized 12 was named Edmondson Village. Thus we still see two neighborhoods with Edmondson in the name, but they are not where they were.

The leader interviewed reported four neighborhood organizations then operating in the immediate vicinity. Her own organization appeared to be a cross between a block organization and a neighborhood organization, with strong representation on her block and modest representation on a couple of adjoining blocks. Although she was confident of the names of the other organizations, she was unsure of their boundaries. During our interview, two local HUD officials came to her door. Vigorous debate ensued between the leader and the two HUD officials about the boundaries of these local organizations. In short, no one appeared to be clear about where the boundaries were.

In Edmondson Village, as in some other parts of town, one finds numerous organizations representing a small area. Since we only interviewed one leader, our comments about the neighborhood boundaries should be considered illustrative of the general type of change being noted here, rather than a definitive description of the changes in this locale.

Morphing to Fit.   In a few instances, neighborhoods reconfigured themselves to meet very specific internal or external political agendas. Sherman Heights provides the clearest case in point. Its boundary shifts, apparently as part of a specific political agenda, are opposite what the stratification perspective leads us to expect.

Sherman Heights.   The 1979 mapping reflected three different segments of Sherman Heights: I, the southernmost; II, the middle; and III, the northernmost. The locals themselves acknowledged differences between the different parts.

Gentrification started in the 1970s; in the late 1970s and the early 1980s, the original gentrifiers began selling out to second-generation gentrifiers. An art teacher at a local university, for example, sold his house to two professionals with young children. In the nearby supermarket after work, blue jeans and work shirts were replaced by suspenders and three-piece suits. In the spring of 1997, plans were announced to close a popular corner store and convert it to an upscale coffee bar.

The shift in population mix from first-generation gentrifiers to second-generation, against the backdrop of a constant student population, resulted in a changeover in the local improvement association as well and an expanded political agenda. The leader we interviewed described "old-timers" being pushed aside in a relatively smooth process by a "new guard." The old-timers were described as "stagnant," with few new ideas, whereas the newcomers were more dynamic and pushed new ideas, such as a special fund created by a local referendum and blessed by the city. The fund came from homeowner taxes, not city coffers. The leader emphasized that amicable relations continued between the "old-timers" and the "new guard."

Sherman Heights sought to create a special locally target fund for, among other purposes, private police patrols. That proposal was approved in the spring of 1995. Much of those funds have been allocated to private patrols, and as of spring 1997 local leaders reported a 20% drop in crime.[13] The focus here is the boundary work undertaken by the local association in preparation for a referendum on its special services proposal.

To position itself more strongly on the proposal, the neighborhood improvement association took three steps. It lopped off the southern section of the neighborhood, Sherman Heights I. The leader indicated that the residents and businesses on and below the boundary street had different concerns; he referred to Sherman Heights II as the "core" area and Sherman Heights I as Sherman Heights South. A 1997 *Baltimore Sun* article reported the neighborhood's southern boundary as the street between sections I and II.

According to the symbolic communities perspective, this distancing amounts to Sherman Heights (SH) fencing itself off from an increasingly different community. During the 1980s, SH I had become more heavily African-American. From 1970 to 1990, SH I went from 8% to 57% African-American, whereas SH II went from 15% to 21% African-American. But the economic difference remained steady. The relative house value score for SH I climbed from 0 to the sixty-ninth percentile over the twenty year-period, whereas SH II's score climbed from the eighteenth to the ninetieth percentile.

These ecological shifts suggest SH II was detaching itself from its increasingly African-American southern sister. But beyond the race-based concerns, the distancing also brought functional advantages. For the special funding legislation to be enacted, a plurality or residents had to vote for it. Given the demographic shifts and the associated variation in views about the appropriate collective prevention efforts (Chapter 7), it seems plausible that homeowners in SH I would be more likely than their northern neighbors to vote against it, either because of the added economic burden the district status would have created or because homeowners in that section would have favored a different type of prevention initiative.[14] Excluding SH I may have eliminated those residents most likely to vote against the proposed special funding initiative.

Crime differences provided an additional functional rationale for disassociating from SH I. Crime differences between SH I and SH II had widened over time. In 1970–1972, both SH I and SH II were at about the eightieth percentile on homicide and about the ninetieth percentile on robbery. Twenty years later, SH II was noticeably lower than SH I on both crimes; 34 percentile points lower on homicide, and 17 percentile points lower on robbery. Given that the locale was planning to mount a broad anticrime initiative and would be paying for resources to be spread over a limited locale, it "made sense" to exclude SH I from the program initiative. The safety produced from the resources expended should be more substantial following the truncation. On the other hand, of course, from

SH I's perspective, such a decision made no sense, because it meant excluding the area that was in most need of added safety services.

To sum up on the excision of SH I, race differences between the core (SH II and III) and southern neighborhood sections support a symbolic communities, place stratification perspective. The removal is an example of a higher-status, whiter locale more firmly separating itself from a lower-status, more African-American area. The leader justified doing so by highlighting the residential and business differences between the locales, but neglected to mention the racial and crime differences. These race and crime dynamics are probably secondary concerns, however, given the plan of the "core" area (SH II) to create a special funding arrangement. There are two reasons the separation serves that goal; it removes homeowners who probably would not support the initiative, and it increases the chances of program success by concentrating resources away from the higher-crime southern tier of the neighborhood. Along a related line, SH I would have placed a disproportionate burden on the proposed arrangement. The higher crime there would have required delivery of a higher portion of services, even though the somewhat lower house prices there would have resulted in a lower per homeowner tax contribution. Furthermore, the excision may have reduced later conflicts about operational strategies between SH I and the other sections. (See Note 14 above.) So the symbolic communities perspective provides a general explanation of the dynamics. But as or more centrally relevant, at least from SH II's perspective, is the strategic reasoning behind these moves. Of course, the two perspectives—macro-sociological and contextual—are complementary, as are the insights they provide.

But when we turn to a simultaneously occurring expansion, strategy appears paramount, and the macro-sociological view appears to be contradicted. At the same time the Sherman Heights Community Association was dissociating itself from SH I—relatively more problem-ridden and racially diverging—it also was *affiliating* more closely with another poorer, African-American neighborhood, Kensington, one neighborhood removed to the east.

The leader for Sherman Heights reported that Spruce—immediately to its east—and Kensington—the next area further east—are "considered part of Sherman Heights." Kensington has been predominantly African-American since at least 1970 and has become more so over the past two decades (74%, 87%, and 88% African-American in 1970, 1980, and 1990, respectively). But Kensington's street crime problems are noticeably less severe than those of SH I. Kensington, for example, was almost 30 percentile points lower than SH I on robbery in 1990–1992.

In effect, by allying with Spruce and Kensington, Sherman Heights may have been trying to position itself as an umbrella group.[15] In each case, the rationale for the alliance was different. The leader argued that ties with Spruce "had always been close—residents live in Spruce and sit on the board of SHCA." In the case of Kensington, the leader explained that Sherman Heights had done conscious outreach: About "three to four years ago an intense effort to reach out was made." The upshot of the outreach, according to the leader, has been leadership development and organizing improvements in Kensington. The March/April 1995 Sherman Heights newsletter reported "KENSINGTON and the 56ers [on 56th Street] are incorporating. The bylaws for the organization should be finalized in March." The Sherman Heights leader acknowledged a separate association for Kensington, one with which they cooperated on issues such as cleanup and crime.

According to the symbolic communities perspective, Sherman Heights's pursuit of a closer relationship with Kensington—serving as an umbrella group for the latter, encouraging its organizing initiatives, and collaborating on specific projects—is an unlikely event. Sherman Heights should be pulling back from Kensington as it was from SH I, reinforcing its boundaries and reputation. The status gap between SH II and Kensington has increased markedly in the past twenty years. While SH II went from the eighteenth to ninety-first to ninetieth housing percentile score from 1970 to 1980 to 1990, Kensington's scores for the same periods were eleventh, sixteenth, and thirty-first percentiles. Although the gap has closed in the past ten years, it is greater than it was in 1970 and far larger than the gap between SH I and SH II. If anything, a "straight" symbolic communities perspective—and the historical boundaries—suggest SH II should have been affiliating with SH I and reinforcing its separation from Kensington, exactly the opposite of what it was doing.

Albeit contrary to stratification theory, the Kensington affiliation nevertheless makes sense *strategically*. Expanding coverage to assist Kensington would seem to be a politically savvy move in planning for a referendum on the proposed special funding initiative. Since Sherman Heights could claim coverage for that locale, the boundaries for the special funding initiative would not look like an attempt to protect a segregated area (Sherman Heights II, III, and Spruce), the segments of which were no more than 21% African-American. Approval from city-level authorities would seem more likely since the area was more integrated after including Kensington. Drawing Sherman Heights leaders to Kensington rather than SH I was a lower crime problem.

Other Examples. A few other neighborhood leaders interviewed presented situations replicating at least the "pullback" portion of the Sherman Heights shift. Fox Point is a predominantly African-American neighborhood of large homes in the northwestern portion of town, bounded on the northwest by a major artery. The leader we interviewed there did not accept that his neighborhood extended below a particular street, as shown in the 1979 map. He insisted the housing mix was different—denser—below this street. The 1990 map accorded with his smaller vision of Fox Point which, he explained, had been larger prior to 1979. According to the leader, the organization decided between 1970 and 1980 to rein in and represent only single or duplex detached units.

The Fox Point pullback may have functional impacts. The area, home to large, one-unit detached houses, had been experiencing a large number of conversions to multifamily dwellings in recent years, according to the district planner interviewed. Sometimes owners followed procedures in making these conversions; sometimes they did not. The leader in this neighborhood reported steps taken by his organization to block conversions. It may be the case that the organization's task was less daunting after excluding the area with the dense-housing mix.

Polk Hill provided another example of a neighborhood retreating to its core area, as Fox Point had done. Polk Hill is a predominantly African-American neighborhood, located in the north-central section of the city, with a small park on its western edge separating it from the next neighborhood. The 1979 and 1990 mappings both included the park as the western boundary. The leader interviewed wanted to draw the western boundary two blocks further east. She also wanted to pull the southern boundary back to exclude a school.

According to the leader interviewed, Polk Hill has "171 homes," and they're "all homeowners." The area she sought to exclude immediately to the west, according to the leader, is more heavily rental. Census figures show the larger area, including the western section, at about 30% homeowners in 1970 and about 50% homeowners in both 1980 and 1990.

Rejection of the western area stems in part from the past. The leader reported Polk Hill evolved as a separate neighborhood in 1970. The area was named after a street in the now-disputed western section and was a rental area of "townhouses." A realtor bought and then sold them to people in 1975 or 1976, and the name was changed to Polk Hill. The new name helped free the locale from the image of its lower-status origins and identify the slightly more upscale market, as happened in another locale a few blocks to the west (see below).

Summary. In short, we have seen one instance of a neighborhood organization abandoning its downscale sections, but simultaneously adding other portions for specific purposes; some other neighborhood leaders reported similar constrictions. These shifts may have been driven somewhat by the symbolic communities processes described by Hunter. The leaders were seeking to more clearly differentiate their locales from lower-income or less stable or more problem-ridden or racially different adjoining locations. But at the same time, a focus on the specific strategies pursued by the leaders provides additional, crucial insights. The alterations pursued can sometimes reflect processes opposite to those suggested by the symbolic communities perspective; such processes only make sense by closely examining the specific context to gain some insight into how the leaders hoped to enhance neighborhood use value.

Resisting Add-Ons. Less complex than the repositioning in Sherman Heights was the situation found in several neighborhoods with areas appended in the 1990 map. Some of the appendages were locations previously labeled unorganized; others were preexisting neighborhoods. Several leaders in our sample resisted these add-ons. They often justified the rejection by referring to differences in homeownership. In one instance, a leader alluded to a status difference. Race issues were never mentioned. Colfax was one neighborhood drawing firm distinctions between itself and an adjoining community perceived as less than equal.

Colfax, developed by the Roland Park Company in the 1920s, does not exactly fit the pattern of its better-known sibling neighborhoods. This may be because the development was only partially completed when the Depression hit, and the original tract was not labeled Colfax until 1949, according to the leader interviewed. It was not clear if the local community group exercised the same powers as such groups in the other communities developed by the Roland Park Company. In the 1990 mapping, the city "added" the area north of Hamlin Avenue, one labeled Unorganized 9 in 1979, and another area as well, around a now demolished hospital. Our interviewee objected to both those changes. He saw the area north of Hamlin Avenue as one where the overall quality and upkeep was not the equal of Colfax's.

It was the case that economic differences existed, as suggested by the leader. Colfax's 1990 house value percentile score was 92; Unorganized 9's was 87. The racial differences, however, were more sizable. Colfax went from 1% to 20% to 41% African-American from 1970 to 1980 to 1990; Unorganized 9 went from 19% to 50% to 77% African-American, integrating and resegregating at a faster rate than Colfax. Adding in this area would make Colfax's own integrated composition more heavily African-American.

The leader's rejection of the proposed merger appears to illustrate the symbolic communities perspective. If the original boundaries could be retained, the neighborhood composition would be less predominantly African-American in a part of town that had been becoming progressively more African-American.

Of course, the vantage point of outside agencies, such as the Department of Planning, may have been diametrically opposed. The merger suggested in the official 1990 neighborhood mapping of Unorganized 9 with Colfax, like the merger discussed earlier in the Smithton area, may have been another instance of boundary work softening the picture of local racial change. Unorganized 9's racial changes in the 1970s and 1980s are less obvious once the area is folded into Colfax. I cannot speak to the intended purpose of the boundary work, not having been privy to the relevant discussions. Planners may just have had to put Unorganized 9 someplace and decided it was most physically similar to Colfax.

Splinters Take Root. A part of a neighborhood may emerge as a separate neighborhood. The separation can come about for any number of reasons. At the most general, the forces behind the separation can either be internal to the neighborhood or external. Conflict theorists such as Logan and Molotch emphasize the manipulation of neighborhood boundaries and identities by outside interests seeking political or economic gain. These examples surfaced. But the externally instigated change may take place for impartial reasons as well. Furthermore, instances emerged where internal actors started the splintering process. Here too a wide range of reasons were at work. Externally and internally driven changes are considered in turn.

Externally Driven Changes. Concocted by realtors in the 1970s, the Hobart Improvement Association represents a classic case of outside agents hoping to create an upscale real estate market. Stretching east of York Road, Hobart is a small, narrow neighborhood of tree-lined streets and detached, large, shingle-style houses. To its north is an upscale shopping area put in a few years back. Not too far away on York Road, the art deco Senator Theatre towers over a smaller cluster of shops. Immediately to the south is Wheeler. The streets there are less tree-lined than Hobart's, and we find modest two-story brick row houses rather than larger, detached, frame houses.

The leader we interviewed in one of the larger homes in Hobart Improvement readily admitted that a realtor sought to distinguish the local housing market from the less prestigious housing just to the south (Wheeler) by promoting the separate neighborhood. Compared to its immediate southern neighbors, Hobart does look different.

But when we look at the overall fabric, differences between the two neighborhoods are noticeable but not as sizable as one might expect. Hobart's house value percentile is about 15 points higher, but Wheeler has more homeowners: 80% in 1990 versus 57% in 1990 for Hobart. Racial differences exist, in the expected direction, but they are not overwhelming. Both were predominantly white in 1970: 95% for Wheeler, 89% for Hobart. By 1980, Hobart was about 43% African-American and stayed at about that level through 1990. Wheeler was 41% African-American in

1980, but continued to integrate, becoming 56% African-American by 1990. It is plausible that the higher house prices in Hobart and the separate identity may have been partially responsible for slowing further racial integration there in the 1980s. The distinctions drawn between these two neighborhoods may illustrate Hunter's point that symbolic community boundaries can retard local racial change processes.

Despite the apparently self-serving motivation of the realty agents carving out Hobart, sometimes external agents detach a section of a neighborhood to funnel resources there. The designation of urban renewal areas represent cases in point. As mentioned above, neighborhoods such as Upton, Harlem Park, and Park Heights became designated urban renewal areas in the 1960s. Of course, the "benefits" provided by urban renewal in these areas have been questioned (40). Nevertheless, the process continued, albeit at a far slower pace, in the 1980s. For example, Garfield Heights, as mentioned above, was severed from Southwest Neighbors so that it could receive targeted funds.

Similarly, the public housing community located in Elmton was separated by planners from the surround in the 1990 map so that the interior community could receive targeted funds. The division, however, may have deepened white Elmtonites' estrangement from their African-American neighbors in the public housing community. The Elmton leader we interviewed suggested that differences between those in the public housing community and surrounding residents may have contributed somewhat to problems in Elmton. I do not know if this leader's views were similar before the mapping partition. Regardless of the impacts on leaders' and residents' views, the new configuration, made for specific funding purposes, accents and symbolically reinforces existing racial differences. These racial differences appeared less extreme, presuming the census data were correct, than I would have expected from the leader's comments. Department of Planning neighborhood statistics for 1990 showed Elmton as 5% African-American, and Elmton Homes, the public housing community, as 36% African-American.

Internally Driven Changes.   Turning from partitions engineered by outside actors to those devised by stakeholders inside the neighborhood, an even more complex array of motives emerges. Sometimes these motives are clear; sometimes they are not.

One case of a neighborhood splitting off, apparently driven by one issue, appeared in South Baltimore.[16] South Baltimore is a large, predominantly blue-collar, white neighborhood. Just to its north sits Federal Hill. Federal Hill sits just south of the Inner Harbor in Baltimore. Federal Hill experienced widespread gentrification in the 1970s; many would now view it as a tonier address. The opening of Oriole Park at Camden Yards, to the north and west of these neighborhoods, in the early 1990s, spurred neighborhood organization initiatives in these locales as they strove to cope with the attendant fan parking problems. By late 1996, supports for the new NFL football stadium poked skyward; it was completed in 1997 and hosted games for the latter portion of the Ravens' schedule that year. Constructing the football stadium erased about 5,000 parking spaces, previously used by fans attending baseball games at Camden Yards just to the north. Parking was an extremely serious issue in the neighborhoods close to these stadia.

In January 1997, responding to a December 1996 article in the *Baltimore Sun* on the Federal Hill neighborhood, a local leader announced the existence of the Federal Hill South neighborhood (16). In existence since the early 1990s, and "grown" from an earlier block club near Riverside Park, the new neighborhood organization claimed a substantial portion of South Baltimore. Splitting off appears to have solved residents' parking problems. "As a distinct neighborhood, the city gave us our own permit parking area, Area 19."[17] The break with South Baltimore achieved a specific functional benefit for residents.[18] The separation was a way for the leaders to cope with a pressing issue: scarce parking.

These functional concerns, however, do not mean that stratification processes are dormant. The name chosen by the new group suggests an effort to borrow prestige from its fashionable neighbor to the north, styling itself as an outgrowth of the latter. Granted, other obvious name choices were unsatisfactory for their own reasons. Riverside was too limiting, referring to the park and a street, suggesting an overgrown block club. North South Baltimore would have been too confusing. The new name, Federal Hill South, helps blur the distinction between the new organization and the nearby, higher-status neighborhood. The blurring fits with Hunter's symbolic communities perspective, with lower-status communities seeking to shrink distinctions between themselves and higher-status adjoining neighborhoods.

But more than borrowed prestige may be at issue here; actual change may be partially responsible as well. The leader's comments advise that the issue was complex. He made the case that demographic changes in the locale—newer, upscale residents; more widespread renovation; and "identification with Federal Hill"—all validated the new name chosen. It was not just a case of inappropriate status climbing. He argued a status shift had taken place due to different in-migrants. I did not have readily available data to check those claims, but this example appears to demonstrate how an overriding quality of life issue for local residents, dynamics linked to rank, and demographic neighborhood change, intertwined as a neighborhood evolved a distinct identity. To focus on just one of these threads would result in missing the richness of the interlocking strands.

Sometimes portions of a neighborhood split off and endure as a separate neighborhood; other efforts prove more transitory. Although we do not know yet the long-term viability of Federal Hill South, three other splinters, two apparently longer term, one more transitory, surfaced in our interviews.

East Parkview emerged as a neighborhood separate from Canton in the 1970s, championed by one local leader in particular. Canton is a predominantly white, blue-collar area, stretching north from the waterfront well east of Fells Point to Patterson Park in East Baltimore. Historically, Canton was home to cannery workers, who walked to work sites near the waterfront (51), and to large numbers of Polish immigrants. Fells Point has a relatively lively bar scene, and numerous bars can be found in nearby East Parkview as well. Since the 1960s, Fells Point, and more recently East Parkview, have been "contested terrain as opposing groups have sought to direct changes in the community to conform to their own competing interests" (51: 137): homeowners, developers, younger urbanites, and preservationists.

Since its founding in the mid-1970s, East Parkview, according to the district planner we interviewed, has become well known in the gay community nationwide as a good place to buy a house. Housing, up until 1990, was cheaper there than in adjoining neighborhoods. But its house value percentile score climbed from 13 in 1980 to 81 in 1990, whereas Canton's went from the twenty-third to the fifty-third percentile. Fells Point's 1990 house value percentile score, 88, was comparable to East Parkview's. By the end of the 1980s, East Parkview, termed by the district planner as a "poor relation of Canton," had reversed its position. The splinter neighborhood has developed a distinct reputation, despite a community organization seen by the district planner as "weak," "nominal," and "dormant most of the time."[19] East Parkview's distinctiveness appeared to depend not on the representing organization, but instead on geographical position, proximity to a better-known neighborhood, and subcultural appeal to the broader gay community At this time, it appears that East Parkview is likely to survive as a distinct locality for the near future at least; alternatively, it may be appended to Fells Point, given the growing sociodemographic similarity of the two on some attributes.[20]

More transitory, but inspired like East Parkview by one local leader, was Moreham. A former leader of the Groveland Improvement Association spearheaded the breakaway effort, cutting Moreham out of Groveland I in the late 1980s.[21] The Groveland leader we interviewed calmly discussed the uprising, noting that when the leader ran out of funds, the larger Groveland association took back the Moreham members with no fuss. Our interviewee, generally guarded in his remarks, did not reveal the issues underlying the breakaway; it may have been no more than personal differences between local leaders. But the splintering lasted less than six years.

The northeast section of town is home also to Burnham, the neighborhood with one of the largest populations in the city. A predominantly white, blue-collar, working-class neighborhood historically, Burnham has experienced some integration in recent years, especially in one section, and more class mixing in the broader locale. In the 1990 mapping, planners detached from Burnham an area called Square One, a four-block by four-block section on the very southern edge of Burnham, bordering Nova on the south. (Nova has been at least 98% African-American since 1990.) The Square One segment is cut off from the rest of Burnham by high-volume streets and a large nonresidential land use. Driving through Square One in mid-1995, I noticed a predominantly African-American population of all ages and a smaller number of elderly whites. Residents there appeared more predominantly African-American than in the rest of Burnham. Department of Planning neighborhood statistics described Square One as over 80% African-American in 1990.[22]

Burnham's leaders—we interviewed two of them together—provided only vague comments on Square One's separation, although they did suggest the differences existed long before 1990. Although Square One was the "oldest part of the community," according to one leader, in the late 1960s or early 1970s there "was a big integration movement—speculators came in, bought homes and converted them into rental units."[23] According to the leader, at the time this happened Square One's leadership concluded that Burnham was not representing their area's interests; Square One felt that the two areas had "totally different issues." The leaders interviewed were not sure about the role that racial concerns may have played in these developments, but suspected they were relevant. Nonetheless, the leaders stressed that despite "bad blood" in the past, since about 1990 the two areas have been "mending fences" and are "talking now."

The above leaders' comments suggest Square One established a separate identity, including a separate organization with a racial makeup different from Burnham's, well before the late 1970s, when our mapping was done and that in recent years the two groups have worked together more closely. The recognition of Square One by planners in the 1990 map trailed these developments by at least a decade. In addition, the 1990 recognition occurs in the context of increasing racial integration in the broader Burnham community. Burnham's overall racial makeup went from 1% to 12% to 36% African American from 1970 to 1980 to 1990, with Square One included.[24] Although the differences in racial makeup between the two are still sizable, they are probably much less than they were a decade ago. In short, the formal recognition of Square One not only lags behind the neighborhood formation but also appears *after* the period of the most notable racial differences between Burnham and Square One, which was probably at least ten years prior.

By labeling Square One a separate area, Burnham's leaders and residents distanced themselves from nearby, predominantly African-American populations. To their southeast is a neighborhood over 60% African-American in 1990; to their northeast is another one, also over 60% African-American. On the immediate southern and eastern boundaries, Burnham's residents are buffered from racial change by a variety of non-residential land uses. But beyond these buffers to the south are neighborhoods with populations more than 75% African-American. Further north are several neighborhoods less than 25% African-American in 1990.

In many ways, in the early 1990s, Burnham was positioned as a "gatekeeper" for further racial change up the two main arterial routes in and out of the city in this quadrant. Symbolically, splitting off Square One from Burnham in 1990 may have more closely aligned the latter's image with the more predominantly white neighborhoods further away from the city center. In short, this may be a case of boundary work linked to efforts to slow recognition of racial change.

Coming of Age.   We interviewed leaders in two locales labeled in 1979 as unorganized, but with functioning organizations by the mid-1990s.[25] One locale illustrates dynamics *opposite* those expected given Hunter's discussion of symbolic communities and place-based stratification processes. The second illustrates contextual disadvantages leaders may experience in making the transition from unorganized to recognized locale.

In the northern section of the York Road corridor, just west of York Road, one finds a neighborhood of shingle-style, detached homes perched on moderate-sized lots. As of 1990, over half the households reported managerial or professional occupations; about one fourth of the population was sixty-five or older. Population has declined from 575 in 1970 to 504 in 1980 to 383 in 1990. The number of households has declined only slightly: 231 to 234 to 214 over the same period. The area is about two thirds homeowners. It was labeled in 1979 by us as Unorganized 19, and in 1990 by the Department of Planning as Maple-Adams. We asked the leader how and why the organization developed. She told us the following.

In the late 1980s, an energetic resident piloted an organizing effort. Why is not clear. According to the leader, who had lived in the area since the 1960s, one goal was to act as "sort of a watchdog," keeping an eye on architectural upkeep. She reported that increasing numbers of elderly householders—reflected in the declining population but steady number of households—were finding it more difficult to keep their homes up.

The locals hoped that an organization could assist them. On the eastern edge of the neighborhood, new construction had arisen about the same time, and residents probably wanted to keep an eye on that as well. Crime was not mentioned as a concern for organizing residents. It seems likely though that residents hoped to address that as well, since crime was increasing along the York Road corridor at about the same time.

Just to the north of Maple-Adams sits Pineland, discussed earlier in the chapter. Symbolic community processes would lead us to expect that Maple-Adams would adopt a name capturing or at least hinting at Pineland's prestige, as Federal Hill South appeared to have done. The prestige differential was reflected in part by differences in house prices: The average 1990 price in Pineland was around $169,000; in Maple-Adams it was around $105,000. Historical precedent for a related name existed. When homes went up in Maple-Adams in the 1920s, the development was called Pine Park. Furthermore, a nearby community newspaper merges Maple-Adams's crime reports with Pineland's. The leader also reported that many outsiders referred to the locale as Pineland. So a name echoing Pineland, such as Pine Park, would seem likely.

Instead, when the organizing residents selected and voted on names, they adopted Maple-Adams, referring to the two main streets in the locale. They deliberately turned their collective back on their more elegant neighbor to the north. Admittedly, the details behind this process are lost. Pineland personnel, with their historically and legally sanctified boundaries, may have expressed frustration about the confusion prior to the organizing effort, and Maple-Adams organizers may have sought to avoid future rancor. Or most of the people at the meeting or meetings in question may have lived on Maple Avenue or Adams Road. Or, having failed to project a clear image in the preceding years, the locals may have opted for distinctiveness over borrowed rank. Nevertheless, the striking point here is that even though historical precedent was available for adopting a name that would have linked the locale with a higher-status neighbor, and even though symbolic community dynamics expect such an outcome, it did not occur. Local considerations outweighed these broader forces.

The constraining influence of local concerns surfaced more clearly in the emergence of an organization from an area we labeled Unorganized 20 in 1979. In East Baltimore, it is bounded on the west by Patterson Park. The location covers several square blocks of densely packed, two- and three-story row houses. The area is much smaller in size than the neighboring neighborhoods.

The leader we interviewed for the Eastern Community Association reported that four people had formed the organization, which covered an area we mapped in 1979 as Unorganized 20, around 1991. They hoped to do something about problems in the area with kids, drugs, and crime. People felt "something had to be done." The leader emphasized that when forming the group, those involved were careful not to "go over" the boundaries of other community associations. They respected these other associations, even though one organization further to the east, had "folded" a year or two earlier, according to our interviewee.

In short, the leader here was limited by the configuration of adjoining organizations, and respected those, even though one was inactive. He also sought to work collaboratively with local coalitions and mentioned those to which the Eastern Community Association belonged. Like the Maple-Adams organizers, he respected his stronger brethren.

Minor Fiddles. As mentioned earlier, neighborhood mappers in the Department of Planning were required to include nonresidential locations in neighborhoods. Consequently, most of the appending of these locations to neighborhoods is not that meaningful. But we did find cases where local leaders sought the change and cases where it caused concern. As an example of the former, the Morgan leader agreed with the city's inclusion in his neighborhood of a storage area for a business. He hoped that its inclusion would allow him to prevent its use as a dumping ground and respond to problems there, such as abandoned cars. In another neighborhood, an older white leader expressed concern on finding that the city had appended a small park to his neighborhood. Even though he liked the park and thought more parents should be out in it playing ball with their kids, he was concerned that the city might expect the local association to cut the grass there and contribute to upkeep. So in these two cases, we see nonresidential appending with markedly different reactions.

Implications: Can Police-Community Partnerships Organize Around Neighborhood Units?

Change versus stability in name and boundaries reflects far more than just ecological shifts versus stability. Local politics and organizational and interorganizational dynamics enter as well. How possible is it, given the patterns seen here, for a police-community partnership to use local neighborhood organizations as the organizing unit, instead of police beats? The patterns seen here suggest what police may expect under worst case and best case scenarios and the scenarios in between. For the in-between scenarios, I suggest a range of dynamics that are likely to influence the development of partnerships. Before committing to a partnership development process centered on existing neighborhoods, police leaders may wish to solicit input from local planners and political scientists to learn how many of the neighborhoods in their city fall into the best case, worst case, and in-between scenarios. The feasibility of initiatives centered on local organizations is likely to vary dramatically not only by community but also from city to city.

Worst Case Scenarios

In worst case scenarios, police may partner with an organization that is only weakly, or perhaps decreasingly, representative of the residents. Instances emerged in this investigation where boundaries and organizational recognition were shifting as racial composition was shifting as well, but not necessarily in ways that acknowledged those shifts. It is not unusual that in a racially changing neighborhood, extant organizations, even though they become decreasingly representative of residents over time, may still produce leaders who are recognized by outside interests (43). The disadvantage is that an outside agency, such as a police department, not knowing the internal dynamics, invests in partnering with the wrong partner. The data reviewed suggest this problem will crop up at a low-to-moderate rate.

Best Case Scenarios

In best case scenarios, police could partner with a stable organization boasting stable and effective leadership, representing all or most of the residential groupings nested in the locale in question, with agreement over time between that organization and adjoining ones on the nonoverlapping and, it is to be hoped, unchanging spatial limits of the area served. If these conditions obtained, police would enjoy several advantages. They would have a clear sense of who their partner is in the community policing enterprise. Questions about organizational legitimacy would not arise. Furthermore, police would have a clear sense of the population targeted for service delivery and the space within which those services are expected. The review here did surface some cases of such stability, particularly in high-status, predominantly white, legally empowered organizations.

At the same time at least one of the current cases—Oakwell—suggests that in such neighborhoods, even though the community character and political profile make it ideally suited to police-community coproduction, such partnering may not work. The reason is the community's expectations. The residents may seek more from the police than the latter can deliver, and so may go on to make alternate arrangements that supplement the police department's services. Communities like these may be more likely to make supplemental arrangements in times of increasing crime rates. As crime generally worsens in a city, it seems more likely that a police department will find it harder to provide the deterrence a high-status, stable, politically connected neighborhood might seek. So, depending on how frequently neighborhoods like Oakwell make supplemental security arrangements, it may turn out that locations ideally suited to coproduction will not partner with police because community expectations are too high.

In-Between Scenarios and Potential Concerns for Partnerships

Depending on the city or county, some number of neighborhoods targeted by the police for partnership development are likely to fall between the worst case scenario—organizations largely unrepresentative of the locale—and the best case scenario—stable and effective organization around a fixed area. What issues are likely to surface for police when dealing with such midrange scenarios? In cases where names or boundaries or both undergo shifts, what obstacles to community policing partnerships are likely to emerge?[26] In what specific ways is delivery of community policing services or coproduction of neighborhood improvements impaired? I suggest the following issues deserve consideration.

1. The police organize their work in terms of beats and districts (31). An organization-centered community policing partnership might work, and over time police officers involved largely in the coproduction might be able to reorient to the neighborhood perspective. But if and as these neighborhood organizations undergo name and leader shifts, or questions arise about the representativeness of such groups, it will be all that much harder for the problem-oriented police to make the shift to a neighborhood-centered perspective. The pull back to a beat-, district-, or precinct-centered framework for organizing the partnerships will be all the stronger.

2. If the police are constantly getting acquainted with new community partners, this not only has implications for their organizational frame of reference but also affects the time they need to develop a working relationship where each side trusts and understands the other. If organizations come and go, each purporting to represent an area, it becomes more difficult for the police to gain insight into the goals and capabilities of the local leaders. In addition, organizational shifts, particularly if they are accompanied by boundary shifts, mean the police must constantly reassure themselves that the group in question legitimately represents the area and population in question.

From the community perspective, if varying organizations move into and out of the coproduction process, due to the boundary and naming work described above, the community leaders must constantly be reassured of officers' trustworthiness. Furthermore, the patterns seen here suggest the locations where organizations are most likely to be in flux are also the communities where residents' distrust of and apprehension about the police are likely to be strongest, creating even greater impediments to partnership building.

To expand on the last point, there are obstacles, on the community side, spawned by these fluctuations in organizations, beyond the task-oriented difficulties created. Attitudes toward the police are more antagonistic in lower-income communities and in communities with more residents of color (22, 46). Residents in such communities think they have excellent reason *not* to trust the police. Such suspicions make it extremely difficult for community policing partnerships to work even in neighborhoods with stable boundaries and organizations. These suspicions will probably run deeper and probably take even longer to overcome if the relevant community actors in the partnership are turning over regularly. Analyses reported earlier showed that boundaries were more likely to change from one mapping to the next in more predominantly African-American communities, and residents were less likely to recognize the original neighborhood name in more predominantly African-American communities. If these results hold generally, it means that service areas will be least clearly defined, and locational identity as it is defined here will be the weakest, in exactly those locales where police are least trusted as partners in the coproduction of safety.[27]

3. If in changing locations—places where neighborhood boundaries are redrawn or representing organizations shift—identification by residents with the locale is weaker, because the neighborhood image is more vague, two possibilities follow: Residents are probably less motivated to contribute to efforts to improve neighborhood safety; and the organization itself is probably less effective—given less experience—at generating widespread involvement in such initiatives. The weaker the image is, the weaker the attachment, and consequently the weaker the results of mobilization efforts. In short, in locales where names or boundaries are shifting, enduring local features probably reduce neighborhood attachment and, in turn, residents' willingness to contribute to collective improvement efforts.

4. Little organizational loyalty builds up over time if the organization is changing all the time. Each new organization needs to relegitimate itself in the eyes of its constituency. This creates not only mobilization difficulties and blocks to leadership legitimacy, but also slows down the process of gaining citizen input on proposed initiatives. It is probably *less* troublesome for residents if a single organization changes leaders fre-

quently, as long as the leaders prove effective and maintain a relatively constant policy direction despite the leadership shifts.

5. When boundaries are in flux, the chances increase that an organization from outside the neighborhood will try to represent that neighborhood. In the face of the relatively dormant East Parkview organization, our respondent there told us of three groups attempting to represent the area, for example. Such dynamics create further impediments to citizen mobilization in support of a legitimate, internal organization.

6. Returning for a moment to the officers' perspective, boundary shifts similarly would retard officers' transition to a neighborhood-based problem arena. The officers in question might redefine the program area, and the relevance of the program elements to the shifting locale, in light of organizational changes. But even if they did, boundary shifts also may slow actual program delivery. Or officers might ignore boundary shifts once programs are under way. Alternatively, in reaction to the fluctuations officers might revert to a district- or beat-based focus, their default organizing unit (31).

7. Some locations are at a perpetual contextual disadvantage. If a neighborhood's layout, history, and boundaries fail to provide a clear identity; if the neighborhood is surrounded by larger, higher-profile locales; if the neighborhood is small and thus has only a small leadership pool to draw on for the leaders of its organization, it is going to have difficulty mobilizing large segments of its population and getting recognition from outside organizations.

In sum, the ongoing shifts in neighborhood boundaries or in the organizations representing them, taking place in numerous locations throughout the city, make it harder for police and community organizations to form partnerships. Such partnerships undergird effective coproduction of public safety. The delivery of appropriate community policing services is also impeded.

The implications of the dynamics reviewed here further compound differences police will have partnering with predominantly lower-income or African-American neighborhoods, particularly if the focus is on reduction of incivilities. The material here suggests name or boundary changes, or both, may be frequent in more predominantly African-American neighborhoods. In addition, we saw (Chapter 4) that incivilities were more likely to increase in lower-income locations. Further, policing work suggests that police officers are most likely to tune out disorderly conditions and behaviors in settings where they are the most frequent—the lower-income communities (31). And it is in lower income and African-American communities where mistrust of police may run the highest (Chapter 7). In short, the instabilities surrounding neighborhood identification and representation described here add to the difficulties already experienced by lower-income or African-American communities in forming such partnerships for the coproduction of public safety.

Integrating with Neighborhood Governance

Some form of decentralized but recognized neighborhood government may provide an answer to some of the difficulties described above. In many cities, several powers, and sometimes funds as well, are delegated to neighborhood units. Neighborhood governance occurs in many different forms (23: 243–244) in different cities, and neighborhood structures have more or less political clout from city to city (7, 9, 12, 60, 61). Some cities have recognized neighborhood councils, with which city hall negotiates. Others have different varieties of neighborhood development corporations. Some cities contain more than one type of neighborhood governance structure.

But the key idea throughout these different forms is that the city government invests a local, representative organization with specific powers and resources. For example, neighborhood councils in many cities have modest funds from the municipal authority and provide input to local leaders on a range of issues (23: 70–71). The amount of power and resources delegated to these organizations varies widely across cities (12). The strength of these units is often inverse to the strength of the ward political system (23: 70). The city of Baltimore, of course, had a strong political ward system, suggesting that powerful neighborhood councils are unlikely to be endorsed there.

But the power of Baltimore's ward-based political machinery has faded considerably. A Baltimore political scientist, when asked to comment on the twenty-seven mayoral candidates campaigning for primary votes in the spring and summer of 1999, blamed the weakness of the pool in part on the demise of ward-based political clubs in the city. Crenson suggested that participation in ward-based politics helped season candidates for future citywide office (50). He urged a restoration of these local political processes. From our perspective, however, the demise of those processes might signal a window of opportunity for installing a formalized neighborhood governance structure.

It is not clear at this time whether a rejuvenated ward political system or officially sanctioned and empowered neighborhood governance would be preferable for Baltimore. Arguing the advantages and disadvantages of each is beyond the scope of this volume. And certainly neighborhood councils, in addition to the advantages they provide through decentralization, create problems as well (23: 72–73). Nevertheless, there may be substantial advantages for the delivery of community policing services in the context of recognized neighborhood councils.

If the city were to officially define neighborhoods, designate the representative organization, suggest guidelines for the local elections to the organization, provide those organizations with maintenance funds, and clearly explain the rights accorded to them, some of the problems noted above regarding delivery of community policing services may diminish. Police personnel would know where the neighborhood began and ended and who represented it. Such clarity should speed up the processes of partnership development: identifying objectives, defining target population and locale, encouraging local mobilization, and agreeing on program elements to be implemented. Since the partnership development process would be embedded in the organizations themselves, stronger commitment from those groups might emerge.

From the police perspective, of course, the impediments noted above would persist. The police will still want to orient toward their default operational stance, around beats and districts. But at least the suggested proposal, by providing the officers with stable community partners who are each linked to a fixed locale, would increase the chances of moving officers away from their focus on administrative units. Of course, in the long run these neighborhood units might be incorporated in police administration. Portland, Oregon, for example, reports crime statistics on a neighborhood-by-neighborhood basis.

In considering community policing service delivery within a neighborhood governance structure, it is instructive to contrast it with the governance surrounding the beat-based community policing program, CAPS, in Chicago, started in 1993; that structure has emerged to facilitate police-community communication and planning. Meetings are held at the beat level, and a community structure has evolved at both the beat and the district level. For example, at the beat level there are beat facilitators, "volunteers from the community who train beat teams in creating community-police partnerships and work on making problem solving happen" (4: 56). At the district level, district advisory committees "composed of residents, business owners and other stakeholders in the community are charged with helping the commander identify broad issues related to crime and disorder" (4: 64). In short, it appears that the ongoing project serves as a vehicle for CAPS to establish neighborhood governance structures, oriented to crime, related issues, and the police department. Will such structures persist and demonstrate continuing utility given that they are oriented around a police administrative unit rather than an ecological unit? What are the implications for the longevity of these governance structures should community policing priorities in the department wane following an administrative shift or a change in the nature of the city's crime problem? Would a neighborhood-based structure be more effective than the current beat-based structure where, despite the facilitators and committees, "resident attendance continues to be a problem in many districts" (4: 54)?

Although reliance on formal neighborhood councils to help create community-police partnerships may alleviate some of the above difficulties, there certainly would be disadvantages as well. Hunter has noted the volatility of definitions of symbolic communities has both advantages and disadvantages. Fixing, legitimizing, and empowering neighborhood units over time takes away the flexibility inherent in the concept of symbolic communities. These definitions can no longer shift or be manipulated to respond to, ignore, or hasten ongoing ecological changes in or surrounding an area.

Nonetheless, despite a potential crippling of some of the functions served by symbolic communities for residents, the advantages of formal neighborhood councils may outweigh the disadvantages—at least in some parts of town. As already mentioned, it would help build community policing initiatives. Turning to broader issues of neighborhood viability, an officially sanctioned and empowered neighborhood and corresponding organization may encourage resident identification with the locale, especially in those parts of town where neighborhood changes have been most common. Attachment to neighborhood, identification with it, and participation in its organization all may increase.

Glowing possibilities aside, one could argue, given the volume of neighborhood change seen here in a short, fifteen-year span, that created neighborhood councils would become increasingly unwieldy over time. As ongoing demographic changes alter perceived community boundaries, neighborhood councils' spatial correspondence with those boundaries may decrease over time, leading them to be viewed as irrelevant by locals. Perhaps such decreasing spatial correspondence could be minimized by mandated review of the boundaries every ten years. But such reviews might lead to the same instability the councils were intended to eliminate in the first place.

Another set of limitations stem from police officers' potential unwillingness to accept such council-based contact organizations. As Klinger has pointed out, police work has a built-in bias against moving away from the territorially focused police work groups centered on beats and districts. But even if we put this concern aside for the moment, police acceptance of the groups perhaps may *decrease* as the organizations become more effective. If organizations put increasing pressure on the police department for services, or for reform, officers may become increasingly antagonistic toward the associations.

As the above discussion suggests, the pros and cons of such a proposal are complex. I am not sure that neighborhood councils represent *the* answer to the difficulties brought to police-community partnerships by neighborhood volatility over time. But they do represent a possibility that may be worth exploring.

Summary

This chapter examined changes in neighborhood naming and bounding, relying primarily on interviews with leaders and census and crime information about those neighborhoods. These processes affect the development of police-community partnerships. These partnerships are important tools for reducing social and physical incivilities and, more generally, for supporting the wide array of collective crime prevention initiatives pursued by community organizations.

The previous chapter revealed that neighborhood organizations pursue an extremely broad array of anticrime initiatives. Their efforts have not been completely co-opted by the attention given in the media and in policy circles to incivility reduction. Aspects of neighborhood fabric such as race; status; and, to a lesser extent, stability affected how residents and leaders viewed both the police and the crime problem. This chapter turned to another feature of neighborhood fabric, changes in boundaries or names, or both. These were revealed by a comparison of 1990 and 1979 neighborhood maps and by leader interviews. These shifts also seem likely to affect the development of police-community partnerships and coproduced public safety more generally (45). Klinger has sketched out a theoretical framework describing how police respond to "minor" crimes and disorder; the framework considers both the way police work is organized and variations in community structure (31). The purpose here was to examine these same issues in light of both the volume and patterning of changes in neighborhood boundaries and names. The first goal was to understand how features of context, including the local political climate, linked to the changes. The second goal was to use the linkages found and explore the implications for both police-community partnership development and the delivery of community policing services.

Examining earlier work on neighborhood naming and bounding suggested several points. Some neighborhoods are more distinctive, with more easily recognized names and boundaries, than others, the clarity of their image based on historical factors, relative economic status, ecological features, or other factors. Other neighborhoods present less vivid images, with boundaries less readily recognized and names less easily recalled. Though neighborhoods represent an important feature of local urban culture, over time the names and boundaries of neighborhoods can shift.

Hunter and others have suggested that relative neighborhood status is one of the most important determinants of neighborhood stability in boundaries and in names. This also appears to be the case for the neighborhoods studied here. But status works as a guarantor of stability for a specific set of complementary functional reasons. More specifically, high-status neighborhoods usually have housing stock and street layouts readily distinguishable from those of the adjoining neighborhoods. A few such instances in our sample were originally designed as "artificial" communities. Such distinctions facilitate clear bounding between them and adjoining locales. That clarity advantages the higher-status neighborhood.

Power and ecology intersect here; this intersection illustrates how attempts to distinguish between impacts arising from a "natural area's" ecology and its position in sociopolitical space would be naïve, as others also have pointed out. But in addition to place distinctiveness, in several instances these high-status neighborhoods have legally empowered local community organizations, deeded by the original developer with particular legal powers. Although much work has stressed how such powerful organizations have advantages in dealing with public officials outside their neighborhood and with other neighborhoods, such powerful organizations also have advantages in dealing with residents in the neighborhood itself. This enhanced capability makes it easier for them to maintain the neighborhood and its house prices. Such enhanced quality probably further enhances neighborhood identity and solidarity.

But stability in naming and bounding also emerges in at least one extremely low status neighborhood. The stability observed emerged from an externally sanctioned name and boundaries, vigorously and repeatedly embraced over several decades by a strong local leader to whom other local leaders deferred. In this case, decisions by external agents at one point in time may have provided an anchor for community identity.

One final finding on place stratification by status also supports earlier work. Several instances appear of slightly higher status locations attempting to differentiate themselves from lower-status nearby locations; that differentiation in this direction is more marked than differentiation in the reverse direction. But this is not uniformly true. At least a couple of instances showed how the blurring and separating might work along very different lines. In one case, a higher-status neighborhood sought to enfold a lower-status, more racially mixed neighborhood. In another instance, a lower-status neighborhood made an effort to distinguish itself from its higher-status, next-door neighbor. The fusing and differentiation in these latter cases operates opposite to the symbolic communities–based arguments. The reasons were the specific functional goals the leaders pursued in these cases. To ignore these goals is to miss an important part of local dynamics. In contrast to the popular saying, demographic context is not everything.

Past work suggests that racial change can result in shifts in neighborhood boundaries and changes in name. I found that in Baltimore as well. Considerable changes in neighborhood racial composition took place in Baltimore neighborhoods during the 1980s. Instances appeared where external agents may have overlooked racial change, may have taken actions effectively masking the degree of change, or may have acted so as to isolate it. The dynamics in each case are complex, and full information about the decisionmaking processes is not available. Again, as with status, the symbolic communities perspective provides partial insight into these cases, but local political dynamics provide important additional explanation.

At least a couple of instances appear where names and boundaries remain intact even as the neighborhood undergoes substantial changes in racial composition. It is not clear why racial succession links to neighborhood boundary or naming shifts only in some circumstances.

Past work also has pointed to other contextual factors leading to name or boundary shifts, and such examples show up here. Local funding needs may demand that outside officials "carve out" a section of a neighborhood. A neighborhood name may become tainted over time, forcing leaders to adopt a new one. Internal leaders may form coalitions as they seek more clout outside of their community. A community may drop an area that has changed in a way that makes it different from the neighborhood core.

From the community perspective, a general theme emerging from the evidence is local leaders' sensitivity to local context; they consider numerous small- and meso-scale features of the locale in making boundary and neighborhood maintenance decisions. Their judgments are highly strategic. This sophisticated decisionmaking appears not only in upper-income, high-status neighborhoods but also in disadvantaged neighborhoods. Many of these leaders are driven by a pragmatism that is neither class nor race bound.

In short, perspectives concentrating on status, political power differentials, racial dynamics, and the neighborhood's physical features help to explain much but not all of the change versus stasis seen here. But focusing just on those issues directs attention away from numerous other examples *that are more contextually bound and strategically driven.* Thus, the frameworks used to approach these issues should be kept broad enough so that significant grounded theorizing, looking beyond a small number of macro-sociological issues, can flourish.

The scope and patterning of changes in neighborhood names and boundaries create special challenges for police personnel seeking to create long-term community policing partnerships between their department and neighborhood constituents. Vehicles for police-community interaction can center either on the police work unit—the beat or the district—or on the neighborhood unit. Whichever model is chosen, the changes viewed here have significant implications for police-community coproduction of safety and order.

Neighborhood volatility—frequent changing of organizations or major changes in neighborhood boundaries—creates problems for community-police partnerships affecting both the community and the police personnel involved. Those complications were noted above. For example, as volatility increases it is more difficult for officers to identify legitimate community representatives, develop working relationships, and agree on the intervention site and program elements. Neighborhoods in some parts of town appear at a particular contextual disadvantage; they are handicapped either by widespread redrawing of neighborhood boundaries in their sector or by powerful, stable nearby neighborhoods, the eminence of which far outweighs their own. The irony appears to be that in exactly those neighborhoods where police-community partnerships are likely to be most needed, the long-term, shift-related impediments to establishing such fruitful partnerships are most widespread.

The volatility of neighborhood names and boundaries cannot be denied. Indeed, a key assumption of the symbolic communities perspective is that such alterations are an essential part of how organizations and individuals adapt to the changes taking place around them. Nevertheless, despite the cognitive, social, and political functions served by such boundary work, it impedes coproduced public safety. Perhaps the volatility should be channeled. Establishment or reinforcement of neighborhood councils may help direct neighborhood change and lessen some of the impediments to successful, long-term police-community partnerships.

Notes

1. The two major changes between the city's procedure and ours were as follows. First, it was required that the city's mapping cover all blocks in the city. Thus, the city often allocated unoccupied residential land, such as small parks, to neighborhoods. It also meant the city was not allowed to submit that an area was unorganized at the time and not covered by an neighborhood association. The 1979 mapping included twenty-six such locations. Second, in the initial mapping, local experts often pointed out that a neighborhood could be composed of several distinct parts. Thus, in a few instances, we mentioned different sections of a neighborhood (e.g., Waltherson I, Waltherson II) and treated them as separate neighborhoods. The 1990 mapping did not allow such segmentation.

2. See the appendix at the end of Chapter 7 for a complete description of the sampling plan.

3. The leader interviews included closed-ended as well as open-ended items; the former were less useful than the latter. In several instances, leaders were will-

ing to talk with us, but did not want to follow the closed-ended question format. In a small number of instances, respondents answered questions with respect to a part of the neighborhood rather than the entire neighborhood. Therefore, the focus here is mostly on the open-ended responses.

4. Hunter is the only researcher of whom I am aware who has carried out a comprehensive, citywide examination of changes in neighborhood names and boundaries.

5. Guest and Lee distinguished between "area" and "neighborhood" in their study of Seattle residents (20). Their term "area" probably falls somewhere between the communities of limited and expanded liabilities.

6. Only 1.8% of our total 1994 respondents provided the "new" 1990 official neighborhood name; not all of our thirty neighborhoods had been renamed by 1990.

7. At the individual level, being able to supply the designated 1979 name was coded 1, all other responses were coded 0. At the neighborhood level, the outcome becomes the proportion of respondents who can supply the designated name. Analyses used generalized hierarchical linear modeling for the nonlinear outcome.

8. Several of our 1994 study neighborhoods were located close to Patterson Park, an extremely large city park on the eastside of town. The neighborhood organizations around the park, and the residents, identified strongly with the park, viewing it as a neighborhood rather than a city facility. Yet not one neighborhood around the park had "Patterson Park" in its name.

9. Analyses with racial dummy variables, using 70% and 80% African-American as the cutoff, for 1980 and 1990, respectively, also were attempted to see if high levels of segregation could predict future residential boundary manipulation. All of these results were nonsignificant. The only result approaching significance ($p < .10$) used 1990 ethnicity and a 70% or higher cutoff. Of the non–African-American neighborhoods, 55% experienced boundary manipulation, compared to 66% of the African-American neighborhoods (phi = .11). In short, focusing on high levels of segregation does not result in a different picture from the results using percentage African-American.

10. We do not know how many of these groups purported to represent the entire neighborhood and how many represented just portions of the neighborhood.

11. "Poor Black neighborhoods are often drawn in stereotypical terms as communities where social and political institutions have badly deteriorated and where antisocial behavior is all too prevalent. . . . In the cities we studied, poor Black neighborhoods and Black neighborhoods of all economic stripes demonstrate relatively high levels of political participation in neighborhood associations" (47: 634).

12. But time marches on. By late 1997, the "Yard" name seems even more widely used by residents and outsiders alike and appears to be, ironically, earning some cachet.

13. It is not known at this time how the drop compares to changes in surrounding neighborhoods or in sociodemographically similar but more distant neighborhoods.

14. Given Podolefsky's model, discussed in Chapter 7, had SH I remained in the proposed district, and its homeowners approved it, they probably would

have favored social problem reduction approaches, rather than victimization prevention approaches. The leader in SH II may have anticipated such differences.

15. Although Sherman Heights and the nearby neighborhoods have been served for at least a couple decades by an umbrella group, according to the Sherman Heights and Spruce leaders relations with the umbrella group have not always been close.

16. South Baltimore was one of our sampled neighborhoods. Although we did not contact the leader from the newly formed neighborhood, I discuss this case because the leader provides some background in his letter to the newspaper.

17. If separate neighborhood organizations are required for permit parking, it seems plausible this might serve as an independent impetus for subneighborhoods to split off.

18. Even though the Federal Hill South leader claimed his organization had been in existence for four years and the area has obtained separate permit parking, the South Baltimore leader we interviewed in early 1995 referred to the group as Riverside and viewed it as mainly concerned with issues around Riverside Park. Given that Federal Hill South was "claiming" a large segment of South Baltimore, it is surprising our South Baltimore leader failed to mention the group.

19. Both the district planner interviewed and the local leader intimated that a particular individual with a high profile locally was partially responsible for the difficulties confronting the local organization.

20. An August 15, 1999, *New York Times* article, reviewing nightlife and dining possibilities in the Fells Point area, lumped East Parkview and Fells Point together (39).

21. Our interviewee did not define Moreham's boundaries.

22. Figures for the separate Square One area were not available for 1980 or 1970.

23. Speculation continues to be a serious problem in the locale. One of the leaders suggested she moved to the neighborhood to help counter what speculators were doing to the neighborhood. Around the time of our fieldwork, a large banner sign was hung on a building announcing "CASH FOR HOMES," only a couple of blocks from the large neighborhood welcome sign. Local leaders protested and the sign was taken down within a couple of weeks. On its web site, the association touts the benefits of homeownership and mentions several programs available to those seeking to own a home.

24. Department of Planning figures for Burnham for 1990, *ex*cluding Square One, report 35–40% African-American. But the department's boundaries for Burnham differed from ours, even if we ignore Square One's removal. In short, it is not possible to recover Burnham's makeup using our boundaries and removing only Square One.

25. As described earlier in the chapter, unorganized areas were not socially disorganized but just not represented by a neighborhood organization at the time of our mapping in 1979.

26. Of course, neighborhood organizations are not the only groups undergoing change; police departments themselves constantly adjust to internal and external alterations. District commanders change, for example. Pressures from external groups, including politicians, vary in their direction and force. Departmental or district-level climates may fluctuate over time. In short, there is instability on *both*

sides of the partnership. Nonetheless, the focus here is solely on the neighborhood side of the partnership.

27. Because this particular form of locational identity is weaker does not necessarily mean other forms also will be weaker. Nor does it mean that the strength of community identification at different levels of aggregation from the one being described here will be weaker.

References

(1) Brower, S. (1996) *Good neighborhoods,* Praeger, Westport, CT.

(2) Chicago Community Policing Evaluation Consortium (1995) *Community policing in Chicago, year 2: An interim report,* Illinois Criminal Justice Information Authority, Chicago.

(3) Chicago Community Policing Evaluation Consortium (1996) *Community policing in Chicago, year 3,* Illinois Criminal Justice Information Authority, Chicago.

(4) Chicago Community Policing Evaluation Consortium (1997) *Community policing in Chicago, year 4: An interim report,* Illinois Criminal Justice Information Authority, Chicago.

(5) Clarke, R. V., and Cornish, D. B. (1985) Modeling offenders' decisions: A framework for research and policy. In *Crime and justice: An annual review of research,* Vol. 6 (Tonry, M., and Morris, N., eds). University of Chicago Press, Chicago.

(6) Covington, J. C., and Taylor, R. B. (1989) Gentrification and crime: Robbery and larceny changes in appreciating Baltimore neighborhoods in the 1970's. *Urban Affairs Quarterly* 25, 142–172.

(7) Crenson, M. (1983) *Neighborhood politics,* Harvard University Press, Cambridge, MA.

(8) DeGiovanni, F. F., and Paulson, N. A. (1984) Household diversity in revitalizing neighborhoods. *Urban Affairs Quarterly* 20, 211–232.

(9) Dilger, R. J. (1992) *Neighborhood politics: Residential community associations in American governance,* New York University Press, New York.

(10) Downs, R. M. (1981) Cognitive mapping: A thematic analysis. In *Behavioral problems in geography revisited* (Cox, K. R., and Golledge, R. G., eds), pp. 95–122. Methuen, New York.

(11) Fee, E. (1991) Evergreen House and the Garrett family: A railroad fortune. In *The Baltimore book: New views of local history* (Fee, E., Shopes, L., and Zeidman, L., eds), pp. 17–38. Temple University Press, Philadelphia.

(12) Ferman, B. (1996) *Challenging the growth machine: Neighborhood politics in Chicago and Pittsburgh,* University of Kansas Press, Lawrence.

(13) Firey, W. (1945) Sentiment and symbolism as ecological variables. *American Sociological Review* 10, 140–148.

(14) Fried, M., and Gleicher, P. (1961) Some sources of residential satisfaction in an urban slum. *Journal of the American Institute of Planners* 27, 305–315.

(15) Gans, H. J. (1962) *The urban villagers,* Free Press, New York.

(16) Gisriel, R. R. (1997) Federal Hill residents are not laughing. *Baltimore Sun* January 11, 11A.

(17) Goldstein, H. (1990) *Problem-oriented policing,* Temple University Press, Philadelphia.

(18) Greene, J. R., and Taylor, R. B. (1988) Community-based policing and foot patrol: Issues of theory and evaluation. In *Community policing: Rhetoric or reality?* (Greene, J. R., and Mastrofski, S. D., eds), pp. 195–224. Praeger, New York.

(19) Guest, A., and Lee, B. A. (1983) Consensus on locality names within the metropolis. *Sociology and Social Research* 67, 374–391.

(20) Guest, A. M., and Lee, B. A. (1984) How urbanites define their neighborhoods. *Population and Environment* 7, 32–56.

(21) Guest, A. M., Lee, B. A., and Stacheli, L. (1982) Changing locality identification in the metropolis: Seattle, 1920–1978. *American Sociological Review* 47, 543–549.

(22) Hagan, J., and Albonetti, C. (1982) Race, class and perception of criminal injustice in America. *American Journal of Sociology* 88, 329–355.

(23) Hallman, H. W. (1984) *Neighborhoods: Their place in urban life,* Sage, Beverly Hills, CA.

(24) Haney, W., and Knowles, E. S. (1978) Perception of neighborhoods by city and suburban residents. *Human Ecology* 6, 201–214.

(25) Heitgard, J., and Bursik, R. (1987) Extracommunity dynamics and the ecology of delinquency. *American Journal of Sociology* 92, 775–787.

(26) Hillery, G. (1955) Definitions of community: Areas of agreement. *Rural Sociology* 20, 111–123.

(27) Hunter, A. (1974) *Symbolic communities,* University of Chicago Press, Chicago.

(28) Hunter, A. (1979) The urban neighborhood: Its analytical and social contexts. *Urban Affairs Quarterly* 14, 267–288.

(29) Janowitz, M. (1951) *The community press in an urban setting,* University of Chicago Press, Chicago.

(30) Keller, S. (1968) *The urban neighborhood,* Random House, New York.

(31) Klinger, D. A. (1997) Negotiating order in police work: An ecological theory of police response to deviance. *Criminology* 35, 277–306.

(32) Kotler, M. (1969) *Neighborhood government,* Bobbs-Merrill, New York.

(33) Land, K. C., McCall, P. L., and Cohen, L. E. (1990) Structural covariates of homicide rates: Are there any invariances across time and social space? *American Journal of Sociology* 95, 922–963.

(34) Lavrakas, P. J., and Herz, E. J. (1982) Citizen participation in neighborhood crime prevention. *Criminology* 20, 479–488.

(35) Lee, B. A., and Mergenhagen, P. M. (1984) Is revitalization detectable? Evidence from five Nashville neighborhoods. *Urban Affairs Quarterly* 19, 511–538.

(36) Lee, T. (1970) Urban neighborhood as social-spatial schema. In *Environmental psychology: Man and his physical setting* (Proshansky, H. M., Ittleson, W. H., and Rivlin, L. G., eds). New York: Holt, Rhinehart and Winston.

(37) Logan, J. R., and Molotch, H. (1987) *Urban fortunes,* University of California Press, Berkeley.

(38) Lynch, K. (1960) *The image of the city,* Massachusetts Institute of Technology Press, Cambridge.

(39) Mansnerus, L. (1999) What's doing in Baltimore. *New York Times* August 15, Travel-1.

(40) McDougall, H. A. (1993) *Black Baltimore: A new theory of community*, Temple University Press, Philadelphia.

(41) Miethe, T. D., and Meier, R. F. (1994) *Crime and its social context*, State University of New York Press, Albany.

(42) Orser, W. E. (1990) Secondhand suburbs: Black pioneers in Baltimore's Edmondson Village, 1955–1980. *Journal of Urban History* 16, 227–262.

(43) Orser, W. E. (1997) Personal communication, July 14.

(44) Orser, W. E. (1991) Flight to the suburbs: Suburbanization and racial change on Baltimore's west side. In *The Baltimore book: New views of local history* (Fee, E., Shopes, L., and Zeidman, L., eds), pp. 203–226. Temple University Press, Philadelphia.

(45) Ostrom, E., Parks, R. B., Whitaker, G. P., and Percy, S. L. (1979) The public service production process: A framework for analysing police services. In *Evaluating alternative law enforcement policies* (Baker, R., and Meyer, F. A., Jr., eds), pp. 65–73. D.C. Heath, Lexington, CT.

(46) Podolefsky, A. (1983) *Case studies in community crime prevention*, Charles C. Thomas, Springfield, IL.

(47) Portney, K. E., and Berry, J. M. (1997) Mobilizing minority communities: Social capital and participation in urban neighborhoods. *American Behavioral Scientist* 40, 632–644.

(48) Relph, E. (1976) *Places and placelessness*, Pion Limited, London.

(49) Ross, H. L. (1962) The local community: A survey approach. *American Sociological Review* 27, 75–84.

(50) Shields, G., and Penn, I. (1999) Candidates a troubled assortment *Baltimore Sun* July 25, 1B [on-line: http://www.sunspot.net; retrieved August 21, 1999].

(51) Shopes, L. (1991) Fells Point: Community and conflict in a working class neighborhood. In *The Baltimore book: New views of local history* (Fee, E., Shopes, L., and Zeidman, L., eds), pp. 121–154. Temple University Press, Philadelphia.

(52) Skogan, W., and Hartnett, S. (1997) *Community policing, Chicago style*, Oxford University Press, New York.

(53) Stiehm, J. (1997) Charles Village celebrates 100th. *Baltimore Sun* February 24, 3B.

(54) Suttles, G. D. (1968) *The social order of the slum*, University of Chicago Press, Chicago.

(55) Suttles, G. D. (1972) *The social construction of communities*, University of Chicago Press, Chicago.

(56) Taylor, R. B. (1997) Social order and disorder of streetblocks and neighborhoods: Ecology, microecology and the systemic model of social disorganization. *Journal of Research in Crime and Delinquency* 33, 113–155.

(57) Taylor, R. B., and Brower, S. (1985) Home and near-home territories. In *Human behavior and environment: Current theory and research*, Vol. 8: *Home environments* (Altman, I., and Werner, C., eds). Plenum, New York.

(58) Taylor, R. B., Brower, S., and Drain, W. (1979) *A map of Baltimore neighborhoods,* Center for Metropolitan Planning and Research, Johns Hopkins University, Baltimore.

(59) Taylor, R. B., Gottfredson, S. D., and Brower, S. (1984) Neighborhood naming as an index of attachment to place. *Population and Environment* 7, 101–111.

(60) Thomas, J. C. (1986) *Between citizen and city: Neighborhood organizations and urban politics in Cincinnati,* University of Kansas Press, Lawrence.

(61) Yates, D. (1973) *Neighborhood democracy: The politics and impacts of decentralization,* Lexington Books, Lexington, CT.

9

Closing Thoughts

This chapter summarizes a few major points from the preceding chapters. It starts by reviewing a couple of key features about the data context. Then we return to the central theoretical questions driving the investigation: What evidence do we find supporting the incivilities thesis, in particular the longitudinal, ecological version? The major findings from the two chapters reviewing community anticrime efforts and neighborhood name and boundary work are revisited. Furthermore, some broad implications for policies of police-community coproduction and neighborhood preservation, as well as some theoretical implications are considered.

Context and Ironies

Recall the comparisons made between Baltimore and other cities. Changes in crime rates for the period 1970–1992, except for perhaps the last four years of the series, do not look dissimilar from shifts in comparably sized cities. Similarly, changes in population, employment, and housing in the 1970s and 1980s look roughly comparable. In short, the structural and crime shifts taking place in Baltimore in the 1970s and 1980s were not atypical.

Such typicality does not guarantee, of course, the external validity of the results found here. Although several key patterns found here have surfaced elsewhere, in places such as Spokane, Chicago, and Minneapolis–St. Paul, the broader external validity of the overall findings remains, as it must, an empirical question. In-depth investigations carried out simultaneously in several different cities would be needed to assess the external validity of what was found here.

Recent changes in Baltimore point out an unanticipated feature of recent history. Our initial expectation was that the 1980s, with increasing crime rates and the crack invasion of the mid and late 1980s, would make an excellent decade in which to explore the impacts of earlier incivilities. But this original presumption was incorrect. It appears the major crime and structural changes took place about a decade earlier.

The bulk of safe neighborhoods in Baltimore disappeared in the 1970s, not the 1980s. Furthermore, the more dramatic structural changes—population losses, decreasing manufacturing jobs in the overall mix, and increasing poverty—appeared in the 1970s, not the 1980s. Chicago neighborhood researchers similarly found the more dramatic increases in structural disadvantage occurred in the 1970s, not the 1980s (16: 41). Numerous crime rates, including homicide, were extremely high around 1980, came down for several years after that, and did not match earlier levels until the 1980s were well over half gone. Looking at the Blocks' and Rosenfeld's data for, respectively, Chicago and St. Louis, I see the same temporal patterns for homicide as was witnessed in Baltimore.

In short, this "background check," although confirming Baltimore's relatively typical scores on many community and crime shifts, revealed two notable ironies. First, the public perception that the city of Baltimore suddenly became much more dangerous, in an unprecedented way, in the late 1980s, was incorrect. What may have been feeding that impression was an increasing gap between the city crime rates and the rates in the rest of the metropolitan area during that period. That differential in violent crime rates widened noticeably beginning in the mid to late 1980s. In addition, the increase in the late 1980s followed several years of declining rates for most crimes.

Second, the Schaefer years (1971–1986) in Baltimore are widely considered a success story for the city: the rebirth of the Inner Harbor, exemplary public-private partnership efforts, revitalized neighborhoods, "dollar houses," and a dramatic rise in Baltimore's national profile. The years following Schaefer's departure, the Schmoke era (1987–1999) are considered much less successful. The irony is that the city experienced substantial decline during the 1970s, the supposed success years, and those declines, for some indicators, may have outpaced the losses of the following decade. Of course, the structural decline Baltimore experienced during the 1970s may have been far more serious were it not for "Hizzoner's" initiatives. The purpose is not to evaluate either the Schmoke or Schaefer administrations, but just to point out that both structural and crime shifts failed to match popular views of the relative success of these two mayors.

Does the Theory Get Support?

Current efforts across the country by community policing officers and problem-solving police officers receive justification in part from the longitudinal, ecological version of the decline and disorder, or broken windows, thesis. Does the theory receive support from the current findings?

Present results generate some support. But that support is neither as consistent across incivilities indicators or as applicable across outcomes as the theoretical statements suggest. The amount of support varies, depending on a host of factors. For each class of outcomes, results provide some support for the longitudinal, ecological version of the incivilities thesis.

Fear, Attachment, and Avoidance

The present results strongly confirm Garofalo and Laub's version of the incivilities thesis focused on fear: Some people are afraid of crime because they see a lot of problems around them. At the individual level, those more fearful than their neighbors are those who see more problems than their neighbors. These overwhelmed residents also see more dangerous places and express less attachment to their locale. But this connection, which the hierarchical models have allowed us to isolate, is a *difference between neighbors, not a difference between neighborhoods*. It is a psychological and social psychological dynamic, rather than an ecological one. The individual-level results reported here are strong and consistent, and have been recently replicated in a reanalysis of a Minneapolis–St. Paul clustered data set (20). Switching to neighborhood dynamics, ecological impacts of earlier incivilities on later changes in neighborhood fear levels, predicted by the Wilson/Kelling/Skogan version of the thesis, do surface for a couple of outcomes. But the explained variance amounts associated with the ecological incivility impacts are modest. Stated differently, the decline and disorder thesis, when it ranges over these psychological outcomes and treats them as ecological outcomes, is partly missing the boat, in part because some of these outcomes vary far more across individuals within the same neighborhood than across neighborhoods. The implications for police fear reduction efforts are several. Consider the following scenario.

Imagine, across a range of neighborhoods, that we could isolate a single condition, such as the amount of graffiti, which completely explained the between-location differences in fear. Imagine further that subsequently we could *completely* eradicate the graffiti.[1] If graffiti were a direct cause of fear, and all residents were aware of their removal, their removal would result in shrinking fear by no more than 4%–15%, depending on the fear breakdown seen in the particular study. In short, under the most optimal conditions, strong limitations on program effectiveness obtain when we focus on between-neighborhoods differences with fear of crime. Such reductions might be substantial, and they might provide data suggesting a powerful program impact (5). I am just pointing out that the focus of the program is on only a modest portion of the total fear problem.

Of course, I am ignoring for the moment the means by which the graffiti are removed. The cleanup campaign may evolve from local community development efforts. Here there might be side effects of the effort itself, such as increased citizen empowerment and more residents getting to know one another through the cooperative effort. These social-psychological outcomes might result in shrinking fear beyond the 4–15% due to graffiti removal itself. By contrast, the removal may occur because community policing officers, after talking with local leaders, enlist city agency personnel to remove the graffiti.[2] In this case the side effects noted above would not accrue.

But the theorists working on this problem maintain that it is the conditions themselves that cause concern. They either do not address how the problem is fixed or argue in favor of a public agency response or initiatives from a public-private partnership. Given such a perspective, we should not presume that additional side effects will necessarily occur. We should not count on shrinking fear beyond the 4%–15% that arises from the conditions themselves.

In short, if public agencies are concerned about reducing residents' fear of crime, and seek to do so by eradicating local ecological conditions that might inspire fear, they are limited to reducing fear only by a small-to-moderate portion. The bulk of the causes of fear arises from differences between residents responding to roughly comparable ecological conditions; these would be largely untouched by a community policing effort built *solely* around the broken windows thesis or a problem-oriented policing framework oriented solely toward grime reduction. Of course, most efforts usually have a significantly higher number of program elements.

To return to a question raised earlier: Yes, we have overecologized fear of crime as a program outcome. But at the same time, the strong individual-level connection can be used to retarget intervention efforts. I have stated earlier that fear and incivilities link very strongly at the individual level. Those who are much more afraid than their neighbors are the ones who are contributing most to fear. These same residents also perceive more serious problems in their neighborhoods. Which causes which is an important question. Does fear ⟶ problems? Do problems ⟶ fear? Or do they feed each other? Or are they both driven by a third process? We do not know at this time.

Assuming residents, including the fearful ones, trust the police—and this is something that varies with the race, stability, and status of the neighborhood (17)—the police want to identify and work with those in a locale whose concerns are the highest. Service delivery, geared toward fear reduction, might be reoriented from a neighborhood focus to an individual focus.[3] The goal is to create some vehicle whereby community policing efforts deliver sufficient reassurances to highly fearful, problem-plagued individuals. The point is to communicate the improvements being made to those whose views of local conditions are most dire. It may be possible to identify those most responsible for locally high fear levels by using calls for service data cross-referenced with actual crime or arrest data.

This suggestion may fit well with current concerns about hot spots. Some hot spots are real hot spots—sites where a bar, a troublesome business, or a tradition of gathering creates real problems. But other places where residents call the police a lot may not be real hot spots. Instead, they may be places where a small number of residents perceive a lot of problems and are concerned. Frequent discrepancies between police-defined hot spots and community-defined hot spots of fear and concern have been documented (13). Consequently, the police may be able—in some types of neighborhoods—to use calls for service data cross-referenced with "real" crime data to determine those places with highly concerned residents, that is, locations with high repeat calls for service but not lots of crime. If fear reduction is the goal, it is those residents who merit being targeted. Of course, moving away from a community-centered perspective and toward a more focused strategy for reactions to crime does not imply abandoning community-focused partnerships around neighborhood stabilization and safety.

For two reasons, these suggestions are offered in a tentative spirit. First, not enough is known about the relationship between perceptions of local problems and actually calling for police service. Being able to locate the most fearful residents successfully, using calls for service data, may not be feasible at this time. But it would seem worth pursuing to learn whether the available archival data permits identifying those in the target population who would benefit most from an intervention, whatever form that community policing intervention might take.

Second, such a strategy will be far less successful in those neighborhoods where residents are less willing to view police as partners in the production of public safety. As Chapter 7 documented, those concerns remain strong in lower-income and predominantly African-American neighborhoods.

The suggestion to focus on fearful individuals is easily misinterpreted. Some have thought I am saying residents just need some attitude adjustment and they will be fine. I am not saying that. I am saying that to most effectively address these problems, actions at the neighborhood level and the streetblock level should be complemented by efforts to identify and work with the individuals who are most at risk.

One leader told us he was concerned about his neighborhood, but at the same time just about ready to leave the city. This was in 1970, after Baltimore had been rocked by race riots in the spring of 1968. One day, mayoral candidate Schaefer arrived unannounced at the leader's door and said, "I hear you are thinking about leaving Baltimore and I want to talk to you about it." Twenty-four years later, that resident was still living in the city and still active in neighborhood initiatives. If we can find those at risk of moving, or at risk of high fear, and address their specific concerns not only through words but action as well, complementing these efforts with streetblock- and neighborhood-focused initiatives, overall gains against such problems should be substantial.

Of course, a discouraging possibility deserves mention. If fear and incivilities-perception efforts are retargeted to focus on individuals scoring high on fear in a setting, there is always the chance—depending in part on what future research shows—that nothing can be done. Those residents who perceive more problems than their neighbors or who are more fearful than their neighbors may be that way because of their age, their mental makeup, or their surrounding social world. If so, their views will not be easily shifted by community police officers knocking on their doors, attendance at local meetings, hand-delivered local newsletters describing improvements, or other efforts to pinpoint their areas of concern and do something about them.

One psychological reaction, however, that *is* more substantially ecological is *perceptions of dangerous places* that most people avoid. Unfortunately, changes on this outcome were not influenced by earlier incivilities levels, and this outcome presents some special policy challenges. There are some neighborhoods where few residents recognize one or more dangerous locations nearby, and there are some neighborhoods where many do. Do policymakers want residents in the latter neighborhoods to no longer view the surround as dangerous? It would seem the answer would depend on the type of place in question, and whether or not those locations are indeed dangerous. If residents nominated locations such as bars, taverns, and large public parks at night, their avoiding of those locations would seem sensible and would not seem to put a dent in their lifestyle. On the other hand, if the places nominated include locations that are part of the daily round for Baltimoreans, such as 7-11 convenience stores, pharmacies, shopping centers, and food markets, this avoidance exacts a significant daily toll.

Even though this outcome was substantially ecological, changes were not affected by earlier incivilities levels. Increasing avoidance was observed in locations with lower status and higher crime at the beginning of the period. So even for the outcome that would seem to have the best chance for supporting the decline and disorder thesis, because of its substantial ecological component, empirical support was wanting. Changes in perceived incivilities accompany changes in avoidance, but neither earlier assessed nor perceived incivilities help predict those changes.

To sum up on this class of outcomes, there are two distinct patterns of results. For the individual-level Garofalo and Laub–Hunter–Wilson version, the data provide extremely strong support. Those who are more fearful than their neighbors, and less locally committed, see more social *and* physical problems surrounding them. At least one perceived incivility links to each of the six outcomes, and often both types do. These individual-level connections explain considerable amounts of outcome variance. When we view the incivilities thesis as a set of propositions telling us about differences between neighbors, strong confirmation is seen here, as has been seen in other studies. The results here go beyond previous studies by confirming for several outcomes contributions of both physical and social incivilities. So the incivilities thesis is more than just a psychological version of social disorganization theory. Important questions remain, however. Can we demonstrate the connection longitudinally? Are we modeling the connection correctly, or does fear cause perceived problems, or is spurious correlation involved?

When we view the incivilities thesis as a set of propositions informing us about differences between neighborhoods on reactions to crime rather than neighbors, support emerges from the current study, but the pattern is not as consistent as theorists had hoped. Lagged longitudinal impacts of incivilities appear, but only for two out of the six outcomes. Further, the associated amounts of explained variance linked to this impact are more modest than had been expected. So there is support, but it is partial.

Crime Changes

Incivilities do result in some changes in later relative crime rates. Homicide shifts, the crime shift least susceptible to measurement problems that generally plague reported crime indicators, increased later in neighborhoods with high assessed incivilities initially. Initial perceived social incivilities linked to later rape changes. And initial perceived physical incivilities linked to later assault changes. But in a frustrating fashion, the linkages depended on the incivilities indicator used and the type of crime in question. These results raise a question. Should community police officers keep up grime fighting to achieve long-term crime reductions? Even though the present study did not evaluate any particular policing program that included as one of its goals the reduction of incivilities as a means of promoting local safety, do the results here have any implications for such programs?

The broadest implication is that police planners and leaders should not automatically privilege a program that focuses on the reduction of incivilities. Results here suggest that if those programs achieve reductions in the "background" rate of incivilities, there may or may not be an impact on later crime shifts. Whether there is an impact may depend on how incivilities are assessed, the particular types of incivilities targeted by program planners, the crime in question, and the time period within which the crime change is assessed. Stated differently, they should not presume a priori that incivility reduction will prove more effective than other strategies, nor should they adopt incivility-reduction approaches in lieu of a more contextually sensitive program.

Community policing and problem-oriented policing can each be likened to a well-stocked toolbox. The incivilities thesis, with its emphasis on grime fighting and harsh responses to minor infractions like panhandling, is encouraging officers to always pull the same couple of tools out of the toolbox: arrest panhandlers; get appropriate city departments involved for housing code violations. No matter what repair is needed, the thesis says, "Use one of the following socket wrenches," even if a screwdriver is needed instead. By blindly following the thesis, community-policing strategists may be overlooking and underusing other effective tools available in the toolbox: mini-stations, security surveys, attendance at neighborhood meetings, foot patrol, and so on. Strategists should feel free to totally ignore zero tolerance zealots, if they think something different would work better.

Baltimore has provided an interesting arena for discussing these issues. From about 1996 to 1999, city council members, including Martin O'Malley, have pushed hard for Baltimore police to adopt zero tolerance policies. Police Commissioner Frazier and Mayor Schmoke, to the credit of both of them, resisted. Although the impacts of zero tolerance policies on street safety may be uncertain, clogged courts and high dismissal rates are far less uncertain. The police department opted for more targeted strategies, such as gun removal and shutting down major drug rings. In November 1999, O'Malley was voted in as mayor. Will zero tolerance flower in Charm City?

In short, grime reduction (or slime reduction–zero tolerance) ought not be adopted axiomatically as part of a policing program, but instead carefully weighed against other potentially effective program elements, from community policing and other policing strategies, to achieve lower crime.

At the same time, the *reverse* dynamics merit attention as well. More dangerous neighborhoods *do* experience larger later increases in deterioration than less dangerous neighborhoods. Earlier robbery levels strongly predict later, higher graffiti levels, and earlier assault levels have a modest impact on later increases in vacant housing. In short, *crime fighting, over time, should result in less neighborhood deterioration.* This confirms some central tenets in work on the impacts of crime on communities (15, 19). *Crime fighting may be more important than grime fighting for long-term neighborhood preservation.* Here I am taking a position directly opposite that advocated by Kelling and Coles. Yes, I agree, the old men playing chess in the park feel better when there are bike officers going by and stopping to chat daily. But the friendly bike officers are probably not going to be enough to make a homeowner stay if the latter is held up at knifepoint on his or her way home.

Neighborhood Decline

Results looking at relative structural decline explored three different pathways of decline: changing stability, changing status, and changing disadvantage. Since only a few variables were used to operationalize these pathways of decline, the current results should be viewed cautiously. Results showed that initial assessed incivilities, but not initial perceived incivilities, contributed to later increases in relative disadvantage. This confirms the "grime leads to decline" manifesto. But two other pathways of decline were not affected by initial incivilities.

Stepping outside the incivilities thesis box for a moment, initial status and initial racial composition were as influential or more influential for later changes in crime and structural decline. Higher initial status made two later crime increases, rape and assault, less likely. And incivilities themselves were more likely to increase over time in lower-status locales. Neighborhoods predominantly African-American at the beginning of the period were more likely to experience later homicide increases, but *less* likely to increase in relative status and *less* likely to become increasingly disadvantaged, relative to other neighborhoods. Incivilities also were *less* likely to increase in the African-American neighborhoods. Stated differently, two of the most fundamental features of neighborhood, status and racial composition, intertwine intimately with the ecological outcomes of interest here, and with the origins of incivilities themselves. The connections for status fit what generally would be expected given the literature on community stratification by socioeconomic levels (6). The race results, however, are more mixed. Some fit the arguments made by McDougall and Wilson about disadvantages accruing to communities because of African-American racial composition; some clearly do not. Further theoretical work is needed to more closely connect incivility dynamics with those dynamics linked to fundamental community features of status, stability, and race.

Issues of Measurement

The present study used incivilities indicators from on-site assessments and from resident surveys. The different types of measures have different causes and different impacts and do not show the expected convergent validity. The lack of convergence is present when examining both cross-sectional and change indicators. The pattern raises strong questions about the idea that neighborhood "disorder" underlies different incivilities scores. It suggests that different indicators refer to a set of only loosely clustered conditions, and the origins of the various conditions may be somewhat independent. The pattern also has implications for program evaluators of incivilities-reduction initiatives. Relying on one type of indicator alone may result in missed program impacts. *Careful on-site assessments should routinely complement survey-based measures of incivilities.*

Incivilities and Structure

Changes in incivilities appear structurally driven. Neighborhoods with higher initial status are less likely to experience increasing incivilities at a later time. The connection holds for both assessed and perceived incivilities indicators. In short, *incivilities may be better interpreted as a result of an economically disadvantaged neighborhood rather than as a symptom of a disorderly or disorganized neighborhood.* Unexpectedly increasing incivilities reflect more than anything else a lower initial neighborhood status. The incivility shifts link only weakly to earlier stability and do not connect consistently to earlier racial composition. Given these strong connections, it is no surprise that some researchers have begun to question the wisdom of incivilities-reduction policies ignoring the broader community infrastructure (2).

Consequently, it is no surprise that efforts drawing some of the strongest interest are those where incivilities reduction has been allied with fundamental infrastructural rebuilding, as in the Sandtown-Winchester demonstration project in Baltimore (8). Economically one of the ten worst-off Baltimore neighborhoods in 1970 and 1980, Sandtown-Winchester has now seen significant land clearing and infusions of new housing, along with extensive local programming geared toward children. That effort has its critics (14: 157), and formal evaluations have not yet taken place. The reported crime data are ambiguous about long-term trends (8). The redevelopment effort covers just a fraction of the neighborhood, so it is not surprising that the changes do not suggest, as yet, any long-term repositioning of the neighborhood in the broader ecology of city neighborhoods.

Nonetheless, the point here is that the effort has a broader focus, incorporating incivilities reduction through infrastructural renewal. Given the exceedingly strong connections seen in these data between status and incivilities, and between status and changes in incivilities, that may be the only long-term, effective strategy for some types of neighborhoods. In many neighborhoods, neighborhood stabilization or revitalization requires attention to infrastructural renewal in the broadest sense as well as incivilities reduction.

The Context Outside the Theory

This volume has sought to provide a broader theoretical context for thinking about processes linked to incivilities and to the impacts of incivilities. Chapters 4 to 6 focused on the connections between neighborhood structure and incivilities and between structure and outcomes. These connections are informed by work on stratification by place and current models of urban political economies. Chapter 7 considered incivility reduction from local leaders' perspectives, grounding that investigation in a well-supported model linking community structure with different types of prevention efforts. Chapter 8 considered longitudinal changes in neighborhood names and boundaries and viewed those findings in the contexts of other work on place stratification and the organization of police work.

Incivilities and Collective Crime Prevention

Despite the considerable attention focused on incivilities reduction as *the* means to enhance neighborhood safety and stability, interviews with neighborhood leaders showed that they continue to pursue a broad array of collective crime prevention initiatives. They have not put all their "eggs" in the incivility-reduction "basket." Efforts to counter incivilities were certainly widespread, but attention to them has not forced out other strategies. Podolefsky has clustered the entire mix of collective strategies, based on data from the late 1970s, into two types: social problem reduction and victimization prevention (17). Both types of mega-strategies were still being pursued by local leaders in the mid-1990s. Also, as he predicted, and as witnessed here, which type of strategy the community pursued depended on the neighborhood fabric.

Of course, the type of incivilities present, and their prevalence, were both strongly determined by neighborhood fabric too. The leader interviews also revealed that the interpretations residents placed on incivilities were likewise context dependent.

In short, when we look beyond incivilities per se, local leaders are continuing to pursue roughly the same mix of collective crime prevention strategies that they have for the past twenty years. Although concerns about drug markets and drug dealing have increased subsequent to the crack invasion of Baltimore circa 1986–1988, which complicated surveillance initiatives, neighborhoods are not pursuing *just* the "new" antidrug strategies highlighted in the literature, such as confrontation. And although many neighborhoods are pursuing incivility reduction, leaders remain concerned about a broad array of issues and underlying conditions and committed to a wide array of strategies. ·

Incivilities, Partnerships, and Changing Neighborhood Ecology

Effective reduction of social and physical incivilities may be accomplished through third-party policing initiatives (3). These efforts are grounded in effective police-community partnerships. Klinger has shown that even though they may be doing community policing, police are biased toward the police administrative unit for organizing their work (9). He also has shown that how the police carry out their work depends on the amount of incivilities in the locale. If the partnerships can be organized around the community administrative units—neighborhood organizations—some of the mobilization difficulties currently confronting partnerships organized around police administrative units might be overcome. The work here builds on prior work on neighborhood naming and boundary work, and extends it to consider the implications of changing neighborhood names and boundaries for how the police view the community and for the development of police-community partnerships. The pattern of changes suggests that higher-status locales prove more stable, for a range of reasons. The reasons for different types of changes depend not only on macro-sociological forces, such as stratification, race, and asymmetries in the stratification process; they also depend on the leader and the local political and organizational context. The volume of changes taking place appears likely to create difficulties for partnership development; the pattern of the changes taking place makes it likely that difficulties will be worst in exactly the locales most in need of effective partnerships. So, complementing Klinger's finding that incivilities are most likely to be ignored by police in exactly the locations where they are most frequent, the work here suggests that because of boundary work and fluctuations in neighborhood identity over time, it will be most difficult to sustain community-police partnerships in just those places most afflicted with incivilities. But even under such constraints, aligning police-community partnerships with neighborhood governance units may be preferable to using the default police administrative unit.

Incivilities, Collective Efficacy, Social Disorganization, Local Social Capital, and Local Political Economy

Those developing the incivilities thesis sometimes have ignored closely related theoretical work in the areas of social disorganization, collective efficacy, local social capital, and communities and crime. Yet some of the processes described by the incivilities theorists at some levels of aggregation are similar to social disorganization concerns, particularly when we concentrate on social incivilities (4). If our understanding is to advance, we need to more precisely understand how the dynamics described by the incivilities thesis, at the streetblock and neighborhood levels, inter-twine with social disorganization more generally.

Incivilities theorists also sometimes have overlooked structural work on urban political economies (e.g., 10, 12). From that work, the concepts of use value and exchange value are quite helpful in better understanding incivilities. Exchange values and shifts in those values as the urban mosaic reconfigures itself over time help us understand how incivilities can "grow" rapidly in particular places. The concept of use value helps us understand why and in what ways incivilities are problematic for different types of residents in different types of locations. Again, if our understanding is to move forward, more careful theoretical integration is needed.

Incivilities theorists have tended to downplay or ignore structural causes of neighborhood decline, causes that lie not only in the neighborhood, but also in the city, and, more importantly, in the broader metropolitan area and in regional, national, and international shifts in population and political economies (6, 7, 12, 18). Such theoretical isolation from urban sociology and political economy is comforting because it insulates us from feelings of powerlessness in the face of enormously daunting challenges. But it provides only a limited view of the dynamics shaping neighborhood life. A narrow perspective may tempt one to oversell the promise of our policing initiatives, as Bill Bratton did when he modestly claimed he could turn around New York City, and "who knows, maybe even the country" (1: xi). Consequently, the temptation is to frame initiatives too narrowly in terms of what needs to be done and too broadly when describing the expected results. Such a formula surely leads to disappointment.

Currently, with declining crime rates from the early 1990s into at least 1998, police departments are, as the journalist Aric Press has put it, "riding that tiger on the way down" and claiming credit for the dropping rates. This was the debate that opened Chapter 3. But as this same journalist pointed out, police departments must be equally prepared to ride that tiger when the rates start going back up (11).

Clearly, the police must do something, and that something cannot be avowedly political. So, although they can team with housing inspectors when visiting delinquent landlords in third-party policing efforts, they cannot align with forces arguing for redevelopment funds for a locale (3). If we adopt a conflict-based perspective and presume that external agents are trying to maximize a neighborhood's exchange value while those in a neighborhood seek instead to maximize functionality, or use value, there is probably very little in the long run that police can do about that dynamic, save to prevent as much crime as they can. And that would be quite a lot.

Notes

1. Of course, it is extremely unlikely that we would be able to identify one condition responsible for explaining all of the between-location differences. I am trying to present a best case scenario here.

2. This assumes, unrealistically of course, that such public funds are available for the effort.

3. I recognize that fear reduction is an extremely thorny policy goal, with possible adverse side effects. I put that discussion aside for the moment.

References

(1) Bratton, W. (1998) *Turnaround*, Random House, New York.

(2) Buerger, M. E. (1994) The limits of community. In *The challenge of community policing* (Rosenbaum, D., ed), pp. 270–274. Sage, Thousand Oaks, CA.

(3) Buerger, M., and Mazerolle, L. G. (1998) Third-party policing: A theoretical analysis of an emerging trend. *Justice Quarterly* 15, 301–328.

(4) Bursik, R. J., and Grasmick, H. G. (1993) *Neighborhoods and crime: The dimensions of effective social control*, Lexington Books, New York.

(5) Duncan, G. J., and Raudenbush, S. W. (1999) Assessing the effects of context in studies of child and youth development. *Educational Psychologist* 34, 29–41.

(6) Gottdiener, M. (1994) *The new urban sociology*, McGraw Hill, New York.

(7) Gottdiener, M. (1994) *The social production of urban space* 2nd ed., University of Texas Press, Austin.

(8) Kennedy, D. M. (1996) Neighborhood revitalization: Lessons from Savannah and Baltimore. In *Communities: Mobilizing against crime, making partnerships work* (*National Institute of Justice Journal August 1996*) (National Institute of Justice, ed), pp. 13–23. National Institute of Justice, Washington, DC.

(9) Klinger, D. A. (1997) Negotiating order in police work: An ecological theory of police response to deviance. *Criminology* 35, 277–306.

(10) LaGory, M., and Pipkin, M. (1981) *Urban social space*, Wadsworth, Belmont, CA.

(11) Langworthy, R. H., ed. (1999) *Measuring what matters*, National Institute of Justice, Office of Community Oriented Policing Services, Washington, DC.

(12) Logan, J. R., and Molotch, H. (1987) *Urban fortunes*, University of California Press, Berkeley.

(13) Maltz, M. (1991) *Mapping crime in its community setting*, Springer-Verlag, New York.

(14) McDougall, H. A. (1993) *Black Baltimore: A new theory of community*, Temple University Press, Philadelphia.

(15) Miller, E. S. (1981) Crime's threat to land value and neighborhood vitality. In *Environmental criminology* (Brantingham, P. J., and Brantingham, P. L., eds), pp. 111–118. Sage, Beverly Hills, CA.

(16) Morenoff, J. D., and Sampson, R. J. (1997) Violent crime and the spatial dynamics of neighborhood transition: Chicago, 1970–1990. *Social Forces* 76, 31–64.

(17) Podolefsky, A. (1983) *Case studies in community crime prevention*, Charles C. Thomas, Springfield, IL.

(18) Sassen, S. (1996) Epilogue: Cities and communities in the global economy: Rethinking our concepts. *American Behavioral Scientist* 39, 629–335 .

(19) Taylor, R. B. (1995) Impact of crime on communities. *Annals of the American Academy of Political and Social Science* 539, 28–45.

(20) Taylor, R. B. (1997) Relative impacts of disorder, structural change, and crime on residents and business personnel in Minneapolis–St. Paul. In *Community crime prevention at the crossroads* (Lab, S., ed), pp. 63–75. Anderson, Cincinnati, OH.

Index